Fault-Tolerant IP and MPLS Networks

Iftekhar Hussain

Cisco Press

800 East 96th Street
Indianapolis, IN 46240 USA

Fault-Tolerant IP and MPLS Networks

Iftekhar Hussain

Copyright© 2005 Cisco Systems, Inc.

Published by:
Cisco Press
800 East 96th Street
Indianapolis, IN 46240 USA

Printed in the United States of America 1 2 3 4 5 6 7 8 9 0

First Printing   November 2004

Library of Congress Cataloging-in-Publication Number: 2002115120

ISBN: 1-58705-126-5

Warning and Disclaimer

This book is designed to provide information about IP and MPLS control-plane fault tolerance. Every effort has been made to make this book as complete and as accurate as possible, but no warranty or fitness is implied.

The information is provided on an "as is" basis. The authors, Cisco Press, and Cisco Systems, Inc. shall have neither liability nor responsibility to any person or entity with respect to any loss or damages arising from the information contained in this book or from the use of the discs or programs that may accompany it.

The opinions expressed in this book belong to the author and are not necessarily those of Cisco Systems, Inc.

Corporate and Government Sales

Cisco Press offers excellent discounts on this book when ordered in quantity for bulk purchases or special sales.

For more information please contact: **U.S. Corporate and Government Sales** 1-800-382-3419 corpsales@pearsontechgroup.com

For sales outside the U.S. please contact: **International Sales** international@pearsoned.com

Feedback Information

At Cisco Press, our goal is to create in-depth technical books of the highest quality and value. Each book is crafted with care and precision, undergoing rigorous development that involves the unique expertise of members from the professional technical community.

Readers' feedback is a natural continuation of this process. If you have any comments regarding how we could improve the quality of this book, or otherwise alter it to better suit your needs, you can contact us through e-mail at feedback@ciscopress.com. Please make sure to include the book title and ISBN in your message.

We greatly appreciate your assistance.

Trademark Acknowledgments

All terms mentioned in this book that are known to be trademarks or service marks have been appropriately capitalized. Cisco Press or Cisco Systems, Inc. cannot attest to the accuracy of this information. Use of a term in this book should not be regarded as affecting the validity of any trademark or service mark.

Publisher	John Wait
Editor-in-Chief	John Kane
Executive Editor	Jim Schachterle
Cisco Representative	Anthony Wolfenden
Cisco Press Program Manager	Nannette M. Noble
Production Manager	Patrick Kanouse
Development Editor	Betsey Henkels
Technical Editors	Don Banks, Rudy Figaro, Liem Nguyen, Mark Szczesniak
Editorial Assistant	Tammi Barnett
Cover Designer	Louisa Adair
Composition	Mark Shirar
Copy Editor and Indexer	Keith Cline
Proofreader	Tonya Cupp

CISCO SYSTEMS

Corporate Headquarters
Cisco Systems, Inc.
170 West Tasman Drive
San Jose, CA 95134-1706
USA
www.cisco.com
Tel: 408 526-4000
     800 553-NETS (6387)
Fax: 408 526-4100

European Headquarters
Cisco Systems International BV
Haarlerbergpark
Haarlerbergweg 13-19
1101 CH Amsterdam
The Netherlands
www-europe.cisco.com
Tel: 31 0 20 357 1000
Fax: 31 0 20 357 1100

Americas Headquarters
Cisco Systems, Inc.
170 West Tasman Drive
San Jose, CA 95134-1706
USA
www.cisco.com
Tel: 408 526-7660
Fax: 408 527-0883

Asia Pacific Headquarters
Cisco Systems, Inc.
Capital Tower
168 Robinson Road
#22-01 to #29-01
Singapore 068912
www.cisco.com
Tel: +65 6317 7777
Fax: +65 6317 7799

Cisco Systems has more than 200 offices in the following countries and regions. Addresses, phone numbers, and fax numbers are listed on the
Cisco.com Web site at www.cisco.com/go/offices.

Argentina • Australia • Austria • Belgium • Brazil • Bulgaria • Canada • Chile • China PRC • Colombia • Costa Rica • Croatia • Czech Republic
Denmark • Dubai, UAE • Finland • France • Germany • Greece • Hong Kong SAR • Hungary • India • Indonesia • Ireland • Israel • Italy
Japan • Korea • Luxembourg • Malaysia • Mexico • The Netherlands • New Zealand • Norway • Peru • Philippines • Poland • Portugal
Puerto Rico • Romania • Russia • Saudi Arabia • Scotland • Singapore • Slovakia • Slovenia • South Africa • Spain • Sweden
Switzerland • Taiwan • Thailand • Turkey • Ukraine • United Kingdom • United States • Venezuela • Vietnam • Zimbabwe

About the Author

Iftekhar Hussain is a technical leader within the Internet Technologies Division at Cisco Systems. For the past several years, Iftekhar has been involved in the design of high availability-related aspects of IP/MPLS networks. He brings extensive industry experience to the subjects of networking and telecommunication, including switching, traffic management, and voice delivery over packet-switched networks. He has a Ph.D. in electrical and computer engineering from the University of California, Davis.

About the Technical Reviewers

Don Banks is a distinguished engineer at Cisco Systems in the IOS Technologies Division, where he is responsible for the development of the IOS high availability architecture. He leads a cross-functional team responsible for providing high availability for Cisco IOS-based platforms with the goal of 99.999 percent availability or better using fault-tolerant techniques. Don has been responsible for the architecture for stateful switchover (SSO/NSF), in-service software upgrade (ISSU) and follow-on high-availability architecture enhancements. Don has six patents filed in the area of high availability. Throughout his career of more than 30 years in the industry, Don has been involved in the design and implementation of new operating systems, networking protocols, storage networking, fault tolerance, as well as hardware platform design while working on research for an IBM Fellow, and at such companies as Amdahl, Tandem, Apple, and Auspex.

Rudy Figaro is a technical leader at Cisco. He works in MPLS and routing, leading software design and development. Rudy has created the architectural design for MPLS high availability. Rudy also led and worked on many software development projects including MPLS IP+ATM, MPLS-TE and Fast ReRoute, GMPLS, Layer 3 and Layer 2 VPNs, and IP multitable support. Recently Rudy has worked on an architecture for virtual routers with focus on high availability, performance, and scaling. Rudy also holds a patent for "Apparatus and Methods Providing Redundant Routing in a Switched Device."

Liem H. Nguyen is a technical leader in the core IP routing development area at Cisco Systems. Before coming to Cisco in 1997, Liem spent 11 years at IBM and 2 years at start-up NetEdge Systems in RTP, North Carolina, as a network communication software developer. He is an alumnus of North Carolina State University, where he obtained his bachelor of science degree in electrical engineering in 1984, and he is quite proud of his Wolfpack, who won the 1983 NCAA Basketball Championship under the reign of Jim Valvano.

Mark Szczesniak is a technical lead engineer for the Cisco Layer 3 Services Group. He is responsible for leading forwarding code development for MPLS. Mark has been with Cisco for 10 years, since the Lightstream acquisition.

Dedications

To my beloved mother, Bibi Jee; wife, Nabila; and children, Noama, Huda, and Ahmed.

Acknowledgments

I am greatly indebted to my technical reviewers—Don Banks, Rudy Figaro, Liem Nguyen, and Mark Szczesniak—for correcting errors and omissions and providing many helpful suggestions. My thanks also go to Bob Thomas, who reviewed the initial book proposal and made a number of useful suggestions; and to Mike Shand, who reviewed the initial draft of Chapter 5 and provided many helpful hints. I appreciate all the useful recommendations from these people, who have immensely enhanced the quality of this book.

I also want to give special recognition to my colleagues Dan Tappan, Trevor Mendez, Ashok Narayanan, Carol Iturralde, Roger Levesque, Jean Philippe Vasseur, Alex Raj, Chao Zhou, Sumit Mukhopadhyay, George Freeman, Robert Hanzl, Michel Khouderchah, Ruchi Kapoor, Syed Kamran Raza, Sami Boutros, and Reshad Rahman for their insightful discussions and suggestions on various issues related to high availability, which enabled me to cover such a broad set of functional areas in this book.

Thanks to Rich Cascio, Tom McKinney, and Paiman Nodoushani for their flexibility, encouragement, and support during the writing of the book.

A big "thank you" goes out to the production team for this book. Jim Schachterle, John Kane, Amy Moss, Christopher Cleveland, and Betsey Henkels have been incredibly professional and a pleasure to work with. I couldn't have asked for a finer team.

Finally, this book would not have been possible without the generous support and understanding of my family.

Contents at a Glance

Introduction   xix

Part I   IP/MPLS Forwarding Plane   3

Chapter 1   Understanding High Availability of IP and MPLS Networks   5

Chapter 2   IP Forwarding Plane: Achieving Nonstop Forwarding   23

Chapter 3   MPLS Forwarding Plane: Achieving Nonstop Forwarding   43

Part II   IP/MPLS Control Plane   65

Chapter 4   Intradomain IP Control Plane: Restarting OSPF Gracefully   67

Chapter 5   Intradomain IP Control Plane: Restarting IS-IS Gracefully   105

Chapter 6   Interdomain IP Control Plane: Restarting BGP Gracefully   137

Chapter 7   MPLS Control Plane: Restarting BGP with MPLS Gracefully   163

Chapter 8   MPLS Control Plane: Restarting LDP Gracefully   187

Chapter 9   MPLS Control Plane: Restarting RSVP-TE Gracefully   225

Part III   High Availability of MPLS-Based Services   251

Chapter 10   Improving the Survivability of IP and MPLS Networks   253

Index   299

Contents

Introduction   xix

Part I   IP/MPLS Forwarding Plane   3

Chapter 1   Understanding High Availability of IP and MPLS Networks   5

Reliability and Availability of Converged Networks   5

Defining Key Terms   6

Availability and Unavailability   6

Reliability and Its Relationship to Availability   6

Fault Tolerance and Its Effect on Availability   7

MPLS Network Components   7

Network and Service Outages   10

Planned and Unplanned Outages   10

Main Causes of Network Outages   10

Design Strategies for Network Survivability   11

Mitigating Node-Level Unplanned Hardware-Related Outages   11

Mitigating Node-Level Unplanned Software-Related Outages   12

Reducing Downtime Related to Unplanned Control-Plane Restart   13

Stateful Switchover and Nonstop Forwarding   15

Reducing Unplanned Downtime Using Component-Level Modularity and Restartability   15

Mitigating Node-Level Planned Outages   17

Mitigating Network Outages Against Link and Node Failures   17

Mitigating Network Outages via Effective Operation and Maintenance Mechanisms   17

Improving Network Security via Fault-Tolerance Mechanisms   18

Scope of the Book   19

References   19

Chapter 2   IP Forwarding Plane: Achieving Nonstop Forwarding   23

Overview of IP Forwarding   23

Classful Addressing   25

Classless Addressing   25

IP Address Lookup   26

Evolution of IP Forwarding Architectures   28

Route Cache-Based Centralized Forwarding Architecture   29

Distributed Forwarding Architectures   30

Cisco Express Forwarding   33

Separation of IP Control and Forwarding Planes   35
IP Control-Plane Stateful Switchover   35
IP Forwarding-Plane Nonstop Forwarding   36
IP Nonstop Forwarding Architecture   36
IP Control-Plane SSO   37
Separation of Control and Forwarding   37
Summary of IP Nonstop Forwarding Operations   37
IP SSO and NSF Capabilities in Cisco IOS Architecture   39
External View of the IP SSO and NSF   40
Summary   41
References   41

Chapter 3   MPLS Forwarding Plane: Achieving Nonstop Forwarding   43
Overview of MPLS   43
MPLS Label Lookup and Forwarding   50
Separation of MPLS Control and Forwarding Planes   53
MPLS Applications   55
MPLS Forwarding Architecture   56
MPLS Control-Plane Stateful Switchover   57
MPLS Forwarding-Plane Nonstop Forwarding   58
MPLS Nonstop Forwarding Architecture   59
External View of the MPLS SSO and NSF   62
Summary   62
References   63

Part II   IP/MPLS Control Plane   65

Chapter 4   Intradomain IP Control Plane: Restarting OSPF Gracefully   67
Internet Routing Architecture   67
OSPF Control- and Forwarding-Plane Components   69
OSPF Control-Plane Restart Approaches   69
Understanding the Detrimental Effects of the OSPF Restart   70
Overview of OSPF Routing   72
OSPF Hierarchical Routing   73
Establishing Adjacencies and Synchronizing Link-State Databases   75
OSPF Link-State Advertisements   76
Mitigating the Detrimental Effects of OSPF Restart   79
OSPF Restart Mechanisms   79
OSPF Restart Signaling Mechanism   80
Modifications to the OSPF Hello Processing Procedure   81
Link-State Database Resynchronization   81

Restarting Router Behavior 84

SPF Calculations 85

Nonrestarting Router (Helper-Node) Behavior 85

Operation of the OSPF Restart Signaling Mechanism 86

OSPF Graceful Restart Mechanism 89

Reliable Delivery of the Grace LSAs on Unplanned and Planned Restart 92

Restarting a Router's Behavior 93

Helper Node's Behavior 95

Operation of the OSPF Graceful Restart Mechanism 96

Comparison of the OSPF Restart Mechanisms 99

Network Deployment Considerations 100

Scenario 1: R1 and R2 Are Restart Signaling/NSF-Capable 101

Scenario 2: R1 Is Restart Signaling- and NSF-Capable, but R3 Is Only Restart Signaling-Capable 101

Scenario 3: R1 Is Restart Signaling- and NSF-Capable, but R4 Is Restart Signaling- and NSF-Incapable 102

Scenario 4: R1 Is Restart Signaling- and NSF-Capable, and R5 Is Graceful Restart- and NSF-Capable 102

Summary 102

References 102

Chapter 5   Intradomain IP Control Plane: Restarting IS-IS Gracefully 105

Understanding the Detrimental Effects of the IS-IS Restart 105

Original IS-IS Restart Behavior 105

Negative Effects of the Original IS-IS Restart Behavior 106

Overview of IS-IS Routing 107

IS-IS Hierarchical Routing 108

Discovering Neighbors and Establishing Adjacencies 109

Establishing Adjacencies Using a Three-Way Handshake 109

Maintaining Adjacencies 110

Link-State Packets 110

LSP Databases 110

Synchronizing LSP Databases 111

Congestion Indication Through the Overload Bit 112

IS-IS Designated Router 113

Mitigating the Detrimental Effects of the IS-IS Restart 113

IS-IS Restart 113

IETF IS-IS Restart Mechanism 115

Restart TLV 116

Timers 118

Restarting Router (a Router with a Preserved FIB) Behavior   118

Nonrestarting Router (Helper Neighbor) Behavior   121

Starting Router (a Router Without a Preserved FIB) Behavior   122

IETF IS-IS Restart Operation   124

Starting Router Operation   124

Restarting Router Operation   126

Cisco IS-IS Restart   128

Cisco IS-IS Restart Operation   130

Comparison of the IS-IS Restart Mechanisms   131

Network Deployment Considerations   132

Scenario 1: R1 and R2 Are IETF IS-IS Restart- or NSF-Capable   132

Scenario 2: R1 Is IETF IS-IS Restart- or NSF-Capable, but R3 Is Only IETF IS-IS Restart-Capable   133

Scenario 3: R1 Is IETF IS-IS Restart- or NSF-Capable, but R4 Is IETF Restart- or NSF-Incapable   133

Scenario 4: R1 and R2 Are Cisco IS-IS Restart- or NSF-Capable   134

Scenario 5: R1 Is Cisco IS-IS Restart- or NSF-Capable and R3 Is Cisco IS-IS Restart- or NSF-Incapable   134

Summary   134

References   135

Chapter 6   Interdomain IP Control Plane: Restarting BGP Gracefully   137

Introduction to Border Gateway Protocol Routing   137

BGP Control- and Forwarding-Plane Components   138

Route Flaps Caused by BGP Control-Plane Restart   138

BGP Restart Process   140

BGP Routing Evolution and Concepts   140

BGP Messages   141

Idle and Established States   142

Exchange of Routing Information   143

Internal and External Speakers   144

BGP Path Attributes   146

AS_PATH and NEXT_HOP Attributes   146

Routing Information Bases of BGP Speakers   148

BGP Route-Selection Process   149

BGP Route Reflection   149

Mitigating the Detrimental Effects of the BGP Restart   150

BGP Graceful Restart Mechanism   151

Exchange of Graceful Restart Capability   151

BGP Graceful Restart Capability Format   153

Restarting BGP Speaker Behavior 154

Helper BGP Speaker Behavior 155

Operation of the BGP Graceful Restart Mechanism 156

Network-Deployment Considerations 158

Scenario 1: R1/R2 Are BGP Graceful Restart- and NSF-Capable 159

Scenario 2: R1 Is BGP Restart- and NSF-Capable, but R3 Is Only BGP Restart-
Capable 160

Scenario 3: R1 Is BGP Graceful Restart- and NSF-Capable, but R4 Is BGP Graceful
Restart- and NSF-Incapable 161

Summary 161

References 161

Chapter 7   MPLS Control Plane: Restarting BGP with MPLS Gracefully 163

MPLS Control- and Forwarding-Plane Components 163

MPLS Network Components 164

Layer 2 and Layer 3 Virtual Private Network Services 164

Forwarding Tables for Layer 2 and Layer 3 VPN Services 166

MPLS Forwarding State Entries 166

Detrimental Effects of BGP with MPLS Restart 166

Review of Chapter 6 Concepts 167

Overview of the BGP as MPLS Control Plane 168

BGP and MPLS Interrelationship 168

BGP Label-Distribution Mechanisms 169

Advertising Labeled BGP Routes 171

Advertising Labeled BGP Routes Through a Route Reflector 171

Withdrawing Labeled BGP Routes 171

Mitigating the Detrimental Effects of BGP with MPLS Restart 173

BGP with MPLS Graceful Restart Mechanism 173

Behavior of a Restarting LSR 175

Behavior of Helper LSRs 178

BGP/MPLS Graceful Restart Operation 179

Network-Deployment Considerations 181

Scenario 1: LSR1 and LSR2 Are Capable of Both BGP with MPLS Graceful Restart
and of NSF 182

Scenario 2: LSR1 Is Capable of Both BGP with MPLS Graceful Restart and of NSF,
but LSR3 Is Capable Only of BGP with MPLS Graceful Restart 182

Scenario 3: LSR1 Is BGP with MPLS Graceful Restart- and NSF- Capable, but
LSR4 Is Both BGP with MPLS Graceful Restart- and NSF- Incapable 183

Summary 183

References 184

Chapter 8   MPLS Control Plane: Restarting LDP Gracefully   187

    Overview of LDP   187

        LDP FEC-to-LSP Association   188

        LDP Peers   189

        Hello Adjacency Establishment   189

        Hello Adjacency Maintenance   190

        LDP Messages   191

        Label Distribution Control Mode (Ordered Versus Independent)   192

        Label Advertisement Mode (Unsolicited Versus On Demand)   192

            Downstream On Demand   193

            Downstream Unsolicited   194

        Label Retention Mode (Liberal Versus Conservative)   194

        Interactions Between LIB, LFIB, and Routing   194

        Establishing Pseudowires (PWs) Using LDP   196

    LDP Control-Plane and Forwarding-Plane Components   197

        LDP Forwarding State   197

        LDP Control-Plane State   198

    Understanding the Detrimental Effects of LDP Restart   198

    Mitigating Detrimental Effects of the LDP Restart   200

        Comparison of LDP Restart Methods   201

    LDP GR Mechanism for Downstream Unsolicited Mode   203

        Initial Capability Exchange   204

        LDP Session Failure   205

        LDP Session Reestablishment and State Recovery   205

        Nonrestarting LSR Behavior   206

        Restarting LSR Behavior   207

    LDP GR Operation in Downstream Unsolicited Mode   208

        Option A: LDP GR Operation for Downstream Unsolicited Mode   209

        Option B: LDP GR Operation for Downstream Unsolicited Mode   212

    LDP GR Mechanism for Downstream On-Demand Mode   213

        LDP GR Common Procedures   213

        Downstream On-Demand Specific LDP GR Procedures   214

            Restarting LSR Behavior for Ingress LSRs   214

            Restarting LSR Behavior for Egress LSRs   215

            Restarting LSR Behavior for Transit LSRs   216

            Nonrestarting LSR Behavior for Ingress Neighbors   217

            Nonrestarting LSR Behavior for Egress Neighbors   218

            Nonrestarting LSR Behavior for Transit Neighbors   218

      Comparison of LDP GR Mechanisms for Downstream Unsolicited and Downstream On-Demand Modes   219

Network Deployment Considerations   220
    Scenario 1: LSR1 and LSR2 Are LDP GR- and NSF-Capable   221
    Scenario 2: LSR1 Is LDP GR- and NSF-Capable, but LSR3 Is Only LDP GR-
     Capable   222
    Scenario 3: LSR1 Is LDP GR- and NSF-Capable, but LSR4 Is LDP
     GR- and NSF-Incapable   222
Summary   222
References   223

Chapter 9   MPLS Control Plane: Restarting RSVP-TE Gracefully   225
Motivations for Traffic Engineering   225
    Traffic-Engineering Capabilities   226
    MPLS Traffic Engineering   226
Overview of RSVP   227
    Path Message   227
    Path State Block   227
    Resv Message   228
    Reservation State Block   229
    Soft State   229
    Using RSVP in MPLS-TE   230
    Generalization of the Flow Concept   230
    LSP Tunnel   231
    LSP_TUNNEL Objects   231
    SESSION_ATTRIBUTE Object   232
    Specifying ERO   233
    RECORD_ROUTE Object   233
    RSVP-TE Soft State   234
    Lifetime of RSVP-TE State   234
     Detecting RSVP-TE Failures   235
RSVP-TE Control-Plane and Forwarding-Plane Components   236
    Detrimental Effects of RSVP-TE Restart   236
    Term Definitions   238
Mitigating the Detrimental Effects of RSVP-TE Restart   238
    RSVP-TE GR Mechanism   239
     Initial Capability Exchange   239
     RSVP-TE Control-Plane Restart   239
     Reestablishment of Hello Communication   240
    Restarting LSR Behavior   241
     Head-End Restarting   243
     Midpoint Restarting   243
     Tail-End Restarting   244
    Nonrestarting Neighbor Behavior   244

RSVP-TE Graceful Restart Operation   245

Network Deployment Considerations for RSVP-TE Graceful Restart   248

Scenario 1: LSR1 and LSR2 Are RSVP-TE GR- and NSF-Capable   248

Scenario 2: LSR1 Is RSVP-TE GR- and NSF-Capable, but LSR3 Is Only RSVP-TE
GR-Capable   249

Scenario 3: LSR1 Is RSVP-TE GR- and NSF-Capable, but LSR4 Is
RSVP-TE GR- and NSF-Incapable   249

Summary   249

References   249

Part III   High Availability of MPLS-Based Services   251

Chapter 10   Improving the Survivability of IP and MPLS Networks   253

Layer 2 and Layer 3 Services over MPLS Networks   254

Provider-Provisioned Virtual Private Networks   254

VPN Tunnels   255

Tunnel Demultiplexing   255

Signaling of the Tunnel Labels and VPN Labels   256

Service Attributes Related to Network Availability   256

Network Fault-Tolerance Techniques   257

MPLS Traffic Engineering   257

MPLS-TE Functional Modules   258

Establishment of an MPLS-TE Tunnel   259

MPLS-TE Tunnel Reoptimization   262

Protecting MPLS-TE Tunnels Against Control-Plane Failures   262

Intra-Area MPLS Traffic Engineering   263

Inter-Area or Intra-AS MPLS Traffic Engineering   264

Inter-AS MPLS Traffic Engineering   264

Layer 3 Virtual Private Networks   265

CE-Based L3VPNs   265

PE-Based L3VPNs   265

PE-Based L3VPN Reference Model   265

VPN Routing and Forwarding Tables   266

PE-to-PE Tunnel   267

Distribution of L3VPN Labels   268

IPv6-Based L3VPN Services   268

Protecting L3VPN Service Against Control-Plane Failures   268

Single-AS MPLS Backbone   268

Multi-AS MPLS Backbone   269

Carrier Supporting Carrier (CSC)   270

Layer 2 Virtual Private Networks   272
    Protecting L2VPN Services Against Control-Plane Failures   274
    Virtual Private Wire Service   274
    Virtual Private LAN Service   275
Network Fault Tolerance and MPLS-Based Recovery   277
    Protection and Restoration   278
    Optical Layer Protection   279
    SONET/SDH Layer Protection   280
    IP Layer Restoration   280
    MPLS Layer Protection—Fast ReRoute   281
    Protecting Bypass Tunnels Against Control-Plane Failures   284
    Interactions Between Different Protection Layers   285
Network Fault Tolerance and MPLS OAM Mechanisms   287
    Bidirectional Forwarding Detection   288
    Motivations   289
        How Does BFD Improve Network Availability?   289
        How Does BFD Improve Network Convergence?   289
    BFD Protocol Mechanics   289
    BFD Applications   290
        Using BFD for Detecting IGP Neighbor Liveness   290
        Using BFD for LSP Data-Plane Fault Detection and Control-Plane
        Verification   291
        Using BFD for PW Fault Detection   292
        Using BFD for MPLS FRR Fault Detection   292
        Using BFD for Fault Detection in the Access Network   293
    BFD Interactions with the IP and MPLS Control-Plane Graceful Restart
    Mechanisms   294
Network Fault Tolerance and In-Service Software Upgrades   295
Summary   296
References   296

Index   299

Icons Used in This Book

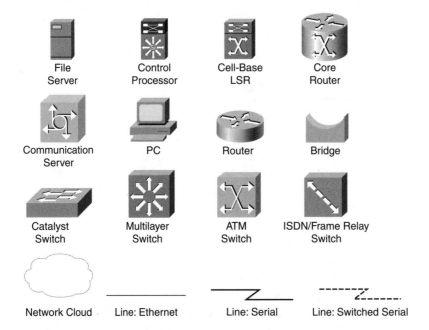

File Server   Control Processor   Cell-Base LSR   Core Router

Communication Server   PC   Router   Bridge

Catalyst Switch   Multilayer Switch   ATM Switch   ISDN/Frame Relay Switch

Network Cloud   Line: Ethernet   Line: Serial   Line: Switched Serial

Command Syntax Conventions

The conventions used to present command syntax in this book are the same conventions used in the IOS Command Reference. The Command Reference describes these conventions as follows:

- **Boldface** indicates commands and keywords that are entered literally as shown. In actual configuration examples and output (not general command syntax), boldface indicates commands that are manually input by the user (such as a **show** command).

- *Italics* indicate arguments for which you supply actual values.

- Vertical bars (|) separate alternative, mutually exclusive elements.

- Square brackets ([ ]) indicate optional elements.

- Braces ({ }) indicate a required choice.

- Braces within brackets ([{ }]) indicate a required choice within an optional element.

Introduction

Multiprotocol Label Switching (MPLS) is the key enabling technology for the widespread deployment of IP networks in core and metro Ethernet applications. Many service providers are looking to migrate their legacy Layer 2 and Layer 3 services onto converged MPLS-enabled IP networks. High availability of IP/MPLS networks is a prerequisite for offering profitable carrier-class services. Although most carrier-class routers do provide an adequate level of hardware redundancy, control-plane software still remains a vulnerable part and cause of a majority of router failures.

Goals and Methods

Router control planes encompass IP routing and MPLS signaling protocols. This book provides an in-depth analysis of mechanisms that help improve the reliability and availability of IP and MPLS control-plane components. The IP/MPLS control-plane architecture and all its restart mechanisms are explained with examples and deployment considerations.

This explanation of IP/MPLS control-plane architecture begins with a service view of the network, moves on to the node-level view by partitioning the network into its constituent network elements, and then advances to the component-level view to explore various techniques that can be used to improve the reliability and availability of each component. The top-down and example-oriented approach facilitates an easy understanding of the constituent components before moving on to more advanced MPLS applications involving multiple components. *Fault-Tolerant IP and MPLS Networks* is your practical guide for understanding, designing, and deploying carrier-class IP/MPLS networks. Salient features of this book enable you to

- Understand a detailed overview of the IP/MPLS forwarding-plane and control-plane protocols, including OSPF, IS-IS, LDP, BGP, and RSVP.

- Comprehend an in-depth analysis of fault-tolerant IP/MPLS control-plane architectures.

- Develop a clear understanding of various high-availability aspects of IP/MPLS networks.

- Learn how to seamlessly deploy IP/MPLS control-plane restart mechanisms.

- Master applying fault-tolerant control-plane architectures in designing and deploying highly reliable and available MPLS applications such as traffic engineering, L2VPNs, and L3VPNs.

- Understand layered architecture of network-level fault-recovery mechanisms (such as optical, SONET, and MPLS) and interactions between different layers.

Who Should Read This Book?

Because an in-depth understanding of recent enhancements to the IP/MPLS control plane is essential for designing and deploying carrier-class services, this book should be of great interest to network engineers, system engineers, and technical managers who want to understand the fault-tolerant aspects of packet-switched networks and how they can effectively design and deploy high-availability IP/MPLS networks.

How This Book Is Organized

Although this book could be read cover to cover, it is designed to be flexible and allow you to easily move between chapters and sections of chapters to cover material of specific interest. There are three parts of this book. Part I, "IP/MPLS Forwarding Plane," covers control-plane stateful switchover and the nonstop forwarding framework. The first three chapters of the book form Part I. Part II, "IP/MPLS Control Plane," focuses on mechanisms that allow IP and MPLS control-plane components to restart gracefully. Chapters 4 through 9 make up Part II. Part III, "High Availability of MPLS-Based Services," includes just Chapter 10, which examines control-plane availability of MPLS applications.

Chapters 2 through 10 are the core chapters and can be covered in any order. If you do intend to read them all, the order in the book is an excellent sequence to use.

The core chapters, Chapters 2 through 10, cover the following topics:

Chapter 2, "IP Forwarding Plane: Achieving Nonstop Forwarding"—This chapter discusses IP forwarding-plane architecure and the control-plane stateful switchover framework to achieve a nonstop forwarding operation across the control-plane failure.

Chapter 3, "MPLS Forwarding Plane: Achieving Nonstop Forwarding"—This chapter describes MPLS forwarding-plane architecture and extends the concepts of the previous chapter to MPLS nonstop forwarding.

Chapter 4, "Intradomain IP Control Plane: Restarting OSPF Gracefully"—This chapter covers two IP control-plane restart mechanisms known as restart signaling and graceful restart, which can be used to reduce the negative effects of the OSPF restart.

Chapter 5, "Intradomain IP Control Plane: Restarting IS-IS Gracefully"—This chapter describes IETF and Cisco IS-IS restart mechanisms for mitigating negative effects of an IS-IS control-plane restart.

Chapter 6, "Interdomain IP Control Plane: Restarting BGP Gracefully"—This chapter introduces the BGP graceful restart mechanism, which allows a BGP speaker to restart without causing route flaps. This chapter covers the case where BGP speakers exchange unlabeled VPN-IPv4 addresses.

Chapter 7, "MPLS Control Plane: Restarting BGP with MPLS Gracefully"—This chapter extends the BGP graceful restart mechanims for the case in which BGP is used for exchanging MPLS-labeled VPN-IPv4 addresses.

Chapter 8, "MPLS Control Plane: Restarting LDP Gracefully"—This chapter describes the LDP graceful restart mechanism for downstream on-demand and downstream unsolicited label-distribution modes.

Chapter 9, "MPLS Control Plane: Restarting RSVP-TE Gracefully"—This chapter covers the RSVP-TE graceful restart mechanism, which helps to lessen the undesirable effects on the MPLS forwarding plane that are caused by an RSVP-TE control-plane restart.

Chapter 10, "Improving Survivability of IP and MPLS Networks"—This chapter discusses how different IP/MPLS control-plane restart mechanisms described in previous chapters can be used to improve availability of an MPLS-enabled IP network against unplanned control-plane failures. Specifically, this chapter examines protection of LSPs against control-plane failures in the context of MPLS-TE, L2VPN, and L3VPN applications. This chapter also briefly touches on a few other fault-tolerance mechanisms, including MPLS FRR, MPLS OAM, bidirectional forwarding detection (BFD), and in-service software upgrade.

IP/MPLS Forwarding Plane

Chapter 1   Understanding High Availability of IP and MPLS Networks

Chapter 2   IP Forwarding Plane: Achieving Nonstop Forwarding

Chapter 3   MPLS Forwarding Plane: Achieving Nonstop Forwarding

Understanding High Availability of IP and MPLS Networks

Until recently, many service providers maintained and operated separate legacy circuit-switched and packet-switched networks. Traditionally, voice services have been offered over circuit-switched networks, commonly known as *Public Switched Telephone Networks* (PSTN). On the other hand, connectivity between enterprises for *virtual private network* (VPN) data applications has been provided over packet-switched networks such as Frame Relay (FR) and *Asynchronous Transfer Mode* (ATM). Of late, many service providers are migrating legacy Layer 2 and Layer 3 services to converged *Multiprotocol Label Switching* (MPLS)-enabled IP networks.[1] This migration toward a common multiservice IP/MPLS network is driven by the necessity to reduce the *capital expenditure* (capex) and *operational expenses* (opex) of both building and operating separate network infrastructures.

This chapter describes major sources of network failures and provides an overview of techniques that are commonly used to improve availability of IP/MPLS networks. In particular, this chapter outlines mechanisms for reducing network downtime due to control-plane failures.

Reliability and Availability of Converged Networks

For service providers, maintaining highly reliable and revenue-generating legacy service offerings is extremely important. So as much as possible, they are interested in migrating legacy services on to IP/MPLS infrastructures without cannibalizing revenue from these services. During migration, they also try to keep network downtime to a minimum (for example, in the order of a few minutes per year) to keep the cost of network outages in check. For example, a 1-minute network outage that affects 100 customers could cost a service provider several hundred thousand dollars.[2] Therefore, it is not surprising to know that network reliability and availability rank among the top concerns of the most service providers. In short, high availability of IP/MPLS networks is a prerequisite to offer reliable and profitable carrier-class services. A well-designed network element, such as a router, facilitates the building of highly available networks and reduces the capex and opex associated with redundant network infrastructures.

Defining Key Terms

Before proceeding further, it would be useful to define some key terms.

Availability and Unavailability

The phrase "availability of a system such as a router or network" denotes the probability (with values in the 0.0 to 1.0 range such as 0.1, 0.2, and so forth) that the system or network can be used when needed. Alternatively, the phrase describes the fraction of the time that the service is available. As a benchmark, carrier-class network equipment requires availability in the range of five-nines (0.99999), which means the equipment is available for service 99.999 percent of the time.

The term *unavailability* is defined as the probability that a system or network is not available when needed, or as the fraction of the time service is not available. An alternative and often more convenient expression (because of its additive properties) for unavailability is *downtime per year*. Downtime in units of minutes per year is obtained through multiplication of unavailability values by minutes in a year (365 days in a year times 24 hours in a day times 60 minutes in an hour). Service providers commonly use yet another expression for unavailability, especially when referring to voice calls. This term is *defects per million* (DPM). DPM measures the number of defective units (or number of failed call attempts) out of a sample size of one million units (1,000,000 call attempts). DPM is obtained by multiplying unavailability by 1,000,000. From these definitions, it follows that 0.99999 availability is equivalent to 0.00001 unavailability, 5.256 downtime per year, or 10 DPM.

Reliability and Its Relationship to Availability

The phrase "reliability of a system or network" is defined as the probability that the system or network will perform its intended function without failure over a given period of time. A commonly used measure of reliability is known as *mean time between failures* (MTBF), which is the average expected time between failures. A service outage caused by a failure is represented as mean time to repair (MTTR). That is the average time expected to be required to restore a system from a failure. MTTR includes time required for failure detection, fault diagnosis, and actual repair. Availability is related to MTBF and MTTR as follows:

$$\text{Availability} = \text{MTBF}/(\text{MTBF} + \text{MTTR})$$

This relationship shows that increasing MTBF and decreasing MTTR improves availability. This means that the availability of a router can be improved by increasing the reliability of its hardware and software components. Similarly, improving the reliability of its constituent elements such as routers, switches, and transport facilities can enhance the availability of a network.

In general, reliability is just one of several factors that can influence the availability of a system. For example, in addition to reliability of constituent network elements, network availability is strongly influenced by the fault-tolerance capability of the network elements, as described in the following section.

Fault Tolerance and Its Effect on Availability

Fault tolerance describes the characteristics of a system or component that is designed in such a way that, in the event of a component failure, a backup or "redundant" component immediately can take its place with no loss of service. Fault tolerance can be provided via software, hardware, or combination of the two. The switch between the failing component and the backup component is opaque to the outside world—from the view outside the system, no failure has occurred.

A network is said to be fault tolerant or survivable if it can maintain or restore an acceptable level of service performance during network failures. Network-level fault tolerance relies on software or hardware to quickly detect the failure and switch to a known backup path/link. The backup paths may be provided at multiple transport layers, including *wavelength-division multiplexing* (WDM), Synchronous Optical Network/Synchronous Digital Hierarchy (SONET/SDH), and MPLS.

As described in the previous section, improving MTBF can increase overall system availability. However, by using redundant components, one can reduce system downtime by orders of magnitude and get closer to the carrier-class goal of five-nines availability while keeping the MTBF and MTTR the same. The effectiveness of a redundancy scheme depends on its switchover success rate (the probability of a successful switchover from active to standby component when the active component fails). Generally, it is difficult to achieve a perfect (100 percent) switchover success rate. In practice, a redundancy scheme that can achieve a 99 percent or better switchover success rate is considered a good design.

To summarize, redundancy is one of the key building blocks for improving high availability. Redundancy not only prevents equipment failures from causing service outages, it also can provide a means for in-service planned maintenance and upgrade activities.

MPLS Network Components

An MPLS-based network consists of routers and switches interconnected via transport facilities such as fiber links (see Figure 1-1). Customers connect to the backbone (core) network through multiservice edge (MSE) routers. The backbone comprises the core routers that provide high-speed transport and connectivity between the MSE routers. An MSE router contains different types of line cards and physical interfaces to provide Layer 2 and Layer 3 services, including ATM, FR, Ethernet, and IP/MPLS VPNs.

Figure 1-1 *Converged IP/MPLS Network Architecture*

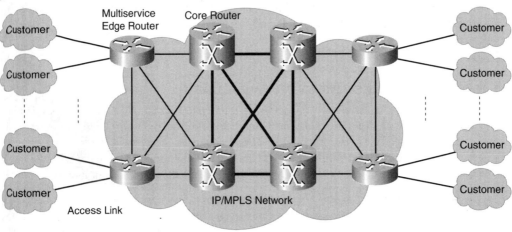

In the incoming direction, line cards receive packets from external interfaces and forward them to the switching fabric (see Figure 1-2). In the outgoing direction, line cards receive packets from the switching fabric and forward them to the outgoing interfaces. The switching fabric, the heart of the router, is used for switching packets between line cards. The IP/MPLS control-plane software, the brain of a router, resides in the control processor card. The phrase *IP/MPLS control plane* refers to the set of tasks performed by IP routing and MPLS signaling protocols. IP routing protocols are used to advertise network topology, exchange routing information, and calculate forwarding paths between routers within (intra) and between (inter) network routing domains. Examples of IP routing protocols include *Open Shortest Path First* (OSPF), *Intermediate System-to-Intermediate System* (IS-IS), and *Border Gateway Protocol* (BGP). MPLS signaling protocols are used to establish, maintain, and release *label-switched paths* (LSP). Examples of MPLS signaling protocols include BGP, *Label Distribution Protocol* (LDP), and *Resource Reservation Protocol* (RSVP). The IP control plane may also contain tunneling protocols such as Layer 2 Tunneling Protocol (L2TP) and Generic Routing Encapsulation (GRE), but these protocols are not covered in this book.

Because redundant network elements add to the overall network cost, service providers typically employ different levels and types of fault tolerance in the edge and core network. For example, the core network is generally designed to protect against core router failures through mesh connectivity. This allows alternative paths to be quickly established and used in the face of a failure. In the core, additional routers and links are used to provide fault tolerance. In contrast, on the edge, often thousands of customers are connected through a single router, and the edge router usually represents a single point of failure. The edge router is what most service providers consider the most vulnerable point of their network after the core is protected. On the edge, instead of using additional routers and links as in the core, redundancy within the edge router via redundant control processor cards, redundant line cards, and redundant links (such as SONET/SDH Automatic Protection Switching [APS]) are commonly used to provide fault tolerance.

Figure 1-2   *Functional Components of Router Architecture*

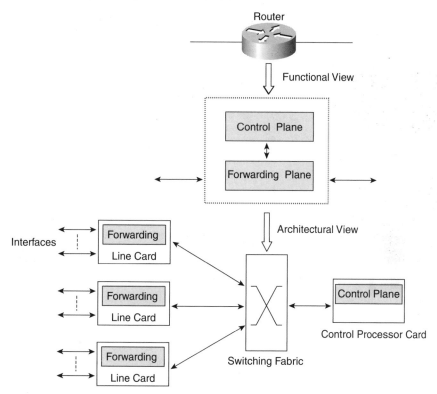

In summary, service (to a customer) downtime can result from failure of the access port, edge links, the edge router, backbone transport facilities, or the core routers. Generally, the core network offers a higher level of fault tolerance than the edge network. The edge router is an important network element because it routes traffic to/from multiple customers to the core network. Therefore, improving the availability of edge routers is extremely important. In short, service providers are looking for truly edge-to-edge reliability, and this includes all of the edge routers as well as the core routers.

Network and Service Outages

A service is the set of tasks performed by the network upon a request from the user such as a voice call, Internet access, e-mail, and so forth. A *service outage* is the users' inability to request a new service or to continue to use an existing service because the service is either no longer available or it is impaired. As discussed previously, availability of a network strongly depends on the frequency of service outages and the recovery time for each outage. A *network outage* is the loss of network resources, including routers, switches, and transport facilities, because of the following:

- Complete or partial failure of hardware and software components
- Power outages
- Scheduled maintenance such as software or hardware upgrades
- Operational errors such as configuration errors
- Acts of nature such as floods, tornadoes, and earthquakes

Planned and Unplanned Outages

Each network outage can be broadly categorized as either "unplanned" or "planned." An unplanned network outage occurs because of unforeseen failures of network elements. These failures include faults internal to a router's hardware/software components such as control-plane software crashes, line cards, link transceivers, and the power supply or faults external to the router such as fiber cuts, loss of power in a carrier facility, and so forth. A planned network outage occurs when a network element such as router is taken out of service because of scheduled events (for example, a software upgrade).

Main Causes of Network Outages

What are the main causes of network outages? As it turns out, several culprits contribute to network downtime. According to a University of Michigan one-year reliability study of IP core routers conducted in a regional IP service provider network, router interface downtime averaged about 955 minutes per year, which translates to an interface availability of only 0.998.[3] As a reference point, a carrier-class router is expected to have a downtime of only 5.2 minutes per year. The same study indicated the following percentages of causes for total network downtime:

- 23 percent for router failure (software/hardware faults, denial-of-service attack)
- 32 percent for link failures (fiber cuts, network congestion)
- 36 percent for router maintenance (software and hardware upgrade, configuration errors)
- The remaining 9 percent for other miscellaneous reasons

According to another study, router software failures are the single biggest (25 percent) cause of all router outages.[4] Moreover, within software-related outages, router control-plane failure is the biggest (60 percent) cause of software failures. The following section provides a brief overview of various node- and network-level fault-tolerance approaches that can help to improve network availability.

Design Strategies for Network Survivability

The reliability and availability of an IP/MPLS network can be examined from two interrelated viewpoints: service and network views. The *service view* deals with satisfying customer expectations such as availability of service and other *service-level agreements* (SLA). The *network view* deals with reducing network equipment and operation costs. Because the main task of a network is to provide user services, the reliability and availability requirements for the network are driven by the service view. An effective network design seeks to satisfy service reliability and availability objectives at the minimum network equipment (capex) and operational (opex) cost.

A packet-switched network consists of interconnected network elements, including routers, switches, and transport links. Network availability depends on the reliability and availability of its network elements. In particular, fault tolerance of router hardware and software components is crucial to deliver user services with negotiated SLAs. A carrier-class router is typically expected to satisfy requirements such as the following:

- No single hardware fault should result in a loss or degradation of user traffic or a loss of control-plane and management functions.

- System downtime should be less than 5.256 minutes per year.

- Line cards, switching fabric, and control processor cards should be redundant with capability to monitor standby cards.

- The control-plane software/hardware module should not be a single point of failure, and the service (forwarding plane) should not be disrupted due to failure of the control plane.

- The router should be capable of service recovery from link/node failures.

Generally, these carrier-class availability requirements are satisfied using a combination of node- and network-level fault-tolerance techniques, as described in the sections that follow.

Mitigating Node-Level Unplanned Hardware-Related Outages

One of the most effective techniques for reducing unplanned hardware-related downtime in a router is the use of redundant hardware components, including line cards, switching fabric, control processor cards, and physical interfaces. Three types of redundancy schemes are commonly used for this purpose:

- **One-for-N (1:N)**—There is one standby component for every N active component.

- **One-for-one (1:1)**—There is a standby component for each active component.

- **One-plus-one (1+1)**—This is similar to the one-for-one scheme except that in the case of one-plus-one, traffic is transmitted simultaneously on both active and standby components. (Traffic is generally ignored on the standby.) An example of one-plus-one redundancy is the 1+1 SONET/SDH APS scheme that avoids loss of data traffic caused by link failure.

A detailed discussion of component redundancy architectures is beyond the scope of this book.

Mitigating Node-Level Unplanned Software-Related Outages

It is apparent that reliability and stability of router hardware and software are absolutely crucial for building reliable and available IP/MPLS networks. As discussed previously, routers use redundant switching fabric, control processor cards, line cards, and interfaces to achieve node-level hardware fault tolerance. Although most routers usually have adequate hardware-component redundancy coverage, the control-plane software still remains a weak link and a prime cause of router failures.

The two most important constituents of the router software are IP and MPLS control-plane protocols. The IP control-plane component consists of IP routing protocols such as OSPF, IS-IS, and BGP, which exchange network topology information and thus help build the IP forwarding state. The MPLS control-plane component is composed of signaling protocols such as LDP, RSVP-TE, and BGP. Label-switching routers (LSR) use information provided by IP/MPLS control-plane components to construct the MPLS forwarding state. The IP forwarding state is used to transfer IP packets from an incoming port of the router to an outgoing port using a destination IP address. In contrast, the MPLS forwarding state is used for moving packets from input to output ports based on label information.

IP and MPLS forwarding tables are collectively referred to as the *forwarding plane*. Because of the time-critical nature of packet-forwarding operations, the forwarding-plane functions are typically distributed on line cards to enhance forwarding performance. In contrast, control-plane tasks are relatively less time critical and therefore often reside on the central control processor card. Because control-plane protocols constitute router intelligence, the control processor serves as host to the router's brain. Because of the pivotal importance of the control-plane functions to the router operation, a control processor is normally protected against failure through 1:1 (active and standby) redundancy.

The existing control-plane software restart and switchover behavior in routers is disruptive and therefore undesirable. When a router detects a software/hardware failure in the active control processor, it switches over to the standby and, in this process, not only restarts its control software but also resets the forwarding plane in the line cards. The end result of this behavior means disruption of data forwarding and the accompanied service outage. Consider, for example, the restart of an IP control-plane protocol such as OSPF or IS-IS. When OSPF or IS-IS restarts, the failing router's *interior gateway protocol* (IGP) neighbors detect this restart and originate LSAs or LSPs to omit links to the restarting router. Upon receiving new LSAs or LSPs, the nonrestarting routers recompute their paths to avoid the restarting router. This shows that the original IP control-plane restart behavior causes unnecessary disruption of traffic in the restarting router, generates extra IGP control traffic, and triggers costly *shortest path first* (SPF) recomputations in nonrestarting routers. Similarly, when the MPLS control plane restarts, LDPs withdraw labels that were advertised prior to this failure. Once again, this behavior results in disruption of the MPLS forwarding. In short, one can say that control-plane restart causes instability throughout the network.

This description clearly shows that the original IP/MPLS control-plane restart behavior is totally unacceptable, particularly when you consider the fact that service providers are deploying more and more IP/MPLS networks to deliver legacy services and customers are expecting a better or comparable level of reliability and availability. Therefore, disruption of the IP/MPLS forwarding plane must be reduced to an absolute minimum. The next section outlines some approaches to achieve this goal.

Reducing Downtime Related to Unplanned Control-Plane Restart

Several types of software redundancy schemes enable you to reduce router downtime resulting from unplanned control-plane failures. One such approach (similar to the 1:1 hardware redundancy scheme) is to instantiate two identical copies of control-plane software on active and standby control processors. The two instances execute independently without any inter-instance communication, and both instances send/receive identical control packets. For example, in the incoming direction, control packets are replicated and passed on to both instances. In the outgoing direction, control packets from the standby instance are discarded.

A second scheme (a variant of the previous approach) is to instantiate two identical copies of the control plane. The two instances execute in complete lock step using inter-instance communication. When a control packet is received, it is processed in identical fashion and at the exact same instant by the active and the standby instance.

A third approach is to instantiate two copies of the control plane on active and standby control processors. The active instance executes, whereas the inactive instance does not. However, the standby instance maintains partial state of the active instance by receiving state synchronization messages. For example, the active instance of an IP routing protocol establishes sessions, exchanges routing information with peers, and helps build and maintain routing/forwarding tables. In contrast, the inactive standby instance does not exchange routing information with external peers. After switchover, the standby instance takes over, reestablishes peer sessions, and resynchronizes its state information. Another variant of the third approach maintains complete state on the standby and can switch over without having to reestablish sessions from the point of view of the neighbors. However, this variant is less scalable because it requires preservation of the complete state.

Table 1-1 describes the advantages and disadvantages of each approach.

Table 1-1 *Advantages and Disadvantages of Software Redundancy Approaches*

Approach	Advantages	Disadvantages
Approach 1 Instantiate two identical copies of the control-plane software on active and standby control processors. The two instances execute independently.	Control-plane failure and resulting switchover hidden from neighbors No requirement for changes to IP/MPLS control-plane protocols	Extra processing burden for replicating control packets Necessity to start both instances at the same time Restriction of precluding software upgrades and downgrades
Approach 2 Instantiate two identical copies of the control-plane software on active and standby control processors. The two instances execute in lock step using inter-instance communication.	Fast recovery time No necessity for protocol changes	Design complexity of synchronizing state Requirement to run two instances synchronously Restriction of precluding software upgrades and downgrades
Approach 3 Instantiate two copies of the control plane on active and standby control processors. The standby instance maintains partial state.	Allows the restarting router to continue to forward across the control-plane recovery Allows for software upgrades	Necessity to reestablish sessions and recover the control-plane state information after the restart Needs protocol extensions

The main strength of the first approach is that the control-plane failure and resulting switchover is hidden from neighbors and therefore does not require any changes to IP/MPLS control-plane protocols. However, this approach has two big drawbacks: extra processing burden for replicating control packets, and the necessity to start both instances at the same time. The second drawback is very restrictive because it precludes software upgrades and downgrades. The key advantages of the second approach are fast recovery time and absence of necessity to make protocol changes. The main disadvantages of this approach are design complexity to synchronize state and the requirement to run two instances synchronously. The latter requirement implies that, like the first approach, the second approach does not allow software upgrades. The main disadvantage of the third approach is the necessity to reestablish sessions and recover control-plane state information after the restart. This requires IP/MPLS protocol extensions and support from neighbors in maintaining their forwarding state while the restarting router comes back.

The third approach, analogous to other two approaches, allows the restarting router to continue to forward across the control-plane recovery. However, unlike the other two schemes, the third approach allows software upgrades, which is a big plus toward achieving the carrier-class availability goals.

Cisco IOS architecture is likely to adopt the third approach and its variants to provide fault-tolerant control-plane software architecture on routers. For example, in the core and on the core side of the edge routers where scalability is extremely important, the third approach can be used because it requires preserving partial control-plane state. In contrast, on the customer side of edge routers where scalability is generally not much of an issue, a variant of the third approach (completely stateful) can be used.

Stateful Switchover and Nonstop Forwarding

The combination of separation of control- and forwarding-plane components, 1:1 redundant control processors, and fault-tolerant control-plane software allows Cisco IOS architecture to make an automatic nondisruptive stateful control-plane switchover upon detection of software/hardware failures in the active control processor. In IOS the term *stateful switchover* (SSO) refers to the aforementioned control-plane redundancy framework that enables nondisruptive automatic SSO of the control plane upon detection of hardware/software failure. The term *nonstop forwarding* (NSF) refers to the capability of a router to continue to forward while its control plane recovers from a fault. NSF requires separation of control- and forwarding-plane functions.

Reducing Unplanned Downtime Using Component-Level Modularity and Restartability

The SSO discussion in the preceding section assumes that control-plane software executes as one or more inseparable components (or processes) that are sharing critical data structures. In that case, because various control-plane components are inseparable and incapable of restarting individually, failure in one component leads to failure of all other components and necessitates control-plane switchover. Therefore, nonrestartable components require stateful redundancy schemes and switchovers to recover from failures (see Figure 1-3).

A software component is said to be *restartable* if it is capable of recovering from fatal runtime errors. In a redundant system, a restartable component that can correctly recover from failures should not require a switchover. However, when a restartable component fails to restart correctly, it should cause a switchover to the standby to recover from failures.

Figure 1-3 *Nonrestartable and Restartable Control-Plane Components*

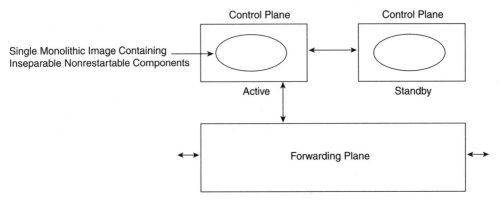

Single Monolithic Image Containing
Inseparable Nonrestartable Components

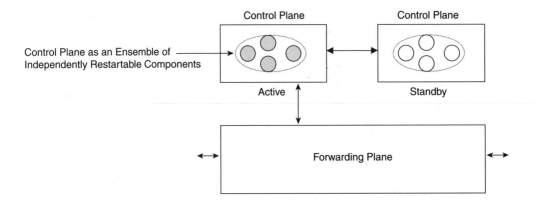

Control Plane as an Ensemble of
Independently Restartable Components

Hence, the component-level restartability complements and extends the SSO approach by providing additional fault-tolerance coverage. In the component-level restartability approach, following system initialization, a system management module instantiates all control-plane components and monitors their health. Upon detecting failure of a control-plane component, the system manager restarts the failed component without disturbing other components or requiring control-plane switchover. After having restarted, the process recovers its preserved state information and resumes normal operation.

It is worth noting that unlike SSO, the process-level restartability approach can be used to improve control-plane availability of routers with single as well as redundant control processors. In a nonredundant control processor scenario, the component restartability-based approach allows a router to recover from unplanned control-plane software component failures. In a redundant control processor case, a combination of SSO and component-level restartability helps improve the overall fault isolation, reliability, and availability of the control plane. In the latter case, for example, a router can recover from minor software component-level faults without requiring switchover to the standby control processor and yet use SSO to recover from major software or hardware faults.

In summary, component restartability is not a remedy for all failure scenarios. For example, if critical data structures of the restartable component are damaged, that component will fail to restart. Complete switchover with redundant hardware components and no shared data (no shared memory) offers a higher level of fault tolerance. You should view these approaches as occurring within a spectrum of approaches to improve high availability, with their own attendant benefits and costs.

In the remainder of this book, it is assumed that the control-plane software runs as a single image containing inseparable nonrestartable components. Discussion of approaches for improving control-plane reliability and availability using component-level modularity and restartability is beyond the scope of this book.

Mitigating Node-Level Planned Outages

As discussed previously, planned events such as software upgrades are a big contributor to network downtime. To deliver carrier-class services, unplanned and planned outages must be reduced. The downtime due to planned events is reduced using an in-service software-upgrade mechanism that allows upgrading the router software without service disruption.

Mitigating Network Outages Against Link and Node Failures

So far this chapter has discussed strategies for reducing downtime caused by unplanned control-plane restart and planned router operations such as software upgrades. Another significant contribution to network downtime comes from link failures. The impact of transport path failures is mitigated by using multilayer protection/rerouting schemes such as SONET/SDH APS and emerging MPLS-based methods such as *FastReRoute* (FRR). With the success of MPLS deployments, the use of MPLS-based recovery schemes is also growing to provide LSP-level protection against link/node failures. Although SONET/SDH-based protection is widely deployed, protection at the lower transport layers is very coarse and can be very wasteful and expensive. In contrast, MPLS-based recovery can provide much finer granularity and presents an efficient, attractive, and complementary alternative to SONET/SDH-based protection.

Mitigating Network Outages via Effective Operation and Maintenance Mechanisms

As service providers move more and more revenue-generating services onto converged IP/MPLS networks, effective MPLS *operation and maintenance* (OAM) mechanisms become an absolute necessity to deliver carrier-class services. This is because service providers rely on robust OAM tools to quickly identify and remove network faults, reduce service downtime, and maintain a high level of network availability. A layered view of IP/MPLS availability architecture is depicted in Figure 1-4.

Figure 1-4 *Dependence of End-to-End IP/MPLS Service Availability on Node and Network Level Availability*

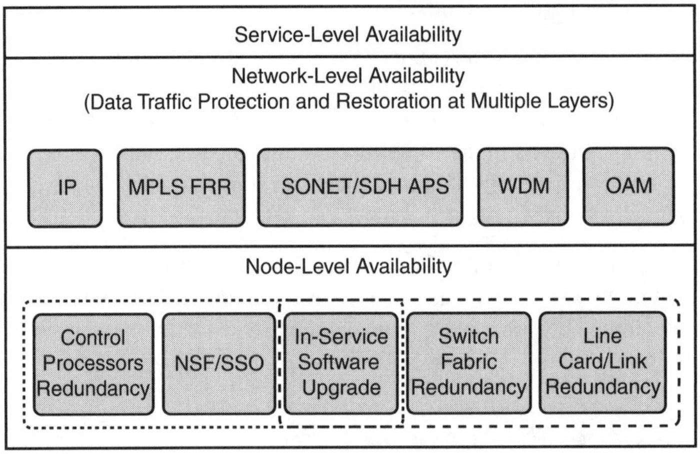

Improving Network Security via Fault-Tolerance Mechanisms

Network resources include routers, switches, hardware, software, data stored on line, data in transit over the network, and so forth. Network security refers to the set of measures taken to protect a resource against unauthorized access. For each resource, the key objectives of security are resource availability, data confidentiality (meaning that information is not made available or disclosed to unauthorized individuals or entities), and data integrity (meaning that information has not been modified in an unauthorized manner). Some exploits that might threaten an IP/MPLS network include attacks on control and forwarding planes, sniffing of data packets, denial-of-service (DoS) attacks, and so forth. In a DoS attack, an attacker seeks to disrupt or prevent the use of a service by its legitimate users. A DoS attack might appear in different forms such as taking network devices out of service by overwhelming the target devices with requests for service or modifying their normal behavior. A DoS attack in which the network is overwhelmed with requests for service is also known as a resource-exhaustion DoS attack. Resource-exhaustion DoS attacks can be mounted against any network resource such as forwarding plane, control plane (for example, control processor), link bandwidth, and so forth.

Because the goal of fault-tolerance mechanisms is to protect a system or network against different types of failures by improving its availability, fault-tolerance mechanisms may also be thought of as defensive techniques against malicious security threats. For example, separation of control plane and forwarding plane (as provided in the SSO/NSF framework) can be used to improve security against some attacks. This, for example, might help to limit DoS attacks against a control plane to that particular component only and might allow the forwarding-plane component to continue to function normally.

In general, to offer network services securely and reliably, security and fault-tolerance mechanisms must be built in to IP and MPLS networks. Examples of common defensive techniques against network security threats include data encryption, authentication, packet filtering, firewalls, separation of control and forwarding planes, intrusion detection, intrusion prevention, and so forth.[5] A detailed discussion of network security mechanisms is beyond the scope of this book.

Scope of the Book

From the discussions in this chapter so far, you know that the design of carrier-class IP/MPLS networks involves reducing both unplanned and planned outages by using a variety of fault-tolerance techniques, including node-level hardware redundancy, control-plane software redundancy, MPLS-layer redundant LSPs, OAM mechanisms, and in-service software upgrades. In short, the reliability and availability of an IP/MPLS network encompasses a broad set of functional areas.

The main purpose of this book is to describe IP/MPLS control-plane fault-tolerance mechanisms that enable you to reduce downtime and improve network availability (by reducing unplanned IP/MPLS control-plane failures). Specifically, this book intends to cover three aspects of the control plane, as follows:

- IP/MPLS forwarding-plane NSF mechanisms that allow a router to continue to forward traffic while its control plane recovers from a failure

- IP/MPLS control-plane restart mechanisms that enable IP/MPLS control-plane components to restart and recover state without disrupting the forwarding plane

- Use of the previous two mechanisms to reduce downtime in the converged IP/MPLS backbone when using MPLS applications such as *traffic engineering* (TE), *Layer 2 VPNs* (L2VPNs), and *Layer 3 VPNs* (L3VPNs).

In the remainder of this book, it is assumed that the control-plane software executes as a single image containing inseparable nonrestartable components. A detailed discussion of process-level modularity and restartability is beyond the scope of this book.

Although for completeness sake fault-tolerance mechanisms such as MPLS FRR, MPLS OAM, and in-service software upgrades are briefly mentioned in a later chapter, a detailed discussion of these mechanisms is also beyond the scope of this book.

References

[1] Heavy Reading Analysts, "2004 Survey of Carrier Attitudes Toward IP/MPLS Backbones and VPNs," *Heavy Reading Report*, Vol. 2, No. 4, January 2004.

[2] Network Strategy Partners, "Reliable IP Nodes: A Prerequisite to Profitable IP Services," White Paper, November 2002.

[3] Ahuja, A., F. Jahanian, and C. Labovitz, "Experimental Study of Internet Stability and Wide-Area Backbone Failures," Proceeding of 29th International Symposium on Fault-Tolerant Computing, June 1999.

[4] Heywood, P., and M. Reardon, "IP Reliability," *Light Reading Report*, March 2003.

[5] Fang, L., "Security Framework for Provider Provisioned Virtual Private Networks," IETF work in progress, July 2004.

CHAPTER 2

IP Forwarding Plane: Achieving Nonstop Forwarding

IP routers contain two interrelated but largely independent components, namely control and forwarding. The IP control plane consists of routing protocols that provide routing information used to build a *Forwarding Information Base* (FIB). The IP forwarding plane comprises a FIB, or forwarding table, that is used to forward packets toward their destination. On the other hand, the IP forwarding plane performs time-critical tasks such as address lookup, packet switching from incoming to outgoing links, and packet scheduling for transmission on the outgoing link. Among these tasks, IP address lookup usually is a major bottleneck in high-performance routers.

This chapter begins with an overview of the FIB and its usage to forward IP packets. After a brief description of the IP address lookup operation, an overview of the trie-based data structures is presented. Trie-based prefix representations are attractive because the performance metrics of the resulting lookup schemes can be conveniently tuned by varying certain parameters. This is followed by an overview of the centralized forwarding architecture paradigm. The discussion continues with analysis of the factors causing performance degradation in the centralized forwarding architecture and trends toward distributed forwarding architecture that avoid such shortcomings. This naturally leads to a description of a fault-tolerant control-plane architecture framework that allows nonstop forwarding operations in a router across its control-plane failure. The chapter concludes with a brief chapter summary.

Overview of IP Forwarding

The Internet is a collection of interconnected networks for forwarding packets between hosts using *Internet Protocol* (IP). IP provides connectionless datagram service without end-to-end delivery guarantees. Throughout this book, unless explicitly stated otherwise, the term *IP* refers to *IP version 4* (IPv4).[1]

In the Internet model, systems that forward IP packets are called *routers*. That is, one of the primary functions of a router is to forward packets toward their final destinations. To accomplish this task, a router needs to make a forwarding decision for each packet to determine the next-hop address and the outgoing link information. The routing information is obtained through routing protocols and is used to build the FIB or forwarding table.

The forwarding process generally consists of three distinct operations:

- Address lookup to determine the outgoing link
- Forwarding packets through the switching fabric when the outgoing link resides on a line card different than that on which the packet was received, or forwarding packets locally without traversing the switching fabric (for example, when the outgoing link is on the same line card)
- Scheduling

The step that involves a forwarding table search using an incoming packet's IP destination address as the search key is called the *address lookup*. The subsequent step of transferring the packet to a link on a different or the same line card using forwarding information retrieved by address lookup is known as *switching*. In the final step, called *scheduling*, the packet is scheduled for transmission on the outgoing link. Figure 2-1 shows the basic sequence of IP forwarding-plane operations.

Figure 2-1 *Basic Operations in IP Forwarding*

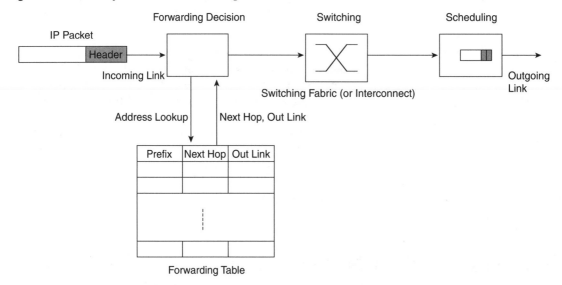

Because IP packets are forwarded based on the IP destination address, the design and complexity of the address lookup operation is influenced by the addressing scheme used. IPv4 addresses are 32 bits long and are partitioned into a network part and a host part (see Figure 2-2). The class of the IP address (denoted as A, B, and C) determines the number of bits in the network and the host part. For example, Class A addresses assign 8 bits to the network part and 24 bits to the host part. Similarly, Class B and Class C addresses assign 16 and 24 bits, respectively, in the network part.

Figure 2-2   *IP Class A, B, and C Addresses*

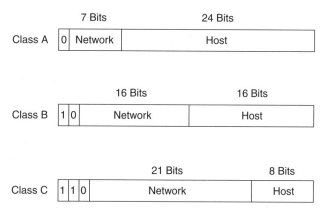

Classful Addressing

The addressing scheme based on partitioning of IP addresses into classes is known as the *classful model*. The classful addressing model corresponds to a two-level routing hierarchy. That is, routers can forward a packet based on the network part of the packet's destination address until it reaches its destination network. Therefore, routers along the path can use a single entry corresponding to network part of the IP destination address (also known as *address prefix*) to forward packets to all hosts attached to a network identified by the address prefix.

The method of representing a group of addresses by prefixes is known as *address aggregation*. To reduce the routing table size, routing tables generally contain prefixes. The classful address scheme allows only 8-, 16-, and 24-length prefixes for Class A, B, and C, respectively. In the Internet, a core router may maintain a large number of routes. For example, a Border Gateway Protocol (BGP) routing table in a core router may contain 100,000 entries and be growing rapidly.

Classless Addressing

To keep the routing table size manageable in core routers, further *address aggregation* is needed. This is achieved using a scheme known as *classless interdomain routing* (CIDR), which allows address prefixes of arbitrary length.[2] CIDR represents addresses as <prefix, length> tuples (also known as *aggregates*), in which length indicates the number of bits in the prefix counting from the far left. For example, 178.214.0.0/18 is an aggregate of length 18. Note that CIDR allows prefixes with lengths smaller than 8. (Such a network prefix is called a *supernet*.) Generally, the shorter the prefix length, the greater the level of aggregation. In summary, address prefixes enable aggregation of routing information and help reduce routing table size.

IP Address Lookup

Although the CIDR scheme helps to reduce routing table size, it makes the address lookup operation more complex in comparison with classful addressing. This is because in classful addressing, prefixes can be only 8, 16, or 24 bits in length and can be found via an exact-prefix-match algorithm using standard search techniques such as binary search. In the case of CIDR, because of arbitrary prefix lengths, prefix search is based on the longest prefix match (or best match) rather than an exact match. Therefore, finding the longest matching prefix involves comparing the prefix bit pattern (value) and the length.

With the growth of the Internet, routing table size, link data rates, and packet-forwarding requirements for a core router have increased substantially. To support packet forwarding at wire speed, high-end routers must be able to perform address lookup operations very quickly. For example, more than half a million address lookups per second are required to support a link with a 1-Gbps data rate. One can easily calculate that to support a 10-Gbps link would require in the order of 5 million address lookups per second. Therefore, design of an efficient address lookup scheme is crucial to meet forwarding requirements of high-end routers. In general, performance of an address lookup scheme is characterized in terms of metrics such as lookup time, update time, and memory consumption. Ideally, you are interested in a scheme with minimum lookup time, minimum dynamic update time, and minimum memory requirement. Because it is difficult to simultaneously satisfy these conflicting design objectives, in practice different design trade-offs are made depending on the relative importance of one performance aspect over the other.

A trie (pronounced as "try") is a tree data structure that uses a radix (or digital base) to decompose a key into digits to organize and search elements in the tree.[3] A trie has two types of nodes: a branch node and element (leaf) node. A branch node has one or more children. A leaf node has no children. One of the most common methods of arranging prefixes is a binary trie.

A trie with a radix 2 is called a binary trie. In a *binary trie*, each node has two children at the most. An example of binary trie for a set of address prefixes P1, P2, P3, P4, and P5 is shown in Figure 2-3. A node that corresponds to a prefix either contains forwarding information or a pointer to it. To find a longest prefix match in a binary trie, the IP destination address (key) is decomposed into binary digits and used to direct the search to left or right according to sequential inspection of bits in the key. In the process of traversing the trie, every time a node marked as prefix is visited, it is remembered as the last longest prefix match. The search terminates when a leaf node is reached and the longest matching prefix is the last longest prefix match. For example, an address lookup for the prefix 111* in binary trie shown in Figure 2-3 would yield prefix P3 as the longest matching prefix.

Although a binary trie provides a simple scheme for arranging and searching arbitrary-length address prefixes, binary tries are not suitable for forwarding at high data rates because of slower lookup times. The slower address lookup times of a binary trie result mainly from its bit-by-bit sequential inspection operation, which may require a large number of memory accesses depending on the prefix length. For example, in the worst case, a binary trie may require 32 memory accesses for 1 address lookup.

Figure 2-3 *Binary Trie*

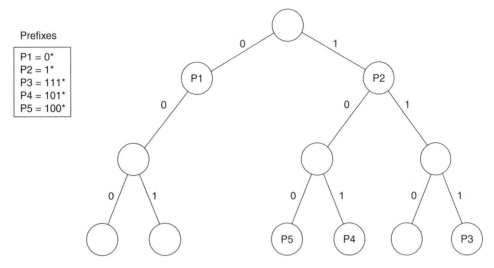

Prefixes

P1 = 0*
P2 = 1*
P3 = 111*
P4 = 101*
P5 = 100*

Inspecting several bits simultaneously can reduce the number of memory accesses and speed up the lookup operations. A trie that allows multiple bits to be inspected simultaneously is known as a *multibit-trie* (m-trie). The number of bits to be inspected is called the *stride*, and the stride can be fixed or variable in each step. An m-trie in which all nodes at a given level have the same stride is called a *fixed-stride m-trie*. An m-trie in which nodes at a given level have different strides is known as a *variable-stride m-trie*. Figure 2-4 shows an example of a variable-stride m-trie. For instance, an address lookup for the prefix 0001* involves using a stride of 2 bits at the first level of the tree and strides of 1 bit at the succeeding levels and would locate P5 as the longest matching prefix.

A fixed-stride m-trie normally has a simpler implementation than a variable-stride m-trie, but it consumes more memory. In general, selection of stride size involves a design trade-off between lookup time and memory usage.[4] For example, larger stride sizes result in faster lookup times but require more memory for storage. Note that with the notion of strides, an m-trie cannot support arbitrary-length prefixes. This problem is usually solved by transforming a prefix length into an equivalent length that can be supported by the strides of the m-trie.

A common prefix-transformation technique used for this purpose is called *prefix expansion*.[5] For example, an m-trie with first stride of 4 bits does not allow prefixes with a length smaller than 4 bits. For instance, to look up a prefix 110* in the previous trie, the prefix is first expanded into two prefixes, 1100* and 1101*. An m-trie of stride s is a trie in which each node has 2^s children. In addition to lookup time and memory consumption, the size of strides also influences the update time. For example, to insert a prefix in a subtrie with a stride s requires the modification, at most, of 2^{s-1} nodes. That means larger stride-size results in greater update times because more entries need to be modified because of prefix expansion.

In general, selection of an optimal stride size is difficult because it depends on a specific prefix distribution. In practice, different heuristics are used for selecting appropriate stride sizes. Examples of commonly used stride patterns include 24-8 (that is, a first-level stride of 24 bits and a second-level stride of 8 bits) and 16-8-8 (that is, a first-level stride of 16, second- and third-level strides of 8). If a majority of prefix entries are expected to have a prefix length of 24 bits or less, for example, using a first stride of 24 bits you can expect to find the best matching prefix in one memory access.[6] In summary, by varying the stride size, a multilevel m-trie provides a flexible way to trade off lookup time, memory requirements, and update time.

Figure 2-4 *A Variable-Stride M-Trie*

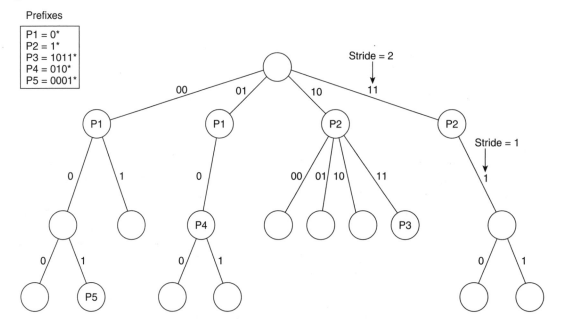

Evolution of IP Forwarding Architectures

An IP forwarding table is a database of destination prefixes and next hops. Each entry in this database describes a set of best paths to a given destination. The objective of IP address lookup is to locate a forwarding table entry that provides the best match for the packet's IP destination address (prefix). The located entry provides the next hop and outgoing link information for forwarding the packet toward its final destination.

Earlier generations of routers were typically based on central forwarding architectures in which the forwarding table was centrally implemented on a general-purpose processor. Because of large memory requirements, the forwarding table was typically stored in (slower) main memory. The centralized forwarding architecture adequately addressed the modest forwarding requirements at that time.

Route Cache-Based Centralized Forwarding Architecture

As link speeds increased, forwarding architectures had to be adapted to meet faster packet-forwarding rates. To keep up with increasing data rates, one of the techniques on which early-generation routers heavily relied was route caching. Route caching is based on the property of temporal and spatial locality exhibited by IP traffic. Temporal locality indicates that there is a high probability of reusing a given IP destination within a short period of time. Spatial locality indicates that there is a good chance of referencing addresses in the same address range. For example, a sequence of packets with the same IP destination address exhibit temporal locality, whereas a sequence of packets destined to the same subnet show high spatial locality.

A cache is generally small but faster (for example, memory access time of less than 50 ns) as compared to the slower main memory (for example, memory access time of less than 100 ns). With a route cache, forwarding of one or more initial packets for a new IP destination is based on slower forwarding table lookup. The result of slower forwarding table lookup for a given IP destination address is saved in the route cache. All subsequent packets for the same IP destination are then forwarded based on a faster address lookup in the route cache.

Route cache performance is commonly characterized in terms of hit ratio, which indicates the percentage of address lookups that were successfully found in the route cache. In general, the hit ratio of a route cache strongly depends on the degree of temporal/spatial locality in the IP traffic and the size of the cache. A route cache–based forwarding architecture may be quite efficient in an enterprise environment where IP traffic exhibits more locality and routing changes are infrequent. However, performance of a route cache–based forwarding architecture severely degrades in the Internet core where traffic typically exhibits much less locality because of the large number of packet destinations and route changes that take place more frequently. Some studies indicate that on the average 100 route changes per second may occur in the Internet core.[7] If routes change frequently, a route cache might need to invalidate corresponding routing entries. This amounts to a reduction in the cache hit ratio.

A lower hit ratio means more and more traffic is forwarded using slower forwarding table lookups. That is, because of a route cache miss penalty, the traffic that would normally be forwarded based on route cache now needs to be forwarded using a slower forwarding table. Some studies have shown that in the Internet core the route cache hits are as low as 50 percent to 70 percent.[8] This means that 30 percent to 50 percent of the lookups are even slower than they would be if there were no caches, because of *double lookups*—a cache lookup followed by another lookup in the slower forwarding table. Moreover, an additional penalty is paid every time there is a route change, because an existing cache entry must be invalidated and replaced with a valid one. Because forwarding table lookups are typically processing intensive, depending on the amount of traffic directed address lookup operations could easily overload the control processor and cause service outage.

Distributed Forwarding Architectures

As the amount of traffic carried by the Internet has grown, routing table size, link data rates, and aggregate bandwidth requirements for a core router have also increased substantially. Although the link data rates have kept pace with the increasing traffic, the packet-forwarding capacity has not been able to match increased data rates. The inability to increase forwarding capacity in relation to link data rates is mainly due to the bottleneck caused by IP address lookup operations. As described earlier, route cache–based forwarding architectures do not perform well in the Internet core. In addition, centralized forwarding architectures do not scale as the number of line cards, link data rates, and aggregate switching capacity increase. For example, a centralized forwarding architecture would require an increase in the forwarding rate to match the aggregate switching capacity. Therefore, address lookup easily becomes the system bottleneck and limits aggregate forwarding capacity.

For these reasons, modern high-performance routers avoid centralized forwarding architectures and route caching. In general, the recent industry trend has been toward distributed forwarding architectures. In a distributed forwarding architecture, address lookup is implemented on each line card either in software (for example, in a dedicated processor) or hardware (for example, in a specialized forwarding engine). Distributed forwarding architectures scale better because instead of having to support forwarding at a system aggregate rate, each line card needs to support forwarding-matching link rates, which typically are a fraction of the system aggregate forwarding capacity and relatively easier to achieve.

One of the key motivations for adopting a distributed forwarding architecture is the desire to separate time-critical and non-time-critical processing tasks. With this separation, non-time-critical tasks are implemented centrally. For example, the collecting of routing information by an IP control plane and the building of a database of destinations to outgoing interface mappings are functions that are implemented centrally. On the other hand, time-critical tasks such as IP address lookup are decentralized and implemented on line cards. Because IP forwarding-related time-critical tasks are distributed and can be independently optimized in each line card according to link data rates, the forwarding capacity of the system scales as the aggregate switching bandwidth and link data rates increase.

The decoupling of routing and forwarding tasks, however, requires separate databases—namely, a *Routing Information Base* (RIB) and a *Forwarding Information Base* (FIB). With this separation, each database can be optimized with respect to appropriate performance metrics. The RIB holds dynamic routing information received through routing protocols as well as static routing information supplied by users. A RIB usually contains multiple routes for a destination address. For example, a RIB might receive the same routes from different routing protocols or multiple routes corresponding to different metric values from the same protocol. Therefore, for each IP destination, the RIB provides a single path or several paths. A path specifies an outgoing interface to reach a certain next hop. When the next-hop IP address is the same as the packet's IP destination address, it is called a *directly attached next-hop path*; otherwise, the path is an indirectly attached next-hop path. The term recursive means that the path has a next hop but no outgoing interface. As described in a later chapter, recursive next-hop paths usually correspond to BGP routes. Because an outgoing interface must be known for the forwarding of a packet toward its destination, recursive routes involve one or more lookups on the next-hop addresses until a corresponding outgoing interface is found. Failure to find an outgoing interface for a next-hop address renders its associated route as unusable for forwarding.

The FIB is a subset of the RIB because it keeps only the best routes that can actually be used for forwarding. The RIB maintains all routes learned through user configurations and routing protocols, but inserts only the best usable routes in the FIB for each prefix based on administrative weights or other route metrics. Unlike a route cache that maintains only the most recently used routes, the FIB maintains all best usable routes in the RIB. In contrast to a route cache that may need to invalidate its entries frequently in a dynamic routing environment, FIB performance does not degrade because it mirrors the RIB and maintains all usable routes. A FIB entry contains all the information that is necessary to forward a packet, such as IP destination address, next hop, output interface, and link-layer header.[10] The RIB is unaware of Layer 2 encapsulation. It just installs the best usable routes in the FIB, but the FIB must have the destination address, next hop, outgoing interface, and the Layer 2 encapsulation to forward the packet. An adjacency provides the Layer 2 encapsulation information required for forwarding a packet to a next hop (identified by a Layer 3 address). An adjacency is usually created when a protocol such as Address Resolution Protocol [ARP]) learns about a next-hop node.[9] The ARP provides a next hop's IP address to Layer 2 address mapping.

A FIB entry maps an IP destination address to a single path or multiple paths. With multiple paths, traffic for the destination can be forwarded over multiple paths. The capability to forward packets to a given destination over multiple paths is known as *load balancing*. The standard packet-scheduling algorithms (such as round-robin, weighted round-robin, and so forth) may be used to distribute or load balance the traffic over multiple paths (see Figure 2-5). The most common form of load balancing is based on a hash of the IP packet header (for example, source and destination address) because this type of load balancing preserves packet ordering better than the various per-packet round-robin methods.

Because FIB forms the time-critical forwarding-plane path through a router, an efficient representation of the FIB is essential to obtain a forwarding architecture that scales with data rates and the number of address prefixes (or FIB entries). In this regard, you are interested in a representation that can be optimized for the smallest address lookup time and lowest memory consumption. In contrast, RIB representation is typically optimized for the smallest update time to handle route changes quickly. For example, to be able to process an average of 100 route changes per second, RIB must be able to perform an insert/delete or modify operation in 10 ms or less.

As described previously, m-trie-based lookup schemes can be tuned with respect to performance metrics such as lookup time, memory consumption, and update time. The ability to customize m-trie-based schemes to a broad range of software and hardware environments makes them very attractive for FIB and RIB implementations. For instance, RIB design can be optimized for faster update times, whereas FIB is used for faster address lookup and lower memory usage.

Figure 2-5   *Example of Per-Packet Load Balancing*

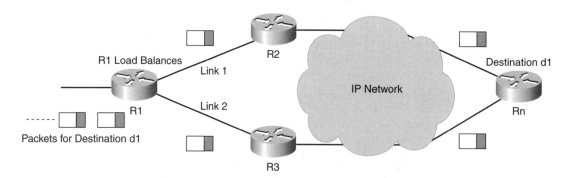

Figure 2-6 shows a generic distributed forwarding router architecture. Because routing information is centralized and forwarding is distributed, for correct and loop-free forwarding behavior, the FIB on each line card must remain synchronized with the latest routing information in the RIB. The process of building the FIB and its synchronization with the RIB consists of the following:

1. Receiving dynamic routing information from protocols and/or static routes from manual configuration.

2. Processing the received routing information builds the RIB.

3. Selecting the best usable routes in the RIB and updating the FIB. The route selection is commonly based on protocol administrative distance and route metrics. If there are multiple routes to a destination from different protocols, a protocol with a smaller administrative distance is preferred. Different protocols define and interpret their route metrics differently. If there were multiple routes to the same destination from a single routing protocol, all candidate routes would have the same administrative distance, but could have the same or different metrics. In that case, the best path or paths (if multiple best paths are kept for load balancing) are selected based on route metrics.

4. Distributing the FIB to the line cards for synchronization. The RIB to FIB synchronization occurs in two stages. First, when router line cards start or reload, the entire FIB is synchronized. Afterward, incremental resynchronization of the FIB takes place as a result of changes in existing routes and addition/deletion of new routes.

Figure 2-6   *Distributed IP Forwarding*

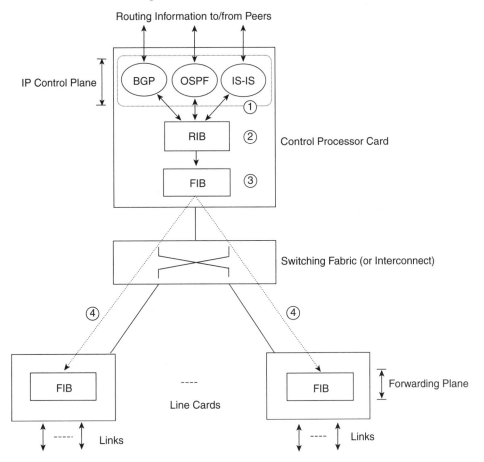

Cisco Express Forwarding

This section covers IP forwarding operations using Cisco Express Forwarding (CEF), which is a sophisticated Layer 3 IP forwarding architecture that provides scalable forwarding performance in a dynamic routing environment. For optimal forwarding, CEF decouples forwarding and routing functions. The forwarding information is maintained in a FIB that mirrors the best usable routing entries in the RIB. The adjacency information is maintained in the adjacency table. CEF forwarding architecture is very flexible and can operate both in a centralized or distributed environment. (Refer to Cisco IOS documentation for more detail.) When operating in centralized mode (for example, on a c7200 router), the FIB and the adjacency tables reside on the router processor card, and forwarding is performed centrally based on the FIB. When operating in distributed mode (for example, on a c12000 router), the FIB and the adjacency tables reside on the line cards, and forwarding is performed on the line cards. In the latter case, all FIB copies are identical on all the line cards. The following is an example of the basic sequence of steps involved in forwarding a packet using CEF, as illustrated in Figure 2-7:

1. The IP packet arrives at an ingress link.

2. The incoming line card extracts the IP destination address and performs a lookup in the FIB to get forwarding information such as next-hop address, outgoing link, and Layer 2 encapsulation.

3. Using information from the previous step, the switching fabric (or interconnect) transfers the packet to the outgoing line card.

4. Finally, the packet is encapsulated with a Layer 2 header and transmitted on the outgoing link.

Figure 2-7   *IP Forwarding Using Distributed CEF*

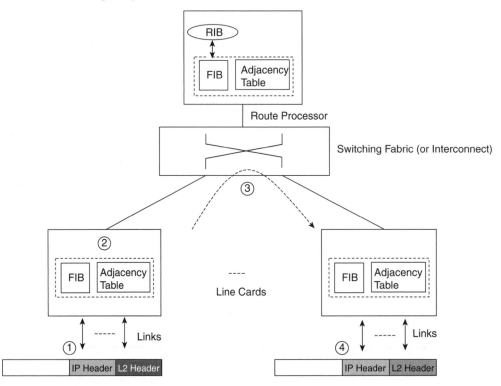

Separation of IP Control and Forwarding Planes

The IP routing can be decomposed into two interrelated but largely independent components: the control and forwarding planes. The control component consists of routing protocols such as *Open Shortest Path First* (OSPF), *Intermediate System-to-Intermediate System* (IS-IS), and *Border Gateway Protocol* (BGP). As described earlier, through routing information exchange the IP control plane provides the information required for building and maintaining routing tables. The IP forwarding plane is responsible for performing time-critical tasks such as address lookup and transferring packets from ingress to egress links. Motivations for the separation of IP control and forwarding planes include the following:

- **Scalability**—The first driving factor for separating control and forwarding is the potential for distributed forwarding architecture and the scalability that this separation enables. For example, with the separation of control and forwarding components, time-critical forwarding-plane tasks can be distributed and optimized for required performance.

- **Fault tolerance**—The term *fault tolerance* refers to the capability of a system to continue to work in the presence of hardware or software failures. (For a more detailed discussion, see Chapter 1, "Understanding High Availability of IP and MPLS Networks.") The second crucial factor for separating the control and forwarding planes is to obtain a fault-tolerant architecture for improving system availability. For example, most router outages result from control-plane hardware/software failures. Therefore, the separation of control and forwarding makes it possible to apply techniques such as stateful switchover of the control plane and nonstop forwarding to design a highly available router, as described in the following sections.

IP Control-Plane Stateful Switchover

In a simplified view, an IP control-plane restart can be described as follows. At first, the IP control-plane components establish sessions with neighbors and exchange routing information for building the RIB and the FIB. After one or more entries in the FIB have been installed, the router is ready to forward traffic for the corresponding prefixes. Now when the IP control plane fails, the router continues to forward traffic using existing FIB entries. (This enables nonstop forwarding, as discussed later.) After a control-plane failure, the IP control-plane component restarts and reestablishes sessions with neighbors for recovering control-plane state. A router is said to be in the recovery period when it is in the process of recovering its control-plane state and updating the existing FIB entries. Some control-plane components might not need to save any state on the standby; instead, the control-plane components recover the state completely from neighbors after the restart. However, other control-plane components might have to save partial state on the standby and recover missing state information from neighbors after the restart. A control-plane component that recovers it state completely from neighbors is referred to as a *stateless component*. A control-plane component that saves some state on the standby is known as a *stateful component*.

Routing protocols reside centrally on the control processor card. Because the control plane is as important to a router as the brain is to the body, the control plane is typically protected through a 1:1 control processor card redundancy. In general, a control processor card may fail due to hardware or the control software failure. When such a failure occurs, an automatic switchover from the active (failed) to the standby (new active) control processor card takes place. Because a control-plane component has been separated from the forwarding component, a failure in the control processor and the resulting switchover need not disrupt the forwarding component. To reduce the effects of a control processor fault and the resulting switchover on the forwarding plane, the following router architecture framework is required:

- Separation of control and forwarding functions
- Control processor card redundancy (for example, 1:1)
- Capability to synchronize configurations and control-plane state from the active to the standby control-plane component

IP Forwarding-Plane Nonstop Forwarding

IP *nonstop forwarding* (NSF) refers to the capability of a router to continue to forward packets while its control plane (here this means IP routing protocols) recovers from failure. It is noteworthy that regardless of whether the IP control plane is stateless or stateful, preservation of the IP forwarding state across the control-plane switchover is a prerequisite for the NSF.

IP NSF capability requires the following architecture framework:

- IP control-plane *stateful switchover* (SSO) capability for stateful components
- The capability of the forwarding components (for example, line cards) to remain unaffected by the control-plane SSO and continue to forward packets using pre-switchover "existing" forwarding information
- After the control-plane switchover, the capability of the routing protocols to restart, recover routing information from neighbors or locally, and update the existing forwarding state
- Recovery of the control-plane state information without causing negative effects such as routing flaps and disruption of the forwarding plane
- Cooperation and support from the neighbors

IP Nonstop Forwarding Architecture

In a highly available router, uninterrupted forwarding operation is of fundamental importance to reduce system downtime. The NSF capability depends on two interrelated capabilities: IP control-plane SSO and the separation of control and forwarding.

IP Control-Plane SSO

As for the IP control-plane SSO, you need two instances of IP control-plane protocols, which are denoted as active and standby instances. Redundant control processors are required to host active and standby instances. The active instance controls the system, whereas the standby assumes the role of the active instance after the switchover. The active instance of the IP control plane executes, whereas the standby instance does not. The standby instance mirrors the complete or partial control state of the active instance by receiving synchronization messages from the active components.

For example, the active instances of IP routing protocols establish sessions, exchange routing information with peers, and help build and maintain the RIB/FIB. In contrast, the standby instances of IP routing protocols do not exchange routing information with external peers. The control-plane components that save complete or partial state information on the standby and keep it synchronized between active and standby instances are called stateful (or SSO-capable) components. After the control-plane restart, the standby instance assumes the active role. During the recovery period, the new active control-plane components recover their state from a locally preserved database or from neighbors and update the forwarding state.

Separation of Control and Forwarding

For NSF operations, separation of control and forwarding is essential; after all, if control and forwarding were not independent, it would be difficult to localize control-plane failures. That is, it would be hard to perform control-plane switchover and recovery without disruption in the forwarding plane.

In addition to separation of control and forwarding, the NSF also requires the capability to maintain the forwarding state across the switchover. Distributed forwarding architecture provides one of the most effective methods to satisfy these requirements. Furthermore, as discussed in detail previously, distributed forwarding architecture helps to avoid forwarding bottlenecks. Thus, distributed forwarding architecture not only helps to improve system scalability but also availability.

Summary of IP Nonstop Forwarding Operations

Now that the architecture framework has been introduced, you can benefit from reviewing a summary of the IP NSF operation. The sequence of steps in the list that follows is not necessarily the one that is followed in a specific implementation (see Figure 2-8). Instead, the steps are meant to convey the main ideas at a functional level.

Figure 2-8 *IP Nonstop Forwarding*

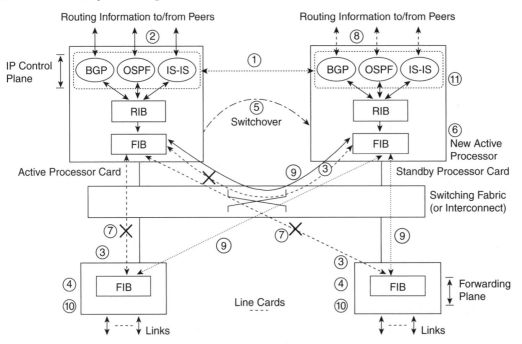

1. The active instance of IP control plane (that is, OSPF, IS-IS, and BGP) starts on the primary control processor. The standby instance of the IP control plane is started on the standby control processor; the standby instance does not execute, but it can receive state synchronization from the active instance. As discussed in Chapter 1, the control plane is considered as a collection of inseperable processes. This means that the restart of one component is always accompanied by the restart of other components. The amount of control-plane state that needs to be preserved on the standby varies from one component to another.

2. The active IP routing protocols establish sessions with peers, start exchanging routing information, and build the RIB.

3. After selecting the best routes in the RIB, the FIB is updated. Initially, the active FIB manager distributes the entire FIB to the line cards and the standby control processor. Afterward, only incremental updates are sent as routing information changes.

4. The line cards populate their FIB tables and start forwarding traffic.

5. Assume a software/hardware failure occurs on the active control processor that causes an automatic control processor switchover.

6. Upon switchover, the standby control processor transitions from the standby to the active role. The standby instance of the IP control plane also changes from the standby to the active role.

7. Upon detecting loss of interprocessor communication (IPC) connectivity (or through other means), line cards learn about the control processor switchover. Each line card marks its existing IP forwarding as needing to be refreshed and starts a timer. The line card, however, continues to use the existing forwarding information. If the existing IP forwarding information is not refreshed before the timer expires (which indicates the completion of the recovery period), it is deleted.

8. The IP routing protocols on the new active control processor reestablish sessions with peers, exchange routing information, and rebuild the RIB and FIB. The procedures that allow routing protocols to reestablish a session and relearn routing information gracefully without causing detrimental effects (such as routing flaps) are discussed in later chapters.

9. The FIB clients connect to the new active FIB manager, which updates the line cards and the new standby control processor with the latest FIB information.

10. The line cards update their forwarding information. Upon stale timer expiration, any forwarding entry still marked as stale is deleted. Thus, during and after the control-plane switchover, the forwarding plane is not disrupted.

11. IP control-plane recovery is complete.

In the remainder of this book, the term *IP forwarding* state is used to denote information stored in FIB entries such as IP destination address (prefix), next-hop address, outgoing interface, and Layer 2 encapsulation. From the preceding discussion, it should be clear that the IP NSF capability requires preservation of the IP forwarding state across control-plane switchover. Unlike FIB, because RIB does not exist in the forwarding path, it need not be preserved across the control-plane switchover. Instead, it can be rebuilt after the switchover. However, current IP control-plane protocols are not capable of rebuilding RIB without disturbing the forwarding plane and causing other negative effects such as routing flaps. To be able to reconstruct the RIB without such detrimental effects, the existing IP routing protocols (OSPF, IS-IS, BGP) have been enhanced. The details of such enhancements are described in chapters dealing with the IP control plane.

IP SSO and NSF Capabilities in Cisco IOS Architecture

IP SSO and NSF in the Cisco IOS architecture provide fault-tolerant control-plane software on Cisco routers, which makes it possible to perform nondisruptive control processor switchover. This capability is achieved through control processor redundancy and Cisco IOS Software enhancements. In Cisco routers, the control processor card is known as a *router processor* (RP). In brief, the Cisco IOS SSO/NSF architecture is based on the following framework:

-   Routers with 1:1 redundant RP cards (active and standby). Examples of routers with redundant RP include c12000, c10000, c7500, and c7600.

-   Routers using distributed CEF.

-   Synchronization of the FIB/adjacency tables from active RP to line cards and the standby RP. Preservation of FIB/adjacency tables across the IP control-plane switchover on line cards and the standby RP.

- Synchronization of router startup, running, and dynamic configurations from active to standby RP. Preservation of synchronized configuration information across the switchover.

External View of the IP SSO and NSF

This section describes the IP control-plane SSO and IP NSF operation from the perspective of neighboring nodes. The following description should be useful to better understand interactions between NSF-capable and NSF-incapable neighbors in the ensuing chapters:

- The IP control-plane SSO capability of a router is not visible to neighbors because it does not involve any protocol message exchange before or after the switchover. In that sense, the IP control-plane SSO capability is internal to the router, and therefore does not depend on support from neighbors (see Figure 2-9). The only thing a neighbor detects is the loss of a protocol session (or protocol adjacency). It has no way to determine the cause of the loss; the loss could be due to any of a number of reasons including a transient, very high traffic load, a change in configuration, SSO, and so forth.

- In contrast, the IP forwarding-plane NSF capability of a router is visible to its neighbors. This is because NSF involves interaction with neighbors both before and after the switchover. These interactions include the exchange of capabilities and the recovery of a partial or complete control-plane state to update the existing forwarding state. As a result, IP forwarding-plane NSF capability is known to its neighbors, and in that sense needs support from neighbors.

Figure 2-9   *Neighbor's View of IP SSO and NSF*

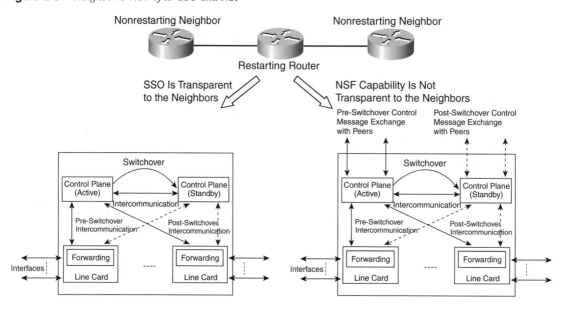

Summary

This chapter provided an overview of IP forwarding and address lookup schemes. This was followed by analysis of centralized- and distributed-forwarding architectures. The chapter then described the IP NSF architecture and explained its functional operation.

References

[1] RFC 1812, "Requirements for IP Version 4 Routers," F. Baker, June 1995.

[2] RFC 1519, "Classless Inter-Domain Routing (CIDR): An Address Assignment and Aggregation Strategy," V. Fuller, T. Li, K. Varadhan, and J. Yu, September 1993.

[3] Knuth, D. *The Art of Computer Programming: Sorting and Searching*, Second Edition (Boston: Addison-Wesley, 1998).

[4] Biersack, E. W., W. Dabbous, and M. A. Ruiz-Sanchez. "Survey and Taxonomy of IP Address Lookup Algorithms." *IEEE Network* (March/April 2001), 8–23.

[5] Srinivasan, V., and G. Varghese, "Faster IP Lookups Using Controlled Prefix Expansion," Proceedings of ACM Sigmetrics '98 (June 1998), 1–11.

[6] Gupta, P., S. Lin, and N. McKeown, "Routing Lookups in Hardware at Memory Access Speeds," Proceedings of IEEE INFOCOM'98 (April 1998), 1240–47.

[7] Labovitz, C., "Scalability of the Internet Backbone Routing Infrastructure," Ph.D. thesis, University of Michigan, 1999.

[8] Huston, L., T. Lyon, G. Minshall, and P. Newman, "IP Switching and Gigabit Routers," *IEEE Communications Magazine*, January 1997.

[9] RFC 826, "An Ethernet Address Resolution Protocol," D. C. Plummer, November 1982.

[10] RFC 3222, "Terminology for Forwarding Information Base (FIB) Based Router Performance," G. Trotter, December 2001.

CHAPTER 3

MPLS Forwarding Plane: Achieving Nonstop Forwarding

The notion of partitioning into control and forwarding components is not restricted to IP routing; it can also be applied to the *Multiprotocol Label Switching* (MPLS) architecture. As this chapter explains, conventional IP control and forwarding components play an important role in MPLS. For example, MPLS label-distribution protocols depend on IP control-plane protocols to communicate with their peers. In some situations (for instance, in the case of *Label Distribution Protocol* [LDP]), MPLS label-distribution protocols learn prefixes for binding labels to these prefixes for establishing label-switched paths. Similarly, MPLS forwarding relies on the conventional IP forwarding component for certain label-related operations such as imposition and disposition.

This chapter builds on and extends the content of the previous chapter. You are encouraged to review Chapter 2, "IP Forwarding Plane: Achieving Nonstop Forwarding," before beginning this chapter. The objective of this chapter is to describe the MPLS *nonstop forwarding* (NSF) operation during control-plane failure and restart. The NSF operation is enabled through separation of control and forwarding to effect a nondisruptive control-plane switchover. To grasp control-plane switchover and NSF concepts, a basic under-standing of MPLS control and forwarding is necessary. To provide the required background, this chapter begins with an introduction of MPLS basics. After the MPLS overview, the chapter describes the stateful control-plane switchover and forwarding-plane architecture framework that enable nonstop MPLS forwarding. The chapter concludes with a summary.

Overview of MPLS

As described in Chapter 2, in conventional IP forwarding each router on a forwarding path makes an independent forwarding decision as packets traverse that path toward their destinations. IP forwarding decision consists of next-hop and outgoing-link information that is obtained by locating a *Forwarding Information Base* (FIB) entry that is the longest prefix match for the packet's IP destination address. In this regard, IP forwarding can be viewed as a process that maps each IP destination address to a next hop. Because each router has a finite number of next hops, IP forwarding can be thought of mapping the set of all packets into a finite number of next hops or equivalently into a finite number of disjointed subsets. As far as IP forwarding is concerned, all packets in a particular subset are indistinguishable and are forwarded in an identical manner. Because packets within a subset are forwarded identically from a router, they traverse the same path in the network. A group of packets that is indistinguishable with respect to a forwarding decision (for example, forwarded in the same fashion and over the same path) is said to form a *forwarding equivalence class* (FEC).[1]

In conventional IP forwarding, as a packet travels toward its final destination, each router along the path examines the packet's IP destination address and assigns it to an FEC. A router typically assigns packets with two different IP destination addresses to the same FEC as long as both IP destination addresses have a common longest prefix matching entry. These packets continue to share a common path as long as they are assigned to the same FEC at each hop. As a set of packets with different IP destination addresses traverses the network, a particular hop might assign these packets to the same or different FEC(s) depending on whether these packets map to common or different longest prefix entries in the forwarding table (see Figure 3-1).

Figure 3-1 *Packets for Destination d1 and d2 Are Mapped to a Common FEC and Traverse the Same Path from R1 to R4*

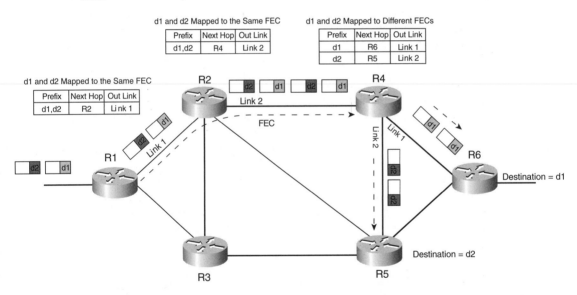

As described previously, IP address lookup is a processing-intensive operation in high-performance routers. This is made worse by the fact that IP forwarding requires a complex IP address lookup operation at each hop along a packet's path. If there were a way to identify FECs and associate each packet to a particular FEC, you would be able to either avoid or simplify the IP address lookup operation. Supposing this is so, then, a router would be able to make an equivalent forwarding decision based on new information instead of having to rely on IP address lookup to accomplish the same.

Along these lines, one way to simplify IP address lookup is to carry extra information, referred to as a *label*, in the packet header. The forwarding technology that uses label information to make its forwarding decision is called *Multiprotocol Label Switching* (MPLS).[1] A label is a short fixed-length value that identifies a particular FEC[2] (see Figure 3-2). The association between a FEC and label is known as *label-to-FEC binding*. The assignment of a packet to an FEC is commonly based on the packet's IP destination address. Generally, however, the FEC assignment can be based on information other than an IP destination address, such as a *virtual circuit identifier* (VCI).[3,4]

The label of an outgoing packet is known as the *outgoing label*. Similarly, the label of an incoming packet is referred to as the *incoming label*. A packet may contain both incoming and outgoing labels, outgoing label but no incoming label, or incoming label but no outgoing label. Generally, a packet may contain one or more labels that are collectively referred to as a *label stack*. The labels in the stack are organized as a *last-in, first-out* (LIFO) stack. An unlabeled packet is said to have a label stack of depth 0. A label stack of depth d corresponds to an ordered sequence of labels <1,2,3 ... d-1, d> with label 1 at the bottom and label d on the top of the stack (see Figure 3-3). For an incoming labeled packet, other than examining the top label on the stack to index the label forwarding table (described later), no other label-stack operation is performed. For an outgoing packet, however, several label-stack operations such as pop (remove the top label), swap (replace the top label with a specified new label), and push (add a specified number of labels on the top of the stack) may be performed.

Figure 3-2 *Label-Stack Entry*

Label = 20 Bits
Exp = Experimental Use, 3 Bits
S = Bottom of Stack, 1 Bit
TTL = Time-To-Live, 8 Bits

Figure 3-3 *Label Stack of Depth d*

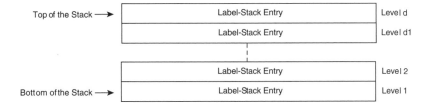

A router that supports MPLS is known as a *label-switching router* (LSR). Suppose you have two LSRs named LSR1 and LSR2. Suppose further that all packets traveling from LSR1 to LSR2, which belong to a particular FEC F1, are identified with a label L1. As far as F1-to-L1 binding is concerned, L1 is the outgoing label for LSR1. With respect to this particular label-to-FEC binding, L1 is the outgoing label for LSR1 and the incoming label for LSR2, or equivalently LSR2 is the downstream LSR and LSR1 the upstream LSR. In MPLS, it is the downstream LSR that selects FEC-to-label mappings and informs the upstream LSRs about the selected labels. The downstream LSR either distributes a label to FEC binding on receipt of an explicit request from the upstream LSR or distributes a label without being solicited when it is ready to forward labeled packets in the FEC. The former label distribution mode is known as *downstream on demand* (DOD) and the latter as the *downstream unsolicited* (DU). To request and distribute labels to FEC bindings, LSRs use procedures commonly referred to as *label-distribution protocols*. MPLS architecture allows several protocols for distributing labels to FEC bindings, such as *Label Distribution Protocol* (LDP), *Border Gateway Protocol* (BGP), and *Resource ReSerVation Protocol* (RSVP). The label-distribution procedures are described in subsequent chapters.

An MPLS network consists of an interconnection of LSRs, and the contiguous set of LSRs defines an MPLS domain. The LSRs at the edge of the MPLS network are called *edge LSRs*. In general, any LSR whose neighbor does not support MPLS is regarded as an edge LSR. In the ingress (incoming) direction, an edge LSR turns unlabeled packets into labeled packets. The action of adding one or more labels (or label stack) is known as *label imposition*. In the egress (outgoing) direction, an edge LSR removes labels and turns labeled packets into unlabeled packets. The action of removing the label stack from a labeled packet is known as *label disposition*.

Unlike edge LSRs, transit LSRs forward only labeled packets. The sequence of LSRs that a labeled packet traverses, starting at the ingress LSR and terminating at the egress LSR, is called *the label-switched path* (LSP). For an LSP, the LSR preceding the egress LSR that pops the label is known as the *penultimate LSR* of the LSP and the action of removing the top label by such an LSR is called *penultimate-hop popping*. The penultimate-hop popping is useful because it eliminates the need to perform extra lookups at the egress LSR (see Figure 3-4).

The label-stack mechanism allows LSPs to be nested within another LSP. An LSP of level d is defined as a sequence of LSRs, which starts at an LSR (ingress LSR) that pushes on a level d label and terminates at an LSR (egress LSR) where the packet is forwarded, based on a label stack of depth smaller than d. From this definition it follows that for an LSP of level d, an LSR preceding the egress LSR may pop (remove) a label instead of the egress LSR and transmit the packet with a label stack of depth $(d-1)$. For a concrete illustration, consider Figure 3-5, which depicts three LSPs. LSP1 and LSP2 have a label stack of depth 1, whereas LSP3 has a label stack of depth 2. LSP1 has LSR1 as the ingress, and LSR6 is the egress LSR; LSP2 has LSR3 as the ingress and LSR6 as the egress LSR; and LSP3 has LSR2 as the ingress and LSR4 as the egress LSR. In the case of LSP3, the level 1 label (the bottom label) is used to nest packets of LSP1 and LSP2, whereas the level 2 label (the top label) is used for forwarding packets of the nested LSPs from LSR2 to LSR4.

Figure 3-4 *MPLS Label-Switched Path*

Prefix	In Label	Next Hop	Out Label	Out Link
d1	5	LSR4	7	4

Transit LSR2 forwards labeled packets.

Prefix	In Label	Next Hop	Out Label	Out Link
d1	7	LSR6	9	3

Transit LSR4 forwards labeled packets.
LSR4 can pop the out label on
behalf of LSR6 if
requested to do so.

Prefix	In Label	Next Hop	Out Label	Out Link
d1	-	LSR2	5	2

Ingress edge LSR1 imposes a
Label of 5 for packets with IP
destination address=d1.

Labled packets →

Prefix	In Label	Next Hop	Out Label	Out Link
d1	9	Router B	-	1

Egress edge LSR6 removes the
label from the outgoing packets.

LSP2   Link 4   LSR4 Link 3

LSP

When LSR4 is performing penultimate-
hop popping, it pops the label on behalf
of LSR6. In the example, packets from
LSR4 to LSR6 on this LSP will not be labeled.

Source

Destination = d1

Link 1

Router A   LSR1   Link 2   LSR6   Router B

Unlabeled Packets →

LSR3   LSR5   Unlabeled Packets →

MPLS Network

Figure 3-5 *MPLS Hierarchical Label-Switched Path*

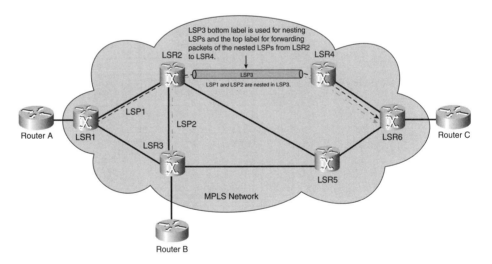

Because MPLS LSPs are unidirectional, a separate LSP in each direction is required for
bidirectional traffic flows. The sequence of LSRs traversed by an LSP can be selected by LSRs
along the path in a hop-by-hop fashion or by explicit specification by the LSR that is the LSP
ingress. An LSP whose path is hop by hop selected using conventional IP routing protocols is
called a *hop-by-hop routed LSP*. An LSP whose path is explicitly specified is called an *explicitly
routed* (or a *traffic-engineered*) LSP. To establish LSPs, MPLS uses label-distribution protocols

such as LDP, BGP, and RSVP-TE. In particular, hop-by-hop routed LSPs are established using LDP, whereas explicitly routed LSPs are established through RSVP-TE.

Multiprotocol in MPLS refers to the fact that it can label switch packets or frames from multiple Layer 3 and Layer 2 protocols.[3,4] MPLS can be implemented over multiple data link layers such as Ethernet, *Point-to-Point Protocol* (PPP), *Frame Relay* (FR), and *Asynchronous Transfer Mode* (ATM). The encoding techniques for label information may vary on different data links.[2] Label-encoding techniques are summarized in Figure 3-6. The fact that MPLS can be implemented over different link-layer technologies implies that MPLS can be supported in IP routers and ATM switches. In particular, ATM switches can be easily adapted for MPLS because there is great similarity between ATM and MPLS forwarding procedures. For example, ATM forwarding is based on swapping *virtual path identifier/virtual circuit identifier* (VPI/VCI) fields in the cell header, whereas MPLS forwarding is based on swapping labels. Therefore, just encoding of labels in VPI/VCI fields without any modifications enables ATM forwarding to function as MPLS forwarding. However, to support MPLS, the ATM switch must also implement an MPLS control plane. An ATM switch that encodes label information in the VPI/VCI fields of the cell header uses an MPLS control-plane component such as LDP to distribute labels to FEC bindings. An ATM switch that forwards cells based on label information (rather than first reassembling cells into frames) is known as *ATM LSR* or *cell-mode LSR*[5] (see Figure 3-7).

Figure 3-6   *MPLS Label Encoding over Different Types of Data Link Layers*

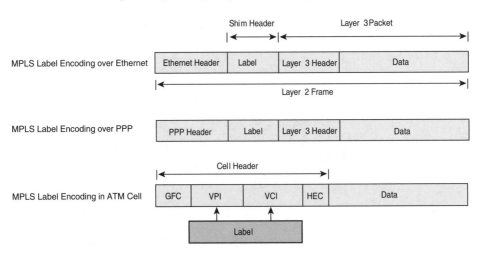

An ATM interface that is controlled by an MPLS control-plane component is called a *label-switching controlled ATM* (LC-ATM) interface. Similarly, an LSR that encodes label information in the shim label header on a frame or cell-based interface and forwards complete frames (first reassembles cells into frames on cell interfaces) is known as a *frame-mode LSR* (see Figure 3-8).

Figure 3-7   *Cell-Based Label-Switching Router*

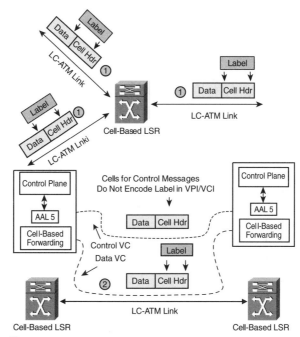

① A cell-based LSR forwards cells using label information encoded
   in the VPI/VCI fields.

② Over an LC-ATM link, labeled packets are transmitted on
   data VCs and the unlabeled control packets on the control VC.

Figure 3-8   *Frame-Based Label-Switching Router*

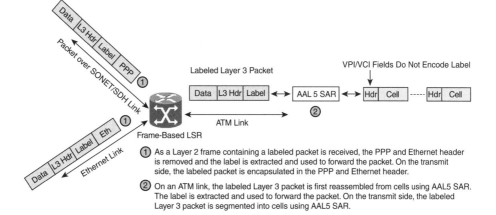

① As a Layer 2 frame containing a labeled packet is received, the PPP and Ethernet header
   is removed and the label is extracted and used to forward the packet. On the transmit
   side, the labeled packet is encapsulated in the PPP and Ethernet header.

② On an ATM link, the labeled Layer 3 packet is first reassembled from cells using AAL5 SAR.
   The label is extracted and used to forward the packet. On the transmit side, the labeled
   Layer 3 packet is segmented into cells using AAL5 SAR.

The remainder of this chapter mainly focuses on the frame-based LSRs. In general, label allocation and management can be implemented per interface or globally (platform wide). A *label space* refers to a set of unique label values. Cell-based LSRs usually support per-interface label space, whereas frame-based LSRs generally implement platform-wide label space.

In contrast to IP forwarding, which reassigns every packet to a particular FEC on each hop, MPLS makes FEC assignments only once, at the ingress edge LSRs. After a packet is mapped to a particular FEC and labeled, all LSRs along an LSP use only label information to make forwarding decisions. Thus MPLS avoids conventional IP address lookup along an LSP, with the exception of ingress edge LSRs or in some cases egress edge LSRs such as in MPLS VPN applications. However, the real benefits of MPLS above and beyond those of IP are the applications it enables, such as *Layer 3 virtual private networks* (L3VPNs), *Layer 2 VPNs* (L2VPN), *traffic engineering* (TE), and *Fast ReRouting* (FRR) of traffic around link/node failures. These applications are possible because MPLS decouples forwarding from control. That is, the same forwarding mechanism (swap, pop, impose) can be used regardless of the application. These advanced applications and features make MPLS an attractive technology for building scalable and reliable networks.

MPLS Label Lookup and Forwarding

In a conventional IP network, forwarding decisions for a packet are made by performing an address lookup in the IP FIB to determine the next hop and the outgoing link. In an MPLS network, however, each LSR maintains a *Label-Switching Information Base* (LFIB) that is separate and distinct from the IP FIB. (Note that with regard to the Cisco IOS architecture, an LFIB may also be referred to as a *Tag Forwarding Information Base* [TFIB] or an *MPLS Forwarding Infrastructure* [MFI].) The LFIB table consists of entries of types such as *next hop label forwarding entry* (NHLFE), *incoming label map* (ILM), and *FEC-to-NHLFE* (FTN) map. The NHLFE contains fields such as next-hop address, label-stack operations, outgoing link, and link-layer header information. The ILM entry associates an incoming label to one or more NHLFE entries. The label of an incoming packet selects a particular ILM entry that in turn identifies NHLFEs. The FTN maps each FEC to one or more NHLFEs (see Figure 3-9). That is, via FTN entries, unlabeled packets are turned to labeled packets. If you refer back to Figure 3-4, LSR1 (the ingress LSR) uses an LFIB entry of type FTN to impose the outgoing label 5 to the incoming unlabeled packets belonging to the FEC d1; LSR4 (the transit LSR) uses an LFIB entry of type ILM-to-NHLFE to swap the incoming label 7 with the outgoing label 9; and LSR6 (the egress LSR) uses an LFIB entry of type ILM-to-NHLFE to dispose the incoming label 9 and forward the unlabeled packets to the next hop.

Figure 3-9   *Label Forwarding Information Base (LFIB)*

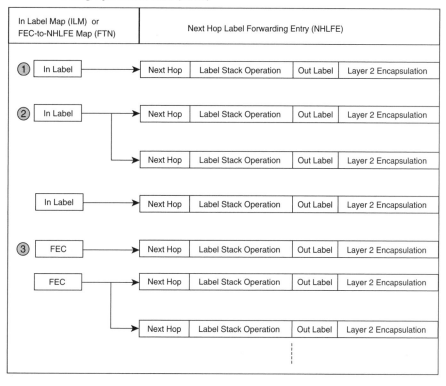

① A label is mapped to an outgoing label.

② For load balancing, an incoming label is mapped to two outgoing labels.

③ An FEC is mapped to an outgoing label.

In general, MPLS forwarding can be characterized in terms of label-imposition, -swapping, and -disposition operations (see Figure 3-10).

- **Label imposition**—This forwarding operation corresponds to the case when a packet is received unlabeled but transmitted as a labeled packet. For example, through a label-imposition operation, an ingress edge LSR turns unlabeled packets into labeled packets. To accomplish this task, the LSR first maps the packet to a particular FEC by performing an address lookup in the IP FIB table and then consults the LFIB table to determine the out label, out link, and Layer 2 encapsulation for the packet.

- **Label swapping**—This forwarding operation is applicable to a transit LSR. In this case, the LSR uses the top label in the incoming packet to find the ILM entry in the LFIB. The ILM entry in turn identifies the associated NHLFE that provides all the information necessary for transmitting the packet. The LSR uses the information in the NHLFE to perform the required label-stack operation, encodes the new label stack, and transmits the packet to the next hop.

Figure 3-10 *Label Imposition, Disposition, and Swapping*

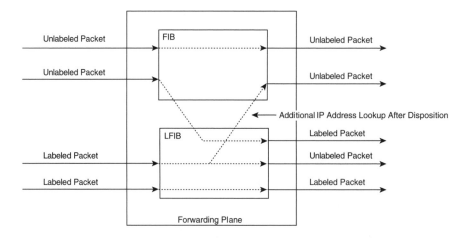

- **Label disposition**—This packet-forwarding case applies to egress edge LSRs (and penultimate-hop LSRs). In this case, the LSR uses the top label in the incoming packet to identify the ILM and the associated NHFLE in the LFIB. The label-stack operation indicates that the packet needs to be transmitted as an unlabeled packet. The LSR strips (pops) the label stack and forwards the unlabeled packet to the next hop. In certain cases (for example, in MPLS VPN applications), an additional IP address lookup might be required to correctly forward the unlabeled packet.

- **IP forwarding**—This forwarding operation corresponds to conventional IP forwarding when label switching is not enabled for certain FECs. When a packet for such an FEC arrives, the router performs a lookup in the FIB to determine the next hop, out interface, and Layer 2 encapsulation. IP forwarding also occurs when LDP is used between two directly connected LSRs where one is an MPLS ingress and the other is an MPLS egress for some FEC. In this case, LDP distributes the Implicit NULL label for the FEC. (An *Implicit NULL* is a label that an LSR may assign and distribute, but which actually does not appear in the packet header; refer to RFC 3031 for further information.)

In summary, the conventional IP forwarding decision is based on examination of the FIB table, whereas an MPLS forwarding decision is based either only on LFIB lookup or the FIB and LFIB. An MPLS forwarding algorithm uses a label-swapping paradigm. Because a major portion of search time is taken up by memory accesses, performance of any lookup algorithm is measured in terms of memory access. Therefore, a smaller number of memory accesses translates to faster search times. MPLS forwarding is simpler than IP forwarding because it uses an exact match on an incoming fixed-length label to locate the forwarding information. Thus, unlike IP address lookup, an MPLS label-switching algorithm can locate the required forwarding information in just one memory access. The simple MPLS lookup operation may be advantageous for routers with less-sophisticated hardware lookup engines. Its inherent simplicity and faster lookup times—and above all its advanced applications such as L3VPN, L2VPN, TE, and FRR—make label switching an attractive technology for building a scalable forwarding architecture. The following sections describe stateful control-plane switchover and the NSF framework.

Separation of MPLS Control and Forwarding Planes

Analogous to conventional IP forwarding, MPLS can also be partitioned into two interrelated but mostly independent functions: control and forwarding. Each LSR supports both control and forwarding functions. The IP control plane consists of only routing protocols such as OSPF, IS-IS, and BGP. The MPLS control plane not only comprises IP routing protocols, but also additional protocols for distributing FEC-to-label bindings that establish LSPs. MPLS architecture has defined multiple label-distribution procedures such as LDP, BGP, and RSVP-TE. These procedures correspond to either extending capabilities of existing protocols, as in the case of BGP and RSVP-TE, or specifying brand new procedures, such as LDP[1].

As described in Chapter 2, decoupling of IP control and forwarding requires two separate databases: the RIB and FIB. Similarly, separation of label-switched control and forwarding requires two distinct databases: the LIB and LFIB. The LIB may be viewed as a counterpart of the RIB for the label-switched traffic. LIB entries are populated from label-distribution protocols. When a label-distribution protocol intends to associate a label with an FEC, it requests an incoming label from the LIB. Thus the LIB manages incoming labels as label-distribution protocols create or delete an FEC to local label binding. Similarly, when a label-distribution protocol learns a label for an FEC, it provides an outgoing label to the LIB. Note that an actual implementation might choose to maintain labels from label-distribution protocols in a common database such as an LIB or in separate databases. In Cisco IOS architecture, for example, each label-distribution protocol maintains its labels in a separate database. Nevertheless, in the following discussion, for the sake of simplicity, the LIB is viewed as a centralized common label database used by all distribution protocols.

An adjacency provides the Layer 2 encapsulation that is required for forwarding a packet on a particular outgoing link. Adjacencies are usually created as ARPs discover the next-hop nodes. It is worth pointing out that the LIB is an element of the MPLS control plane, whereas adjacencies are a part of the forwarding plane. Therefore, the LIB does not deal with adjacencies.

The structure of the LFIB table is described in the preceding section. The construction of LFIB entries requires information that is provided by both IP routing and label-distribution protocols (via LIB). For example, FEC-to-next-hop mapping is provided by IP routing protocols, FEC-to-label mapping is supplied by the label-distribution protocols, and adjacencies are created through ARP. The MPLS forwarding plane is responsible for label-stack operations (imposition, disposition, and swapping), the indexing of the LFIB table using the incoming label, and transferring labeled packets from incoming to outgoing links. As described previously, some of these operations include conventional IP address lookup. Therefore, the motivations for separation of IP control and forwarding components—namely, scalability and fault tolerance—also apply to MPLS control and forwarding components:

- **Scalability**—When control and forwarding planes are separate, forwarding-plane tasks that are time critical can be distributed, resulting in better forwarding performance.

- **Fault tolerance**—The separation of control and forwarding allows localization and containment of faults. More importantly, separation of control and forwarding improves system availability by allowing application of techniques such as stateful switchover and NSF.

To summarize, the MPLS control plane is a superset of the conventional IP control plane. The MPLS control plane can be thought of as made up of two subcomponents: the IP routing protocols and the label-distribution protocols (see Figure 3-11). Each LSR must support both subcomponents because collectively they provide all the information required for constructing the FIB and LFIB. Similarly, the MPLS forwarding plane is a superset of conventional IP forwarding. The MPLS forwarding plane can be viewed as composed of two subcomponents: the FIB and LFIB. As far as the MPLS forwarding plane is concerned, an LSR might need to consult only LFIB or a combination of the FIB and LFIB to make a forwarding decision.

Figure 3-11 *MPLS Control and Forwarding Planes*

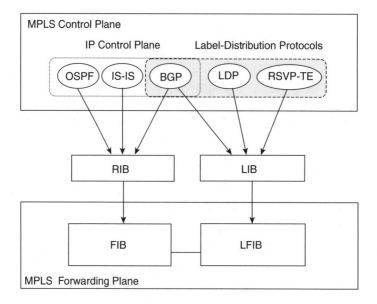

MPLS Applications

MPLS enables a diverse set of advanced applications, including TE, L2VPNs, and L3VPNs. In the following list, these applications are briefly introduced along with the control-plane components used by each application. A more detailed description of these applications, particularly from the perspective of control-plane restart, is given in Chapter 10, "Improving Survivability of IP and MPLS Networks." Generally, distinct applications use a different set of control-plane components. A summary of MPLS applications and corresponding control-plane components is depicted in Figure 3-12.

- **IP over MPLS**—IP over MPLS refers to the forwarding of Layer 3 packets over hop-by-hop routed LSPs that are established through LDP.

- **Traffic engineering (TE)**—The MPLS-TE application enables establishment of LSPs along explicit paths, which are either specified by the user or derived from network topology information provided by OSPF or IS-IS routing protocols. The enhanced OSPF and IS-IS allow constraint-based path computation and selection; without these enhancements, TE would compute the same paths as IP routing.

- **Fast ReRoute (FRR)**—The MPLS FRR provides a mechanism to establish backup tunnels and quickly reroute traffic from protected TE LSPs onto the backup tunnels on detection of local link and node failures. The backup tunnel (also known as the *bypass tunnel*) is established using RSVP-TE.

- **Layer 3 virtual private network (L3VPN)**—The MPLS VPN application allows sharing of the service provider's MPLS transport network among multiple customer private networks. MPLS VPN uses LDP or RSVP-TE to establish LSPs between provider edge LSRs and BGP for distributing customer FEC to label bindings.

- **Layer 2 virtual private network (L2VPN)**—The L2VPN allows establishment of emulated virtual circuits to transport various Layer 2 frames (such as Ethernet, FR, ATM, and PPP) across the MPLS backbone network. The information for virtual circuits is exchanged through LDP. The LSP that may carry traffic from multiple emulated virtual circuits can be an LDP-established hop-by-hop routed LSP or RSVP-TE-established explicitly routed LSP. Note that in the Cisco IOS architecture, L2VPN is also referred to as *Any Transport over MPLS* (AToM).

Figure 3-12 *MPLS Applications and Their Control-Plane Components*

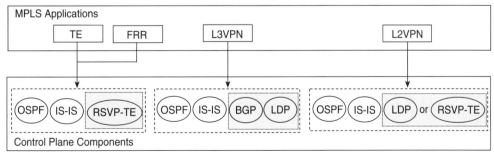

MPLS Forwarding Architecture

You have seen earlier that to make forwarding decisions, edge LSRs consult not only LFIB but also FIB tables. Although the label-based forwarding procedure is simple and conducive for high-performance forwarding, nevertheless edge LSRs still must perform conventional IP address lookups during label-imposition and sometimes during label-disposition operations. If you consider an LSR that is to act as a transit LSR for all traffic, in theory the LSR should be able to forward all traffic based on the LFIB. In practice, however, typically each LSR is configured for forwarding a mix of labeled and unlabeled IP traffic. To sum up, in a general case MPLS forwarding may be considered to contain label-switching and conventional IP forwarding components. Therefore, as a corollary to discussions from the Chapter 2, MPLS forwarding should also be distributed for an overall scalable forwarding performance. In this fashion, once again, time-critical IP and label lookup operations are decentralized and distributed on each line card. Based on these premises, a generic MPLS distributed forwarding architecture is depicted in Figure 3-13. A quick examination of MPLS forwarding architecture reveals that it is an extension of conventional IP forwarding. For example, LIB and LFIB can be thought of as counterparts of RIB and FIB, respectively.

As in the case of conventional IP forwarding, because the MPLS control plane is centralized but forwarding is distributed, forwarding information in the FIB/LFIB must remain synchronized with the latest information in the RIB/LIB for correct and loop-free forwarding operations. The complete process of building the FIB/LFIB and its synchronization with the RIB/LIB can be summarized as follows:

1. Receive dynamic routing information from protocols and/or static routes from manual configuration. Allocate a local label on request from label-distribution protocols and receive remote label mappings from label-distribution protocols.

2. Process the received routing information and thereby build the RIB. Similarly, process the local and remote label bindings to build the LIB.

3. Select the best usable routes in the RIB and thereby derive the FIB. Construct the LFIB using information in the LIB and FIB.

4. Distribute the FIB/LFIB to the line cards. The distribution of FIB/LFIB occurs in two stages. First, when the router line cards start or reload, the entire FIB/LFIB is distributed. Afterward, incremental resynchronization of the FIB/LFIB takes place as a result of changes in existing routes and the addition/deletion of new routes and label bindings.

Figure 3-13 *MPLS Distributed-Forwarding Architecture*

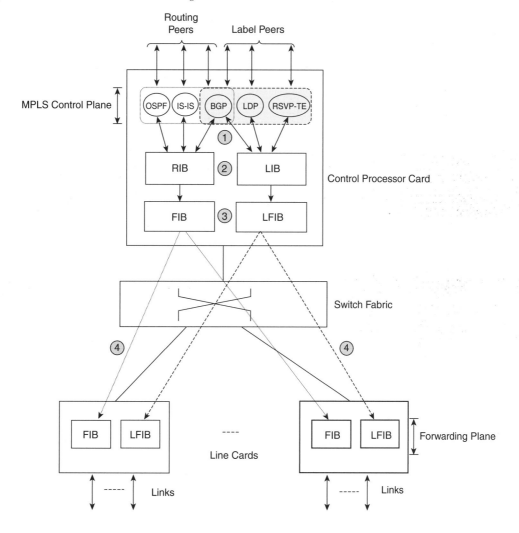

MPLS Control-Plane Stateful Switchover

From the previous discussion, it should be evident that the MPLS control plane is an extension of the IP control plane. Generally, MPLS control-plane components (LDP, BGP, RSVP) are *stateful*, which means the active instance of these components save some state to the standby. (The nature of the saved state is discussed in the following chapters.) After MPLS control-plane failure and switchover, MPLS control-plane components on the new active restart, reestablish sessions with neighbors, and recover missing control-plane state. As discussed shortly, MPLS forwarding state is preserved across the control-plane switchover to allow uninterrupted packet forwarding. An LSR is said to be in the recovery period when it is in the process of recovering its control-plane state and updated MPLS forwarding state.

Analogous to conventional IP control-plane stateful switchover (SSO), MPLS control-plane SSO refers to the control-plane redundancy architecture that enables automatic SSO from the active to the standby control processor on hardware/software failures in the active control-plane instance without disrupting MPLS forwarding. Therefore, with so much commonality between IP and MPLS frameworks, it makes sense to use IP/MPLS control-plane SSO and nonstop forwarding (NSF) schemes to improve the overall availability of the LSR.

To support the MPLS control-plane SSO, the following architecture framework is required:

- Separation of control and forwarding functions
- Redundant control processor cards
- The capability to synchronize configurations and control protocols' related states from the active to the standby control-plane components

MPLS Forwarding-Plane Nonstop Forwarding

MPLS NSF refers to the capability of an LSR to continue to forward packets while its control plane recovers from failure. It is important to note that irrespective of whether the MPLS control-plane components are stateful or stateless, preservation of the MPLS forwarding state (and IP forwarding state when appropriate) across the control-plane switchover is a prerequisite for the MPLS NSF operation.

The MPLS NSF capability requires the following architecture framework:

- MPLS control-plane SSO capability.
- The capability of the forwarding components to remain unaffected from the control-plane switchover and to continue to forward packets using pre-switchover "preserved" forwarding state information. In a generic case, this corresponds to preserving IP FIB and LFIB tables and being able to use them in the distributed forwarders across the control-plane switchover.
- After the control-plane switchover, the capability of the routing protocols and label-distribution protocols to restart, recover routing and required label information from neighbors, and update the "preserved" FIB/LFIB forwarding state.
- The recovery of state information needs to take place without causing negative effects such as routing flaps, incorrect delivery of labeled packets (a security issue), and disruption of LSPs.
- Cooperation and support from the neighbors.

MPLS Nonstop Forwarding Architecture

MPLS control-plane SSO requires two instances (active and standby) of IP routing protocols and label-distribution protocols. The active instances reside on the active control processor that controls the system. The standby instance resides on the standby control processor that maintains state for the stateful components and waits to become active following a control-plane switchover. The active instances of IP routing protocols and label-distribution protocols establish sessions, exchange routing information with peers, and help build the RIB/FIB and LIB/LFIB. The standby instances of IP routing protocols and label-distribution protocols neither exchange routing information with external peers nor process data packets. That is, the standby acquires sufficient information (state) from the active so that after the control-plane switchover the new active can recover the control-plane state and validate the forwarding state.

MPLS control-plane SSO alone is not adequate for NSF capability. The additional necessary framework is enabled by separation of control and forwarding, which allows preservation of the IP/MPLS forwarding state and use of this information for uninterrupted packet forwarding across the control-plane switchover (see Figure 3-14). The following sequence of steps is not necessarily the one that is followed by a specific implementation, but is instead a functional description of the main components:

1. The active instance of IP routing protocols and label-distribution protocols starts on the active control processor. The standby instance of the control plane is started on the standby control processor. However, the standby instance does not process packets, but can receive state information from the active instance.

2. The FIB clients on line cards connect to the active FIB manager (or server). The standby instance of the FIB on the standby control processor also connects. Similarly, LFIB clients on line cards establish connections with the active LFIB manager (or server). The active FIB and LFIB are responsible for distributing IP forwarding and label-switching forwarding information to FIB clients on line cards and the standby control processor, respectively. Assuming FIB and LFIB are empty at this time, no forwarding information is sent to the line cards and the FIB client on the standby control processor.

3. The active IP routing protocols and label-distribution protocols establish sessions with peers, start exchanging routing information and label information, and build the RIB/LIB.

4. After selecting the best usable routes, the RIB installs the usable routes in the FIB. The information from locally allocated in labels and remotely learned out labels is used to populate the LIB. LFIB is derived from the LIB (FEC-to-label mappings) and FIB (FEC-to-next-hop mappings). Initially, the entire FIB and LFIB are distributed to the line cards and the standby control processor. (Some implementations might choose to distribute to a line card only the forwarding state, which is necessary for forwarding on that line card.) Afterward, only incremental updates are sent as routing information, and labels to the FEC bindings change.

5. The line cards start forwarding traffic.

6. Assume a software/hardware failure occurs in the active control processor that causes an automatic control processor switchover to the standby.

7. On switchover, the standby control processor transitions to the active role. The standby instance of the control-plane components also make a transition to the active role.

8. On detecting loss of connectivity (or through other means), line cards learn about the control processor switchover. Each line card marks its existing IP forwarding and label forwarding state as stale, and starts a stale timer. Each line card continues to use the preserved forwarding information (considered valid but marked as stale). If the stale IP forwarding and label forwarding information is not validated before the stale timer expires, it is deleted.

9. The IP routing protocols and label-distribution protocols on the new active control processor reestablish sessions with peers, exchange routing/label information, and rebuild the RIB/FIB and LIB/LFIB. The following chapters discuss the procedures that allow routing and label-distribution protocols to reestablish sessions and relearn routing and label information without causing detrimental effects such as routing flaps and forwarding disruption.

10. The FIB clients connect to the new active FIB server, which validates and updates the line cards and the new standby control processor with the latest FIB information. Similarly, LFIB clients connect to the new active LFIB server, which updates the line cards and the new standby control processor with the latest LFIB information.

11. The line cards update their IP forwarding and label forwarding information. Upon the stale-timer expiration that marks the end of the recovery period, any forwarding entry still marked as stale is deleted. Thus, during and after the switchover, the forwarding plane is not disrupted.

12. MPLS (including IP control components) control-plane recovery is complete.

From this description, it becomes clear that MPLS NSF capability in a generic case requires preservation of not only the label-switching forwarding state but also the conventional IP forwarding state. In other words, IP NSF is a prerequisite for MPLS NSF. In theory, if a system is used completely as a transit LSR for all the traffic, it could achieve NSF by preserving only the label forwarding state of the form (in label, out label, next hop) in the LFIB. In general, however, with ingress/egress LSRs or when LSRs are forwarding a mixture of unlabeled and labeled traffic, both the FIB and LFIB need to be preserved. Analogous to IP routing protocols, the existing label-distribution protocols (LDP, BGP, RSVP-TE) are not capable of restarting without disrupting the MPLS forwarding plane. The details of such protocol enhancements that help restart label-distribution protocols gracefully are described in following chapters.

Figure 3-14 *MPLS Nonstop Forwarding*

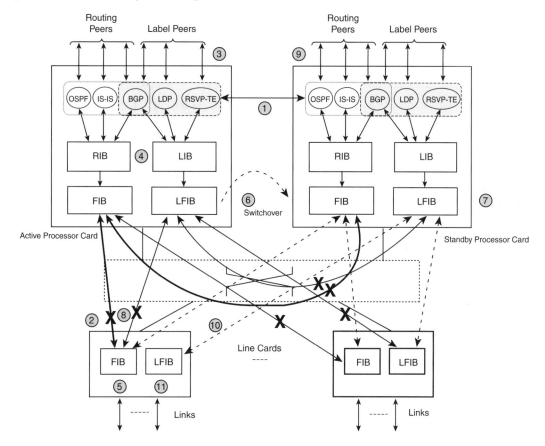

In the remainder of this book, unless stated otherwise, the term *MPLS control plane* refers to label-distribution protocols BGP, LDP, and RSVP-TE, and the term MPLS forwarding plane refers to LFIB. In particular, the MPLS forwarding state refers to entries of the following types:

- **Ingress LSP**—FEC, push (outgoing label), next hop
- **Transit LSP**—Incoming label, swap (outgoing label), next hop
- **Egress LSP**—Incoming label, pop (label stack), next hop

The MPLS SSO and NSF features of the Cisco IOS architecture provide fault-tolerant control-plane software on Cisco LSRs, which enables nondisruptive control processor switchover. This MPLS SSO/NSF capability is achieved through control processor redundancy and Cisco IOS Software enhancements. In summary, Cisco IOS MPLS SSO/NSF features are based on following framework:

- Routers and LSRs with 1:1 redundant RP cards.

- Routers and LSRs with distributed CEF and label-switching capabilities.

- For distributed architectures, synchronization of the FIB and LFIB from the active RP to line cards and standby RP. Preservation of FIB and LFIB tables across the control-plane switchover on line cards and the standby RP. For centralized forwarding architectures, synchronization and preservation of FIB and LFIB on the standby RP.

- Synchronization of router startup, running, and dynamic configurations from the active to standby RP. Preservation of synchronized information across the switchover.

External View of the MPLS SSO and NSF

Analogous to IP control-plane SSO, the MPLS control-plane SSO capability of an LSR is not visible to neighbors because it does not involve any protocol message exchange before and after the switchover. The only thing a neighbor detects is the loss of a protocol session (or protocol adjacency). It has no way to determine the cause of the loss; the loss could be caused by any number of events, including a transient, very high traffic load, a change in configuration, SSO, and so forth.

The MPLS forwarding-plane NSF capability of an LSR is visible to its neighbors. This is because MPLS NSF involves interaction with neighbors both before and after the switchover. These interactions include the exchange of graceful restart capabilities, the recovery of control-plane state, and validation of the preserved forwarding state.

Summary

This chapter provided an overview of MPLS, particularly those aspects required for understanding concepts related to NSF. After the MPLS overview, the chapter described the MPLS control-plane SSO and the architecture framework of the forwarding plane NSF. To sum up, this chapter extended to MPLS the IP SSO/NSF concepts that were described in Chapter 2.

References

[1] RFC 3031, "Multiprotocol Label Switching Architecture," R. Callon, E. Rosen, and A. Viswanathan, January 2001.

[2] RFC 3032, "MPLS Label Stack Encoding," E. Rosen et al., January 2001.

[3] Martini, L., et al., "Encapsulation Methods for Transport of Layer 2 Frames Over IP and MPLS Networks," Internet draft, work in progress.

[4] Martini, L., et al., "Transport of Layer 2 Frames Over MPLS," Internet draft, work in progress.

[5] RFC 3035, "MPLS Using LDP and ATM VC Switching," B. Davie, et al., January 2001.

PART II

IP/MPLS Control Plane

Chapter 4   Intradomain IP Control Plane: Restarting OSPF Gracefully

Chapter 5   Intradomain IP Control Plane: Restarting IS-IS Gracefully

Chapter 6   Interdomain IP Control Plane: Restarting BGP Gracefully

Chapter 7   MPLS Control Plane: Restarting BGP with MPLS Gracefully

Chapter 8   MPLS Control Plane: Restarting LDP Gracefully

Chapter 9   MPLS Control Plane: Restarting RSVP-TE Gracefully

CHAPTER 4

Intradomain IP Control Plane: Restarting OSPF Gracefully

This chapter describes two Open Shortest Path First (OSPF) restart approaches that enable you to reduce the negative effects of the original OSPF restart: restart signaling and graceful restart. An *adjacency* is a relationship between neighboring routers that enables the exchange of routing information. The time that expires between a router restarting and reestablishing adjacencies is called a *graceful restart*. Although restart signaling and graceful restart use different mechanics, both approaches have the same goals: to have neighboring routers retain adjacencies with the restarting router and continue to forward data traffic across the restart. If you examine the mechanisms from a bird's-eye view, you see that both restart mechanisms require protocol extensions and support from neighbors.

This chapter begins with a description of the detrimental effects resulting from the original OSPF restart behavior. This is followed by an overview of the OSPF routing and descriptions of the OSPF restart mechanisms. The key concepts of each restart mechanism are elaborated through operational examples and network-deployment scenarios. The chapter concludes with a summary.

Internet Routing Architecture

To reduce the amount of routing information that must be maintained and transmitted by routers, hierarchical routing architecture is used to partition the Internet into smaller-sized entities known as *autonomous systems* (see Figure 4-1). An autonomous system (AS) is a collection of networks under a common administration that share a common routing strategy. An AS is divided into one or more smaller entities known as *routing domains*. A routing domain is a set of networks that use the same routing protocol. Between autonomous systems, routing information is exchanged using an exterior gateway protocol such as *Border Gateway Protocol* (BGP), which is described in a later chapter. Inside an AS, routing information within a routing domain (intradomain) is exchanged through an *interior gateway protocol* (IGP) such as *Open Shortest Path First* (OSPF) or *Intermediate System-to-Intermediate System* (IS-IS). (Chapter 5, "Intradomain IP Control Plane: Restarting IS-IS Gracefully," supplies more information on IS-IS.)

Figure 4-1 *Internet Routing Hierarchy*

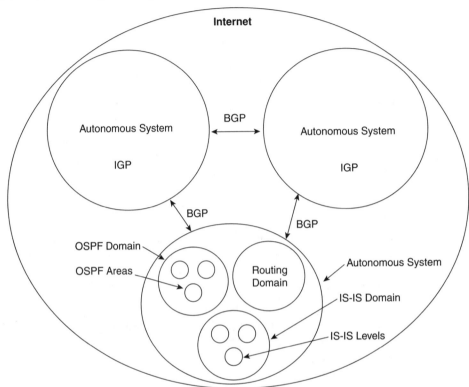

Each routing domain is divided into even smaller networks known as *OSPF areas* or *IS-IS levels*.

OSPF and IS-IS are the members of the general class of routing protocols known as link-state protocols. The key component of a *link-state* protocol is the distributed database that describes the routing topology of the network—the map of the interconnection of routers in the routing domain.

To build and maintain synchronized databases on every router, the link-state protocol demands that each router in the routing domain periodically transmit its local piece of the topology information as *link-state advertisements* (LSA). The OSPF flooding procedure ensures that every LSA is propagated to all routers (as determined by the flooding scope of the LSA). From self-originated and received LSAs, each router pieces together a *link-state database* (LSDB).

Taking the LSDB as input, at regular intervals or when the network topology changes, each router independently runs the *Shortest Path First* (SPF) algorithm to construct a tree of shortest paths. The SPF tree contains routes to each destination internal to the routing domain and to some external destinations. The SPF tree contains information for the entire routing path (a concatenation of links and routers from source to destination). However, IP forwards hop by hop based on the next-hop and outgoing-link information. The SPF tree is needed for routing calculations, but it holds much more information than actually required to forward IP data packets. Therefore, the SPF tree is transformed into another data structure referred to as the *Routing Information Base* (RIB).

OSPF Control- and Forwarding-Plane Components

As discussed in Chapter 2, "IP Forwarding Plane: Achieving Nonstop Forwarding," in general the RIB might maintain routes for multiple routing protocols such as OSPF, IS-IS, and BGP. To improve forwarding performance and availability, the RIB is in turn mapped to another data structure known as the *Forwarding Information Base* (FIB). The RIB may retain all learned routes, whereas the FIB keeps only the best of the selected usable routes. As described in Chapter 2, IP routing protocols and the RIB reside on the control processor and make up the IP control plane. The FIB resides on the line cards (the active and the standby control processor also have a copy of the FIB) and forms the IP forwarding plane. The separation of control and forwarding planes not only results in a scalable forwarding architecture, it also improves fault tolerance of the router. If a router's faults are confined to the control plane, for example, the separation of control and forwarding components makes it possible to preserve the FIB and use it for forwarding across the IP control-plane restart. Similarly, separation of the control and forwarding components in a distributed forwarding architecture allows faults in the forwarding plane to be confined to the single failing line card and not propagated to other parts of the forwarding plane or the control plane. In this type of failure scenario, although any packets that need to traverse the failing line card are dropped, forwarding in other line cards is not affected (which is much better than dropping data packets in all line cards). The term *nonstop forwarding* (NSF) refers to the capability of a router to continue forwarding across the control-plane restart.

OSPF Control-Plane Restart Approaches

As discussed in Chapter 1, "Understanding High Availability of IP and MPLS Networks," control-plane restart schemes can generally be categorized into two classes: mechanisms that require protocol extensions and mechanisms that do not. In the former case, the control-plane restart is externally visible to the neighbors, and the restarting router requires support from its neighbors. For example, neighbors must retain their forwarding state and continue to forward packets to the restarting router as normal, while the restarting router recovers its control-plane state and validates the preserved *forwarding state* (FIB). In this case, the restarting control-plane component is stateless (or is stateful but has preserved only partial state) and needs to recover the missing control-plane state from its neighbors.

For mechanisms that do not require protocol extensions, the control-plane restart in a router is not externally visible to its neighbors. Therefore this scenario does not necessitate any changes to the protocols. In this case, the restarting control-plane component preserves its complete control-plane state and therefore does not need to recover it from neighbors. In this case, it is assumed that even if the restarting control-plane component has not preserved any state (stateless) or has preserved partial state (stateful), it can recover its missing state without requiring any externally visible changes to the protocols.

The OSPF restart mechanisms described in this chapter belong to the class that requires protocol extensions. The Cisco IS-IS restart mechanism, which is described in Chapter 5, is an example of the mechanism that belongs to the class that does not require protocol extensions. In general, the IP and MPLS control-plane restart mechanisms described in this book require protocol extensions. At this point, if you need more explanation of these concepts, you might want to review the IP forwarding-plane architecture described in Chapter 2.

Understanding the Detrimental Effects of the OSPF Restart

OSPF uses Hello packets to discover neighbors and establish neighbor relationships. Hello packets are also used to ensure two-way connectivity between *adjacent* routers. After two-way connectivity has been established, the two neighbors may form an adjacency (a relationship between neighboring routers for the purpose of exchanging routing information). After an adjacency has been established, the two neighbors exchange routing information to initially synchronize their LSDBs. After a router has synchronized its LSDB with all neighbors, the router is ready to forward data packets.

OSPF database synchronization adopts two forms: the initial and the continual incremental synchronization. The initial database synchronization takes place between adjacent neighbors when they form an adjacency. After the initial LSDB synchronization is complete, further resynchronization is accomplished through the incremental asynchronous reliable updates (or flooding). The OSPF flooding mechanism keeps LSDB synchronized in the presence of network topology changes. Whenever a new adjacency is established or an existing adjacency is torn down, for example, the routers associated with the adjacency issue new LSAs to inform other routers about the network topology change. These LSAs are reliably flooded to ensure that the LSDB remains resynchronized. One of the reasons for insistence on keeping the LSDB synchronized is that routing calculations are based on the LSDB. And if the LSDB itself does not reflect the state of the actual network topology, it increases the likelihood of erroneous forwarding. To avoid the possibility of incorrect forwarding such as black holes, OSPF recalculates routes whenever content of the LSDB changes.

When the OSPF in a router restarts, neighbors with adjacencies to the restarting router learn about the OSPF restart. How does a neighboring router find out about the OSPF restart? A neighbor detects the restart event on an adjacency when the associated hold timer expires, or when it receives a Hello packet containing incomplete information. For example, the Hello does not mention the receiving router in the neighbor list.

When neighbors learn about the OSPF restart, they cycle their adjacencies to the restarting router through the down state. To keep the LSDB synchronized, a change in adjacency state (up to down) forces the neighboring routers to advertise new LSAs. The complete reliable flooding and installation of these LSAs in the LSDB will force the SPF to run in the entire area or routing domain.

In the original OSPF specification, the main objective of this protocol behavior was reducing the possibility of incorrect forwarding by routing around the restarting router while its database is being resynchronized. This OSPF protocol behavior is necessary in the case of a restarting router that is incapable of preserving its FIB across the restart. This inability is due to the fact that if traffic is allowed to pass through such a restarting router, there is an increased likelihood of incorrect forwarding because of an incomplete database and the FIB. Therefore, to reduce the possibility of incorrect forwarding, such as routing loops and black holes, OSPF deliberately routes around the restarting router.

The OSPF behavior of deliberately routing around an NSF-capable restarting router is very undesirable. This is because if the network topology does not change and the restarting router is able to preserve its FIB across the restart, it is safe and more convenient to retain the restarting router on the forwarding path. When the restarting router is NSF-capable, there are three major undesirable effects of adhering to the original OSPF restart behavior:

- First, in spite of the fact that the restarting router would have continued to forward data packets correctly, by routing around it data traffic passing through the restarting router is disrupted.

- Second, if the alternative forwarding path is not found, the data traffic passing through the restarting router is unnecessarily dropped.

- Third, to make the situation even worse, the restarting router quickly re-forms adjacencies with its neighbors. The appearance of a new adjacency (down to up) on the neighboring routers causes them to reissue new LSAs containing links to the restarting router, which again triggers SPF runs throughout the entire area or routing domain.

An abrupt disappearance and reappearance of an adjacency is referred to as an *adjacency flap*. Upon receiving new LSAs, other routers now bring back the restarting router on the forwarding path and again start directing traffic to the restarting router. In short, the whole episode of the adjacency flap causes detrimental effects in the IP control plane and the forwarding plane. For example, the adjacency flap causes a generation of excessive control traffic and disruption of data traffic. These detrimental effects of OSPF restart are depicted in Figure 4-2. For example, when R5 restarts, all routers in the area (or routing domain) must recalculate their routes.

Figure 4-2 *Adjacency Flap and Its Detrimental Effects Caused by Original OSPF Restart Behavior*

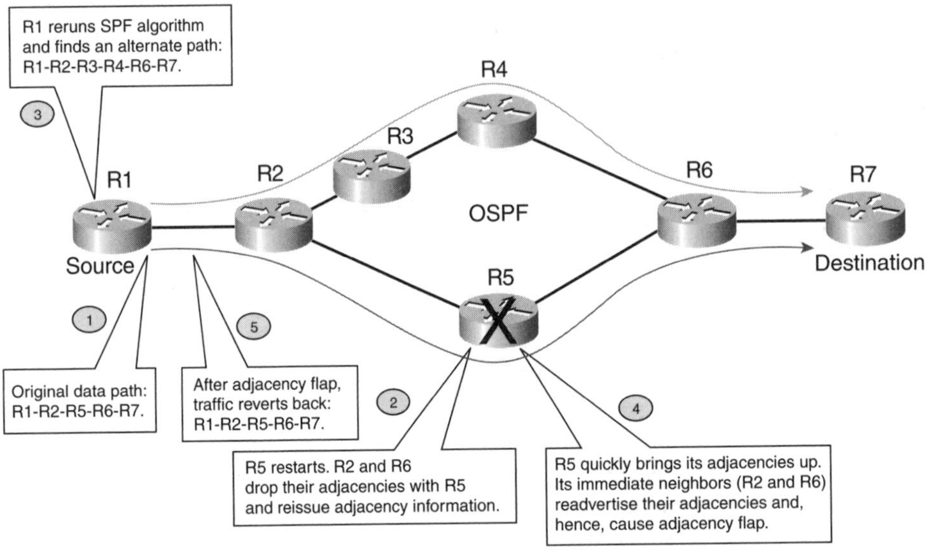

Overview of OSPF Routing

An *interior gateway protocol* (IGP) is a routing protocol that is used to exchange routing information between routers inside a routing domain. (Sometime the term *routing domain* is used interchangeably with the AS.) OSPF and IS-IS are two of the most popular IGPs. OSPF belongs to the class of routing protocols known as *link-state protocols*.[1] Because of features such as fast convergence time (typically less than few hundred milliseconds) and reduced link bandwidth requirements for control messages (typically less than 1 percent of link bandwidth), link-state protocols are increasingly being deployed in enterprise and service provider networks.

The primary requirement of a link-state routing protocol is to maintain a synchronized LSDB within the routing domain. To satisfy this central requirement, each OSPF router in the routing domain advertises its LSAs that are reliably propagated throughout the routing domain. (As you see shortly, each LSA has a flooding scope, which may restrict its propagation to smaller portions only.) Using LSAs that are both self-originated and received, each router constructs an LSDB. Strictly speaking, routers might not have synchronized LSDBs during a brief period of convergence. In the steady state, however, each router should have a synchronized LSDB.

OSPF uses the Dijkstra algorithm (also known as the *SPF algorithm*) to compute a tree of the shortest paths to internal and external destinations. Each route in the SPF tree contains routing information for the entire path. However, as mentioned earlier, you need only enough information to be able to forward to the next hop. Therefore, the SPF tree is converted to another data structure, the RIB. To improve forwarding performance and availability, the RIB in turn is mapped to another data structure, the FIB. (See Chapter 2 for more details on the FIB architecture.) Figure 4-3 shows a functional view of the OSPF routing.

Figure 4-3   *Functional View of the OSPF Operation*

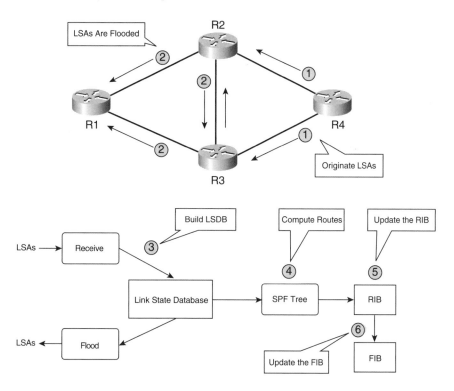

OSPF Hierarchical Routing

To manage network resources such as routing table size in a scalable manner, OSPF uses a hierarchical routing scheme by partitioning a routing domain into groups of smaller networks called *areas*. A 32-bit area ID uniquely identifies each area. All OSPF areas physically attach to a special area known as the *backbone area*. Areas that are physically noncontiguous to the backbone area attach through virtual links. The backbone area is always assigned an area ID of zero (0.0.0.0)—(see Figure 4-4). Inside a given OSPF area, routing is flat, which means that all routers within the area have an identical LSDB, and each router knows about every network segment within that area.

Because an area's LSAs are not flooded across its boundary, that area's topology information is not visible to other areas. How do routers forward packets to destinations in another area? As you learn shortly, routers that attach to multiple areas leak interarea routing information. Hence, by segmenting the network topology information into smaller pieces, OSPF hierarchical routing reduces the routing table size. For example, because the size of an area is much smaller than the routing domain, the size of the area's LSDB is considerably reduced. Because area-specific LSAs are not flooded across that area's boundary, the amount of flooding traffic is also reduced. In addition, summary LSAs aggregate area routing information at an area boundary, which further reduces the number of interarea routing entries.

Figure 4-4   *OSPF Hierarchical Routing Model*

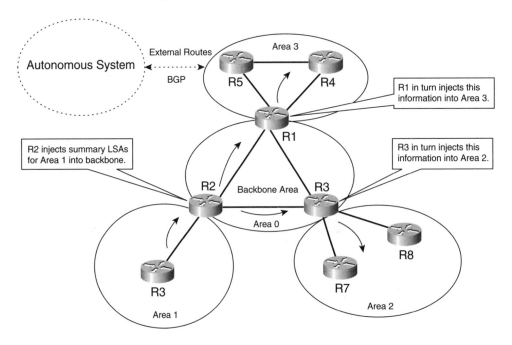

Area Border Routers (ABRs) – R1, R2, R3
Autonomous System Border Router (ASBR) – R5

With the introduction of areas, OSPF classifies routers according to their special routing function:

- **Internal routers**—Have all attached network interfaces within the same area
- **Area border routers (ABR)**—Attach to multiple areas and leak summarized interarea routing information
- **Backbone routers**—Have an interface to the backbone area
- **AS boundary routers (ASBR)**—Exchange routing information with other autonomous systems

Establishing Adjacencies and Synchronizing Link-State Databases

OSPF uses the Hello protocol to establish and maintain neighbor relationships. After coming up, an OSPF router first discovers neighbors by sending OSPF Hello packets periodically (default is every 10 seconds). On point-to-point and broadcast interfaces, neighbors are discovered dynamically by sending Hellos to a well-known multicast address called *ALLSPFRouters*. In contrast, on *nonbroadcast multiaccess* (NMBA) interfaces such as Frame Relay and ATM, OSPF neighbors are typically discovered via configuration. An OSPF router learns about the existence of a neighbor when it receives a Hello from the neighbor. The OSPF Hello protocol ensures that neighboring routers can communicate bidirectionally.

To assist neighboring routers in checking the existence of the two-way connectivity, each router lists all recently seen neighbors in its Hello packets. Therefore, when a router finds its own router ID listed in the neighbor's Hello packet, this confirms the establishment of two-way connectivity with the neighbor. The confirmation of two-way connectivity is important because it prevents the possibility of black holes resulting from link failures in one direction. To guard against these sorts of routing errors, OSPF only forwards over bidirectional links. OSPF prevents these sorts of routing errors by omitting unidirectional links in the LSAs and then excluding them from routing calculations. That is why when a router does not find itself listed in the neighbor's Hellos, it resets any existing adjacency with that neighbor.

As mentioned earlier, an adjacency is a relationship between neighboring routers for the purpose of exchanging routing information. Each adjacency has an associated hold timer known as a RouterDeadInterval. If a router does not receive another Hello within the RouterDeadInterval, it thinks that the neighbor is dead and deletes the adjacency. From this behavior it follows that maintenance of adjacencies not only requires timely reception of Hello packets but also the presence of correct information in the Hellos.

After having discovered neighbors, two routers may form an adjacency. Adjacencies are formed through the exchange of OSPF Database Description and Link-State Request packets. The Database Description packets exchange is also known as the *database exchange process*. Each Database Description packet describes the set of LSAs that are currently being held in the sender's LSDB. After having exchanged Database Description packets with a neighbor, a router learns about the LSAs that are currently missing or out-of-date in its own LSDB. The router then requests the missing and out-of-date LSAs from the neighbor by sending Link-State Request packets. In response to Link-State Request packets, the neighbor responds with Link-State Update packets. Each Link-State Update packet may contain one or more LSAs. The Link-State Update and Link-State Acknowledgment packets implement the reliable update mechanism. To acknowledge reception of LSAs, OSPF uses Link-State Acknowledgment packets. It is the explicit acknowledgment of the received LSAs that makes flooding reliable. Note, however, that the delivery of OSPF packets itself is not guaranteed because of the unreliable nature of the IP transport. A single Link-State Acknowledgment packet can be used to acknowledge multiple LSAs. If the Link-State Update packet is lost, it is retransmitted. For each adjacency, OSPF maintains a list of LSAs that have been transmitted but not acknowledged. The unacknowledged LSAs are retransmitted at intervals until they are either acknowledged or the adjacency is removed.

Two neighbors are considered fully adjacent and ready for forwarding when all outstanding Link-State Request packets have been acknowledged. The progression of conversation between neighbors as they form adjacencies is represented as neighbor states and maintained in the neighbor data structure. Initially, the two routers start in the down neighbor state. After having exchanged Hello packets, the neighbor state transitions to two-way, which indicates establishment of bidirectional communication between the two neighbors.

The adjacency between two routers starts to form in the exstart state. Then the two neighbors establish a master and slave relationship. As soon as two routers learn about their master/slave status, the neighbor state moves to exchange state. In the exchange state, each router describes its entire LSDB to the neighbor by sending Database Description packets. Link-State Request packets may also be sent to ask for the neighbor's more recent LSAs. An adjacency in the exchange or greater neighbor state can send and receive all types of OSPF routing protocol packets. At this stage, the flooding procedure starts and the two routers begin to synchronize their LSDBs. The LSDB synchronization completes when all outstanding Link-State Request packets have been acknowledged. At that point, the neighbor state transitions to full and the two routers are said to be *fully adjacent*. Now the adjacency is ready for forwarding data packets and is advertised in the LSAs. Because the existence of adjacency is a prerequisite for routing exchange, LSDB synchronization only occurs between adjacent routers.

In general, not every pair of neighboring routers forms adjacencies. Routers connected by point-to-point links always form adjacencies. However, on broadcast and NBMA networks such as ATM and Frame Relay, all routers form adjacencies with the designated router (DR) and the *backup designated router* (BDR), if it exists.

Every broadcast and NBMA network elects a DR that generates network LSAs on behalf of the associated network and has other special responsibilities in the running of the protocol. The DR is elected through the Hello protocol. On a broadcast network with n routers, $n(n - 1)$ pair of neighbor relationships are required. With the notion of DR, instead of having to form adjacencies and synchronize LSDB between every pair of neighbors, routers now can form adjacencies and synchronize with a single router. Hence the notion of DR helps to reduce the number of adjacencies required on a broadcast or NBMA network. The reduced number of adjacencies in turn helps to lessen the amount of routing protocol traffic and the size of the LSDB. In addition to the DR, there might be a BDR on each broadcast and NBMA network. Like the DR, the BDR is also adjacent to all routers on the network and becomes the DR when the previous DR fails. The BDR is important because if there were no BDRs on a network, when a new DR became necessary, new adjacencies would have to be formed between the new DR and all other routers on the network. Therefore, the existence of the BDR improves fault tolerance of the network against a DR failure and enables a smoother transition to a new DR.

OSPF Link-State Advertisements

Every OSPF router originates one or more different types of LSAs to describe routing information. Each LSA has a fixed 20-byte header that contains fields such as LS age, LS type, advertising router, LS sequence number, and LS ID. The LS ID uniquely distinguishes an LSA of a router from other self-originated LSAs of the same LS type. The sequence number field is used to determine which LSA is more current. When there are multiple instances of an LSA, the LSA instance with the higher sequence number is considered to be more recent. The combined three fields of LS type, LS ID, and advertising router uniquely identify an LSA in the LSDB.

A new instance of an LSA may be issued in response to a number of events, such as on expiration of the LSA refresh timer, an interface state change (up or down), a change of DR, or when a neighbor's state changes to or from the full state. The flooding procedure starts when an Link-State Update packet has been received. Each Link-State Update packet carries a collection of LSAs one hop farther from the originating router. For each LSA contained in the Link-State Update packet, the receiving router performs a number of checks, such as an LSA's checksum validation and examination of the LS type and the LS age fields.

After installing a new or more recent LSA and acknowledging its receipt with a Link-State Acknowledgment packet, the router floods the LSA out of pertinent interfaces (as determined by the LSA's flooding scope). Through the repetitive update process, each LSA is reliably propagated throughout the routing domain. Note that an LSA that has reached the value of MaxAge is purged from the LSDB and excluded from routing calculations. After the initial LSDB synchronization has been done, further resynchronizations are ensured through the reliable flooding procedure.

OSPF LSAs can be broadly classified as follows:

- Router LSAs (LS type = 1)
- Network LSAs (LS type = 2)
- Network summary LSAs (LS type = 3)
- ASBR summary LSAs (LS type = 4)
- AS external LSAs (LS type = 5)
- Type 7 LSAs (used to import limited external route information in not-so-stubby areas, as described in sections that follow)

Depending on its role in the routing hierarchy, an OSPF router may originate LSAs of one or more types. (See Table 4-1 for details.) All OSPF routers originate router LSAs, whereas only ABRs originate summary LSAs. Each type of LSA conveys a certain level of routing information such as intra-area, interarea, or external, and is targeted for a specific set of routers (see Figure 4-4). For example, router LSAs and network LSAs are propagated only within an area. In contrast, AS external LSAs are propagated through the routing domain (excluding stub areas). An area that has a single exit point from the area and is incapable of carrying transit traffic is known as a *stub area*. A majority of LSDBs consist of AS external LSAs. These LSAs are not flooded into the stub areas. Thus stub areas are useful when it is desirable to reduce the LSDB size and memory requirements caused by limited resources on routers internal to these areas. Because AS external LSAs are not flooded into or throughout stub areas, in stub areas routing to AS external destinations is based on default routing, which is considered to be very restrictive in some deployments. The restriction of a stub area can be alleviated by using an area referred to as a *not-so-stubby area* (NSSA). In contrast with a stub area, the NSSA has the additional capability of importing external routes in a limited fashion through the type 7 LSAs.

Table 4-1   *Summary of OSPF LSAs*

LSA Type	Name	Originated By	Flooding Scope
1	Router LSAs	All routers	Router LSAs describe router active interfaces and are flooded within an area.
2	Network LSAs	DR	Network LSAs describe lists of attached routers on the network and are flooded within an area.
3, 4	Summary LSAs	ABR	A summary LSA describes a route to a destination outside the area (that is, an interarea route). The destination described by each summary LSA is either an IP prefix (type 3 summary LSAs) or an ASBR (type 4 summary LSAs). Summary LSAs (type 3 and type 4) are originated by ABRs and flooded within the LSA's associated area. For example, each ABR originates a summary LSA for each of its attached areas (nonbackbone areas) into the backbone area. These summary LSAs are flooded within the backbone area and received by other ABRs. Thus an ABR within the backbone area may receive multiple summary LSAs for the same destination flooded by different ABRs. It selects the best summary LSAs for the destination and re-advertises this interarea destination into its attached areas through its own summary LSA. That is how interarea routing information is leaked across area boundaries.
5	AS external LSAs	ASBR	An AS external LSA describes a route to a destination in another AS. These LSAs are flooded in all nonstub areas of the AS.
7	Type 7 LSAs	ASBR	Type 7 LSAs are used for importing external routing information into NSSAs. These LSAs are flooded throughout the NSSAs.

OSPF uses a four-level routing hierarchy with a decreasing order of preference in the path-selection process:

- **Intra-area paths**—Correspond to destinations within the same area. Intra-area paths are calculated based on routing information gathered within the area from router LSAs and network LSAs.

- **Interarea paths**—Pertain to destinations in other OSPF areas. These paths are learned through the examination of received summary LSAs (which are leaked by ABRs into their attached areas).

- **Type 1 and Type 2 external paths**—Refer to destinations external to the routing domain. These paths are learned through the examination of received AS external LSAs (injected by ASBRs).

The OSPF hierarchical routing model allows routers within an area to select the best exit area border router for interarea destinations and routers internal to the AS to pick the best exit ASBR for external destinations. Generally, installing a new LSA in the LSDB triggers routing calculations. In other words, as long as the content of the new LSA differs from the old instance, installing such an LSA in the LSDB requires routing recalculations. Two instances of the same LSAs are considered to have different content at these points: whenever the options field changes, when one of the LSA instance's LS age is set to MaxAge but the other is not, when the length field changes, or when the body of the LSA (excluding LS sequence number and LS checksum) changes.

Mitigating the Detrimental Effects of OSPF Restart

As discussed in Chapter 1, router downtime can be caused by unplanned and planned faults. An unplanned OSPF restart is caused by the unexpected hardware or software component failures of a router. Examples of unplanned OSPF restart include a control-plane software crash, control processor switchover because of unexpected hardware or software failures, and so forth. A planned OSPF restart is caused by scheduled maintenance events such as an in-service software upgrade. Therefore, to reduce a network's overall downtime, the OSPF restart mechanisms must be designed for planned and unplanned situations.

OSPF Restart Mechanisms

This section describes two OSPF restart mechanisms: restart signaling and graceful restart. Before delving into the nitty-gritty details, it would be helpful to get a high-level view of the two approaches. To begin with, it is important to note that even though their mechanics are very different, both approaches attempt to achieve the same goal—to allow OSPF to restart in the least-disruptive manner after a planned or unplanned outage. Specifically this means that the neighbors must retain their adjacencies and continue forwarding on those adjacencies across the neighbor's restart. Although the restarting router loses all its OSPF adjacencies, it continues to forward packets based on the preserved FIB. Therefore, after restarting, the restarted router must re-form all prerestart adjacencies, synchronize the LSDB on these adjacencies, and update the FIB with any new forwarding information. And to keep things in perspective, all these tasks must be accomplished without causing adjacency flaps and the ensuing harmful effects. From this discussion it should be clear that to meet these objectives, not only does the restarting router need to preserve the FIB, but the neighboring router must also cooperate by retaining its adjacencies and continue to forward on those adjacencies.

The neighbors should also allow the restarting router to re-form adjacencies and resynchronize its LSDB. In a few words, to be able to restart OSPF in a graceful manner, you need to make behavior changes both in the restarting router and its neighbors. This is precisely what the two OSPF restart mechanisms are all about. For example, both restart mechanisms require protocol extension and support from neighbors. The mechanics of each approach are described in the following sections.

OSPF Restart Signaling Mechanism

In a simplified view, the OSPF restart signaling mechanism can be described as follows. During neighbor discovery, the neighboring routers exchange restart capabilities. After the OSPF restart, the restarting router informs its neighbors by saying "My OSPF has restarted; however, I have managed to preserve the FIB across the restart. Please don't reset your adjacencies to me, and keep these adjacencies on your forwarding paths." The neighboring routers acknowledge by saying "We are retaining our adjacencies and are expecting you to re-form these adjacencies and resynchronize LSDB shortly. To avoid forwarding into black holes by retaining incorrect adjacencies on the forwarding paths, if you fail to start LSDB resynchronization within a certain time period, we will reset these adjacencies."

From this functional description, it follows that to reduce the harmful effects of the OSPF restart, the restarting router must be able to inform its neighbors before any adjacency expires. The restart signaling mechanism has three main goals:

- Inform its neighbors about the OSPF restart and prevent them from resetting their adjacencies

- Re-form adjacencies and correctly resynchronize its LSDB with the neighbors after the restart

- Reliably determine when the LSDB is completely synchronized with all neighbors to reduce the possibility of forwarding loops resulting from premature routing calculations using an incomplete LSDB

The following paragraphs describe the mechanics of the restart signaling mechanism that are used to accomplish these objectives.

The restart signaling mechanism defines a new bit, called the Restart Signaling (RS) bit, in Hello packets.[3] After OSPF restart, the restarting router sets the RS bit in the Hello packets to inform its neighbors about the restart and to prevent them from resetting their adjacencies. The RS bit is encoded in the *extended option type length value* (EO-TLV) that in turn is carried in the optional opaque data structure known as the *link local signaling* (LLS). The LLS data block is optional and therefore might not be present in every Hello.[4]

A new bit, known as the L bit, is introduced in the options field to indicate the presence of the LLS data block. When a neighbor receives a Hello packet with the RS bit set, the neighbor knows that the sender has restarted and managed to preserve its FIB across the restart. The neighbor maintains its adjacency with the restarting router and continues to forward data packets on the retained adjacency. To achieve this behavior, the nonrestarting router needs to change its Hello processing. Before describing the details of those changes, it is useful to examine the original OSPF Hello processing procedure.

The original Hello processing procedure works as follows. When a router receives a Hello packet that does not mention the router in the neighbors list, it moves the neighbor state from full to init and resets the adjacency. As mentioned earlier, the restarting router loses its adjacencies across the restart. Therefore, upon restarting it does not know its previously known neighbors. In the process of rediscovering neighbors, the restarting router sends Hello packets without correct neighbor-list information. If neighbors were to process these Hellos according to the original Hello procedure, they would reset their adjacencies with the restarting router (which is obviously very undesirable).

Modifications to the OSPF Hello Processing Procedure

To stop neighbors from resetting their adjacencies with the restarting router, the restart signaling mechanism modifies the Hello processing procedure in the neighbors as follows. When a router receives a Hello packet with the RS bit set, if the adjacency is in the full state, the router omits the two-way connectivity check. The end result of this modification is that even if the restarting router's Hellos contain incomplete information, its neighboring routers do not reset their adjacencies with the restarting router. In addition to ignoring the two-way connectivity check, the restart signaling mechanism also requires the neighboring router to quickly acknowledge receipt of a Hello with the RS bit set with a Hello with the RS bit clear. The neighbor's Hello not only acknowledges receipt of the Hello with the RS bit set, but also helps the restarting router to relearn its previously known neighbors quickly. A new bit, known as the *RestartState bit*, is defined in the neighbor data structure to record the fact that a Hello with the RS bit has been received from a restarting neighbor. This bit is set when a Hello with the RS bit set is received from the neighbor.

In summary, after having received a Hello with the RS bit set, the neighbor maintains its adjacencies with the restarting routers that are in the full state, and quickly acknowledges it with its own Hello with the RS bit cleared.

Link-State Database Resynchronization

Suppose following the OSPF restart the restarting router has managed to inform its neighbors by sending Hellos with the RS bit set before the adjacency is removed (RouterDeadInterval expires). Upon receipt of the Hello packet with the RS bit clear, the restarting router is expected to resynchronize its LSDB with the neighbor. However, there is one small problem. The original OSPF specification does not allow a neighbor to resynchronize its LSDB without first moving the neighbor state from full to exstart.

Again, this behavior is very undesirable because any time the neighbor state moves from the full to exstart state, a corresponding adjacency is also reset. The restart signaling mechanism proposes to use a different method, known as an *out-of-band* (OOB) resynchronization procedure.[5] The objective of the OOB resynchronization procedure is to allow the initial LSDB resynchronization without resetting adjacencies.

How does the restarting router know whether its neighbor is capable of performing OOB resynchronization? The answer is quite simple. The restart signaling mechanism defines a new bit in the EO-TLV, which is referred to as *LSDB Resynchronization* (LR) bit. Routers capable of supporting the OOB LSDB resynchronization procedure advertise their OOB resynchronization capability by setting the LR bit in both Hello and Database Description packets. The LR bit is stored in the neighbor's data structure (along with other bits in the standard options field). When desired, the restarting router can obtain a neighbor OOB capability by examining the stored LR bit information. After having received Hello packets with the RS bit set and responding with its own Hellos, the nonrestarting neighbor expects the restarting router to initiate the OOB LSDB resynchronization procedure.

To avoid having to wait indefinitely for the restarting router to start the OOB resynchronization and to reduce the possibility of black holes because of forwarding on incorrect adjacencies, the neighboring router uses a local timer. This timer, referred to as the *ResyncTimeout*, defines the time interval within which the restarting router must initiate OOB resynchronization to prevent neighbors from resetting their retained adjacencies. When a router receives a Hello packet with the RS bit set, it sets the RestartState bit and starts the ResyncTimeout timer. If the restarting router initiates the OOB LSDB procedure with the neighbor while its ResyncTimeout timer is running, the neighbor cancels the ResyncTimeout timer. Otherwise, the neighboring router clears the RestartState bit and resets the adjacency when the ResyncTimeout timer expires.

How does the restarting router initiate the OOB LSDB resynchronization? To initiate OOB LSDB resynchronization with a neighbor, the restarting router first examines the LR bit in the neighbor's data structure. If the neighbor is OOB capable, the restarting router sets the OOBResync bit for the neighbor to true, forces the neighbor state to exstart, and sends Database Description packets to the neighbor with the R bit set. The OOBResync is a new bit in the neighbor data structure. When set to true, it indicates that the router is currently performing OOB LSDB resynchronization. While the OOBResync bit is set to true, Database Description packets are sent with the R bit set.

The R bit is a new bit in the Database Description packet's field containing the *Init* (I) bit, the *More* (M) bit, and the *Master/Slave* (MS) bit (not to be confused with the LR bit in the EO-TLV). When a neighboring router receives a Database Description packet with the R bit set while its ResyncTimeout timer is running, it cancels the ResyncTimeout, sets the OOBResync bit to true, and forces the neighbor state from full to exstart. While the OOBResync bit is true, the adjacency is not reset as state transitions to or from the full state.

During the OOB resynchronization procedure, Database Description packets are processed a little differently than according to the original OSPF specification (see Figure 4-5).

The two routers then synchronize their LSDB using standard OSPF procedure. For example, they exchange Database Description and Link-State Request packets. When OOB LSDB with a neighbor is complete, the corresponding OOBResynch bit is cleared.

How does the restarting router determine that its LSDB is fully synchronized? It is fully synchronized when all its adjacencies have reached the full state. Why is it important to know that LSDB synchronization has completed? This is important because calculating routes based on incomplete LSDBs can cause forwarding loops and black holes. It is for this reason that the restarting router does not recalculate its routes or update the preserved FIB until its LSDB has been synchronized with all neighbors. The OSPF restart behavior for the restarting and nonrestarting router using the restart signaling mechanism is described in the following sections.

Figure 4-5   *Processing Procedure of the Database Description Packets During OOB LSDB Resynchronization*

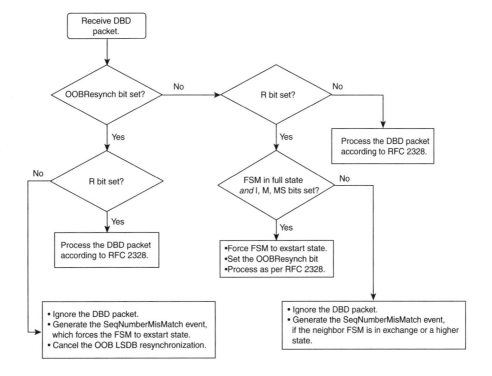

Restarting Router Behavior

Suppose a router restarts due to a planned or unplanned outage. The router manages to preserve its FIB and continues to forward data traffic while OSPF is restarting. Further assume that the router can restart and is ready for communicating with OSPF neighbors before any adjacency on neighbors shared with the restarting router expires. After restarting, the router marks all preserved FIB entries as stale and starts a *refresh timer* (a time period within which stale entries must be updated to avoid being deleted after the restart). However, the router still continues to use the stale FIB entries to forward data packets.

To prevent neighboring routers from resetting their adjacencies, the restarting router quickly sends Hellos with the RS bit set on each interface that is capable of supporting the restart signaling mechanism. After having sent Hellos with the RS bit set, the restarting router expects to get acknowledgments from neighbors in the form of Hello packets with the RS bit clear. After having received the acknowledgment from a neighbor, the restarting router is now certain that the concerned neighbor is retaining its adjacencies.

Then the restarting router attempts to resynchronize its LSDB with the neighbor using the OOB procedure. To determine the neighbor's OOB capabilities, the restarting router examines the neighbor data structure. If the neighbor is determined to be OOB capable, the restarting router starts the resynchronization procedure by setting the OOBResynch bit and forces the neighbor state to exstart. The adjacency is not reset when the neighbor state transitions from full to exstart. If the neighbor is not OOB capable, normal OSPF restart takes place.

After neighbor state has moved to exstart, the restarting router uses the standard OSPF database exchange procedure to synchronize its LSDB. The restarting router asserts itself as the master and starts sending initial Database Description packets with the R bit set, in addition to the I, M, MS bits. After having established the master/slave relationship with the neighbor, the neighbor state moves to exchange. In the exchange state, each router describes its entire LSDB to the neighbor by sending Database Description packets and asks for the neighbor's more recent LSA by sending Link-State Request packets.

While OOBResynch bit is set to true, the restarting router sends Database Description packets with the R bit set in the standard options field. After all outstanding Link-State Request packets have been acknowledged, the LSDB synchronization is complete and the neighbor state moves to the full state.

Upon entering the full state, the restarting router clears the OOBResynch bit in the neighbor data structure and the R bit in the Database Description packets. To put an upper limit on the OOB database exchange process, the restarting router starts a timer upon initiating the OOB LSDB resynchronization procedure. If this timer expires before the LSA database synchronization is complete, the restarting router cancels the OOB LSDB procedure and reverts back to the normal OSPF restart procedure by clearing the R bit in the Database Description packets and resetting the adjacency.

In summary, OOB LSDB resynchronization uses the standard database exchange procedure except that it modifies the processing of the Database Description packets and allows transitioning to and from the full state without resetting the adjacency.

SPF Calculations

To avoid SPF computation churn resulting from an OSPF restart, the restarting router does not originate a new version of router or network LSAs when the *finite-state machine* (FSM) state transitions to or from the full state with the OOBResynch bit set. During OOB LSDB resynchronization, the restarting router may receive its self-originated LSAs that it had originated before this restart.

As per the original OSPF specification, the receiving router should either update or purge these LSAs from the routing domain. To update these LSAs without triggering SPF calculations on other routers, the router needs to ensure that new instances of the self-originating LSAs are identical to those originated before the restart. This assumes that the restarting router has all the required information for building new instances of these LSAs. If the required information is unknown, normally a router should flush such self-originated LSAs. If the restarting router was able to preserve its FIB across the restart, however, flushing of unknown self-originated LSAs is undesirable because it causes other routers to reroute around the restarting router, even though the restarting router has preserved the FIB across the OSPF restart.

As discussed previously, forwarding loops and black holes might occur if routes are calculated based on incomplete LSDB information. Therefore, to avoid forwarding loops, the restarting router does not modify or flush the received self-originated LSAs but instead accepts them as valid. The restarting router delays regeneration of the self-originated LSAs until the LSDB has been synchronized with all neighbors. Moreover, the restarting router neither recalculates routes nor updates the preserved FIB until its LSDB has been completely synchronized. The restarting router's initial LSDB resynchronization is complete when all its adjacencies have reached the full state. As normal OSPF behavior, the router performs any further LSDB re-synchronization through flooding. When the initial LSDB resynchronization is complete, the restarting router runs the SPF algorithm, updates the FIB entries, and flushes all invalid self-originated LSAs. When the refresh timer expires, the restarting router removes FIB entries that are still marked as stale.

Nonrestarting Router (Helper-Node) Behavior

Upon receipt of a Hello with the RS bit set from the restarting router, the nonrestarting neighbor skips the two-way connectivity check provided the adjacency is in the full state. The nonrestarting router immediately sends a Hello with the RS bit cleared, sets the RestartState, and starts the ResyncTimeout timer. The restarting router is expected to initiate the OOB LSDB procedure before the ResyncTimeout timer expires. However, if the restarting router is unable to initiate the OOB LSDB procedure, the nonrestarting router reverts to the normal OSPF restart behavior by resetting the adjacencies.

Now suppose that while the ResyncTimeout timer is active, the nonrestarting router receives a Database Description packet with the R bit set. The nonrestarting router sets the OOBResynch bit to true, cancels the ResyncTimeout timer, and forces the neighbor FSM state from full to exstart without resetting the adjacency.

Following master/slave negotiations, the two neighbors exchange Database Description packets. While the OOBResynch bit is set, the nonrestarting router sends all Database Description packets with the R bit set. After successfully exchanging the Database Description packets, the adjacency state moves to loading, and the router requests the latest information from the neighbor by sending Link-State Request packets. When the link-state request list becomes empty, the initial LSDB database resynchronization is complete, and the adjacency moves to full state.

Upon entering the full state, the restarting router clears the OOBResynch bit and clears the R bit in the Database Description packets. To avoid adjacency flap, the nonrestarting router does not originate a new version of router or network LSAs when the adjacency state transitions to or from the full state with the OOBResynch bit set. After the adjacency has been successfully formed, the restarting router reverts to normal OSPF behavior. The processing of Database Description packets during OOB resynchronization is summarized in Figure 4-5.

To set an upper limit on the OOB database exchange process, the nonrestarting router starts a timer upon initiating the OOB LSDB resynchronization procedure. If this timer expires before the LSA database synchronization is complete, the nonrestarting router cancels the OOB LSDB procedure and reverts to the normal OSPF procedures by clearing the R bit in the Database Description packets and resetting the adjacency.

Operation of the OSPF Restart Signaling Mechanism

This section describes operation of the OSPF restart signaling mechanism using the network diagram shown in Figure 4-6. Both routers support the restart signaling mechanism and are NSF-capable.

Figure 4-6   *Example of the OSPF Restart Signaling Operation*

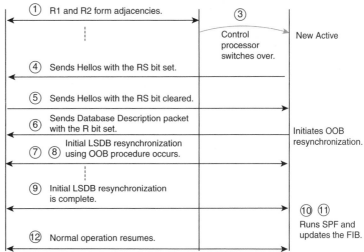

The sequence of steps that follows is not necessarily followed by a specific implementation. This description is intended to provide a simplified functional view:

1. R1 and R2 discover each other via Hellos, exchange parameters such as RouterDeadInterval, form adjacencies, and perform initial LSDB synchronization. To advertise their OOB LSDB resynchronization capability, R1 and R2 set the LR bit in the OSPF options field of the Hello and Database Description packets to indicate the presence of an LLS data block and with the LR bit set. The LR bit information is stored in the neighbor's data structure, which can be used later to check the neighbor's OOB LSDB resynchronization capability. After LSDB synchronization, R1 and R2 select routes and populate their FIB.

2. Suppose an IP forwarding path exists from "source" to "destination" passing through R1 and R2, and data traffic is being forwarded along this path.

3. Assume OSPF in R2 restarts, because R2 is NSF-capable, and it continues to forward packets along the routes learned before restart.

4. After restart, R2 marks all OSPF-related FIB entries that were preserved across restart as stale and starts a stale timer. However, R2 continues to use stale entries for forwarding. Assume R2 is ready for exchanging Hellos with its neighbor before the RouterDeadInterval (default value 40 seconds) for the adjacency expires. Because R2 is capable of OOB LSDB resynchronization and would like R1 to maintain the adjacency to R2 that it established prior to this restart, R2 sends a Hello packet with the RS bit set. Because R2 does not preserve an adjacency-related state across the OSPF restart, the neighbor list in the Hellos might be empty.

5. R1 receives Hellos with the RS bit set, skips the two-way connectivity check with the restarting neighbor, leaves the neighbor state in full state, sets the RestartState bit, starts the ResyncTimeout timer, and immediately replies with a unicast Hello with the RS bit cleared. If the restarting neighbor does not initiate an OOB LSDB resynchronization procedure before the ResyncTimeout expires, R1 resets its adjacencies with the restarting neighbor.

6. On receiving a Hello with the RS bit cleared, R2 creates a neighbor data structure. Assuming R1 and R2 are connected by a point-to-point interface, R2 moves the state to exstart. On a broadcast network, R2 runs a delayed DR/BDR election process to allow it to relearn its neighbors and moves the neighbor state to exstart. To initiate an OOB LSDB resynchronization procedure, R2 checks the LR bit in the neighbor's data structure to determine whether R1 is OOB capable. Because R1 is OOB capable, R2 sets the OOBResynch bit for R1, forces the FSM to exstart, and sends an initial Database Description packet with the R bit and the I, M, MS bits set.

7. R1 receives a Database Description packet with the R bit set, checks the OOB LSDB resynchronization capability of R2, and further processes the packet as shown in Figure 4-5. Assume the OOBResynch bit for the neighbor (R2) is clear, and its neighbor state is in full state. R1 sets the OOBResynch bit for the neighbor, cancels the ResyncTimeout timer, and moves the neighbor state to exstart; otherwise, it continues to process the Database Description packet as per normal OSPF procedure. When R1's neighbor state transitions to or from the full state with the OOBResynch bit set, it does not originate a new router LSA or network LSA.

8. When the previous steps are completed, R2 and R1 resynchronize their LSDBs. On completion of the LSDB resynchronization with R1, R2 clears the OOBResynch bit. Because R1 is the only neighbor, this also marks the completion of the initial LSDB resynchronization. In general, however, the restarting router LSDB must resynchronize LSDBs with all neighbors. When the OOBResynch bit is not set, all Database Description packets are sent with the R bit cleared. When R2's neighbor state transitions to or from the full state with the OOBResynch bit set, it does not originate a new router LSA or network LSA. During OOB LSDB resynchronization, R2 may receive self-originated (such as router, network, or AS external) LSAs. Under normal processing, such LSAs are

flushed from the routing domain. However, in this case, to avoid undesirable negative effects due to the premature aging of such LSAs, R2 accepts these LSAs as valid but marks them stale.

9. R1's neighbor FSM reaches the full state. It clears the OOBResynch bit to mark the completion of the OOB LSDB resynchronization procedure and reverts to normal OSPF procedures.

10. After OOB LDDB resynchronization, R2 reconstructs its self-originated LSAs. These newer self-originated LSAs are compared with the existing (marked stale) self-originated LSAs. If the newer LSAs are identical to the existing LSAs, these LSAs are updated by clearing the stale flag, but these LSAs are not flooded. (They are updated based on regular periodic refresh timers.) However, if the new instances of LSAs differ from the stale LSAs, the new instances are installed in the LSDB and flooded to the neighbors. On the expiration of a stale timer, the remaining stale self-originated LSA entries are deleted from R2's LSDB and flushed from the routing domain.

11. R2 computes the routing table and updates the RIB, refreshing the stale IP forwarding state. Upon the FIB stale timer expiration, any entry still marked as stale is removed.

12. At this stage, recovery from OSPF restart is complete.

OSPF Graceful Restart Mechanism

The OSPF graceful restart mechanism seeks to achieve the same goals as the restart signaling mechanism, as follows:

*   Maintain established adjacencies across the restart
*   Have neighbors retain these adjacencies on their forwarding paths
*   Ensure LSDB resynchronization after the restart[6]

Similar to the restart signaling mechanism, the graceful restart mechanism requires some enhancements to the OSPF routing protocol to realize these goals.

To sum up concisely, the OSPF graceful restart mechanism defines a new link-local opaque LSA called *grace LSA*, which is meant for direct neighbors.

A router that is capable of OSPF graceful restart sends grace LSAs to its neighbors to indicate its intention to perform OSPF graceful restart. The restarting router encapsulates the grace LSA in the Link-State Update packet and transmits it on all OSPF interfaces to neighbors reliably or unreliably, depending on the nature of the restart (planned or unplanned). The planned and unplanned restart events and their implications on the reliable delivery of the grace LSAs are discussed later in this chapter.

The grace LSA may contain multiple fields such as grace period, graceful restart reason, and IP interface address. These fields are encoded in the *type length value* (TLV) format. The grace period field indicates the number of seconds that the neighbors (or the helper nodes) should continue to advertise the restarting router as fully adjacent, irrespective of the state of the LSDB synchronization between the restarting router and its neighbors. The grace period begins when the restarting router originates the grace LSA (sets the age field to zero) and ends when the LS age field exceeds the value of the grace period or when the grace LSA is flushed. The grace period TLV must always be present in all grace LSAs.

The maximum time between distinct originations of any particular LSA is referred to as *LSRefreshTime*. For example, if the LS age field of one of the router's self-originated LSAs reaches the LSRefreshTime value, a new instance of the LSA is originated. The default value of LSRefreshTime is set to 30 minutes (1800 seconds). To avoid other routers from aging out LSAs originated by the restarting router, the grace period should not exceed LSRefreshTime (1800 seconds). The graceful restart mechanism suggests a default value of 120 seconds for the grace period.

The restarting router initially sets the LS age field in the grace LSA to zero, which is continuously incremented with the passage of time until it reaches the MaxAge. The current value of the LS age field indicates the time elapsed since the grace LSA was originated. Because the grace period duration is derived from the LS age field, the DoNotAge bit is never set in the grace LSA.

The graceful restart reason TLV is used to indicate the reason for the restart. For example

- 0 (unknown)
- 1 (software restart)
- 2 (software reload/upgrade)
- 3 (switch to redundant control processor)

For this reason, TLV must always appear in a grace LSA. The information in the reason TLV may be useful for fault diagnostics and gathering router failure statistics.

The restarting router's IP interface address associated with the grace LSA is contained in the IP interface address TLV. The helper node requires this information to identify the restarting neighbor on broadcast or NMBA network segments.

After restart, the restarting router sends grace LSAs on all interfaces (even though at that stage it may neither have adjacencies nor any knowledge of pre-restart adjacencies, as described later in this chapter). By sending grace LSAs, the restarting router essentially informs its neighbors that "I have restarted; however, I have managed to preserve the FIB across the restart. Please allow me some time (the grace period) to successfully complete this restart. During the grace period, retain your existing established adjacencies with me and continue to advertise them in your LSAs. I will inform you about the successful completion of the restart procedure by flushing the grace LSAs. However, abort the graceful restart procedure and revert back to the normal restart procedure if either the grace LSAs are not flushed before the grace period expires or in the meantime the network topology changes."

The expiration of the grace period indicates that the restarting router is having trouble completing the restart procedure. Therefore, to reduce likelihood of black holes, the neighbors take a safer course of action by resetting the concerned adjacencies and rerouting data traffic on those adjacencies around the restarting router. Why abort the graceful restart procedure because of a change in the network topology? The logic here is that if the network topology changes during a restart procedure, the restarting router might not be able to update its FIB in a timely fashion. If this is so, there is a possibility of forwarding loops or black holes. Therefore, to avoid possible forwarding loops because of an incorrect FIB, it is safer to revert to the normal OSPF restart procedure.

After having received the grace LSAs from the restarting router, the neighbors cooperate by maintaining their established adjacencies with the restarting router and by keeping those adjacencies on the forwarding path.

It is worth noting that during the initial neighbor-discovery and adjacency-establishment procedure, the graceful restart-capable neighboring routers do not exchange restart capabilities. This means that the restarting router does not know a priori whether a given neighbor is capable of the graceful restart. As a consequence, there is no guarantee that a given graceful restart attempt will succeed.

Other than the behavior changes during the graceful restart procedure described in this section, the restarting router and its neighbors behave in the same way as any other OSPF router. For example, the restarting router discovers neighbors using the Hello protocol, reestablishes adjacencies, and performs the initial LSDB exchange through exchange of Database Description packets. However, in the grace period, the restarting router changes its OSPF processing as follows: The restarting router does not originate LSAs of type 1 through 5 and type 7. This is because to avoid forwarding loops, the restarting router wants other routers to use its pre-restart–originated LSAs. Even though the restarting router runs the SPF algorithm to bring up OSPF virtual links (for example, to reduce the possibility of forwarding loops because of incomplete LSDB), it does not update the preserved FIB.

Similarly, in the grace period, the helper node also changes its behavior somewhat. For example, unless either the network topology changes or the grace period expires, it continues to advertise adjacencies with the restarting router as if the neighbor had never restarted.

Upon successful completion of the graceful restart, both routers revert to normal OSPF processing. How do a restarting router and its neighbors determine successful completion of the graceful restart? Insofar as the restarting router is concerned, it knows that the graceful restart has been successfully completed when it has re-formed all its pre-restart adjacencies (or equivalently when its LSDB has been synchronized with all pre-restart neighbors).

As for the neighbors, the restarting router informs them about the completion. For example, to indicate the successful completion of the graceful restart to its neighbors, the restarting router flushes its grace LSAs (sets the LS age field to the MaxAge value). When a neighbor receives a grace LSA with the LS age set to MaxAge from the restarting router, it ceases to play the helper function and reverts back to the normal operation. If for some reason the restarting router cannot successfully reestablish adjacencies with all neighbors before the grace period expires, the graceful restart procedure is aborted. The graceful restart procedure is also aborted if the network topology changes during the grace period. When the graceful restart procedure is aborted, the helper nodes reset their adjacencies with the restarting router and reroute around the restarting router. Similarly, when a graceful restart procedure aborts, the restarting router resets its adjacencies and removes the preserved FIB.

During graceful restart, the restarting router and its neighbors play slightly different roles. These roles are described in the following sections. First, however, it is useful to clarify some of the differences between planned and unplanned restarts.

Reliable Delivery of the Grace LSAs on Unplanned and Planned Restart

The OSPF restart may be planned or unplanned:

- **Planned restart**—The reason for restart is known *a priori*, such as a scheduled software upgrade.

- **Unplanned restart**—The restart reason is unknown *a priori*, such as unexpected software failure and control processor hardware failure.

Irrespective of whether the restart is planned or unplanned, the restarting router must be able to send a grace LSA before its neighboring routers time out their adjacencies.

In general, transmission of a grace LSA is reliable in the sense that its reception is explicitly acknowledged. However, the delivery of a grace LSA is not guaranteed because OSPF Link-State Update packets, which carry grace LSAs, are transported over IP. To make the delivery of grace LSAs robust against any packet loss, the grace LSAs require repeated (a predetermined number of times) transmission until acknowledged. However, this remedy might not be adequate to ensure the success of the graceful restart attempt in the case of an unplanned restart if neighbors do not process grace LSAs before Hellos.

In handling unplanned and planned restarts, the main difference lies in the origination timings of the grace LSAs. In the case of a planned restart, because it is a planned event, the restarting router can control the origination of the grace LSAs more easily. For example, in this case the restarting router can determine when adjacencies are due to expire. To ensure that neighbors will not time out their adjacencies unexpectedly, the restarting router can first refresh the hold timers of adjacencies before attempting the graceful restart. However, the situation is quite different in the case of an unplanned restart. With unplanned restarts, the restarting router does not even know about the existence of adjacencies, let alone when the hold timers of adjacencies are due to expire. Because the restarting router has no information about neighbors, it is unable to send Hellos containing correct information. Therefore, if the restarting router attempts to discover neighbors and re-form adjacencies before having informed the neighbors about the graceful restart, it is asking for a trouble. This is because unless neighbors are informed about the graceful restart first, neighbors will reset their adjacencies on receiving Hellos with incorrect information. Therefore, a restarting router undertaking unplanned graceful restart must originate grace LSAs before sending any Hello packets.

Restarting a Router's Behavior

The OSPF graceful restart mechanism defines two modes of operation for a restarting router: normal and graceful restart. The restarting router's behavior can be succinctly described in terms of a two-state *finite-state machine* (FSM). A change in a router's mode of operation corresponds to the FSM state transitions. A state transition is caused by the occurrence of one or more events. Whenever an event occurs, the router performs a set of actions either while staying in the same state or transitioning to the next state. The events and actions related to the restarting router behavior are described in Figure 4-7 and Table 4-2.

Table 4-2   *Events and Actions Associated with the Restarting Router's Graceful Restart Behavior*

Event	Description
E1	OSPF software restarts (unplanned and planned).
E2	All the restarting router's adjacencies have been reestablished. To determine pre-restart adjacencies that need to be reestablished, the restarting router examines its self-originated pre-restart router LSAs and network LSAs.
E3	The grace period has expired.
E4	A router LSA has been received from a neighbor that is inconsistent with the pre-restart self-originated router LSA. For instance, a neighbor's router LSA does not have a link to the restarting router, whereas the self-originated pre-restart router LSA has a link to the neighbor. This shows either that there is a network topology change during the graceful restart or the neighbor is not capable of graceful restart.

Action	Description
A1	The restarting router transmits a grace LSA on each interface before sending Hellos. The grace LSA is retransmitted until acknowledged (for a planned restart) or for a predetermined number of times (for an unplanned restart). The restart reason in the grace LSA is set to 1 (software restart) for a planned restart and 0 (unknown) or 3 (switch to redundant control processor) for an unplanned restart. To avoid aging out the restarting router's LSAs, the grace period is set to a value less than LSRefreshTime (default 120 second).
A2	Ensures the preservation of the FIB across the restart. Marks preserved FIB entries as stale. However, continues to use them for forwarding across the restart.
A3	Does not originate LS type 1 through 5 and type 7 LSAs.

continues

Table 4-2   *Events and Actions Associated with the Restarting Router's Graceful Restart Behavior (Continued)*

A4	Does not modify or flush the received self-originated LSAs, but instead accepts them as valid.
A5	Upon receipt of Hellos, if the router determines that it was a DR for a segment before this restart, it re-elects itself as DR.
A6	Runs the OSPF algorithm (to keep the virtual link operational), but does not update the FIB.
A7	Re-originates its router LSAs for all attached areas. Re-originates its network LSA on all segments where the router is acting as DR.
A8	Runs the OSPF algorithm, updates the FIB, and originates summary LSAs, type 7 LSAs, and AS external LSAs as appropriate.
A9	Removes any remaining FIB entries still marked as stale.
A10	Flushes all invalid self-originated LSAs and self-originated grace LSAs.
	In all other respects, the router behaves like any other standard OSPF router. For example, it discovers neighbors through Hellos, carries out the database exchange procedure to initially synchronize its LSDB, and keeps it synchronized through asynchronous flooding.

Initially, the router is operating in the normal mode. While operating in normal mode, the router follows the standard OSPF procedure. As a result of an unplanned or a planned OPSF restart, the router transitions to the graceful restart mode. In the graceful restart mode, the restarting router changes its processing behavior (see Figure 4-7). Otherwise, the router behaves just like any other OSPF router. For example, the restarting router discovers neighbors via Hellos, re-forms adjacencies, and performs initial LSDB synchronization using normal OSPF procedures. When all adjacencies are re-formed, the router flushes its grace LSAs and reverts to normal operation.

Figure 4-7   *Finite-State Machine Depicting the Restarting Router's Graceful Restart Behavior*

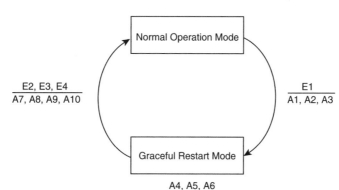

Helper Node's Behavior

The graceful restart mechanism also defines two modes of operation for a neighboring router: normal and helper. The neighbor's graceful restart behavior is depicted in Figure 4-8, and the associated set of events and actions is described in Table 4-3.

Figure 4-8   *Finite-State Machine Depicting the Helper Node's Graceful Restart Behavior*

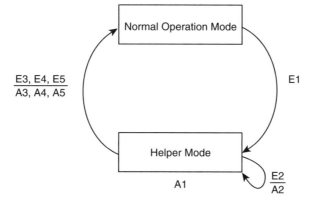

Initially, the neighboring router is operating in the normal mode. When the router receives a grace LSA, it carries out certain tests, and if these tests are passed the router transitions to the helper mode. While in the helper mode, the router continues to announce adjacency to the restarting neighbor so long as there is no topology change or the grace period does not expire.

Upon successful completion of the graceful restart procedure (on seeing grace LSAs flushed), the router reverts to normal operation.

Table 4-3   *Events and Actions Associated with the Helper Node's Graceful Restart Behavior*

Event	Description
E1	Receives a grace LSA and carries out certain tests. Upon the successful passing of these tests • There is an established adjacency with the restarting router. • The content of LSAs of type 1 through 5 and type 7 has not changed since the neighbor has restarted. • The grace period has not expired. • The router itself is not in the graceful restart mode. • The local policy of the router allows it to act as helper node.
E2	Receives a grace LSA while in helper mode.
E3	Graceful restart has been successfully terminated. (Grace LSAs are flushed.)
E4	The grace period has expired (which indicates unsuccessful termination of the graceful restart).
E5	The network topology has changed (for example, a new instance of type 1 through 5 or type 7 LSAs has been installed).
Action	**Description**
A1	Maintains the adjacency with the restarting router during the grace period.
A2	Accepts the grace LSA and updates the grace period.
A3	Recalculates the DR for the segment.
A4	Re-originates its router LSAs for the area of the segment. If acting as DR, re-originates the network LSA.
A5	If the segment is a virtual link, re-originates the router LSA for the virtual link's transit area.

Operation of the OSPF Graceful Restart Mechanism

This section describes the operation of the OSPF graceful restart in the event of an unplanned outage. The planned outage case is not described because its operation is similar to the unplanned case for the most part. Figure 4-9 shows the network topology.

Figure 4-9   *Example of the OSPF Graceful Restart Operation*

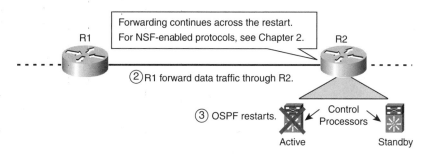

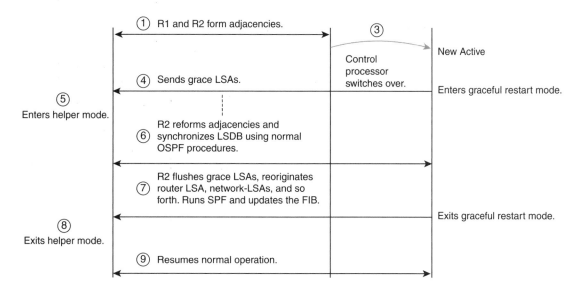

Both routers are assumed to support the graceful restart mechanism. The restarting router is assumed to preserve the FIB and other state information, such as the grace period and cryptographic sequence number for an interface, across the restart. The sequence of steps described is not necessarily the one followed by a specific implementation. These steps are meant to provide a functional-level description of the hitless restart mechanism:

1. R1 and R2 discover each other using OSPF Hellos, form adjacencies, and perform initial LSDB synchronization. After LSDB synchronization, R1 and R2 compute routes and populate the FIB.

2. Suppose an IP forwarding path exists from "source" to "destination" passing through R1 and R2, and data traffic is being forwarded along this path.

3. Assume OSPF in R2 restarts because of an unplanned outage. Furthermore, assume that R2 has preserved the FIB, cryptographic sequence for each OSPF interface, and the grace period across the restart. Using the preserved FIB, R2 continues to forward data across the restart.

4. After restarting the OSPF software, R2 marks the preserved FIB as stale. It continues, however, to use the preserved FIB information. Before sending any Hellos, R2 originates a grace LSA on each interface with the restart reason set to 0 (unknown) or 3 (switch to redundant control processor). For robust delivery, the grace LSAs may be transmitted a predetermined number of times until acknowledged. To avoid timing out the restarting router's LSAs, the grace period is kept smaller than LSRefreshTime (default 1800 seconds). The graceful restart mechanism suggests a default value of 120 seconds (2 minutes) for the grace period.

   As discussed previously (see events E3 and E4 in the Table 4-2), the restarting router aborts the graceful-restart procedure either when the grace period expires or when the network topology changes. A neighbor that is not graceful restart-capable ignores any grace LSAs it has received. This means it might take up to the grace period to discover that a neighbor is not graceful restart capable. The restarting router does not know ahead of time whether its neighbors are graceful restart-capable. The restarting router assumes that all neighbors are graceful restart-capable and proceeds with the graceful-restart procedure. Subsequently, if the restarting router discovers that a neighbor is not graceful restart-capable, it aborts the graceful restart procedure with all neighbors and reverts to the normal restart procedure.

5. Upon receipt of the grace LSA, R1 enters the helper mode and maintains its adjacencies with R2 during the grace period. That is, R1 continues to advertise R2 in its LSAs because it is fully adjacent and conceals R2's restart from other routers. Other than this, the helper node behaves just like any other OSPF router.

6. Using standard OSPF procedures, R2 forms adjacencies and synchronizes the LSDB. In the grace period, however, R2 does not modify or flush self-originated pre-restart LSAs. Instead, R2 accepts them as valid, and it does not originate type 1 through 5 or type 7 LSAs (when neighbor state transitions to full). Furthermore, although R2 runs the OSPF calculations, it does not update the FIB.

7. Assume R1 and R2 have synchronized their LSDBs within the grace period. After R2 has synchronized its LSDB with all neighbors (only R1 in this case), R2 flushes its grace LSAs to signal neighbors about the successful completion of the graceful restart procedure. R2 re-originates router LSAs on all attached areas and network LSAs on segments where acting as DR, recalculates the routes, and updates the FIB. When it recalculates and updates, R2 removes entries that are still marked as stale. In addition, R2 re-originates summary LSAs, type 7 LSAs, and AS external LSAs as appropriate, and flushes all invalid self-originated LSAs. For more details, see Figure 4-7 and Table 4-2.

8. When R1 determines that grace LSAs originated by R2 are being flushed, it exits the helper mode and reverts to the normal OSPF procedures. R1 re-originates router LSAs and network LSAs (if acting as a DR on the segment). For more details on the complete set of actions, see Figure 4-8 and Table 4-3.

9. Graceful restart is complete. R1 and R2 return to normal operation.

Comparison of the OSPF Restart Mechanisms

The two approaches share many similarities, including the following:

*   Both have the goals of retaining adjacencies with neighbors and continuing to forward across the restart.

*   Both require protocol extensions.

*   Both require support from neighbors.

*   Both can be used for unplanned and planned restarts.

In terms of mechanics, however, these restart approaches differ significantly, as follows:

*   The restart signaling-capable restarting router sets the RS bit in Hellos to prevent its neighbors from resetting their adjacencies.

*   In contrast, the graceful restart-capable restarting router sends grace LSAs to inform its neighbors about the restart.

*   The restart signaling-capable neighboring routers exchange restart signaling capabilities. For example, neighboring routers become aware about each other's restart capabilities by examining the LR bit in Hellos and Database Description packets. This means the restarting router knows the restart capabilities of all neighbors ahead of time. Therefore, the restarting router attempts to restart gracefully only if all neighbors are capable of supporting the restart signaling mechanism.

*   In contrast, in the case of the graceful restart mechanism, neighboring routers do not exchange graceful restart capabilities. This means that the restarting router does not know a priori whether a given neighbor is capable of the graceful restart. The restarting router sends grace LSAs on all interfaces (assuming and hoping that all neighbors are capable of graceful restart). As a consequence, there is no guarantee that the restarting router will gain cooperation from all neighbors and that a given graceful restart attempt will succeed. The inability of a single neighbor to cooperate causes the graceful restart procedure to abort and revert to the normal OSPF restart procedure.

*   As discussed previously, regardless of whether the restart is planned or unplanned, the restarting router must be able to inform its neighbors before neighbors time out their adjacencies to the restarting router. In the case of the restart signaling mechanism, the new bits (for example, the RS bit and the LR bit) and corresponding processing modifications

are introduced in the required context. For instance, bits in the Hello packets are used to modify Hello processing. Similarly, to modify processing of the Database Description packets, flags in the Database Description packets are examined.

- In contrast, in the case of the graceful restart mechanism, the delivery of grace LSAs is not guaranteed because the OSPF Link-State Update packets containing grace LSAs are transported over IP (which does not provide assured delivery). Therefore, if the Link-State Update packet carrying grace LSAs is lost, after waiting for the grace period and without receiving an acknowledgment, the restarting router cancels the graceful restart. In the case of planned restart, grace LSAs can be transmitted reliably using the normal OSPF flooding procedure. With unplanned restarts, the restarting router does not even know about the existence of adjacencies, let alone when the hold timers of adjacencies are due to expire. Because the restarting router has no information about neighbors, it cannot send Hellos containing correct information.

  If the restarting router were to discover neighbors and re-form adjacencies, neighbors would reset their adjacencies on receiving Hellos with incorrect information. This means the restarting router undertaking unplanned graceful restart must reliably originate grace LSAs before sending Hellos. To improve robustness of grace LSA transmission in the face of potential packet loss, grace LSAs are transmitted repeatedly for a predetermined number of times until acknowledged. Therefore, in the unplanned restart case, even if neighbors have received grace LSAs before Hellos, the graceful restart procedure can still fail if a neighbor processes Hellos before the grace LSA. This might happen, for example, because grace LSAs and Hello packets are processed in different contexts.

To sum up, both approaches have similar goals but use quite different mechanics to achieve these goals. In theory, either approach can be used to handle planned or unplanned restarts gracefully. As to the standardization status of the two approaches, after extensive and prolonged discussions, the IETF OSPF Working Group has voted in favor of the graceful restart mechanism. That means that only the graceful restart mechanism will be published as a proposed standard. One of the arguments that consistently favored the graceful restart mechanism was its simplicity. For example, the graceful restart mechanism is considered to support the planned restart in a manner that requires minimal and backward-compatible changes to the OSPF specification.

Network Deployment Considerations

In actual network deployments, routers with diverse control- and forwarding-plane capabilities are likely to coexist for some time. Some routers may be capable of supporting OSPF control-plane restart mechanisms but incapable of preserving the FIB across the restart. This section describes interoperability scenarios for the OSPF restart signaling and graceful restart mechanisms. Although the mechanics vary, in principle the restart signaling and the graceful restart mechanisms are similar. For want of space, only interoperability scenarios for the restart signaling mechanism are described. The discussions generally apply, however, to both restart mechanisms.

Scenario 1: R1 and R2 Are Restart Signaling/NSF-Capable

Because the restarting router and its neighbors are restart signaling- and NSF-capable, the IP forwarding plane is not disrupted when either R1 or R2 restarts (see Figure 4-10). In other words, OSPF restart in either R1 or R2 will not cause harmful effects. Hence, for maximum benefit, the restarting router and its neighbors must be restart signaling- and NSF-capable.

Figure 4-10 *OSPF Restart Signaling and Graceful Restart Interoperability Scenarios*

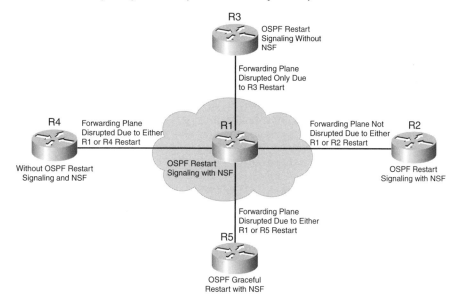

Scenario 2: R1 Is Restart Signaling- and NSF-Capable, but R3 Is Only Restart Signaling-Capable

In this case, when OSPF restarts in R1, its IP forwarding plane is not affected. This is because R3 is OSPF restart signaling-capable and in helper mode maintains its adjacencies with R1 across the restart. However, when OSPF in R3 restarts because R3 is not NSF-capable, following restart it transmits Hello with the R4 bit cleared. Upon receipt of Hellos with the RS bit cleared, R1 reverts to normal OSPF restart behavior—resets the adjacency, regenerates LSAs informing other routers about this topology change, and reroutes around R1. Therefore, when a router is restart signaling-capable but NSF-incapable, it does not reduce negative effects on other routers. However, such a router would still help to reduce negative effects by acting as a helper node when its neighbors restart. Figure 4-10 illustrates these interactions.

Scenario 3: R1 Is Restart Signaling- and NSF-Capable, but R4 Is Restart Signaling- and NSF-Incapable

In this case, OSPF restart in either R1 or R4 does not reduce the negative effects on other routers. So to achieve any meaningful benefit from an OSPF restart signaling-capable router, its neighbors must at least be capable of supporting the OSPF restart signaling mechanism.

Scenario 4: R1 Is Restart Signaling- and NSF-Capable, and R5 Is Graceful Restart- and NSF-Capable

The OSPF restart signaling and graceful restart mechanisms are not interoperable. Therefore, this configuration reduces to the previous scenario. That is, OSPF restart in either R1 or R5 would not lessen the negative effects on other routers. In other words, for deriving any benefit from an OSPF restart signaling- or graceful restart-capable router, its neighbor must at least be able to support the same OSPF restart mechanism.

Summary

This chapter described the undesirable effects OSPF restart can have on IP control and forwarding planes. Two approaches that address these problems were described: OSPF restart signaling and OSPF graceful restart. The operation of each approach was illustrated through examples. A comparative analysis of the two approaches was presented. In addition, several practical deployment scenarios for OSPF restart mechanisms were described.

References

[1] RFC 2328, "OSPF Version 2," J. Moy, April 1998.

[2] Moy, J., *OSPF Anatomy of an Internet Routing Protocol*. Boston: Addison-Wesley, 1998.

[3] Zinin, A., A. Roy, and L. Nguyen, "OSPF Restart Signaling," Internet Draft, Work in progress.

[4] Friedman, B., et al., "OSPF Link-Local Signaling," Internet Draft, Work in progress.

[5] Nguyen, L., A. Roy, and A. Zinin, "OSPF Out-of-Band LSDB Resynchronization," Internet Draft, Work in progress.

[6] RFC 3623, "Graceful OSPF Restart," J. Moy, P. Pillay-Esnault, and A. Lindem, November 2003.

Intradomain IP Control Plane: Restarting IS-IS Gracefully

This chapter describes two mechanisms that enable you to reduce the negative effects of the *Intermediate System-to-Intermediate System* (IS-IS) restart. The chapter begins with an overview of IS-IS routing focusing primarily on concepts necessary for a better understanding of the proposed restart mechanisms. Two mechanisms are described: IETF and Cisco IS-IS restart. Both mechanisms help to reduce the detrimental effects caused by the IS-IS restart. In this regard, the strengths and weaknesses of each approach are also discussed. In addition, the key concepts underlying each approach are illustrated through operational examples and deployment scenarios. The chapter concludes with a chapter summary.

Understanding the Detrimental Effects of the IS-IS Restart

Similar to the *Open Shortest Path First* (OSPF) protocol, the IS-IS protocol is a link-state protocol for intradomain routing. (For more details on OSPF, see Chapter 4, "Intradomain IP Control Plane: Restarting OSPF Gracefully.") In a link-state protocol, each router in the routing domain maintains a synchronized topology database that describes the interconnection of routers within an area or domain and reachable destinations. To build a synchronized topology database, each router initially originates and subsequently re-advertises its local piece of topology information periodically, which is propagated throughout the area or routing domain through flooding. Based on the topology database, each router computes the shortest paths for all known destinations. (A *path* is a sequence of connected routers and links between a source and a destination.) The calculation of the shortest paths is a processing-intensive task because it involves running the Dijkstra algorithm (also referred to as *Shortest Path First* [SPF] algorithm) to construct a tree of shortest paths.

Original IS-IS Restart Behavior

To ensure loop-free forwarding, any change in the network topology typically necessitates a recomputation of the shortest paths. In general, network topology changes result from hardware and software failures of links and nodes. For instance, when an IS-IS router restarts because of a failure in the control-plane software, its immediate neighbors drop all existing peering relationships (adjacencies) with the restarting router and reissue their new local topology information, omitting links (adjacencies) to the restarting router. To reduce the chances of incorrect forwarding, upon detecting a change in the network topology, other routers recalculate their SPF paths to avoid the restarting router. The router control software generally consists of IP routing protocols (IS-IS, OSPF, BGP) and is generally referred to as the *IP control plane*. The IP forwarding component consists of a *Forwarding Information Base* (FIB), which is commonly known as the *IP forwarding plane*.

When following the original IS-IS specification, the IS-IS restart behavior assumes that the IP control plane and the IP forwarding plane are not separate. This implies that an IP control-plane restart is always accompanied by the IP forwarding-plane restart. This in turn implies that the IP forwarding state cannot be preserved across the IS-IS restart. Such assumptions generally might have been valid in earlier-generation routers (and hence would rightly justify the restart behavior as outlined in the original IS-IS specification). Typically, however, such assumptions are no longer valid. This is because presently most routers are based on a distributed forwarding and centralized control architecture. This means that the control-plane functions are centrally implemented on a dedicated control processor while the forwarding-plane functions are distributed on line cards. In other words, control and forwarding functions are separate, making it feasible to preserve the forwarding state, and therefore can continue to forward across the control-plane restart. The capability of a router to continue forwarding across the control-plane restart is referred to as *nonstop forwarding* (NSF). For further details on the IP NSF and *stateful switchover* (SSO) architecture, see Chapter 2, "IP Forwarding Plane: Achieving Nonstop Forwarding."

Negative Effects of the Original IS-IS Restart Behavior

Now that a restarting router is NSF-capable, it is desirable that its immediate neighbors maintain their adjacencies and not remove the restarting router from the forwarding path. Therefore, the original IS-IS restart behavior is no longer suitable in this case because it leads to a number of undesirable effects. When a router following the original IS-IS protocol specification restarts, for example, its neighboring routers detect the restart and hence cycle their adjacencies to the restarting router through the down state. The change in adjacency state (up to down) causes the neighboring routers to advertise new topology information via *link-state packets* (LSP). This in turn triggers SPF algorithm runs in other routers through the area or domain to find alternative forwarding paths around the faulting router. As a result, data packets are forwarded on alternative paths, which will cause disruption of forwarding on those routes.

This sequence of events has two main detrimental consequences. First, even though the restarting router would have continued to forward data packets (because it is NSF-capable), by removing it from the forwarding paths other routers disrupt traffic passing through the restarting router. Second, if alternative forwarding path(s) were not found, the data traffic passing through the restarting router would be unnecessarily dropped. To make it even worse, the restarting router quickly reacquires adjacencies with its neighbors. The appearance of new adjacency (down to up) on the neighboring routers causes them to reissue new LSPs, which again triggers SPF runs throughout the area or domain. A quick disappearance (up to down) and reappearance (down to up) of an adjacency is commonly referred to as an *adjacency flap*. That is, the adjacency is first withdrawn and then immediately re-advertised.

In summary, an adjacency flap causes several negative effects:

- **In the control plane**—Following IS-IS restart, for example, SPF runs throughout the domain and generates excessive control traffic.

- **In the forwarding plane**—For example, the data traffic passing through the restarting router is disrupted.

- **In the control plane**—For example, when neighbors reestablish an adjacency with the restarting router, they reissue new LSPs, again triggering SPF runs throughout the entire area or routing domain.

Figure 5-1 illustrates the effects of an adjacency flap.

Figure 5-1   *Adjacency Flap and Its Detrimental Effects Caused by an IS-IS Restart (a Restart That Follows the Original IS-IS Specification)*

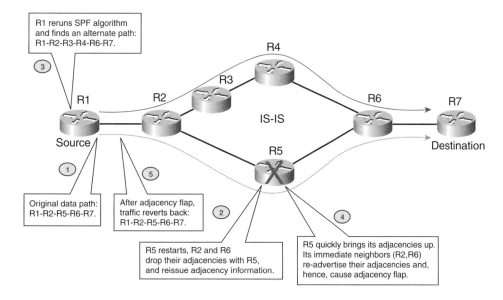

Overview of IS-IS Routing

IS-IS is a link-state *interior gateway protocol* (IGP) for intradomain routing.[1] The IS-IS protocol was originally designed for routing in an *Open Systems Interconnection* (OSI) environment. However, with the growing number of networks using IP routing, IS-IS has been enhanced to handle forwarding of IP data packets. The enhanced IS-IS protocol is known as *Integrated IS-IS*.[2] The main advantages of the Integrated IS-IS protocol include the capability to forward both IP and OSI data packets and the simplicity of managing a single routing protocol in a dual-routing (IP and OSI) environment. The latter option, in which two independent protocols are run, is known as *ships in the night* (a term that refers to ships passing silently in the night without the crews knowing about each other). Currently, IS-IS is primarily used as an IP routing protocol. The remainder of this chapter deals with the use of IS-IS in an IP environment.

Network resource requirements such as routing table size and bandwidth overhead caused by control messages generally grow linearly as the network grows. Although network resources are bound to increase as the network size increases, it is desirable to keep the affected resource growth rate as low as possible. In this regard, hierarchical routing has proven to be very effective.

IS-IS Hierarchical Routing

In hierarchical routing, networks are partitioned into smaller pieces that in turn are recursively arranged into levels. Inside one of the lowest-level partitions, all routers have complete knowledge of the network topology of that partition but have a limited view of the network topology in other partitions. For that reason, routers at a lowest-level partition rely on higher-level routers for forwarding data packets to destinations in other partitions. In particular, IS-IS uses a two-level hierarchical routing scheme (see Figure 5-2). Level 1 routers know the complete topology of their own areas and hence are used for routing intra-area destinations. Level 2 routers have the knowledge of level 2 topology (which includes routers in other areas and even other domains) in addition to level 1 topology of their own areas. Therefore, level 2 routers are used to forward data packets for interarea or interdomain destinations.

Figure 5-2 *IS-IS Hierarchical Routing Model*

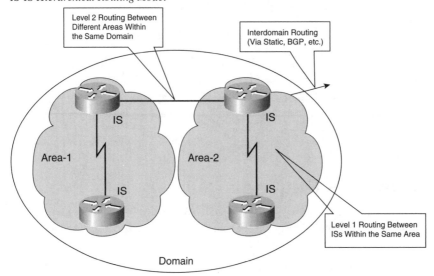

For example, when a level 1 router has data packets to forward to a destination within its own area, it forwards the packets toward the destination. When the destination is not within the same area, however, the level 1 router forwards packets to the nearest level 2 router. Level 2 routers may also advertise external addresses (destinations that can be reached through routers in other domains). Note that level 2 routers do not exchange routing information with external routing peers. The external reachability information is typically learned through *Border Gateway Protocol* (BGP) or manual configurations (via reachable address objects). The external reachable addresses are injected and propagated into the IS-IS routing domain through LSPs.

Discovering Neighbors and Establishing Adjacencies

To establish adjacencies (peer relationships), neighbors are first discovered through Hello packets. Level 1 adjacencies are formed between routers that are in the same area (share a common area address). In contrast, level 2 adjacencies are formed between any pair of level 2 routers regardless of area addresses. For example, routers in the same area can establish both level 1 and level 2 adjacencies. However, routers in different areas can only establish level 2 adjacencies. To establish and maintain adjacencies between neighboring routers, IS-IS uses three types of Hello packets:

- **Level 1 LAN IS-IS Hello**—Used to establish adjacencies between level 1 routers on broadcast LANs

- **Level 2 LAN IS-IS Hello**—Used to establish adjacencies between level 2 routers on broadcast LANs

- **Point-to-point IS-IS Hello**—Used to establish adjacencies on point-to-point links at both level 1 and level 2

In summary, on broadcast circuits (interfaces) there are separate versions for lev-el 1 and level 2 IS-IS Hellos (IIHs). However, there is only one type of point-to-point IIH for both level 1 and level 2.

Establishing Adjacencies Using a Three-Way Handshake

The original IS-IS specification does not use a three-way handshake to establish adjacencies on point-to-point links. The absence of a three-way handshake means that if a point-to-point link fails in one direction, the link failure is detected only on one side. The router on the other side, unaware of the one-way connectivity, tries to send data packets in the failed direction (which means traffic is black holed).

To avoid problems caused by one-way connectivity, point-to-point adjacencies must be established through three-way handshake extensions.[3] The three-way handshake defines a new *type length value* (TLV) called a *point-to-point three-way adjacency*, which is optionally included in point-to-point IIH packets (see Figure 5-3).

Whereas there is an obvious necessity for using a three-way handshake on a point-to-point adjacency, there is no such need on a broadcast adjacency. This is because broadcast circuits use an implicit three-way handshake by virtue of the fact that the broadcast adjacency only transitions to the up state if it finds its own MAC address being reported in the neighbor's IIH.

Figure 5-3 *The Optional Point-to-Point Three-Way Adjacency TLV*

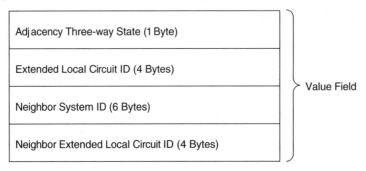

Adjacency Three-way State (1 Byte)

Extended Local Circuit ID (4 Bytes)

Neighbor System ID (6 Bytes)

Neighbor Extended Local Circuit ID (4 Bytes)

Value Field

Maintaining Adjacencies

Each adjacency has an associated holding timer. To maintain an adjacency, Hello packets are sent every Hello-timer seconds to update the adjacency holding timer. If a Hello packet is not received before the holding timer expires, the adjacency is torn down. In addition, if anything in the Hello packet changes (such as system ID or reporting of three-way handshake status), the adjacency is re-initialized (recycled through the down state).

Link-State Packets

When adjacencies are established, level 1 and 2 peer routers can exchange routing information. IS-IS uses LSPs to exchange routing information. There are two types of LSPs: level 1 LSPs, which are transmitted by level 1 routers, and level 2 LSPs, which are transmitted by level 2 routers. For example, routers that have both level 1 and level 2 adjacencies transmit both types of LSPs. Each level 1 router transmits its local piece of topology information by issuing level 1 LSPs. The level 1 LSPs are propagated only within the area. Similarly, level 2 routers transmit their local piece of topology information by advertising level 2 LSPs. Unlike level 1 LSPs, the level 2 LSPs are propagated throughout the routing domain. Both level 1 and level 2 LSPs are refreshed whenever the affected network topology changes or the periodic timers expire.

LSP Databases

An LSP database provides a map of the network topology (for example, the interconnection of routers). The collection of all level 1 LSPs within an area defines the level 1 LSP database for the area. Similarly, the collection of all level 2 LSPs within a domain constitutes the level 2 LSP database for the domain. A level 1 router maintains only a level 1 LSP database. Similarly, a level 2 router keeps only a level 2 LSP database. However, a router that is involved in level 1 and level 2 routing maintains both types of LSP databases. By taking LSP database packets as the input, each router runs the SPF algorithm to compute the shortest paths to all known destinations (see Figure 5-4). A separate instance of the SPF algorithm is run for each level database. For example, a router that is involved in level 1 and level 2 routing runs two instances of the SPF algorithm. The output of the SPF calculations is used to populate the FIB. The FIB tables are used for the actual forwarding of data packets.

Figure 5-4   *Functional View of the IS-IS Routing*

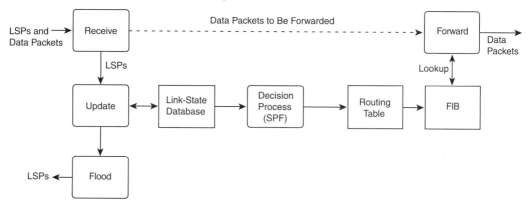

Synchronizing LSP Databases

Because route calculations are based on the LSP database, for correct and loop-free forwarding the LSP database must remain synchronized. IS-IS uses sequence number packets to ensure that neighboring routers have the latest LSPs from each other. IS-IS uses four types of sequence number packets:

- Level 1 complete sequence number packet (CSNP)
- Level 2 CSNP
- Level 1 partial sequence number packet (PSNP)
- Level 2 PSNP

Each CSNP has a range, and the entire set of CSNPs has a contiguous range covering all LSPs in the database. A CSNP contains information such as the ID, sequence number, and checksum of the LSP. When a router receives a CSNP that does not mention a particular LSP ID that would fall in that range, the receiving router knows that the sender did not have it. The missing LSPs are transmitted to the sender. Periodic transmission of all LSPs guarantees LSP database synchronization. In addition, IS-IS uses CSNPs as an efficient way to synchronize databases by avoiding the unnecessary exchange of LSPs that both routers already have. In summary, even if CSNPs are lost in the process of transmission, LSP databases will still be synchronized, although synchronization will require the exchange of more LSPs.

A PSNP contains the most recent sequence number of one or more LSPs. Although the primary use of a PSNP is to acknowledge receipt of LSPs, it can also act as an implicit request for LSPs. For example, if the receiving router has more recent LSPs than those reported in the PSNP, it transmits the most current LSPs to the sender.

Each circuit has a set of flags for each LSP: *send sequence number flags* (SSNflags) and *send routing message flags* (SRMflags). These flags are used to indicate LSPs that need to be transmitted or acknowledged. For example, when set, the SSNflag indicates that a PSNP needs to be sent (acknowledging the receipt) for that LSP. Similarly, when set, the SRMflag indicates that the corresponding LSP needs to be transmitted. The SRMflag is cleared upon receipt of the packet that acknowledges the LSP transmission. Failure to clear SRMflags results in a retransmission at the next LSP transmission interval (5 seconds by default). SRMflags are not set on an external interface that forms an adjacency with a router in another domain.

LSPs are issued as a result of changes in topology, such as an adjacency up or down event, and then reissued on expiration of a periodic timer (30 seconds by default). Upon receipt of an LSP, the receiving router examines fields such as sequence number and checksum with the stored instance of the LSP to determine whether the received LSP contains new, old, or duplicate information.

IS-IS uses flooding to ensure that LSPs are reliably propagated through the area (in the case of level 1 LSPs) or domain (in the case of level 2 LSPs). In flooding, every router transmits each received LSP (discarding duplicates) to all its neighbors, except for the sending neighbor. If a router receives a copy of its own LSP with a sequence number higher than what it currently has, it increases its own LSP's sequence number to be one higher and refloods a new instance of the LSP. The receipt of such an LSP indicates that there are LSPs in the routing domain that the router originated before the last time it was restarted. In general, events such as reception of new LSPs that cause the content of the LSP database to change trigger an SPF algorithm run.

Congestion Indication Through the Overload Bit

Sometimes the size of an LSP is too large to fit in the receive buffer, and sometimes a reduction in link bandwidth and processing overhead resulting from control messages is desired. In these cases, routers may fragment a single logical LSP into a number of smaller LSPs. If so, each fragment carries the same source ID, but has a different LSP number field. The fragment with LSP number 0 (not to be confused with the LSP sequence number) carries information such as the database Overload (OL) bit that is important for SPF calculations.

For example, the SPF algorithm does not consider any LSP from a router whose LSP number 0 (also known as the *zeroth LSP*) with a nonzero remaining lifetime is not present in the LSP database. Similarly, under certain situations a router might not have enough memory to store the entire LSP database. The LSP database OL bit is designed to handle the case in which a router knows that it cannot store the entire LSP database and therefore might have inconsistent information.

When a router is unable to store a received LSP, it ignores the LSP, enters a waiting state, and starts a timer. To inform other routers about this condition, the congested router originates an LSP number 0 with the OL bit set. Because SPF calculations disregard all LSPs from a router whose zeroth LSP has the OL bit set, other routers omit forwarding paths through the congested router. While in the waiting state, the router continues to run the SPF algorithm as normal. The receipt of another LSP that the router cannot store resets the waiting timer. When the waiting timer expires, the router clears the OL bit in the LSP number 0 and returns back to the normal operation.

IS-IS Designated Router

On a broadcast LAN with n routers, there are n(n – 1) adjacencies. Instead of synchronizing the LSP database between every pair of neighbors, IS-IS elects a designated router (referred to as *designated IS* or DIS). The DIS has the highest priority among all other routers on that LAN. If multiple routers have the same priority, the router with the highest numeric MAC address value wins. With the introduction of DIS, each router needs to maintain only a single link to the DIS instead of (n – 1) links. The DIS generates LSPs (and afterward periodically regenerates) reporting links to all routers on behalf of the LAN.

Mitigating the Detrimental Effects of the IS-IS Restart

This section describes two different approaches to reduce the negative effects resulting from the original IS-IS restart behavior. The first approach, referred to as the *IETF IS-IS restart mechanism*, extends the IS-IS protocol and requires that both the restarting router and its neighbors (also known as *helper nodes*) be restart-capable.[4] As a result, for an adjacency when both neighbors are not IETF IS-IS restart-capable, the IS-IS restart behavior on that adjacency reverts back to normal operation (which means the adjacency is re-initialized).

The second approach, referred to as the *Cisco IS-IS restart mechanism*, does not make any observable protocol changes. That is, the IS-IS restart on a router is hidden from its neighbors. To conceal the IS-IS restart event from other routers, this approach requires that some IS-IS–related state information be preserved across the restart.[5]

IS-IS Restart

Before delving into details, it would be useful to understand what the IS-IS restart mechanism is trying to accomplish and for what purpose. In this regard, we can say that the IS-IS restart mechanism attempts to achieve three main goals:

- Keep the adjacency state up across the IS-IS restart
- Have immediate neighbors set their SRMflags
- Determine when the LSP database resynchronization is complete

The first objective of keeping the adjacency state up across the IS-IS restart ensures that detrimental effects caused by adjacency re-initialization can be avoided.

The second objective is having immediate neighbors set their SRMflags to ensure LSP database resynchronization after the restart. For this reason, both the IETF and the Cisco restart mechanisms make certain that neighbors set their SRMflags following the restart. For example, after restart, the restarting router that supports the IETF IS-IS restart mechanism transmits a special message to its neighbors (which is equivalent to saying "Please set your SRMflags"). The special message is retransmitted until acknowledged by neighbors. The acknowledgment is equivalent to saying "Okay, I have set my SRMflags." Similarly, a restarting router that supports the Cisco IS-IS restart mechanism transmits a special CNSP to set SRMflags in neighbors. It is worthwhile to note that this is not a change to the existing IS-IS protocol. The setting of SRMflags in neighbors is important because it ensures that neighbors will transmit their LSPs (and thus the database will eventually be synchronized).

Note, however, that the setting of SRMflags alone is not sufficient for database synchronization. The restarting router also needs to know "when" its LSP database has synchronized. This is important because without this knowledge, the restarting router might attempt to recalculate SPF paths prematurely. It would help to recall that a restarting router preserves its FIB across the restart and continues to forward data traffic based on the preserved FIB. If there is no other topology change in the network, the restarting router can continue to forward using preserved FIB without any black holing of the traffic. If a change does occur, however, there is the possibility of black holes or forwarding loops. Therefore, recomputing SPF paths before the LSP database is completely resynchronized will yield incorrect paths and, through the FIB update, you will replace the "valid" FIB (which is preserved across the restart) with the "invalid" one.

Therefore, the third important objective of IS-IS restart mechanism is to determine when LSP database resynchronization is complete. The set of CSNPs describes LSPs that are currently in possession of each neighbor. Therefore, to know exactly which LSPs are required for database synchronization, the restarting router needs a reliable way to have all its neighbors transmit their set of CSNPs.

LSP database synchronization is complete when the restarting router has received all required LSPs. The IETF IS-IS restart provides a reliable method to determine when the LSP database synchronization is complete. For example, when a neighbor receives the special message ("Please set your SRMflags"), in addition to setting SRMflags it also transmits a set of CSNPs to the restarting router. The restarting router keeps on resending the special message ("Please set your SRMflags") until both an acknowledgment ("Okay, I have set my SRMflags and will send you the set of CSNPs") and a complete set of CSNPs have been received. The restarting router records the set of LSP IDs contained in the first complete set of CSNPs received over each interface. When the list of LSP IDs becomes empty, the restarting router knows that the LSP database synchronization is complete with its neighbors.

Unlike the IETF restart, the Cisco IS-IS restart procedure does not provide any reliable mechanism to determine when LSP database synchronization is complete. (Instead, it uses certain heuristics for this purpose.)

IETF IS-IS Restart Mechanism

The IETF IS-IS restart mechanism addresses two IP control-plane (specifically the IS-IS component) failure cases, referred to as the *restarting* and *starting routers*. In the remainder of this chapter, the phrases restarting router and starting router mean the following:

- **Restarting router** refers to a router that has preserved its IP FIB across the control-plane restart. In this scenario, the objective of the IETF restart protocol enhancements is to do away with the unnecessary adjacency flap and its associated side effects.

- **Starting router** refers to a router that has not preserved its FIB across the control-plane restart. In this scenario, the objective of the IETF restart is to eliminate temporary black holes that could be created by the presence of stale LSPs that the starting router previously might have generated before this start.

In case of starting or restarting, the IETF restart mechanism provides a reliable way to determine when the LSP database synchronization is complete.

When a router that supports the original IS-IS specification restarts, its neighbors detect the restart event and re-initialize their adjacencies (cycle through the down state) to the restarting router. This restart behavior is necessary to make sure that appropriate protocol actions are invoked. For example, SRMflags are set to ensure LSP database synchronization. However, as described earlier, cycling of an adjacency through the down state causes a number of detrimental side effects. For example, as neighboring routers recycle their pertinent adjacency, they generate LSPs to advertise a change in the topology. Setting of SRMflags by the neighboring routers is highly desirable because it ensures LSP database resynchronization. However, regeneration of LSPs by the neighboring routers is highly undesirable because it triggers SPF rerun through the area or the routing domain.

The IETF IS-IS restart mechanism allows a restarting router to inform its neighbors to retain their adjacencies (which avoids the associated harmful side effects) and yet set SRMflags (which ensures LSP database synchronization). The restarting router achieves this through inclusion of a new optional TLV in IIH packets. After the restart, the restarting router sets certain fields in the restart TLV that essentially say "Please don't re-initialize your adjacency to me, but do set your SRMflags, and do send me a set of CSNPs." Upon receipt of Hellos containing the restart TLV, the nonrestarting neighbor maintains its adjacency to the restarting router, sets the SRMflags, and acknowledges it with an IIH packet with certain fields set in the restart TLV. The neighbor's IIH packet says "Okay, I have maintained my adjacency to you, I have set the SRMflags, and you should expect to receive a set of CSNPs." To avoid premature route computations and the ensuing incorrect forwarding, the restarting router needs to know when its LSP database has synchronized. By having each neighbor send a set of CSNPs, the IETF IS-IS restart mechanism provides a reliable way to ascertain when the LSP database synchronization is complete.

In summary, the IETF IS-IS restart mechanism introduces enhancements in the original IS-IS restart behavior through protocol extensions (for example, restart TLV and timers). The new restart behavior avoids adjacency re-initialization and prevents nonrestarting neighbors from regenerating their LSPs, which in turn avoids SPF reruns in routers throughout the area or domain. Even though the concerned adjacency is not re-initialized, by setting the SRMflags LSP database resynchronization is still ensured. The restart TLV, timers, and restarting and nonrestarting behaviors are described in the sections that follow.

Restart TLV

This is a new TLV that an IS-IS router uses to indicate its capability to support the IETF IS-IS restart mechanism. The IS-IS routers that can support this capability are required to include the restart TLV in all IIH packets. Figure 5-5 shows the format of the restart TLV.

Figure 5-5   *IS-IS Restart TLV Format*

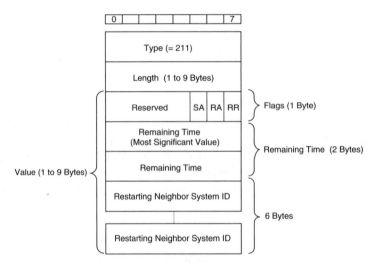

Figure 5-5 shows the following elements:

- **Restart Request (RR)**—Bit 7 in the flags field (1 byte) is defined as the Restart Request (RR) flag. After restart a router capable of supporting this mechanism sets the RR flag to inform its neighbors that a restart is in progress and therefore they must not re-initialize an existing up adjacency to the restarting router. In addition, the RR flag is used to request setting of SRMflags and transmission of a set of CSNPs from neighbors.

- **Restart Acknowledgment (RA)**—Bit 6 in the flags field is defined as the Restart Acknowledgment (RA) flag. On receipt of an IIH packet with RR flag set, an IETF IS-IS restart-capable neighbor acknowledges it with an IIH packet in which the RA flag is set and the RR flag is cleared. Because the remaining time and the restarting system ID fields are not required unless the RA bit is set, the valid range of the length field is 1 to 9 bytes. Therefore, the value field may contain only the flags field, or the flags and remaining time fields (this combination is used by implementations based on an earlier version of the IETF IS-IS restart specification that did not define the restarting system ID field), or flags, remaining time, and the restarting system ID fields.

- **Suppress Adjacency Advertisement (SA)**—Bit 5 in the flags field is referred to as the Suppress Adjacency Advertisement (SA) flag. By setting this flag, a starting router requests its neighbors to re-initialize their existing up adjacencies (from previous instantiations) to the relevant router and suppress advertisement of those adjacencies. The main reason to suppress an adjacency is to eliminate the possibility of temporary black holes that might result from incorrect LSP database information.

  This sort of condition might arise, for example, if the starting router has originated LSPs in previous instantiations and other routers still possess the stale LSPs. Because after start the starting router re-initializes its LSP fragment sequence numbers, pre-start copies of its LSP might appear "newer" (contain larger sequence numbers) than the actual new post-start LSPs. In this situation, other routers think that they have the latest LSPs from the starting router and start forwarding traffic toward the starting router. As a result, the data traffic is black holed.

  The solution to this problem is to have neighbors delay advertisement of the concerned adjacency until the starting router has been able to propagate newer versions of LSPs. Therefore, when a neighbor receives an IIH packet with the SA bit set, if an adjacency exists in an up state on that interface with the sender, it suppresses advertisement of the concerned adjacency in its LSPs. The nonstarting neighbor continues to suppress advertisement of the concerned adjacency until an IIH packet with the SA bit clear has not been received from the starting router. In addition, while an adjacency advertisement is suppressed, the nonstarting neighbors exclude that adjacency from the SPF calculations.

- **Remaining time**—This 2-byte field specifies the adjacency remaining holding time in seconds. Upon receipt of an IIH packet from a restarting neighbor with the RR flag set, an IETF IS-IS restart-capable router responds with its own IIH packet with the remaining time field set to the current value of the time (in seconds) remaining on this adjacency to its expiration. Through the remaining time field, the restarting router learns about how much time it has left to successfully complete restart before the adjacency expires.

- **Restarting neighbor system ID**—This field contains the system ID of the neighbor that is acknowledging the RR flag by setting the RA flag. Implementations based on earlier versions of the IETF restart mechanism might not include this field in the TLV when the RA is set.

Timers

The IETF IS-IS restart mechanism defines three timers, referred to as T1, T2, and T3, for a restarting/starting router.

- **T1 timer**—This is a per-interface timer with a typical value of 3 seconds. After restarting, a router starts a T1 timer and sends an IIH packet with an RR bit set. If an acknowledgment is not received from the neighbor within T1, this timer resets and an IIH packet is re-sent with an RR bit set. This timer may be allowed to expire for a preconfigured number of times. A starting router uses a T1 timer in a similar fashion except that the first IIH packet (after adjacency has reached the up state) has the SA bit set but the RR bit cleared. After the T1 timer's first expiration, in subsequent IIH packets both SA and RR bits are set. If the T1 timer expirations exceed a predefined value, the restart/start procedure is aborted.

- **T2 timer**—This is a per-LSP database timer (with a typical value of 60 seconds) that indicates the maximum time a router can wait for its LSP database synchronization. A level 1/2 router maintains a separate instance of this timer for each level. This timer is started when a router restarts or starts and is cancelled when the associated LSP database is synchronized. A starting or restarting router may use the T2 timer.

- **T3 timer**—This is a system-wide timer that indicates the time a router can wait before declaring LSP database synchronization failure by setting the OL bit in its LSP. When a router restarts, it initializes the T3 timer to 65,535 seconds and afterward sets it to the minimum of the remaining times received in IIH packets with an RA bit set. Through the T3 timer, the restarting router keeps track of the maximum time it can wait before an adjacency times out. In other words, this is the maximum time at hand in which the restart must be completed before an adjacency expires. While a T3 timer is running, transmission of IIH packets based on normal procedures is inhibited to avoid unnecessary adjacency initialization. After a T3 timer has expired or been cancelled, transmission of IIH packets (with the RA, SA, and RR bits cleared) resumes using normal Hello procedures. The T3 timer is used only by a restarting router.

Restarting Router (a Router with a Preserved FIB) Behavior

This section describes the restarting router behavior during an IS-IS restart. The starting router behavior is described later. When the restart is complete, normal IS-IS procedures are followed. The IETF IS-IS restart mechanism divides the restart process into four steps or phases: adjacency reacquisition, database synchronization, LSP generation and flooding, and SPF computation. For the following discussion, assume the point-to-point adjacencies are established via a three-way handshake.[3]

Adjacency Reacquisition

After restart, the first step toward IS-IS recovery is reacquisition of the adjacencies before the adjacency holding timers expire. An IETF IS-IS restart-capable router initializes the T3 timer to 65,535 seconds, starts the T2 timer for each level of the LSP database, starts the T1 timer on each interface, and sends an IIH packet containing the restart TLV with the RR flag set (SA and RA bit cleared) on all circuits. By setting the RR bit in the restart TLV, the restarting router explicitly informs its neighbor about adjacency reacquisition. Assuming point-to-point adjacencies are established via a three-way handshake, when transmitting a point-to-point IIH packet the restarting router also sets the point-to-point adjacency state value to initializing. This action ensures that reception of an IIH packet with the RA bit set (which acknowledges the RR bit) will cause the point-to-point adjacency to move from the initializing to up state.

After sending an IIH packet with the RR bit set, the restarting router expects to receive an acknowledgment in the form of an IIH packet with the RR bit set. When a T1 timer for an interface expires, it is restarted, and an IIH packet with the RR bit set is retransmitted on that interface. The T1 timer may expire a preconfigured number of times. If the T1 timer expires more times than the configured number, the adjacency is considered failed and the restart procedure is aborted.

Upon receipt of an IIH packet with the RR bit set, a nonrestarting neighbor is expected to set its SRMflags and send a complete set of CSNPs. On receiving both an acknowledgment and a complete set of CSNPs on an interface, the restarting router cancels the associated T1 timer. While the T3 timer is active, transmission of IIH packets based on the normal algorithm is inhibited, to prevent adjacency from re-initializing. When the T3 timer expires or is cancelled, transmission of IIH packets with the RR, RA, and SA bits cleared based on normal procedures resumes.

Depending on the restart capabilities of a neighbor, the IIH packet from that neighbor might or might not contain the restart TLV. On receipt of an IIH packet, as in the normal case, the restarting router establishes the local adjacency. If the received IIH contains a restart TLV with the RA bit set, the restarting router records the receipt of acknowledgment over that interface and sets the T3 timer to the minimum of the current value and the value in the remaining time field. The absence of restart TLV in the received IIH packet indicates that the neighbor is incapable of supporting the IETF IS-IS restart mechanism. In this case, as per normal IS-IS restart behavior, it re-initializes the adjacency and sets the SRMflags. Because in this case delivery of a CSNP is not guaranteed on the point-to-point interface, the T1 timer is cancelled without waiting for a complete set of CSNPs. In the case of a local-area network (LAN) interface, however, if the restart TLV is not contained in the received IIH packet, the T1 timer is not cancelled because database synchronization can still occur as long as at least one of the neighbors on the LAN restarts. If this does not occur, the T1 timer is eventually cancelled after the configured number of failed attempts.

LSP Database Synchronization

After having informed neighbors about its restart and received acknowledgments from the neighbors, the restarting router is guaranteed to receive a complete set of CSNPs from its neighbors. The CSNPs describe the set of LSPs that are currently present in each neighbor's database. When the restarting router has received these LSPs, its database is considered synchronized with the neighbors (as described next).

As a part of the normal CSNP processing procedure, the restarting router records the set of LSP IDs contained in the first complete set of CSNPs along with the associated remaining lifetime values received over each interface. An LSP ID with a zero remaining lifetime is not recorded in the list because it has expired and does not need to be reacquired. As the restarting router receives an LSP from neighbors, it removes the corresponding LSP ID entry from the list. In addition, when the remaining lifetime for an LSP ID entry in the list expires, that LSP ID entry is also removed from the list. With the progression of time, this list should become empty, which indicates that the LSP database is completely synchronized with its neighbors. When the list of LSP IDs becomes empty, the associated T2 timer is cancelled.

LSP Generation and Flooding

As mentioned earlier, after restart the restarting router starts a system-wide T3 timer and an instance of the T2 timer for each level of the LSP database. Generally, information from a level 1 SPF may be required to update level 2 LSPs and vice versa. Therefore, to propagate the required information from one level to another, the SPF algorithm is run as soon as database synchronization is complete on that level. However, the FIB is derived using information from level 1 and level 2 databases. Therefore, to reduce the possibility of using incorrect forwarding information and to avoid black holes, the FIB is not updated until both databases have been completely synchronized. When an LSP database synchronizes, the associated T2 timer is cancelled and the SPF algorithm is run (at this stage, the FIB is not updated) to enable propagation of interlevel routing information. When all T2 timers have been cancelled or expired (indicating that LSP database synchronization is complete on both levels), the T3 timer is also cancelled.

A change in the contents of the LSP database triggers SPF computations. Therefore, to avoid unnecessary route computations in other routers, the restarting router should ensure that it regenerates its own LSPs that are the same as those it generated before this restart. To meet this requirement, the restarting router does not regenerate and flood its own non-pseudo-node LSPs, nor does it update its FIB until each level's LSP database is synchronized.

Under normal operation, when a router receives a copy of its own LSP, which it might have generated previously but is no longer doing so, it purges that LSP from the entire domain by flooding it with a zero lifetime. This situation can occur, for example, when a router resigns as DIS and might receive copies of its own LSPs that it had generated while acting as a DIS. However, while the T2 timer is running, when an IETF IS-IS restart-capable restarting router receives its self-originated LSPs that are currently not present in its LSP database, it does not purge them. The changed behavior results because while T2 is running, the router might not yet have acquired all its adjacencies or propagated interlevel information. Because the restarting router's database information might still be incomplete, it must not take the normal action of purging those LSPs. When timer T2 expires or is cancelled, the SPF algorithm is run to update the *Routing Information Base* (RIB) for that level. After each level LSP database has synchronized, all interlevel routing information has been exchanged and the FIB has been updated, the restarting router regenerates and floods its own LSPs. At this stage, all those LSPs that were not purged earlier while waiting for database synchronization now must be purged.

In some cases, the T3 timer expires before all T2 timers have expired. When this happens, it indicates that the LSP database synchronization is taking longer than the minimum of the neighbor adjacency timers. (Recall how the T3 timer is set.) Because the router knows that it has an incomplete LSP database, it should act as if it were overloaded. The behavior to keep all adjacencies up and set the OL bit is desirable because it is less disruptive than just dropping all adjacencies. Hence, if the T3 timer expires before all T2 timers have expired, two events occur:

- First, the restarting router floods its own zeroth LSP with the OL bit set to inform other routers about this condition. On receiving zeroth LSPs with the OL bit set, other routers avoid using the restarting router in their SPF computations. The OL bit is cleared when the associated T2 timer expires.

- Second, to prevent neighbor adjacencies from expiring, the restarting router resumes transmission of normal IIH packets with the RR, RA, and SA bits cleared. A nonrestarting router does not refresh the adjacency holding timer upon receipt of an IIH packet other than the first with the RR bit set.

SPF Computation

When an instance of the T2 timer expires, SPF computations are carried out on the corresponding-level LSP database. After SPF computations have been performed, the interlevel routing information may be exchanged from one level to another within the restarting router. The FIB tables are not updated until all T2 timers have been cancelled and the T3 timer has been cancelled.

Nonrestarting Router (Helper Neighbor) Behavior

Upon receiving an IIH packet containing a restart TLV with the RR bit set, an IETF IS-IS restart-capable router knows that its sender has restarted. To identify an existing point-to-point or LAN adjacency in the up state, the receiving router compares the system ID or source LAN address. If a matching point-to-point or LAN adjacency is found, it takes the following actions, which are summarized as follows and described subsequently:

1. The state of the adjacency is left unchanged.

2. A router transmits an IIH packet when the periodic Hello timer expires.

3. Under specific circumstances, the router initiates transmission of a complete set of CSNPs and sets SRMflags on that interface for all LSPs in its database.

In Step 1, the state of the adjacency is left unchanged. (That is, it is not re-initialized.) If this is the first IIH packet with the RR bit set, the concerned adjacency is marked as being in the restart mode. Under normal operation, on receiving an IIH packet, the adjacency holding timer is set to the value received in the holding time field. However, the adjacency holding timer is not updated unless this is the first IIH packet with the RR bit set.

The main purpose of introducing the restart mode flag is to record the information that the first IIH with RR bit set has been received, the adjacency timer has been updated, and that the reception of another IIH packet with the RR bit set does not cause the adjacency timer to be re-updated.

The restart mode flag is cleared upon receipt of an IIH packet with the RR bit reset. By not re-updating the adjacency holding timer while the restart mode flag is set, the nonrestarting neighbor can maintain the adjacency long enough for the restart to complete successfully. However, this avoids the possibility of maintaining an adjacency indefinitely that might be caused by successive restarts. The restart mode flag setting does not affect the normal adjacency state transitions.

- Normally in Step 2, a router transmits an IIH packet when the periodic Hello timer expires. However, now it immediately (that is, after some random delay but before transmitting any LSPs or CSNPs) responds with an IIH packet over the corresponding interface. On the transmitted IIH packet, the RA bit is set, the RR and SA bits are cleared, and the remaining time field is set to the current value of the adjacency holding timer.

- In addition, in Step 3, if the interface on which the IIH with the RR set was received is a point-to-point interface or the receiving router has the highest level n router priority among the IETF IS-IS restart-capable routers (excluding the restarting router), the router initiates transmission of a complete set of CSNPs and sets SRMflags on that interface for all LSPs in its database. Setting the SRMflags ensures that the LSP database synchronization takes place. The delivery of CSNPs makes it possible to determine completion of LSP database synchronization.

- However, if there is no matching adjacency in the up state, it processes the IIH packet as normal; that is, the receiving router re-initializes the adjacency (which ensures the LSP database synchronization because SRMflags are set by this action) and sets the RA bit when responding with its own IIH packet.

Starting Router (a Router Without a Preserved FIB) Behavior

The IETF IS-IS restart mechanism treats the case of starting and restarting routers a little differently. After starting, an IETF IS-IS start-capable router starts a T2 timer for each level of LSP database on each interface and sends IIH packets with the SA bit set and the RR bit clear. By setting the SA bit and clearing the RR bit, the restarting router explicitly informs its neighbors as follows: "Please do re-initialize your existing up adjacencies to me. However, don't advertise the concerned adjacency until I request you to do so by clearing the SA bit in my IIH packets."

As mentioned previously, adjacency advertisements are suppressed to prevent temporary black holes caused by inconsistent LSP database information. When the starting router retransmits IIH packets on each interface, the SA bit remains set (and RR bit cleared) until the concerned adjacency has transitioned to the up state. Note that irrespective of the SA bit settings, a neighboring router is not expected to acknowledge (with the RA bit set in the IIH packet) until it receives an IIH packet with the RR bit set.

Another difference exists in restarting and starting router behaviors that are involved with the T1 timer usage. For example, a restarting router starts a T1 timer on each interface after restart. In contrast, a starting router does not do so until an adjacency has attained the up state. When an adjacency attains the up state, a T1 timer is started and IIH packet is sent with the SA bit set and the RR bit clear. When the T1 timer expires for the first time, it is restarted and an IIH packet is retransmitted with both the SA and RR bits set.

The normal adjacency formation process does not provide a reliable procedure for acquiring a set of CSNPs from a neighbor. To acquire a set of CSNPS reliably, the starting router sets the RR bit to force neighbors to acknowledge the request for CSNPs with the RA bit set in their IIH packets. Acquisition of a set of CSNPs is important because it provides a reliable way to ascertain when LSP database synchronization is complete. Therefore, after having sent an IIH packet with the RR bit set, the starting router expects to receive an acknowledgment in the form of an IIH packet with the RR bit set and a set of CSNPs. Until a set of CSNPs is received, the starting router knows that its database is incomplete. Therefore, as soon as each adjacency reaches the up state and before CSNPs are exchanged, the router transmits its zeroth LSP with the database OL bit set. By doing so, the starting router intends to inform other routers that its database synchronization is incomplete. Upon receipt of the zeroth LSP with the OL bit set, other routers take the starting router out from the forwarding paths.

There is a separate OL bit for each level, and both OL bits are set and cleared together. The objective of setting both OL bits simultaneously is to make an allowance for an interlevel routing exchange within the node. For example, level 2 might need to wait for database synchronization at level 1. Therefore, both OL bits remain set until both databases are completely synchronized. For each adjacency in the up state, on expiration of the T1 timer, the timer is restarted and the IIH packet is retransmitted with both SA and RR bits set. On a given interface, the T1 timer is cancelled upon receiving both an acknowledgment (RA bit set) and a complete set of CSNPs. If a T1 timer expires more than the configured number of times, the concerned adjacency is considered to have failed and the start procedure is aborted.

After receiving the set of CSNPs from all neighbors and having synchronized both LSP databases, both T2 timers are cancelled and both OL bits are cleared simultaneously. From this time onward, normal IIH packets (with RR, RA, and SA bits clear) are transmitted.

Independent of any T2 timer status, the starting router generates and floods its own LSPs (including the zeroth LSP, except that the OL bits remain set while T2 timers are running) following normal procedures. Similarly, as the starting router learns new routes, it runs the SPF algorithm and updates the RIB and the FIB following normal procedures.

IETF IS-IS Restart Operation

This section describes the operation of the IETF IS-IS restart mechanism. For clarity, the starting and restarting router cases are described separately. Figure 5-6 shows the network diagram for this example. Both routers are assumed to be IETF IS-IS restart- and NSF-capable (able to preserve IP forwarding state across IS-IS restart). R1 and R2 are interconnected via point-to-point links, and the point-to-point adjacencies are established using the three-way handshake procedure. The sequence of steps described in the next section might not necessarily be followed by a specific implementation. These steps are just meant to provide a functional-level description of the IETF IS-IS restart mechanism.

Starting Router Operation

Figure 5-6 shows the network diagram for the starting router case, and the corresponding sequence of steps follows.

Figure 5-6   *Example of the IETF IS-IS Restart Operation for the Starting Router Case*

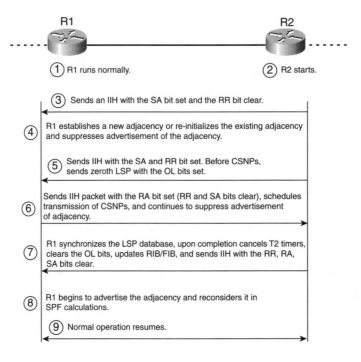

1. Assume R1 is running normally. (That is, LSP databases have been fully synchronized.)

2. Suppose R2 starts.

3. On starting, R2 activates the T2 timer for each level database and establishes adjacencies by transmitting IIH packets containing a restart TLV with the SA bit set and the RR bit clear.

4. On receipt of the IIH packet with the SA bit set and the RR bit clear, R1 follows the normal procedure for an adjacency establishment. That is, if there is no existing adjacency on the concerned interface, R1 establishes a new adjacency. Otherwise, it re-initializes the existing adjacency. Unlike the normal procedure, however, R1 suppresses advertisement of the adjacency in its LSPs and, to prevent temporary black holes, it excludes that adjacency from the SPF calculations.

5. When an adjacency transitions to the up state, R2 starts the T1 timer and transmits an IIH packet with the SA bit set and the RR bit clear on that interface. When the T1 timer expires for the first time, it is restarted and an IIH packet is retransmitted with both the SA and RR bits set. As a result of having sent an IIH packet with the RR bit set, R2 expects to receive both an acknowledgment and a set of CSNPs from the neighbor over the concerned interface. Because R2 knows that its database is incomplete, immediately after establishing the adjacency but before the CSNPs exchange, it transmits the zeroth LSP with the OL bits set. This ensures other routers (including R1) in the domain remove R2 from their forwarding paths.

6. Upon receipt of the IIH packet with the RR bit set, R1 maintains the established adjacency state, sends an IIH packet with the RA bit set (RR and SA bits clear), sets SRMflags, sets the restart mode flag (if previously clear), updates the hold time, and schedules transmission of a complete set of CSNPs on that interface. In addition, because the SA bit is set in the received IIH packet, R2 continues to suppress the adjacency advertisement and excludes it from the SPF calculations.

7. Upon receiving both an acknowledgment and a set of CSNPs, R2 cancels the associated T1 timer. Now R1 and R2 exchange LSPs and synchronize their databases. When the database synchronization is complete at both levels, R2 cancels all T2 timers and simultaneously clears both OL bits. From this point on, R2 transmits IIH packets with the RR, RA, and SA bits clear. Irrespective of T2 timers, as R2 learns new routes it runs the SPF algorithm and updates the RIB and the FIB.

8. Upon receiving the RR bit cleared, R1 clears the restart mode flag. As in the received IIH packet, the SA bit is clear (indicating the end of adjacency suppression), and R1 begins to advertise the concerned adjacency in its own LSPs and reconsiders it in the SPF calculations.

9. Normal operation resumes.

Restarting Router Operation

Figure 5-7 shows the network diagram for the restarting router case and the corresponding sequence of steps follows.

Figure 5-7   *Example of the IETF IS-IS Restart Operation for the Restarting Router Case*

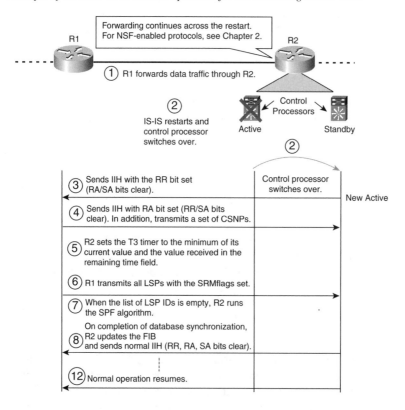

1. Assume at this stage that R2 is running normally and can forward data traffic. Suppose a forwarding path exists from "source" to "destination" passing through R1 and R2, and that data traffic is being forwarded on this path.

2. Assume R2 restarts. Because R2 has preserved the FIB, it continues to forward data packets on the routes learned before this restart.

3. Upon restarting, R2 attempts to reacquire adjacencies. It initializes the T3 timer, starts the T2 timer for each level LSP database, starts the T1 timer on each interface, and transmits an IIH packet with the RR bit set (RA and SA bits clear) on each interface. Because point-to-point adjacencies are assumed to use a three-way handshake, R2 sets the adjacency state value to initializing before transmitting an IIH packet on a point-to-point interface.

4. Upon receipt of the IIH packet containing a restart TLV with the RR bit set (RA and SA bits clear), R1 finds an existing point-to-point adjacency in the up state. R1 maintains the adjacency state, sets the restart mode flag, updates the hold time, sets SRMflags, and schedules transmission of a complete set of CSNPs. In addition, R1 responds with an IIH packet with the RA bit set and the RR bit cleared, and with the remaining time field set to the current value of the adjacency holding timer.

5. On receiving an IIH packet containing a restart TLV with the RA bit set, R2 records the receipt of acknowledgment over that interface and sets the T3 timer to the minimum of its current value and the value received in the remaining time field. When both an acknowledgment and a complete set of CSNPs have been received on an interface, R2 cancels the T1 timer for the interface. However, if both CSNPs and acknowledgment have not been received, R2 restarts the T1 timer and retransmits an IIH packet with the RR bit set (RA and SA bits clear). If the T1 timer expires more than configured the number of times, the adjacency is considered to have failed and therefore the restart procedure is aborted.

6. The update process in R1 scans the LSP database to find all LSPs with SRMflags set and transmits all LSPs.

7. After having received sets of CSNPs on each interface, R2 is waiting for the LSPs reported in sets of CSNPs received on all interfaces (which may be different for different interfaces). As part of normal CSNP processing, R2 records the set of LSP IDs contained in all the sets of CSNPs along with the associated nonzero remaining lifetime values. Because LSPs with zero remaining lifetimes have expired, there is no need to acquire them. As R2 receives an LSP, it removes the corresponding LSP ID entry from the list. With the progression of time, this list becomes empty, which indicates that the LSP database is fully synchronized. When the list of LSP IDs becomes empty, R2 cancels the associated T2 timer and runs the SPF algorithm (the FIB is not updated at this stage) to allow propagation of interlevel routing information between levels in R2.

8. When all T2 timers have been cancelled, indicating complete LSP database synchronization on both levels, R2 cancels the T3 timer, updates the FIB tables, regenerates and floods its own LSPs, purges all its own LSPs (received while waiting for database synchronization) that are no longer contained in the database, and resumes transmission of the normal IIH packets with the RR, SA, and RA bits cleared.

9. If T3 expires before all T2 timers have expired, this indicates an adjacency has expired before the LSP database is completely synchronized. R2 transmits its own zeroth LSP with the OL bit set to prevent other routers from using R2 in their forwarding paths. The OL bit is eventually cleared when the associated T2 timer expires.

10. Upon receipt of an IIH packet with the RR bit clear, R1 clears the restart mode flag. This marks the completion of successful restart.

11. After restart, R2 regenerates its own LSPs, which should be the same as those generated before this restart. Therefore, reception of R2's LSPs should not trigger SPF calculations on R1 and other routers in the domain.

12. Normal operation resumes.

Cisco IS-IS Restart

The IETF IS-IS restart mechanism extends the IS-IS protocol and requires that both the restarting router and its neighbors be able to support these capabilities. In contrast, the Cisco IS-IS restart mechanism does not make any externally observable protocol changes. That is, the IS-IS restart on a router is hidden from its neighbors. First, this mechanism requires transmission of IIH packets quickly following the restart before an adjacency's hold time expires. Second, to conceal the restart event following the restart, this mechanism relies on the capability of the restarting router to transmit IIH packets containing exactly the same information as existed before the restart. Therefore, to mask the IS-IS restart event from other routers, this approach requires preservation of some IS-IS adjacency-related state information across the restart.

Although the IETF restart mechanism uses protocol extensions to affect changes in the restart behavior, the Cisco restart takes a different approach to satisfy the three objectives stated previously:

- First, to prevent SPF runs throughout the routing domain caused by a change in an adjacency state, none of the existing up adjacencies between the restarting router and its neighbors should be initialized across the restart.

- Second, to ensure LSP database synchronization, the restarting router needs to have some way to make neighbors set their SRMflags for all LSPs.

- Third, to prevent temporary black holes that might result from incorrect or incomplete information, the restarting router should have a reliable way to determine when its database synchronization is complete.

The restarting routers supporting the Cisco IS-IS restart meet the first objective by transmitting IIH packets (which appear the same as they were before restart) before an adjacency expires. A router running with the Cisco IS-IS restart meets the second objective through transmission of a CSNP containing the special LSP. However, this mechanism does not meet the third objective because it cannot invoke transmission of CSNPs on point-to-point interfaces. Note the IETF IS-IS restart achieves this through protocol extensions (RR and RA bits). In the absence of a reliable way, the Cisco IS-IS restart uses heuristics such as monitoring the arrival rate of LSPs. For example, when the arrival rate of LSPs falls below a certain predefined threshold value, the database synchronization is deemed complete.

The Cisco IS-IS restart mechanism preserves some IS-IS adjacency-related state information across the IS-IS restart. This information is needed to transmit IIH packets after the restart to make IIH packets appear exactly the same to neighbors as before the restart. After restart, the restarting router sends regular IIH packets (without the restart TLV) containing correct information using a state preserved across the restart.

On receipt of IIH packets with correct information, as usual nonrestarting neighbors update their adjacency holding timers. Because there is no detectable change in IIH packets after the restart, the fact that the router has restarted is completely concealed from its neighbors. To accomplish this, however, the restarting router must restart quickly and transmit IIH packets before neighbors drop adjacencies caused by timeouts. If the restarting router takes too long to restart and fails to transmit IIH packets before an adjacency expires, the neighbor will drop the adjacency (resulting in negative effects).

As discussed earlier, normally when an IS-IS restarts its neighbors re-initialize their adjacencies and set SRMflags for all LSPs in their databases to ensure database synchronization. However, when a router supporting a Cisco IS-IS restart mechanism restarts, because neighbors are unaware of the restart event, they fail to set the SRMflags. To address this problem, following the restart, the restarting router transmits an empty CSNP that causes SRMflags to be set on all LSPs in the neighbors' databases. However, this alone does not solve the problem completely because the restarting router still does not know whether a neighbor has actually received the empty CSNP and set its SRMflags.

To get this confirmation, the Cisco restart-capable router sends a CSNP containing reference to a "special" LSP. The restarting router owns the special LSP, which has never been propagated before. The main idea is to get a confirmation of the CSNP receipt by having the neighbor request the special LSP. Clearly, if the neighbor already has the special LSP, it may not request it. Therefore, for this approach to work, the special LSP must not exist in the neighbors' databases. After receiving a CSPN referencing the special LSP from the restarting router, the neighbor is expected to request the special LSP through a PSNP. Now when the restarting router receives a PSNP asking for the special LSP, it interprets this request as an acknowledgment of the CSNP, which in turn ensures that the neighbor has set all SRMflags.

The special CSNP covers the entire range of LSP IDs and must be transmitted as a single fragment. This is because the sender of the special CSNP receives only a confirmation of the fragment that contains the special LSP. Therefore, if the CSNP is broken into multiple fragments and some fragments are lost, SRMflags for LSP IDs contained in the lost fragments will not be set. That in turn might jeopardize eventual database synchronization, because CSNP exchange provides an efficient mechanism for LSP database synchronization by inhibiting the unnecessary exchange of information that both routers already have.

Therefore, after transmitting the CSNP containing a special LSP as a single fragment and after having received the PSNP requesting the special LSP, the sender knows that the neighbor has set SRMflags for all LSPs and is expecting to receive all LSPs. To avoid exchange of LSPs that it already has (essentially to clear SRMflags on neighbors), the restarting router is programmed to send normal CSNPs (without any reference to the special LSP). The exchange of normal CSNPs cannot be combined with a special CSNP because of a single-fragment requirement, as described earlier. Therefore, after sending the special CSNP, the restarting router transmits the set of normal CSNPs.

Cisco IS-IS Restart Operation

This section illustrates the operation of the Cisco IS-IS restart mechanism, using the network diagram shown in Figure 5-8. Both R1 and R2 are Cisco IS-IS restart/NSF-capable and are interconnected via point-to-point links.

Figure 5-8   *Example of the Cisco IS-IS Restart Operation*

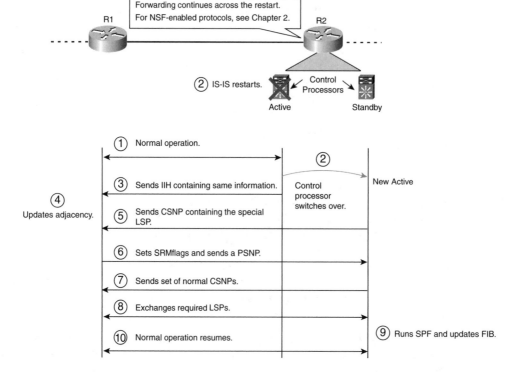

1. Assume using normal IS-IS procedures, R1 and R2 have synchronized their databases and are ready for forwarding. Suppose a forwarding path exists from "source" to "destination" passing through R1 and R2, and data traffic is being forwarded on this path.

2. Assume R2 restarts and was able to preserve IP forwarding as well as adjacency-related state information across the restart. Therefore, it continues to forward data packets using the preserved forwarding state.

3. After it restarts and before any adjacency expires, R2 transmits IIH packets on all interfaces using correct adjacency-related state information.

4. Upon receiving an IIH packet, R1 updates the relevant adjacency timer without even noticing R2's restart.

5. To have the neighbor set SRMflags for all LSPs (ensuring database synchronization), R2 transmits the CSNP containing the special LSP. The special CSNP is transmitted as a single fragment.

6. Upon receipt of the CSNP (covering the entire range of LSP IDs) and containing the special LSP, R1 sets SRMflags for all LSPs. In addition, R1 transmits a PSNP requesting the special LSP from R2.

7. After sending the CSNP containing the special LSP and having received its confirmation through the PSNP requesting the special LSP, R2 sends a set of normal CSNPs so that R1 does not unnecessarily transmit those LSPs that it already possesses.

8. Upon receiving a normal set of CSNPs, R1 clears the SRMflags for those LSPs that R2 already claims to have. For the remaining LSPs with SRMflags set, R1 transmits the corresponding LSPs.

9. Following normal procedures, R2 synchronizes its database. Because R2 does not have any reliable method to determine when its database is complete, it uses heuristics such as a timer or waits until the LSPs' rate of arrival falls below a certain threshold. Upon completion of the database synchronization, R2 runs the SPF algorithm and updates the FIB tables. To avoid causing a routing flap in other routers, R2 regenerates its own LSPs, which are the same as those generated before this restart. Therefore, reception of R2's LSPs should not trigger SPF calculations on R1 and other routers in the domain.

10. Normal operation resumes.

Comparison of the IS-IS Restart Mechanisms

The advantages of the IETF IS-IS restart approach include scalability (does not require IS-IS–related state preservation across the restart) and standards-based implementation. Disadvantages of this approach are that it requires IS-IS protocol extensions and support from its neighbors (helper nodes). To elaborate on this further, consider a router R1 in a provider's network that is peering with an R2 that might be managed by another provider or a customer. The IETF IS-IS restart mechanism requires that both R1 and R2 support this capability. However, the customer or the network provider might not always be willing to upgrade, or R2 might not be upgradeable.

An advantage of the Cisco IS-IS restart approach is that it does not require support from neighbors. Therefore, unlike the IETF IS-IS restart, a Cisco IS-IS restart- and NSF-capable router handles the case, whereas its neighbors are not IS-IS restart-capable. However, Cisco IS-IS restart might be less scalable than the IETF IS-IS restart, because some IS-IS-related state information must be preserved across the restart. Another drawback of this approach is the lack of a reliable mechanism to determine when database synchronization is complete. Note that the Cisco IOS architecture supports both IETF and Cisco-specific IS-IS restart mechanisms.

Network Deployment Considerations

Presently, the majority of deployed routers in large networks are not capable of control-plane restarts without disrupting the forwarding plane. To improve system and network availability, such routers must be upgraded with software that allows the control-plane restart without disturbing the forwarding plane. The majority of customers are expected to adopt a phased approach for upgrading their networks. In a heterogeneous multivendor network, therefore, routers with different sets of control-plane restart capabilities may exist. For instance, some of the routers might be able to support IS-IS restart; however, because of the system architecture or for other reasons, the routers might not be NSF upgradeable. As a result, routers with different sets of control- and forwarding-plane restart capabilities are likely to coexist for some time.

With respect to control and forwarding capabilities, routers can be classified as follows:

- **IS-IS restart- and NSF capable**—A router that supports either the IETF or the Cisco IS-IS restart mechanism and is capable of preserving the IP forwarding state across the IS-IS restart.

- **IS-IS restart-capable but NSF-incapable**—A router that supports either the IETF or the Cisco IS-IS restart mechanism but is incapable of preserving the IP forwarding state across the IS-IS restart.

- **IS-IS restart- and NSF-incapable**— A router that does not support either the IETF or the Cisco IS-IS restart mechanism, nor is capable of preserving the IP forwarding state across the IS-IS restart.

- **IS-IS restart-incapable but NSF-capable**—A router that does not support either an IETF or a Cisco IS-IS restart mechanism, but is capable of preserving the IP forwarding state across the IS-IS restart.

The interoperability scenarios involving the IETF and the Cisco IS-IS restart mechanisms are described in the following sections.

Scenario 1: R1 and R2 Are IETF IS-IS Restart- or NSF-Capable

Because both the restarting router and its peers are IS-IS restart- and NSF-capable, the IP forwarding state remains undisturbed due to IS-IS restart in either R1 or R2 (see Figure 5-9). Hence, IS-IS restart in either router does not cause negative effects in the network. Therefore, for maximum benefit from the IETF IS-IS restart mechanism, the restarting router and its neighbors must be both IS-IS restart- and NSF-capable.

Figure 5-9   *IETF IS-IS Restart Interoperability Scenarios*

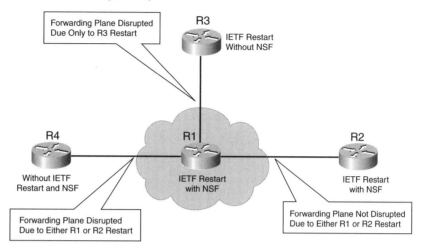

Scenario 2: R1 Is IETF IS-IS Restart- or NSF-Capable, but R3 Is Only IETF IS-IS Restart-Capable

In this case, when the IS-IS control plane in R1 restarts, its forwarding plane is not affected. This is because R3 is IS-IS restart-capable and maintains the adjacency across the IS-IS restart in R1. That is, R3 learns (for example, via the restart TLV) about the IS-IS restart in R1 and plays the helper-node role through maintaining its adjacencies with R1. However, when IS-IS in R3 restarts, it transmits IIH packets with the RR bit cleared, because it is not capable of NSF.

On receipt of IIH packets with the RR bit cleared, R1 reverts back to normal procedure (see Figure 5-9). That is, R1 initializes the adjacency, regenerates its own LSP informing other routers about this topology change, and recomputes its forwarding paths avoiding R3. In other words, if a router supports only the IS-IS control-plane restart mechanism but is incapable of preserving an IP forwarding state (FIB) across the IS-IS restart, when IS-IS restarts in such a router it does not reduce the negative effects on other routers. However, it does help reduce such negative effects (by acting as a helper node) when its IS-IS restart- or NSF-capable neighbor(s) restarts.

Scenario 3: R1 Is IETF IS-IS Restart- or NSF-Capable, but R4 Is IETF Restart- or NSF-Incapable

In this case, IS-IS restart in either R1 or R4 would not minimize the negative effects on other routers (see Figure 5-9). In other words, to derive any benefit from an IETF IS-IS restart- and NSF-capable router, its neighbor(s) must also be capable of supporting at least the IETF IS-IS restart mechanism.

Scenario 4: R1 and R2 Are Cisco IS-IS Restart- or NSF-Capable

The interoperability scenario involving Cisco IS-IS restart- and NSF-capable routers has already been described (see Figure 5-10). In this case, unlike the IETF IS-IS restart mechanism, the nonrestarting neighbor is not required to be Cisco IS-IS restart-capable or IETF IS-IS restart-capable. However, when both routers are Cisco IS-IS restart- and NSF-capable, data-plane forwarding remains unaffected by an IS-IS control component restart in either R1 or R2. The maximum benefit is achieved whenever the faulting router is Cisco IS-IS restart-capable. (It does not require its neighbors to be.)

Figure 5-10 *Cisco IS-IS Restart Interoperability Scenarios*

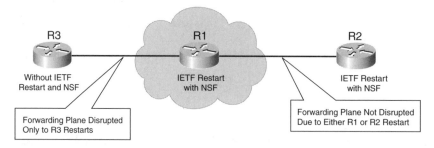

Scenario 5: R1 Is Cisco IS-IS Restart- or NSF-Capable and R3 Is Cisco IS-IS Restart- or NSF-Incapable

This interoperability scenario is a subset of the previous one. In this case, when the IS-IS control plane in R1 restarts, the forwarding plane in neither R1 nor R3 is disrupted (see Figure 5-10). This is because the restart of R1 is hidden from its neighbors, and therefore R3 does not re-initialize its adjacency across the restart. However, when R3 restarts, because it is not IS-IS restart-capable, its neighbors re-initialize their adjacencies with R3. This causes all the undesirable negative effects on other routers. This interoperability scenario, however, is important from a practical deployment point of view to address cases involving routers that do not support such capability or that might not be upgradeable.

Summary

This chapter began with an overview of the IS-IS protocol followed by a description of the undesirable effects on control and forwarding planes caused by IS-IS restart. Then two approaches to reduce these negative effects were described: the IETF IS-IS restart and the Cisco IS-IS restart. Both restart mechanisms were illustrated through operation examples and interoperability scenarios. The strengths and weaknesses of each approach were also described.

References

[1] ISO 8473, "Intermediate System to Intermediate System Intra-Domain Routing Information Exchange Protocol for Use in Conjunction with the Protocol for Providing the Connectionless-Mode Network Service," ISO/IEC 10589, 2001.

[2] RFC 1195, "Use of OSI IS-IS for Routing in TCP/IP and Dual Environments," R. Callon, December 1990.

[3] RFC 3373, "Three-Way Handshake for Intermediate System to Intermediate System (IS-IS) Point-to-Point Adjacencies," D. Katz and R. Saluja, September 2002.

[4] RFC 3847, "Intermediate System to Intermediate System (IS-IS)," M. Shand and L. Ginsberg, July 2004.

[5] Cisco Systems, Inc. "Cisco Non-Stop Forwarding (NSF)," http://www.cisco.com.

CHAPTER 6

Interdomain IP Control Plane: Restarting BGP Gracefully

This chapter describes a procedure, referred to as the Border Gateway Protocol (BGP) graceful restart mechanism, which allows a BGP speaker to restart without causing route flaps. The chapter starts with an overview of BGP routing with a focus on those concepts that are pertinent to the graceful restart mechanism. This is followed by a description of the mechanics of the graceful restart mechanism. Subsequently, operation of the graceful restart mechanism is explained in detail. The key concepts of the restart mechanism are further elaborated through deployment scenarios. The chapter concludes with a brief summary.

Introduction to Border Gateway Protocol Routing

The Internet is a collection of a large number of autonomous systems in which each *autonomous system* (AS) consists of a set of interconnected routers that are managed by a single technical administration. BGP plays a crucial role in routing traffic in the Internet because BGP is the de facto standard for interdomain routing.[1] BGP routers, known as *BGP speakers*, establish sessions with each other to exchange routing information. BGP employs *Transmission Control Protocol* (TCP) to deliver protocol messages reliably. After a BGP session has been established, BGP peers are ready for exchanging routing information.

BGP routing exchange occurs in two phases: bulk and incremental. Initially, after the session has formed, BGP peers exchange complete routing information with each other. Afterward, however, only incremental routing updates are sent in response to routing changes. When a BGP speaker learns about a new route, if the decision process has selected the route as the best route, the speaker advertises that route to its peers. Similarly, when a route is no longer available, the speaker withdraws the previously advertised route. As compared with the periodic update of the entire routing table, the incremental update approach is more efficient because it consumes reduced link bandwidth and control processor resources.

BGP Control- and Forwarding-Plane Components

Just as with the *interior gateway protocols* (IGP) such as the *Open Shortest Path First* (OSPF) and *Intermediate System-to-Intermediate System* (IS-IS; (see Chapter 4, "Intradomain IP Control Plane: Restarting OSPF Gracefully," and Chapter 5, "Intradomain IP Control Plane: Restarting IS-IS Gracefully"), BGP can be decomposed into control- and forwarding-plane components. The BGP control-plane component establishes the session, builds a *Routing Information Base* (RIB) by exchanging routing information with BGP peers, and selects the best routes for its own use and for advertising to peers. Each BGP speaker periodically runs the decision process to select the best routes for each destination prefix. The decision process takes the BGP routes stored in the RIB as input, applies local policies, and selects the best routes for each destination. The selected routes are installed in the *Forwarding Information Base* (FIB) and also advertised to peers.

The IP forwarding plane is composed of the FIB. Note that the FIB contains not only BGP-derived forwarding state (routes), but also the IGP routes. Therefore, the BGP forwarding-plane component that comprises only the BGP routes may be viewed as a subset of the FIB. The BGP control-plane component resides on the control processor, whereas the forwarding-plane component resides on the line cards. (See Chapter 2, "IP Forwarding Plane: Achieving Nonstop Forwarding," for more details on IP forwarding-plane architecture.)

Keeping the incremental update approach of the BGP in mind, in a stable routing environment BGP speakers should need to send a few updates now and then. Ideally, in the absence of any further routing changes, the BGP speakers will not have to send incremental routing updates. In practice, however, the situation is quite different because typically the BGP routing environment is far from stable. For example, some studies show that the BGP environment exhibits significant route fluctuations[2] (in the order of millions of updates) .

Route Flaps Caused by BGP Control-Plane Restart

BGP routing instability is commonly measured in terms of route flapping events per second. A route flap is a rapid change in the state of a route, such as an advertisement abruptly followed by a withdrawal, or vice versa. The origins of route flaps can generally be traced back to router hardware and software faults (such as BGP control-plane restart, router configuration errors, and link failures). This chapter covers mainly route flaps that result from BGP control-plane restart.

Now that you know about route flaps, the discussion can turn to why route flaps are so undesirable. For one, route flaps are undesirable because such route fluctuations can severely degrade network performance. Perhaps it might be best to illustrate this point through an example. Consider two BGP speakers, R1 and R2, in Figure 6-1. Assume these speakers have established a BGP session, exchanged routing information, selected the best routes, installed those routes in the FIB, and are forwarding data traffic. Now suppose the BGP control plane in R1 restarts, and as a result BGP session with R2 is lost. BGP requires that whenever a BGP session is closed (normally or abnormally), all routes learned or advertised on that session must be deleted. Insofar as the forwarding plane is concerned, this means the associated forwarding state must be removed from the FIB. Therefore, as soon as R2 detects failure of the BGP session with R1, R2 withdraws all concerned routes from its peers that it had previously learned from R1 and advertised to its peers and removes those routes from its FIB.

Figure 6-1   *Detrimental Effects of the BGP Control-Plane Restart*

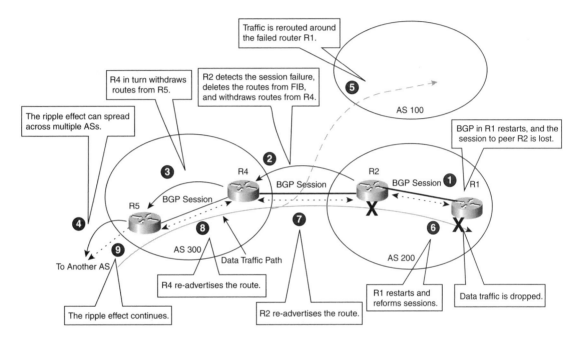

In the meantime, peers of R2 (unaware of the fact that R1 has restarted) keep sending data packets to R2 on the failed route, which is discarded in R2. Now coming back to the route-withdrawal process, upon receiving an Update message from speaker R2, the peers of the speaker R2 in turn withdraw those routes from their peers. Hence the route withdrawal sequence continues and its ripple effect can spread across multiple routing domains. In other words, a single BGP restart event can cause a long sequence of updates as the BGP speakers explore alternative paths around the restarting speaker. Eventually, R2 and other speakers find alternative paths, and the traffic on the failed routes begins to flow on the alternative path. Until that happens, data traffic on the failed routes will be continuously black holed.

Now suppose after restarting, R1 quickly reforms a BGP session with R2 and re-exchanges complete routing information. As before, R2 runs the decision process, selects the routes received from R1 as the best routes, installs the routes in its FIB, and advertises these routes to its peers. Once again, this process causes a long sequence of updates while speakers attempt to find out the new best routes. When R2 and its peers determine these new routes to be the best, they again start forwarding traffic on these routes.

In summary, BGP control-plane restart causes route flaps that can lead to creation of forwarding loops and extra control traffic. The propagation of routing updates consumes more link bandwidth and control processor resources on BGP speakers in multiple domains. The increased control processor activity resulting from rapid routing updates is commonly referred to as *the churn*. This example demonstrates that the BGP restart events and the ensuing route flaps can degrade overall network performance.

BGP Restart Process

Before learning about a mechanism that can mitigate harmful effects of route flaps, you need to understand the original BGP restart behavior. When BGP in a speaker restarts, to avoid forwarding into the black hole the nonrestarting BGP peers withdraw routes derived from the failed BGP session. The objectives of this deliberate protocol behavior are to prevent other speakers from forwarding traffic to the restarting speaker (which is assumed to be incapable of forwarding across the restart) and to inform other speakers quickly about the failure to enable them to find alternative paths.

This protocol behavior is necessary for a speaker that is incapable of preserving its FIB across the restart. This is because, as discussed earlier, if the data traffic is allowed to use the failed routes, it will be black holed. Therefore, to reduce the possibility of packet loss, BGP deliberately withdraws routes to find alternative paths around the restarting router. However, the situation is quite different when a speaker is capable of preserving its FIB and uses it for forwarding across the BGP restart. The term *nonstop forwarding* (NSF) refers to the capability of a router that can continue to forward across the control-plane restart. If the restarting speaker is NSF-capable and the network topology does not change during the restart period, it would be safe and feasible to retain the restarting router on the forwarding path. In this case, route flaps can be avoided because there is no need to inform routers about the failure. To achieve this objective, however, the original BGP restart behavior needs to be modified. For example, unlike the original restart behavior, a restarting speaker's peers should not withdraw routes on detection of a BGP session failure when the restarting peer is capable of forwarding across the restart.

BGP Routing Evolution and Concepts

As outlined previously, the Internet is a collection of interconnected autonomous systems. The Internet uses different types of routing protocols for destinations within the AS (commonly called *intra-AS routing*) and external to the AS (commonly called *inter-AS* or *interdomain routing*), as depicted in Figure 6-2.

Intra-AS routing is performed via IGPs such as OSPF and IS-IS, whereas inter-AS routing is achieved through exterior gateway protocols. BGP version 4 (BGP-4) is the de facto exterior gateway protocol for inter-AS routing. The BGP has evolved from an earlier inter-AS routing protocol called *Exterior Gateway Protocol* (EGP) and has gone through several revisions since its introduction in 1989. The latest version, BGP-4, is the most widely deployed exterior gateway protocol. BGP-4 introduced several new features such as the notion of classless IP address (referred to as *IP prefix*) and route aggregation. In the remainder of this chapter, the term *BGP* specifically refers to the BGP version 4.

Figure 6-2   *Intra-AS and Inter-AS Routing*

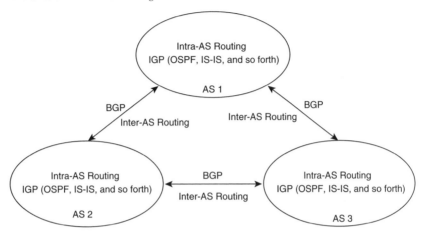

BGP Messages

BGP views the Internet as a collection of interconnected autonomous systems. Routers that exchange routing information via BGP are known as *BGP speakers*. BGP routing information a exchange consists of set of IP destination addresses, which are referred to as the *network layer reachability information* (NLRI). Before routing information can be exchanged, the pair of BGP speakers must establish a BGP session. To ensure reliable message delivery, a BGP session uses TCP.

BGP uses four types of protocol messages: Open, Update, Notification, and Keepalive. Open and Keepalive messages are used to establish and maintain a session, respectively. After the TCP connection has been formed, each speaker sends an Open message to negotiate session parameters. The Open message contains several fields:

- Version (protocol version)
- My autonomous system (AS number of the sender)
- Hold time (maximum time that is allowed to elapse between the receipt of successive Keepalive or Update messages before the sender is considered to be dead)
- BGP identifier (IP address of the loopback interface on the sender)

If the Open message is acceptable, the receiver sends back a Keepalive message to confirm acknowledgment of the Open message. After the BGP session has been formed, the peers keep it alive either by exchanging Update messages, or if there are no Update messages to exchange, by sending Keepalive messages periodically. If a Keepalive or an Update message is not received from a peer within hold time, that peer is considered dead (unreachable). To avoid unintentional expiration of the hold timer, successive Keepalive messages are typically sent within one third of the hold-time interval. This means, for example, if three successive Keepalive messages fail to reach the peer, by definition the hold time has expired and the peer will drop the session.

Idle and Established States

BGP protocol operation can be described in terms of a *finite-state machine* (FSM). There is one FSM for each BGP session. BGP starts off in the idle state (see Figure 6-3). When a local BGP speaker is in the idle state, it does not accept TCP connection requests from remote speakers. When the system operator triggers the start event on the local speaker, it initiates a TCP connection request to the remote speaker, starts to listen for TCP connection requests from the remote speaker, and transitions to the connect state. If the TCP connection request succeeds, the local speaker sends the Open message, transitions to the opensent state, and waits for an Open message from the remote peer. If the local BGP speaker receives a Keepalive message, it changes to the established state. This marks the successful establishment of a BGP session. In the established state, a BGP speaker can exchange Update, Keepalive, and Notification messages with the remote peer.

Figure 6-3   *BGP Session Finite-State Machine*

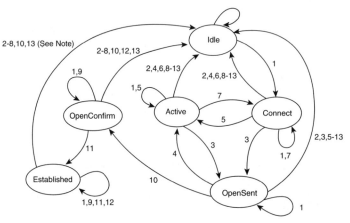

BGP Events:

1- BGP Start
2- BGP Stop
3- BGP Transport Connection Open
4- BGP Transport Connection Closed
5- BGP Transport Connection Failed
6- BGP Transport Connection Fatal Error
7- Connect Retry Timer Expired

8- Hold Timer Expired
9- Keep Alive Timer Expired
10- Receive Open Message
11- Receive Keep Alive Message
12- Receive Update Message
13- Receive Notification Message

Note: Whenever BGP transitions from established to idle state, it closes the TCP connection and withdraws all routes learned on that connection.

Whenever a BGP speaker encounters any problem, it sends a Notification message and transitions to the idle state. More importantly, any time a BGP speaker changes its state from established to idle, it closes the TCP connection and deletes all routes derived from that connection. As discussed previously, this particular protocol action results in route flaps. The next section describes a mechanism that allows a BGP speaker to restart and reestablish sessions in a graceful manner.

Exchange of Routing Information

After having established the session, the two BGP peers are ready for exchanging routing information. Initially, BGP peers exchange complete routing table information with each other. After the initial routing information transfer is complete, only incremental updates are exchanged as a result of routing changes.

The BGP incremental update approach requires less link bandwidth and fewer control processor resources as compared to the periodic exchange of the entire routing table. Routing information is exchanged between pairs of BGP peers in the Update message. In general, an Update message can be used to advertise a single feasible route, or to withdraw multiple unfeasible routes, or to simultaneously advertise a feasible route and withdraw multiple unfeasible routes.

A feasible route is the association of the path attributes (contained in the Path Attributes field) with one or more IP destination prefixes (contained in the NLRI field). The Update message contains fields such as NLRI (to advertise a set of reachable IP destination address prefixes), Path Attributes, and Withdrawn Routes (see Figure 6-4).

Figure 6-4   *BGP Update Message*

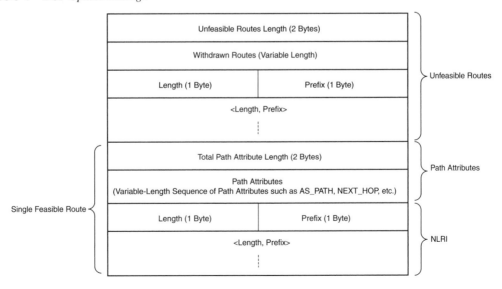

For a feasible route, each destination is advertised as an IP address prefix in the NLRI field and encoded as a <length, prefix> tuple. The Path Attributes field contains a set of path attributes, and each attribute is encoded as an <attribute type, attribute length, attribute value> triple. All path attributes contained in the Path Attributes field apply to all the IP prefixes in the NLRI field. That is why an Update message can advertise a single feasible route. In contrast, because BGP can unambiguously identify a route to be withdrawn based on its destination address prefix in the Withdrawn Routes field, an Update message can withdraw multiple routes simultaneously. When there is no route to be advertised, the NLRI field is either not present or is empty.

Internal and External Speakers

BGP speakers can be categorized as internal or external. When a session that is formed between speakers in different autonomous systems, it is known as the *external BGP* (eBGP) session and the two speakers are external peers to each other. Similarly, when a BGP session that is formed between two speakers in the same AS, it is referred to as the *internal BGP* (iBGP) session. In this case, the two speakers are internal peers.

How does a speaker know whether its peer is internal or external? During the BGP session-establishment process, the two speakers exchange AS numbers that help to determine whether a peer is internal or external. For example, when a speaker receives an AS number that is the same as its own, the speaker knows that the peer is internal and vice versa.

In what other aspects do iBGP and eBGP differ? For one, BGP requires that an eBGP session be established between directly connected routers, but there is no such restriction for iBGP sessions. Another important difference lies in the way BGP advertises and processes routes on iBGP and eBGP sessions. For example, when a BGP speaker receives a route advertisement on an eBGP session, the receiving speaker can re-advertise this route on both iBGP and eBGP sessions (see Figure 6-5).

In contrast, if the route advertisement were received on an iBGP, the receiving speaker could have re-advertised this route to external but not to the internal peers (see Figure 6-6). From this description, it follows that to ensure propagation of routing information to all BGP speakers inside an AS, a full iBGP session mesh must be maintained. The requirement to maintain a full mesh of iBGP sessions introduces certain scalability issues. A practical solution to this problem is described later.

Figure 6-5   *BGP Advertisements on eBGP Sessions*

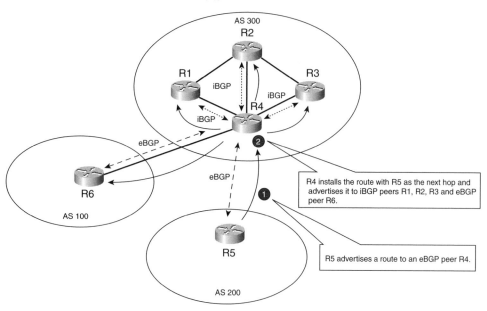

Figure 6-6   *BGP Advertisements on iBGP Sessions*

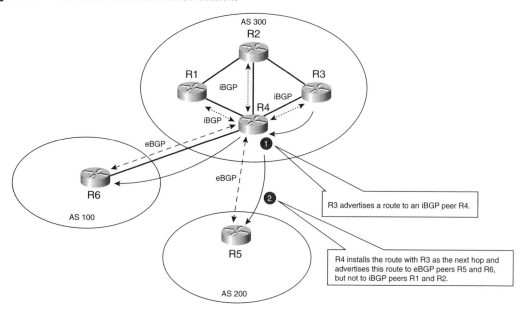

BGP Path Attributes

There are four types of BGP path attributes, as follows:

- **Well-known mandatory**—An attribute that is recognized by all BGP implementations and must be included in every Update message.

- **Well-known discretionary**—An attribute that is recognized by all BGP implementations but its inclusion in every Update message is optional.

- **Optional transitive**—An attribute that may not be known to all BGP implementations and its inclusion in every Update message is optional. A receiver should accept it and then pass it on to the other BGP peers.

- **Optional nontransitive**—An attribute that may not be known to all BGP implementations. Its inclusion in every Update message is optional. If not recognized, a receiver should silently ignore it and not pass it to other BGP peers.

AS_PATH and NEXT_HOP Attributes

This section briefly describes two important attributes known as AS_PATH and NEXT_HOP. AS_PATH is a well-known mandatory path attribute that must be present in every Update message. This attribute identifies the autonomous systems traversed by routing information contained in the Update message. The numbers of traversed autonomous systems are recorded either as an ordered sequence (called AS_SEQUENCE list) or as an unordered sequence (called AS_SET list). When a BGP speaker originates a route to an external peer, it includes its own AS number in the AS_PATH attribute of the Update message. In contrast, whenever a BGP speaker originates a route to an internal peer, it includes an empty AS_PATH attribute (AS_PATH attribute with a Length field set to 0) in the Update message. When a BGP speaker advertises a route learned from an internal peer to an external peer, it includes its own AS number in the AS_PATH attribute list. However, when a BGP speaker advertises a route learned from an internal peer to another internal peer, it does not modify the AS_PATH attribute (see Figure 6-7).

The information contained in the Update message allows a BGP speaker to construct a topology graph that describes the relationships (interconnections) of the various autonomous systems. In particular, BGP uses the AS_PATH attribute to construct a loop-free AS topology graph. For example, a BGP speaker does not accept an Update message when it finds its own AS number in the AS_PATH attribute. In addition, the selection of best routes during the BGP decision process (which is described later) is based on path attributes. For instance, when there are multiple routes to choose from, BGP prefers the route with the shortest AS_PATH attribute. Thus a BGP speaker can influence interdomain routing behavior by manipulating the AS_PATH attribute. To apply certain input and output policies (filtering) and to manipulate path attributes (to influence decision process), the candidate routes must first be identified. A BGP speaker often uses the AS_PATH attribute to identify a set of routes that match the specified criterion.

Figure 6-7   *BGP AS_Path Attribute Advertisement*

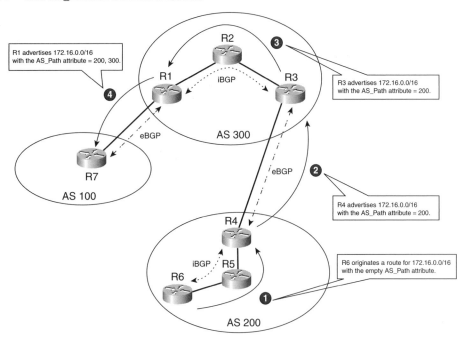

The NEXT_HOP attribute is a well-known mandatory path attribute that must also be present in every Update message. This path attribute contains the IP address of the border BGP router that is to be used as a next hop when forwarding traffic for destinations contained in the NLRI field of the Update message.

It is important to note that the notion of next hop in BGP is quite different from that in IGPs. In IGPs, for example, next hop always specifies the IP address of the directly connected neighbor. However, this is not always true for the BGP. For instance, when a route is learned from an external peer, the BGP next hop for this route is the IP address of the external peer. If this learned route is in turn advertised to internal peers, the received NEXT_HOP attribute is passed on without any modifications. The BGP next hop for a route originated inside the AS is the IP address of the router that originated the route (see Figure 6-8).

From this description, it follows that the BGP next hop does not always represent the IP address of a directly connected neighbor. For example, R1 and R4 are not directly connected and yet R4 is a BGP next hop for R1. For the case when the BGP next hop is not directly connected, to be able to forward a data packet, the immediate next hop that leads to the BGP next hop must be found. A BGP speaker determines the immediate next-hop interface associated with the address contained in the NEXT_HOP attribute by performing one or more lookups in the IGP routing table. Because a BGP route with an unreachable NEXT_HOP is considered inaccessible, it is excluded from the BGP decision process.

Figure 6-8 *BGP NEXT_HOP Attribute Advertisement*

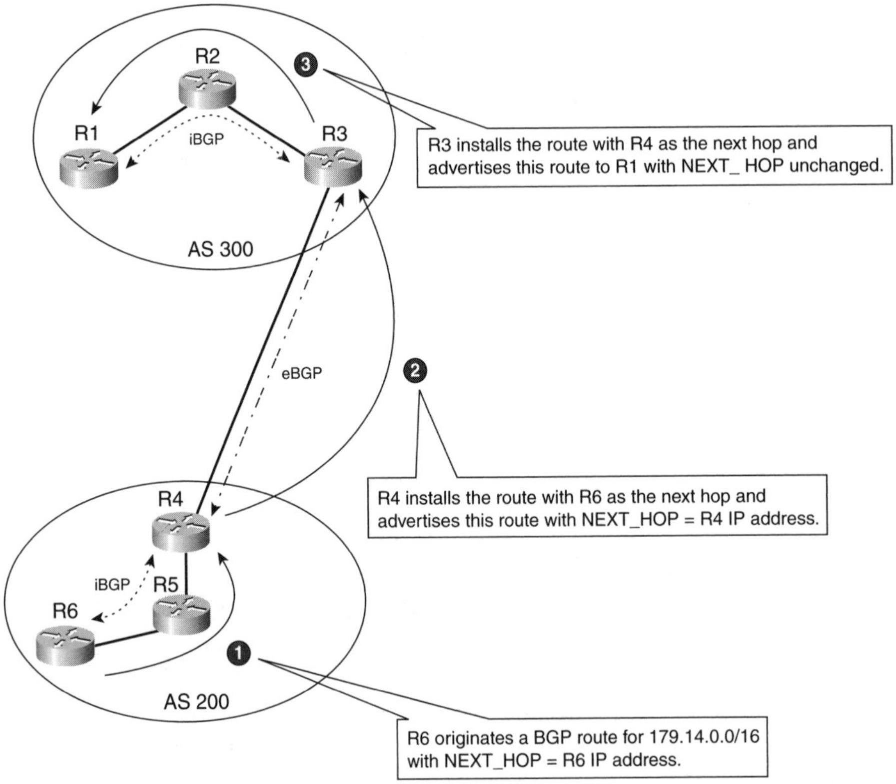
R2
R1
iBGP
R3
3
R3 installs the route with R4 as the next hop and advertises this route to R1 with NEXT_ HOP unchanged.
AS 300
eBGP
2
R4
R4 installs the route with R6 as the next hop and advertises this route with NEXT_HOP = R4 IP address.
iBGP
R5
R6
1
AS 200
R6 originates a BGP route for 179.14.0.0/16 with NEXT_HOP = R6 IP address.

Routing Information Bases of BGP Speakers

Each BGP speaker maintains three different RIBs to store routes. The RIBs can be categorized as Adj-RIBs-In, Adj-RIBs-Out, and Loc-RIB. The Adj-RIBs-In contains the unprocessed routes that have been received from peers. The routes in the Adj-RIBs-In are used as input to the BGP decision process. The Loc-RIB contains the routes that have been selected by the BGP decision process for use in the local speaker. The routes in the Loc-RIB are in turn installed in the FIB that is used for forwarding data packets.

The Adj-RIBs-Out contains routes that have been selected for advertisements to peers via Update messages. Although conceptually there are three distinct copies of RIBs, in practice an implementation actually may maintain only one copy of the RIB.

BGP Route-Selection Process

BGP takes Adj-RIBs-In as input and goes through a three-phase decision process to select and advertise the best routes for each destination. In the first phase, a BGP speaker determines a degree of preference for each route learned from a neighbor. The degree of preference for a route is either based on a path attribute (such as LOCAL_PREF) or on a preconfigured local policy. In the second phase, the decision process selects the best routes out of all available routes for each destination and installs the selected routes in the Loc-RIB. A route with an unfeasible BGP next-hop address is excluded in the second phase of the decision function. The third phase takes routes in the Loc-RIB as input, processes them (performs outgoing filtering and attribute manipulation to affect the desired routing behavior), and selects routes for the Adj-RIBs-Out. The routes in the Adj-RIBs-Out are advertised to peers. A functional view of the BGP routing components is depicted in Figure 6-9.

Figure 6-9   *Functional View of the BGP Operation*

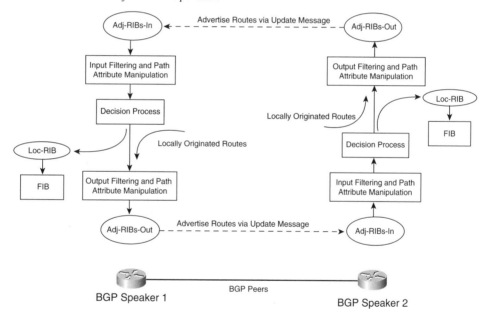

BGP Route Reflection

As mentioned earlier, a route advertisement that is received on an iBGP session is not re-advertised to other internal peers. Therefore, for propagating external routing information to all BGP routers inside the AS, a full iBGP session mesh is required. For a large AS, say in the order of several hundred iBGP sessions, it becomes impractical to manage such a large number of sessions. To avoid iBGP session mesh and yet still be able to propagate routing information to all BGP routers inside the AS, the route reflector (RR) concept is used.[3] The RR is a BGP speaking router that performs the RR function (see Figure 6-10).

Figure 6-10 *BGP Route Reflection Function*

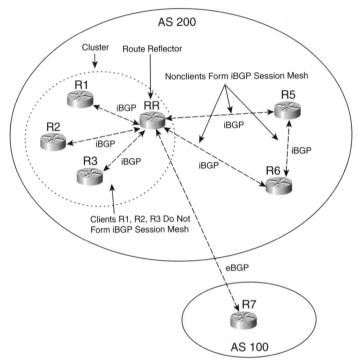

The internal peers of the RR router are called *clients*. An RR router along with its clients forms a *cluster*. All other BGP peers of the RR, which are not part of the cluster, are referred to as *nonclients*. A full session mesh is maintained between the RR and the nonclients. The clients do not peer outside their own clusters. A RR performs the route reflection function as follows:

- A route that is received from an external peer is reflected to all client and nonclient peers.

- A route received from a nonclient peer is reflected to all client peers only.

- A route received from a client peer is reflected to all other clients excluding the originator.

Mitigating the Detrimental Effects of the BGP Restart

To sum up the earlier discussion, BGP restart causes route flaps, which can lead to transient black holes and increased consumption of link bandwidth and control processor resources. Thus route flaps can degrade the overall network performance.

The source of route flaps can be traced back to the BGP restart behavior—specifically, deletion of routes derived from the failed session. As mentioned previously, peers withdraw routes from a restarting speaker to find alternative paths to avoid forwarding traffic into a black hole. However, if the restarting router were capable of preserving the FIB across the restart and there were no changes in the network while the RIB is being rebuilt and before the FIB is updated, it would be relatively safe without causing black holes and loops to keep forwarding. In general, black holes and forwarding loops are always possible in any network; however, in a network that is relatively stable during the recovery, forwarding based on the preserved FIB should not be an issue. In that case, it will not be necessary or desirable to withdraw routes from the restarting peer. Therefore, it would be possible to eliminate route flaps if somehow the restarting speaker could inform peers about its capability to preserve the FIB across the restart. And the peers in turn, instead of withdrawing routes on detection of the restart, could continue to forward while the concerned speaker restarts and reestablishes its BGP sessions. In that case, with the exception of peers, the BGP restart event could be concealed from all other speakers. The BGP graceful restart mechanism, as described in the next section, proposes a solution along similar lines.

BGP Graceful Restart Mechanism

Normally when the BGP control plane in a router restarts, its BGP sessions to the peers are lost. Upon detection of the BGP session failure, peers withdraw all routes associated with the failed session. The neighboring routers first withdraw, but then quickly re-advertise the affected routes as their peer restarts. This set of actions leads to route flaps. The aforementioned BGP behavior is based on the fact that the restarting router is incapable of forwarding across the restart. However, if the faults were confined to the control plane and the restarting router was capable of preserving the FIB across the control-plane restart, it would be desirable to keep the restarting router in the forwarding path and avoid route flaps.

Exchange of Graceful Restart Capability

The BGP graceful restart mechanism defines protocol extensions that allow a speaker to indicate NSF capability to its peers during the initial BGP session-establishment process.[4] For this purpose, a new BGP capability known as *graceful restart capability* is defined that is carried in the Open message. The neighboring speakers exchange graceful restart capability in the Open message during BGP session establishment. When a speaker is capable of preserving the FIB across a BGP control-plane restart, it announces its capability to preserve the concerned forwarding state in the graceful restart capability, which is tantamount to saying, "For each address family listed here, I am capable of preserving the associated forwarding state across the BGP restart. When my BGP control-plane restarts, please continue to forward data traffic to me as before, and don't withdraw routes for the aforementioned address families. If I don't reestablish the failed session within a certain time (as indicated in the Restart Time field), you should delete all routes that were being retained across the restart and stop forwarding traffic on those routes."

As a result of having exchanged the graceful restart capability, when a router restarts that had previously expressed its capability to preserve the FIB across the restart, its neighbors retain routes learned from the restarting router, but mark them as stale. Assuming the restarting router is ready for communicating with peers within the previously advertised restart time, it reestablishes a BGP session and again exchanges graceful restart capability exchange in the Open message.

In the new graceful restart capability exchange, the restarting router informs its neighbors whether it was actually able to preserve its forwarding state, which it had indicated in the previous (pre-restart) graceful restart capability. Assuming the restarting router actually had managed to preserve the pertinent forwarding state, the peers exchange routing information again, select the best routes, and update the FIB. Because peers do not withdraw routes and keep the restarting router on the forwarding path, traffic passing through the restarting router is not disrupted. This means that, other than the immediate peers who act as helper nodes, the BGP restart event is completely concealed from all other speakers. Thus the BGP graceful restart mechanism helps to eliminate the negative effects of the normal BGP restart.

An observant reader might ask what if things do not go as smoothly as planned during the restart. For example, suppose a router had indicated its capability to preserve the forwarding state for an address family (say IPv4), but actually could not preserve it across the restart. The neighbors honoring the pre-restart capability exchange and unaware of the actual situation would continue to forward IPv4 data traffic, which would be black holed. After restarting, the restarted router realizes that it actually cannot preserve the forwarding state for the concerned address family and indicates so by clearing a certain bit (the F bit, as described later) in the post-restart graceful restart capability. Upon receiving the new graceful restart capability, the neighbors will immediately remove the concerned routes and stop forwarding traffic on those routes. Thus even if something goes wrong during the restart, the BGP graceful restart mechanism provides a way out by reverting to the normal restart procedure.

The graceful restart capability exchange between neighboring speakers implies that the restarting speaker must be NSF-capable and that the restarting router and its neighbors must be able to support the graceful restart procedure. As long as a router can act as a helper node for the restarting neighbor, but its own BGP control plane does not restart, the BGP graceful restart mechanism does not care whether the helper node itself is NSF-capable. In general, however, BGP restart can occur in any BGP router in the network. Therefore, for a least-disruptive BGP restart operation, all BGP speakers should be graceful restart- as well as NSF-capable.

Suppose, for instance, that the restarting speaker and all its peers can support the graceful restart mechanism. Furthermore, suppose the restarting speaker is not capable of preserving its FIB across the restart. When the BGP control plane on this speaker restarts, it causes route flaps and the associated harmful effects. In this case, because the restarting speaker is NSF-incapable, peers withdraw routes to avoid forwarding data traffic into the black hole. After the restart, the restarting speaker reforms BGP sessions, the peers relearn routes from the restarting peer, and then these peers announce these routes to their own peers.

All this could have been avoided had the restarting router been NSF-capable. In general, the BGP restart mechanism can be supported on routers with or without the capability to preserve the FIB across the restart. However, as explained later, for maximum benefit, all BGP routers must be able to support not only the graceful restart extensions but must also be NSF-capable. Nonetheless, supporting the BGP graceful restart mechanism alone without NSF capability does have utility. For instance, such a router still enables the neighbor to restart in a graceful manner by acting as a helper node.

BGP Graceful Restart Capability Format

The format of the graceful restart capability is shown in Figure 6-11. It contains multiple fields such as Restart Flags, Restart Time in Seconds, Address Family Identifier (AFI), Subsequent Address Family Identifier (SAFI), and Flags for Address Family. Restart Flags is a 4-bit field; however, only the most significant bit, referred to as Restart State (R) bit, is defined. A BGP graceful restart-capable speaker sets this bit to 1 to announce the fact that it has restarted. Upon receipt of graceful restart capability with the R bit set, the receiving peer no longer waits for the arrival of the End-Of-RIB marker from the restarting speaker before advertising route information to the speaker.

Figure 6-11 *BGP Graceful Restart Capability*

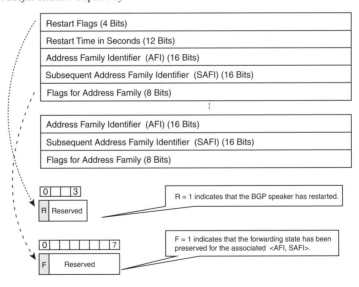

The BGP graceful restart mechanism defines an Update message with no reachable NLRI and an empty, withdrawn NLRI as the End-Of-RIB marker. A BGP speaker sends the End-Of-RIB marker to indicate to its peers the completion of the initial routing update. The End-Of-RIB marker helps to speed up the routing convergence.

The Restart Time in Seconds field specifies the time taken by the sender to reestablish the BGP session after a restart. For a graceful restart operation, the restart time should be smaller than the hold time. This is because if the graceful restart operation takes longer than the hold time, the restarting speaker's peers would consider it to be dead (unreachable) and would terminate their BGP sessions to the restarting speaker.

The AFI field identifies the network layer protocol (such as IPv4, IPv6) for which the support of the graceful restart capability is being advertised. Therefore, for each address family, a separate AFI field is included to identify each such address family. The SAFI field provides further information about the address family being advertised in the AFI field, such as NLRI for unicast forwarding, NLRI for multicast forwarding, and NLRI with MPLS labels.[5]

The Flags for Address Family field contains flags for the <AFI, SAFI> fields. A BGP speaker indicates its capability to preserve the forwarding state for each address family by including the appropriate <AFI, SAFI> information in the graceful restart capability during pre-restart session establishment. As discussed earlier, it is possible that a speaker can support graceful restart extensions, but is NSF-incapable. When a sender includes the graceful restart capability in the Open message, however, and the <AFI, SAFI> field is missing, it indicates that the sender supports the graceful restart mechanism, but is incapable of preserving the FIB across the restart.

The most significant bit in the Restart Flag field is referred to as the *Forwarding State (F) bit*. After the restart, the restarting BGP speaker sets the F bit to 1 for each <AFI, SAFI> for which it was able to persevere the forwarding state across the restart. For example, suppose a speaker had previously (before restart) indicated its capability to preserve a forwarding state by including <AFI, SAFI> for IPv4 and IPv6 address families. If the router is actually able only to preserve the IPv4 forwarding state across the restart, it sets the F bit (to 1) for the IPv4 address family, but clears it (to 0) for the IPv6 address family.

The BGP graceful restart mechanism requires special protocol behavior from a graceful restart-capable router and its neighbors. In the following sections, the term *restarting speaker* refers to a router whose BGP control-plane component has restarted, and the term *helper speaker* refers to a router that peers with the restarting router.

Restarting BGP Speaker Behavior

During initial BGP session establishment (before BGP restart), the speaker advertises its capability to preserve the forwarding state for an address family by including <AFI, SAFI> fields in the graceful restart capability. In addition, the speaker advertises the estimated time it will take to reestablish the session after a BGP restart. The following discussion assumes that the speaker not only supports graceful restart extensions, but also is capable of preserving its forwarding state across the restart.

When the BGP control plane in the speaker restarts, it continues to forward data traffic using the preserved FIB. After restarting, for each address family for which the restarting speaker had expressed its capability to preserve a forwarding state before the restart, the speaker checks whether it was actually able to preserve the relevant forwarding state across the restart.

Assuming this is the case, the restarting speaker now marks the BGP-derived forwarding state as stale and starts a stale timer. The restarting speaker, however, continues to use the stale information for forwarding. The objective of the stale timer is to avoid retaining the stale forwarding information indefinitely. Then the restarting speaker attempts to reestablish a session with its peers and exchanges the graceful restart capability. The restarting speaker sets the R bit (value 1) to inform its peers about the BGP control-plane restart. In addition, for each address family for which the restarting speaker was able to preserve the forwarding state across the BGP restart, it sets the F bit (value 1) to indicate the fact that the restarting speaker was able to preserve forwarding state for the corresponding address family across its BGP restart.

After the BGP session has been reestablished, the restarting router receives BGP Update messages from its peers and rebuilds its Adj-RIBs-In. Note that RIB is not preserved across the restart; therefore, the restarting speaker rebuilds its RIB through routing information exchange with the peers after the restart. Because route selection cannot take place until the RIB is rebuilt completely, for each address family the restarting router defers its route-selection process until it has received the End-Of-RIB marker from all its peers. In fact, the restarting speaker does not need to wait for End-Of-RIB markers from those peers that have restarted and those that are not graceful restart capable, because these peers are not expected to send or not capable of sending the End-Of-RIB marker.

To avoid waiting for the arrival of End-Of-RIB markers and deferring the route-selection process indefinitely, the restarting router uses a (configurable) delay timer. When the delay timer has expired, the route-selection process is run even though all the End-Of-RIB markers may not have been received yet. After the restarting router has selected the routes, it updates its Loc-RIB, FIB, Adj-RIBs-Out and advertises selected routes to peers. On completion of the initial update for an address family, the restarting speaker sends an End-Of-RIB marker to all its peers.

Recall that after restarting, the speaker had marked all preserved routes as stale and started a stale timer. After the restarting speaker had rebuilt the RIB and run the decision process, all valid routes should have been updated in the FIB. If some forwarding entries are still marked as stale, these correspond to invalid routes that need to be removed. Therefore, when the stale state timer expires, any remaining stale forwarding entries are deleted.

Helper BGP Speaker Behavior

Upon detection of the BGP session failure with the graceful restart-capable peer, the helper speaker starts the restart timer. The value of the restart timer is exchanged in the graceful restart capability during the initial session establishment (prior to peer's restart). For each address family, the helper speaker retains all routes received from the restarting peer for which the restarting peer had previously expressed its capability to preserve the forwarding state across the restart. The helper speaker marks the aforementioned routes as stale and starts a stale timer. While the restart timer is running, the helper speaker continues to use the stale routes for forwarding data traffic and waits for the restarting peer to reestablish the session. If the restarting peer does not reestablish the BGP session before the restart time expiration, the helper speaker deletes the stale routes that were being retained across the restart. Otherwise, when the BGP session has been successfully reestablished, the helper speaker cancels the restart timer and processes the newly received graceful restart capability. If the F bit for an address family is not set, or if the address family is absent in the newly received graceful restart capability, or if the graceful restart capability is not advertised at all in the newly received Open message, the helper speaker immediately removes the stale routes learned from the restarting router. Otherwise, for each address family that appears with the F bit set, the helper peer continues to retain the stale routes.

The helper speaker advertises BGP updates from the Adj-RIBs-Out to the restarting peer, and upon completion of the initial update for an address family, it sends an End-Of-RIB marker. After having updated the RIB and run the decision process, the restarting speaker in turn advertises new routes. The helper speaker replaces the stale routes by the routing updates received from the restarting speaker. Upon receipt of the End-Of-RIB marker from the restarting speaker for an address family, the helper speaker runs the decision process and updates the routes for that address family.

At this stage, all valid routes for the concerned address family should have been updated. Therefore, when the End-Of-RIB marker is received for an address family, any routes that are still marked as stale are immediately removed. To avoid waiting for arrival of all the End-Of-RIB markers and retain stale routes indefinitely, the restarting router uses a (configurable) stale timer. As mentioned earlier, the stale timer is started on detection of the session failure. When the stale timer expires, the helper speaker router deletes all routes that are still marked as stale.

Operation of the BGP Graceful Restart Mechanism

This section describes the operation of the BGP graceful restart mechanism using the network diagram shown in Figure 6-12. Both routers R1 and R2 are assumed to be graceful restart-capable as well as NSF-capable. The sequence of steps described in this section is not necessarily followed by a specific implementation. The objective of this description is to provide a functional view of the BGP graceful restart operation.

Figure 6-12 *Example of the BGP Graceful Restart Operation*

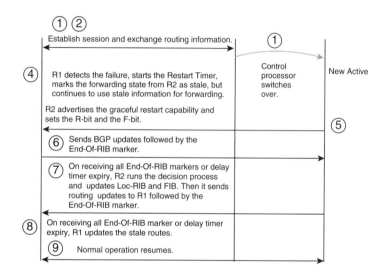

1. R1 and R2 establish BGP session and exchange the graceful restart capability to indicate their capability to preserve forwarding state during BGP restart. For the sake of brevity, suppose that only IPv4 addresses are supported. In general, however, the same procedure applies to other address families such as IPv6.

2. R1 and R2 exchange routing information using normal BGP procedures.

3. Assume in R2 the BGP control-plane restarts and the control processor switches over.

4. R1 detects the failure of the BGP session with R2. Because R1 knows that that R2 is capable of preserving the forwarding state across the restart, R1 starts the restart timer within which R2 is expected to reestablish the session. However, R1 retains the routes received from R2 for all the address families that were advertised by R2 in the graceful restart capability before its BGP restart, marks these routes as stale, and starts a stale timer. R1 continues to use the stale routes for forwarding while the restart timer is running. R1 waits for R2 to reestablish the BGP session. If the BGP session were not established within restart time, R1 would delete all stale routes from R2.

5. Assume R2 is able to preserve the BGP-related forwarding state across the restart for the IPv4 address family. After restarting, R2 marks the preserved forwarding state as stale and starts a stale timer, but continues to use the stale information for forwarding. R2 tries to establish the BGP session with R1. During the session-reestablishment process, R2 includes the graceful restart capability with the R bit set. In addition, because R2 was able to preserve the forwarding state for the IPv4 address family, it sets the F bit for the IPv4 address family. In general, R2 would need to set the F bit for each address family for which it was able to preserve the forwarding state.

6. On BGP session reestablishment, R1 stops the restart timer and processes the newly received graceful restart capability from R2. Because the F bit for the IPv4 address family is set, R1 continues to retain the forwarding state marked as stale. However, if the F bit for an address family were not set in the newly received graceful restart capability, R1 would have immediately removed all stale routes from R2 for that address family. For each address family, R1 sends BGP updates from its Adj-RIBs-Out to R2. Upon completion of the initial update for an address family, R1 sends the End-Of-RIB marker to R2.

7. R2 receives BGP Update messages from its peers, processes these messages, and rebuilds its Adj-RIBs-In. However, R2 defers (for a configurable time) its BGP route-selection process for an address family until it receives an End-Of-RIB marker from all its nonrestarting peers. After R2 has done the route selection, it updates its Loc-RIB, FIB, and Adj-RIBs-Out and advertises its routes to its peers. On completion of the initial update for an address family, R2 in turn sends an End-Of-RIB marker to all its peers. To avoid deferring route selection indefinitely, R2 uses a delay timer. When the delay timer expires, R2 runs the route-selection process, even if not all End-Of-RIB markers have been received.

8. R1 replaces the stale routes in Adj-RIBs-In with the routing updates received from R2. On receiving the End-Of-RIB marker for an address family, R1 deletes any routes from R2 that are still marked as stale for that address family. R1 runs the decision process and updates the Loc-RIB, FIB, and Adj-RIBs-Out. To avoid waiting indefinitely for the arrival of all the End-Of-RIB markers and to avoid retaining stale routes, the helper speaker uses a (configurable) stale timer. When the stale timer expires, R1 deletes all routes still marked as stale.

9. Normal operation resumes.

Network-Deployment Considerations

As discussed earlier, two capabilities are essential to the successful operation of the graceful restart mechanism:

- Capability to support graceful restart protocol extensions
- Capability to preserve forwarding state across the restart

Insofar as the restarting speaker is concerned, the BGP graceful restart mechanism requires that it must not only be able to support graceful restart extensions, but also be NSF-capable. As far as the helper speaker is concerned, BGP graceful restart requires that it must be graceful restart-capable (support protocol extensions); however, it is not required to be NSF-capable. This means that BGP graceful restart-related protocol extensions and behavior could be supported in routers with or without the capability to preserve the forwarding state across the restart.

One may ask, "What is the use of graceful restart capability without NSF capability?" The fact that a router can be BGP restart-capable but NSF-incapable has very important practical utility, because in real network deployments not all routers may be capable of supporting the preservation and using it for forwarding state across BGP restart. By being able to support graceful restart extensions and able to act as a helper node, such routers can still help to reduce the harmful effects of a BGP restart in peers. However, when a BGP restart can occur in any speaker in the network, to derive the most benefits from BGP graceful restart capability, all BGP speakers must be BGP graceful restart- and NSF-capable. In general, NSF capability is relatively more important for an edge router than a core router. This is because the core network is generally designed to protect against core router failures by being mesh connected. This allows alternative paths to be quickly established and used in the face of a link/node failure. That is, in the core network, redundant routers and additional links are used to provide fault tolerance. In contrast, on the edge, often thousands of customers will be connected via a single router. Thus the edge router usually represents a single point of failure.

Another aspect that needs careful examination when deploying BGP graceful capability is interaction between IGP and BGP. In many routers, IP control-plane components such as OSPF, IS-IS, and BGP not only reside on the same control processor, but are also tightly coupled. This means that every BGP restart is accompanied by the OSPF and IS-IS restart and vice versa. In such situations, to reduce the negative effects of BGP and IGP restart, routers should be capable of supporting not only BGP but also IGP restart capabilities (described in Chapters 4 and 5). In terms of NSF capability, this means, the router must be able to preserve the BGP-derived forwarding state as well as the IGP-derived forwarding state. When both BGP and IGP restart, because BGP relies on IGP for TCP connectivity and for determining the next-hop reachability, it is better to wait for IGP convergence before carrying out the BGP route selection. On the surface this seems to pose a problem for BGP in terms of increasing the convergence time. In practice, however, this should not be the case because IGPs typically converge much faster (for example, in the order of seconds) than BGP (for example, in the order of minutes). The following interoperability scenarios involve peers with diverse sets of graceful restart and NSF capabilities.

Scenario 1: R1/R2 Are BGP Graceful Restart- and NSF-Capable

You have already examined this scenario in the previous section. In this case, because the restarting speaker and its helper peers are BGP graceful restart- and NSF-capable, the BGP-related IP forwarding state is not affected by the BGP control-plane restart in either speaker (see Figure 6-13). Therefore, to derive a network-wide benefit from the BGP graceful restart capabilities, all BGP speakers in the AS must be graceful restart-capable as well as NFS-capable.

Figure 6-13 *BGP Graceful Restart Interoperability Scenarios*

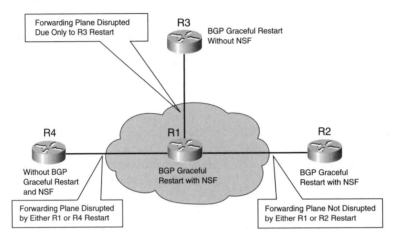

Scenario 2: R1 Is BGP Restart- and NSF-Capable, but R3 Is Only BGP Restart-Capable

This scenario is important for the deployment in which a BGP peer is graceful restart-capable but does not support NSF capability. In this case, when the BGP control plane in R1 restarts, R1's forwarding plane is not affected because R1 is graceful restart- and NSF-capable, and R3 being graceful restart-capable can act as the helper speaker. However, the situation is different for BGP restart in R3. Because R3 is NSF-incapable, it would have advertised this (for example, by not advertising <AFI, SAFI> in the graceful restart capability) during session establishment before the restart. Therefore, upon detection of session failure with R3, R1 reverts to the normal BGP restart behavior. This means that R1 immediately removes all routes learned from R3 and withdraws those routes from peers. Therefore, BGP restart in a speaker that is BGP graceful restart-capable but that is incapable of preserving the IP forwarding state across the restart does not reduce the negative effects. However, a speaker that is graceful restart-capable but NSF-incapable does help to reduce harmful effects by acting as the helper node when a BGP graceful restart- and NSF-capable peer restarts (see Figure 6-13).

Scenario 3: R1 Is BGP Graceful Restart- and NSF-Capable, but R4 Is BGP Graceful Restart- and NSF-Incapable

In this case, BGP restart in either speaker does not mitigate the negative effects on other speakers. This means that to get any benefit from a BGP graceful restart- and NSF-capable speaker, at a minimum its peers must be BGP graceful restart-capable.

Summary

This chapter described the BGP graceful restart mechanism, which allows a BGP speaker to restart without causing undesirable effects on the forwarding and control plane. For a clear insight into the BGP graceful restart mechanism, its operation was explained through multiple deployment scenarios.

References

[1] RFC 1771, "A Border Gateway Protocol 4 (BGP-4)," T. Li and Y. Rekhter, March 1995.

[2] Labovitz, C., R. Malan, and F. Jahanian, "Internet Routing Stability," IEEE/ACM Trans. Networking, 515–528, October 1998.

[3] Halabi, S., *Internet Routing Architectures*, Second Edition. (Indianapolis: Cisco Press, 2000).

[4] Sangli, S., et al., "Graceful Restart Mechanism for BGP," IETF Draft, Work in progress.

[5] RFC 2858, "Multiprotocol Extensions for BGP-4," T. Bates, R. Chandra, D. Katz, and Y. Rekhter, June 2000.

CHAPTER 7

MPLS Control Plane: Restarting BGP with MPLS Gracefully

Chapter 6, "Interdomain IP Control Plane: Restarting BGP Gracefully," described the *Border Gateway Protocol* (BGP) graceful restart mechanism for the case when BGP is used to distribute IP routes. This chapter examines the harmful effects of the BGP restart when BGP is used to distribute labeled IP routes. This chapter also describes a mechanism to reduce the negative effects of BGP with MPLS restart.

The material in this chapter builds on the concepts covered in Chapter 3, "MPLS Forwarding Plane: Achieving Nonstop Forwarding," and in Chapter 6. Therefore, before proceeding with the description of BGP with an MPLS restart mechanism, this chapter summarizes some key concepts from those two chapters.

MPLS Control- and Forwarding-Plane Components

Even though IP and MPLS forwarding schemes are quite different, the two are similar in many ways. For example, conventional IP routers forward packets by looking up the IP destination address in the *Forwarding Information Base* (FIB). In contrast, a *label-switching router* (LSR) makes its forwarding decision by performing a label lookup in the Label *Forwarding Information Base* (LFIB).

The forwarding state in the FIB is derived from the routing information distributed by IP control-plane protocols such as OSPF, IS-IS, and BGP. The forwarding state in the LFIB is derived from the label information distributed by the MPLS control-plane protocols such as *Label Distribution Protocol* (LDP), *Resource ReSerVation Protocol* (RSVP), and BGP. In short, the FIB contains the IP forwarding state derived from multiple routing protocols, whereas the LFIB holds the MPLS forwarding state derived from multiple label-distribution protocols.

To set up a proper context for the BGP with MPLS restart discussion, the following section provides an overview of a few concepts from Chapter 3.

MPLS Network Components

An MPLS network is composed of the interconnection of LSRs, namely, edge and transit LSRs. Edge LSRs reside at the boundary of an MPLS network. In the ingress to the MPLS network, an edge LSR turns unlabeled packets over to the labeled packets. To accomplish this, the edge LSR performs an IP address lookup in the FIB to map the IP address to a particular *forwarding equivalence class* (FEC). After the FEC has been determined, the LSR looks in the LFIB to obtain both the FEC-to-outgoing label mapping and the outgoing interface.

In the egress direction, the edge LSR strips off the labels of the packets and sends them out as unlabeled. In this case, the LSR uses the top label (incoming label) to perform a label lookup in the LFIB to determine the out-label stack operation (which should indicate a pop operation to strip off the label stack completely). In some cases, the egress edge LSR does not usually receive a labeled packet. In such cases, the LSR before the egress LS (known as the *penultimate LSR*) pops the label (referred to as the *penultimate-hop popping*) and sends an unlabeled packet to the egress edge LSR. For complete details, see Chapter 3.

Depending on the application, an LSR might perform one or more additional IP address lookups before forwarding the packet. For example, when an egress LSR associates a single label to a set of IP routes by aggregating them into one route, the egress LSR usually requires one or more additional IP lookups to de-aggregate the route and forward packets on a more specific route. Unlike edge LSRs, because transit LSRs receive and transmit labeled packets, they need to perform only label lookups.

Layer 2 and Layer 3 Virtual Private Network Services

A *virtual private network* (VPN) is a set of customer sites interconnected over a shared network infrastructure (known as the *VPN backbone*). The backbone consists of a packet-switched network and customer devices connected to the edge LSRs via attachment circuits such as a Frame Relay (FR) data link connection identifier (DLCI), an *Asynchronous Transfer Mode* (ATM) *virtual path identifier/virtual circuit identifier* (VPI/VCI), an Ethernet port, a *virtual LAN* (VLAN), a *Point-to-Point Protocol* (PPP) connection on a physical interface, and so forth. Two types of VPN services can be offered by the edge LSRs: Layer 2 and Layer 3 services (see Figure 7-1).

- In the case of Layer 2 services, when an edge LSR receives a frame from a customer, it determines how to forward the packet by considering both the packet's incoming link and the Layer 2 information in the frame header, such as the FR, ATM, and Ethernet header. This type of VPN service is called a *Layer 2 virtual private network* (L2VPN).

- In the case of Layer 3 services, when an edge LSR receives a packet from a customer, it determines how to forward the packet by considering both the packet's incoming link and the Layer 3 information in the packet's header, such as the IP header. This type of VPN service is called a *Layer 3 virtual private network* (L3VPN). In L3VPNs, a customer may attach to an edge LSR using a Layer 2 service such as an FR DLCI, an ATM VPI/VCI, and an Ethernet port. However, Layer 2 services in this case are terminated at the edge LSR where the customer's IP packets are removed from any Layer 2 frames.

- In the case of MPLS-based VPNs, the backbone consists of an MPLS-enabled IP network and a label-switched path (also known as *tunnel*) is used to send traffic from multiple customers across the VPN backbone from one edge LSR to another. The tunnel is established using LDP or RSVP. Within a tunnel, traffic that belongs to a particular VPN is identified using an additional MPLS label known as a *VC label* (or *inner label*).

- In the case of L3VPNs, VC labels are signaled using BGP.

- In the case of L2VPNs, VC labels may be signaled using LDP or BGP.

- In the case of L3VPNs, the edge LSRs use a Layer 3 FIB and LFIB to forward customer packets.

- In the case of L2VPNs, the edge LSRs use a Layer 2 FIB and LFIB to forward customer frames. The Layer 2 FIB is derived from the information distributed by Layer 2 protocols such as Ethernet, ATM, and FR. For example, in the case of Ethernet, the Layer 2 FIB uses *Media Access Control* (MAC) addresses and VLAN tags to forward Ethernet frames.

- Irrespective of L2VPN or L3VPN services, the transit LSRs in both cases use LFIB to forward labeled packets.

Chapter 10, "Improving Survivability of IP and MPLS Networks," provides a more detailed description of L2VPNs and L3VPNs.

Figure 7-1   *MPLS-Based Layer 2 and Layer 3 VPN Services*

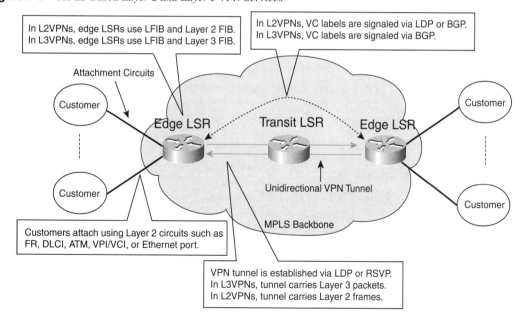

Forwarding Tables for Layer 2 and Layer 3 VPN Services

From descriptions in the previous sections, it follows that depending on whether an LSR is functioning as a transit or edge LSR, it consults the LFIB alone or both the Layer 3 FIB and LFIB or Layer 2 FIB and LFIB.

In the context of BGP, this means that to support *nonstop forwarding* (NSF), the restarting LSRs must be able to preserve the pertinent forwarding state across the BGP restart. For example, because an edge LSR may use the Layer 2/3 FIB and LFIB, it must be able preserve both the Layer 2/3 FIB and LFIB across the BGP restart. In contrast, because a transit LSR uses only the LFIB for forwarding, it needs to preserve only the LFIB across the BGP restart.

In general, because the forwarding state in the Layer 2/3 FIB and LFIB is derived from multiple protocols, the LSR must be able to preserve both the Layer 2/3 FIB and LFIB across the restart of any control-plane components, including BGP, LDP, and RSVP.

The remainder of this chapter assumes Layer 3 services, which means that an edge LSR needs the Layer 3 FIB and MPLS LFIB to forward packets.

MPLS Forwarding State Entries

A *label-switched path* (LSP) is the sequence of LSRs that a labeled packet traverses (starting at ingress LSR, passing through transit LSRs, and terminating at an egress LSR). LSPs are established through protocols, such as LDP and RSVP. If you were to traverse along an LSP and examine the MPLS forwarding state in each LSR, you would find a slightly different form of forwarding state entry in the edge and transit LSRs.

In the remainder of this chapter, the term *MPLS forwarding state* refers to these entries of the form ingress edge LSR (FEC, out label, next hop), egress edge LSR (in label, FEC, next hop), and transit LSR (in label, out label, next hop).

Detrimental Effects of BGP with MPLS Restart

As discussed in Chapter 6, when the BGP in a router restarts, it leads to harmful effects in IP forwarding- and control-plane components. When BGP is used to distribute MPLS labels, a BGP route withdrawal is also accompanied with the associated label withdrawal. Therefore, a BGP restart disrupts both IP and MPLS forwarding/control-plane components (see Figure 7-2).

Figure 7-2   *Detrimental Effects of BGP with MPLS Control-Plane Restart*

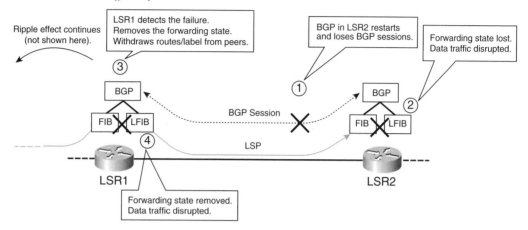

For BGP with MPLS restart, to avoid negative impacts on the MPLS forwarding plane you need to extend the BGP graceful restart mechanism to account for label information. The BGP restart procedure that considers the MPLS forwarding state in the graceful restart capability exchange is referred to as the *BGP with an MPLS graceful restart mechanism*.

Review of Chapter 6 Concepts

Because this chapter extends the BGP restart concepts of Chapter 6 to MPLS, this section contains a summary of the relevant concepts from that chapter. Chapter 6 described the harmful effects of the BGP control-plane restart on the IP control and forwarding planes. You learned that when BGP in a router restarts, the restarting router loses its BGP sessions. On discovering a BGP session failure with the restarting router, neighbors withdraw routes derived from the failed BGP session. If the BGP restarts quickly, after restarting the router attempts to reestablish BGP sessions with peers and exchange routing information. The peers relearn routes from the restarting router and as a result re-advertise routes that were withdrawn a short time before.

A route withdrawal that is abruptly followed by re-advertisement is termed a *route flap*. As discussed previously, BGP route flaps are undesirable for a number of reasons, including the initiation of forwarding that leads to packet loss and the injection of extra control traffic that consumes link bandwidth and control processor resources.

Chapter 6 also discussed the main reason that BGP neighbors withdraw routes from the restarting peer—to avoid forwarding data traffic into the black hole created by the restarting router. The assumption is that the restarting router is incapable of preserving the forwarding state across the restart and hence cannot forward across the restart. Under this assumption, the correct course of action is to withdraw failed routes as soon as possible to inform other BGP speakers about the failure. With this information, BGP speakers can explore alternative paths so that potential packet loss can be reduced.

Nonstop forwarding refers to the capability of a router to preserve its FIB and continue to forward data traffic across the control-plane restart. How can the NSF capability of a router influence the BGP restart behavior? If a restarting router is NSF capable, instead of withdrawing routes as normal to avoid the black hole, with the NSF capability of the restarting router the peers can continue to forward across the BGP restart. Because routes are not withdrawn, data traffic continues to flow as normal across the restart. Therefore, NSF capability not only reduces data packet loss, it also helps to eliminate route flaps that result from BGP restart. To achieve the goals of reducing data packet loss and eliminating route flaps, however, the restarting router must inform its peers about its NSF capability before the restart. In turn, the peers must modify their normal BGP restart protocol behavior.

Chapter 6 described the BGP protocol extension, which is called the *BGP graceful restart mechanism*. This protocol extension allows a speaker to indicate its NSF capability to the peers during the process of an initial BGP session establishment. When such a speaker restarts, its peers retain routes learned from the restarting speaker, mark them stale, but continue to use the stale forwarding state. To prevent peers from deleting the stale routes, the restarting speaker is expected to restart and reform BGP sessions with peers within a negotiated restart period. The restarting speaker can avoid forwarding-plane disruption as well as route flaps caused BGP restart if it performs the following functions: preserves its forwarding state across the BGP restart, reestablishes BGP sessions, and completes routing information updates within the negotiated recovery period.

Overview of the BGP as MPLS Control Plane

MPLS architecture allows multiple protocols for distributing label information between LSRs.[1] MPLS label-distribution protocols are based on either extending the capabilities of existing protocols, as in the case of BGP and RSVP-TE, or explicitly defining new protocols for this purpose, as in the case of LDP. Chapter 6 focused on BGP as an IP control-plane protocol. This chapter mainly focuses on the role of BGP as a label-distribution protocol. LDP and RSVP are described in Chapter 8, "MPLS Control Plane: Restarting LDP Gracefully," and Chapter 9, "MPLS Control Plane: Restarting RSVP-TE Gracefully," respectively.

BGP and MPLS Interrelationship

As discussed earlier, MPLS-based L3VPNs use LDP or RSVP to set up label-switched paths called *VPN tunnels* between edge LSRs to send VPN traffic across the MPLS backbone. Because each tunnel can transport traffic from multiple customers, within a tunnel traffic that belongs to a particular VPN customer is identified using an additional label known as a *VC label*. In this case, the tunnel has just two labels: an outer label and an inner label. The outer label is signaled using a label-distribution protocol such as LDP or RSVP-TE. The inner label is signaled through BGP.

The main points about the BGP and MPLS interrelationship are summarized in the following list to help you better understand why BGP failure can affect MPLS:

- The FIB holds *interior gateway protocol* (IGP)-learned prefixes (routes).

- LDP is used to associate and distribute labels for the IGP routes. RSVP can also be used for this purpose, but is not discussed in this chapter.

- LDP-assigned labels are held in the LFIB.

- BGP-learned routes are held in the FIB.

- BGP is used to associate and distribute labels for the BGP routes.

- The LFIB holds BGP-assigned labels.

- In the case of L3VPN services, a BGP-assigned label is known as the *inner label*, and an LDP (or RSVP)-assigned label is referred to as the *outer label*.

- The outer (top) label is also known as the tunnel label, and the inner (bottom) label is also known as the VPN label.

- The ingress edge LSR pushes *two* labels (an inner and an outer label).

BGP label-distribution procedures are described in the following section.

BGP Label-Distribution Mechanisms

Originally BGP-4 was capable of distributing only IPv4 routes. Later on, however, extensions were defined that enabled BGP-4 to support routes for multiple address families such as IPv4, IPv6, IPX, and so forth. This was achieved by defining two new optional transitive attributes: Multiprotocol Reachable NLRI (MP_REACH_NLRI) and Multiprotocol Unreachable NLRI (MP_UNREACH_NLRI).[2]

The MP_REACH_NLRI attribute is used for advertising a set of reachable destinations (prefixes) and the associated BGP next-hop information. In contrast, the MP_UNREACH_NLRI attribute is used to withdraw a set of unreachable destinations. For example, a BGP speaker can withdraw a previously advertised route by listing the NLRI of the previously advertised route in the Withdrawn Routes field of an Update message. These attributes are shown in Figures 7-3 and 7-4 and briefly described in the following list:

- The *Address Family Identifier* (AFI) identifies the network layer protocol (such as IPv4 and IPv6) associated with the NLRI.

- The *Subsequent Address Family Identifier* (SAFI) field provides further information about the address family being advertised in the AFI field, such as whether the NLRI is unicast, multicast, or whether the NLRI has associated MPLS label information.

Figure 7-3   *Multiprotocol Reachable NLRI (MP_REACH_NLRI) Attribute*

Address Family Identifier (AFI) (2 Bytes)
Subsequent Address Family Identifier (SAFI) (1 Byte)
Length of the Next Hop Network Address (1 Byte)
Number of SNPAs (1 Byte)
Length of the first SNPA (1 Byte)
First SNPA (Variable)
Length of the second SNPA (1 Byte)
Second SNPA (Variable)

Length of the last SNPA (1 Byte)
Last SNPA (Variable)
Network Layer Reachability Information (NLRI) (Variable) Based on the SAFI Value, NLRI Is Encoded as a \<Length,Prefix\> or \<Length,Label,Prefix\>

Figure 7-4   *Multiprotocol Unreachable NLRI (MP_UNREACH_NLRI) Attribute*

Address Family Identifier (AFI) (1 Byte)
Subsequent Address Family Identifier (SAFI) (1 Byte)
Withdrawn Routes (Variable)

Advertising Labeled BGP Routes

BGP uses Update messages to distribute routing information. In the case of BGP with MPLS, each route also has associated label information. Both the route and the associated label information are carried in the same Update message using the MP_REACH_NLRI attribute. Figure 7-5 shows the format for the NLRI with MPLS label(s). The AFI indicates the address family of the route, and the value of the SAFI field indicates whether an NLRI has an associated label. The Length field indicates the length of address and label(s) in units of bits. The Label field contains one or more MPLS labels (or label stack). Each label is encoded in 3 bytes with the higher 20 bits containing the label value.[3,4]

Figure 7-5   *NLRI Format with the MPLS Label Stack*

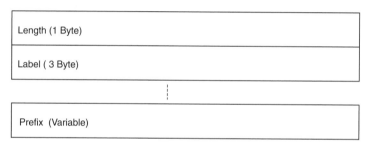

Advertising Labeled BGP Routes Through a Route Reflector

In some cases, BGP label distribution between BGP speakers may also involve a route reflector (RR). As described in Chapter 6, an RR helps to avoid interior BGP (iBGP) session mesh and yet ensures propagation of BGP routing information to all BGP speakers inside an autonomous system (AS). The RR transparently reflects the label information along with the route.

Withdrawing Labeled BGP Routes

To withdraw a previously advertised route and the associated label mapping, the BGP speaker either advertises a new route-to-label mapping with the same NLRI as in the previously advertised route or lists the NLRI of the previously advertised route in the Withdrawn Routes field of an Update message with the label field set to 0x800000. The BGP label-distribution procedures for the case of adjacent and nonadjacent edge LSRs are shown in Figures 7-6 and 7-7, respectively.

Figure 7-6 *BGP Label Distribution Between Adjacent LSR Peers*

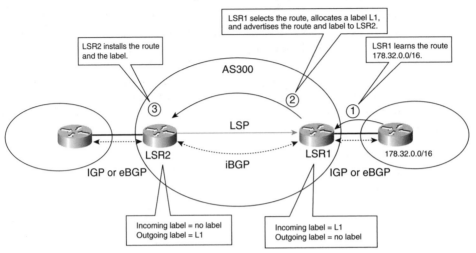

Figure 7-7 *BGP Label Distribution Between Nonadjacent Edge LSRs*

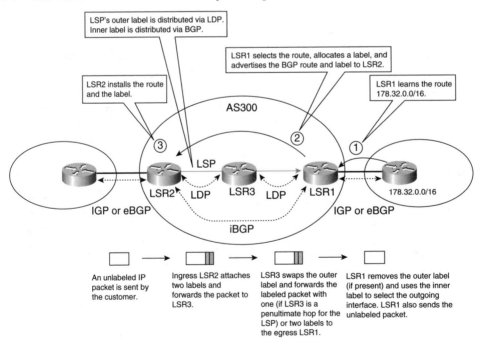

Mitigating the Detrimental Effects of BGP with MPLS Restart

In Chapter 6, you learned that the BGP graceful restart mechanism allows a speaker to announce its capability to preserve the BGP-related IP forwarding state across the BGP restart.

The BGP with the MPLS graceful restart mechanism[5] extends the BGP graceful restart procedure to MPLS. In essence, during the establishment of the pre-restart BGP session, an LSR informs its peers about its capability to preserve the MPLS forwarding state across the BGP restart. When the LSR restarts, its peers retain labels learned from the restarting LSR, mark them stale, but continue to use them for forwarding. After restart, the restarting LSR exchanges label information with peers that allows the MPLS forwarding state to be refreshed. As a result, the forwarding-plane disruption is avoided, as shown in Figure 7-8.

Figure 7-8   *BGP with MPLS Graceful Restart Behavior*

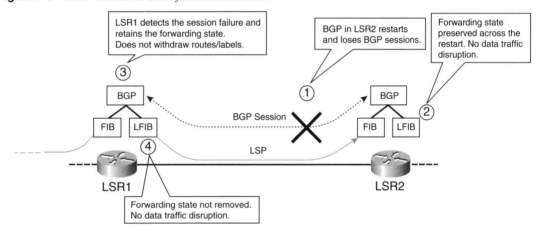

BGP with MPLS Graceful Restart Mechanism

BGP with MPLS graceful restart depends on the use of the graceful restart capability.[6] In terms of protocol behavior, the main difference between BGP graceful restart and BGP with MPLS graceful restart lies in the processing of the SAFI field. By examining the SAFI field, a receiver determines whether the sender is capable of preserving an IP or MPLS forwarding state.

For each address family, a separate <AFI, SAFI> pair is required to advertise IP and MPLS capability. For example, if an LSR is capable of preserving both a BGP-derived IPv4 and an MPLS forwarding state, it needs to include two <AFI, SAFI> fields. In short, an LSR can express its capability to preserve IP and MPLS forwarding states across the BGP restart by including the appropriate <AFI, SAFI> fields.

For now, the discussion is restricted to MPLS. By including the graceful restart capability in the Update message and setting the <AFI, SAFI> fields, the LSR indicates the following: "For each address family listed in the graceful restart capability, I am capable of preserving the MPLS forwarding state across the BGP restart. When my BGP control-plane restarts, please do not withdraw labels for these address families, but continue to use those labels for forwarding data packets as normal. After restarting, if I am not able to reestablish the session within the allowed time (restart time), or if I explicitly indicate my inability to preserve the MPLS forwarding state for the previously advertised address families across the restart, please immediately delete the concerned MPLS forwarding state that you have retained across the restart."

As a result of this message exchange, when BGP in the LSR restarts, its peers retain labels exchanged with the restarting LSR. This behavior allows the LSR to restart and reestablish sessions without any disruption. After a session has been reestablished, the LSRs exchange label information, which enables both the restarting LSR and its peers to refresh their stale MPLS forwarding state. From the interactions between a restarting LSR and its peers, it follows that the BGP with MPLS graceful restart mechanism requires support from peers. The details of protocol mechanics are described in the paragraphs that follow.

A BGP speaker advertises its capability to preserve an IP and MPLS forwarding state for a given network layer protocol through the AFI and SAFI fields in the graceful restart capability. For example, a value of 1 in the AFI field indicates IPv4, a value of 2 indicates IPv6, and so forth.[7]

Similarly, a value of 1 in the SAFI indicates a unicast NLRI, and a value of 4 indicates an NLRI with MPLS labels. (See Table 7-1.) For example, to advertise the capability to preserve the forwarding state for unicast IPv4 prefixes, a BGP speaker sets the AFI to 1 and the SAFI to 1. Similarly, for expressing the capability to preserve the MPLS forwarding state for IPv4 prefixes, the AFI field is set to 1 and the SAFI is set to 4. After restart, the restarting speaker sets the Forwarding State (F) bit in an <AFI, SAFI> pair to indicate whether the MPLS forwarding state has been preserved for that address family across the BGP restart. BGP graceful restart capability contains a number of fields and flags (for details, see Chapter 6) such as restart flag (which indicates if BGP has restarted) and restart time (which indicates the estimated time taken by the restarting speaker to reestablish the BGP session) .

Table 7-1   *Subsequent Address Family Identifier Field Values*[8]

SAFI Value	Description
0	Reserved
1	NLRI used for unicast forwarding
2	NLRI used for multicast forwarding
3	NLRI used for both unicast and multicast forwarding
4	NLRI with MPLS labels
5–127	Unassigned
128–255	Private use

When the graceful restart capability is included, but <AFI, SAFI> fields are not present, this indicates that even though the LSR supports the graceful restart procedure, it is incapable of preserving the IP and MPLS forwarding state across the restart. When an LSR can support the BGP with an MPLS graceful restart procedure but is NSF-incapable, such an LSR helps to reduce the negative impact of BGP restart on neighbors. It does not, however, diminish the harmful effects on the MPLS forwarding plane caused by its own BGP restart. This is discussed later in the chapter. The following section briefly describes BGP with MPLS restart protocol behavior for the restarting LSR (the LSR whose BGP has restarted) and helper LSR (peer of the restarting LSR). Before proceeding further, you would do well to review the BGP graceful restart mechanism in Chapter 6.

Behavior of a Restarting LSR

During the initial BGP session establishment, the LSR advertises its capability to preserve the MPLS forwarding state by setting the <AFI, SAFI> fields in the graceful restart capability. In addition, the LSR advertises the estimated time it will take to reestablish the session after a BGP restart. The following discussion assumes that the LSR not only supports BGP with MPLS graceful restart extensions, but the LSR also is capable of preserving IP and MPLS forwarding states across the restart.

After having informed its neighbors about graceful restart capabilities, when the BGP control plane in an LSR restarts, the LSR continues to forward data traffic using the preserved MPLS forwarding state (LFIB). After restarting, for each address family for which the restarting LSR had expressed its capability to preserve the MPLS forwarding state before the restart, the LSR checks whether it was actually able to preserve the concerned forwarding state across the restart.

An LSR needs to preserve MPLS-related or both IP- and MPLS-related forwarding state depending on whether the LSR is an edge or transit LSR. For the sake of the following discussion, assume that the restarting LSR is an edge LSR. Suppose that the restarting LSR has preserved its MPLS forwarding state across the restart. After restarting, it marks the BGP-derived MPLS forwarding state. It continues, however, to use the stale information for forwarding data traffic. To avoid retaining the stale forwarding information indefinitely, the LSR starts the state stale timer. The restarting LSR attempts to reestablish BGP sessions with its peers and exchange the BGP graceful restart capability. The restarting LSR sets the R bit (value 1) to inform peers about its BGP control-plane restart. In addition, for each <AFI, SAFI> pair (with the SAFI = 4 indicating NLRI with label information) for which the LSR was able to preserve the MPLS forwarding state across the restart, it sets the F bit (value 1) to indicate that it has preserved the concerned MPLS forwarding state.

After the BGP session has been reestablished, the restarting LSR receives Update messages from peers and rebuilds its Adj-RIBs-In. Because route selection must wait until the RIB is rebuilt completely, for each address family the restarting LSR defers its route-selection process until it has received the End-Of-RIB marker from all peers. The restarting LSR does not need to wait for End-Of-RIB markers from peers, because those markers have either restarted or are graceful restart-incapable. This is because those peers are either not expected to send or are incapable of sending the End-Of-RIB marker. To avoid waiting for the arrival of End-Of-RIB markers and deferring the route-selection process indefinitely, the restarting router uses a (configurable) delay timer. When the delay timer has expired, the route-selection process is run regardless of the fact that not all the End-Of-RIB markers may have been received. After the restarting LSR has selected the best routes, the LSR updates its Loc-RIB, FIB, and Adj-RIBs-Out and advertises routes and the locally (incoming) assigned labels to its peers.

As discussed previously, depending on the role of the restarting LSR as an edge or transit router, the MPLS forwarding state may consist of <FEC, out label, next hop> for an ingress LSR, <in label, out label, next hop> for a transit LSR, or <in label, FEC, next hop> for an egress LSR. Edge LSRs perform the role of both ingress and egress LSRs and thus contain forwarding state entries in both the first and last format.

After restart, the restarting LSR relearns the outgoing label-to-FEC (NLRI in the Update message) mapping from the nonrestarting LSR and then updates/replaces the corresponding stale entry in the LFIB. Regarding the FEC-to-incoming label mapping, the restarting LSR has two options: re-advertise the same label that was preserved across the restart or allocate a new local label and then advertise the new local label-to-FEC mapping. Each approach has advantages and disadvantages. For example, the first approach has the advantage that FEC-to-incoming label mappings are not changed after the restart, but consume more memory. In contrast, the second approach obviates the need for preserving and managing the FEC-to-incoming label mappings across the LDP restart, but consumes more labels. In particular, if the restarting LSR does not have at least as many unallocated as allocated labels during the restart, the second approach could lead to label depletion. If the restarting LSR chooses the second option, for a short period it may have two incoming labels for an FEC in the LFIB, namely, the stale and the new one. Even though there are two incoming label mappings for an FEC, the FEC will have a single outgoing label and the next hop. Hence, there is no danger of incorrect forwarding. On completion of the restart procedure, pre-restart stale FEC-to-incoming label mappings are deleted (see Figure 7-9).

In summary, the restarting LSR relearns the FEC-to-outgoing label mappings from downstream peers. For the incoming label mappings, the restarting LSR either reclaims the pre-restart incoming label mappings (marked stale) from the preserved forwarding or allocates a new incoming label mapping. Suppose a unidirectional LSP is passing through the restarting LSR B, with LSR A and LSR C acting as the upstream and the downstream LSRs for the LSP. Suppose the concerned LSP has an incoming and outgoing label pair of (L1, L2) in LSR A, (L2, L3) in LSR B, and (L3, L4) in LSR C (see Figure 7-10). In this example scenario, LSR B is the restarting LSR, whereas LSR A and C are helpers. After restart, LSR B relearns L3 from LSR C and re-advertises either L2 or a new label to LSR A. The LSR A receives either L2 or a new label and updates the out label for the LSP. Similar concepts apply for LSPs in the other direction.

Figure 7-9 *MPLS Forwarding State Across BGP Graceful Restart*

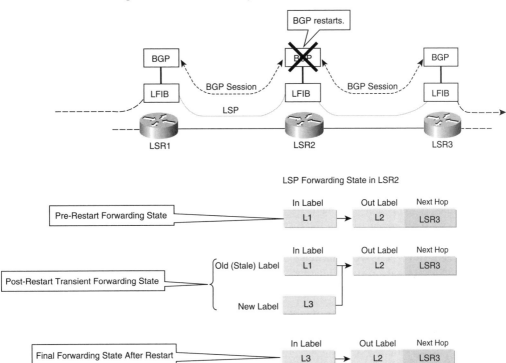

Figure 7-10 *Example of Label-Recovery Procedure*

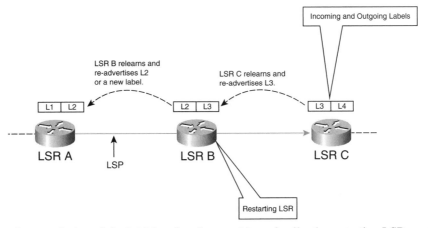

On completion of the initial update for an address family, the restarting LSR sends an End-Of-RIB marker to all its peers. As mentioned earlier, upon restarting the LSR marks all preserved MPLS forwarding state as stale and starts a stale timer. Because the RIB/LIB has been rebuilt and the decision process run, all valid forwarding states should have been updated in the FIB and the LFIB updated. If some LFIB entries are still marked as stale, these correspond to invalid forwarding states that need to be removed. (A similar procedure applies to the IP forwarding state, but is not included here.) Therefore, when the stale state timer expires, any remaining stale LFIB entries are deleted.

Behavior of Helper LSRs

As soon as an LSR detects the failure of a BGP session to a graceful restart neighbor, it starts the restart timer. For each address family for which the restarting peer had expressed its capability to preserve the MPLS forwarding state across the BGP restart, the helper LSR retains all FEC-to-label mappings learned from the restarting LSR. The helper LSR marks the concerned MPLS forwarding state as stale and starts a stale timer. While the restart timer is running, the helper LSR waits for the session to reestablish and continues to use the stale forwarding information. If the restarting peer does not reestablish the BGP session before the expiration of the restart timer, the helper LSR immediately deletes the stale MPLS forwarding state. However, if the restarting LSR manages to reestablish a BGP session on time, the helper LSR cancels the restart timer and processes the newly received graceful restart capability.

For each address family with the F bit set, the helper LSR continues to use the stale MPLS forwarding state. However, if any of these conditions exist, the helper LSR immediately removes the stale MPLS forwarding state:

- The F bit for an address family is not set.
- The address family is absent in the newly received graceful restart capability.
- The graceful restart capability is not present in the newly received Open message.

To allow the restarting LSR to rebuild the RIB and recover FEC-to-out label mappings, the helper LSR advertises BGP routes and the locally assigned labels to the restarting LSR. When the update for an address family is complete, the helper LSR sends an End-Of-RIB marker. After having received the updates and run the decision process, the restarting LSR in turn advertises new routes and the associated labels information back to the helper LSR. After receiving updates from the restarting LSR, the helper LSR replaces/updates the stale routes and labels (FEC-to-out label mappings). On receipt of the End-Of-RIB marker from the restarting LSR for an address family, the helper LSR runs the decision process and updates the routes for that address family. At this stage, all valid routes and the associated labels for the concerned address family should have been updated. Therefore, when the End-Of-RIB marker is received for an address family, labels that are still marked as stale are immediately removed. To avoid waiting for the arrival of all the End-Of-RIB markers and retaining stale MPLS forwarding state indefinitely, when the stale timer expires, the LSR deletes all stale MPLS forwarding entries.

BGP/MPLS Graceful Restart Operation

This section describes the operation of the BGP with an MPLS graceful restart mechanism using the network shown in Figure 7-11. The following discussion assumes that LSR1 and LSR2 are capable of both BGP with MPLS graceful restart and NSF. The following sequence of steps does not necessarily indicate the processing steps of a specific implementation. This description is intended to provide a functional view.

1. During BGP session establishment, LSR1 and LSR2 exchange BGP restart capability to indicate their capability to preserve the MPLS forwarding state during BGP restart (by including <AFI, SAFI> pairs). The graceful restart capability contains fields such as the following:

    a. Restart flags (R flag set to 1 to indicate that BGP restart)

    b. Restart time (time it will take for the sender to reestablish a BGP session after restart)

    c. Flags for the address family (F bit set to 1 to indicate that the forwarding state for the <AFI, SAFI> pairs has been preserved across the restart)

    In the case of MPLS, the SAFI contains a value of 4, which indicates that the NLRI has associated label information. For the sake of simplifying the description, this section only considers NLRI for the IPv4 address family. In general, however, a similar procedure applies to the other address families.

2. LSR1 and LSR2 exchange routing information using normal BGP procedures.

3. Assume BGP in LSR2 restarts.

4. LSR1 detects failure of the BGP session with the LSR2. Because LSR1 a priori knows that LSR2 is NSF-capable, it immediately starts the restart timer. And for each address family for which LSR2 has expressed its capability to preserve MPLS forwarding state prior to the restart, LRR1 retains the MPLS forwarding state derived from LSR2, but marks them as stale and starts the stale timer. While the restart timer and the stale timer are running, LSR1 continues to use the stale forwarding information. After restarting, LSR1 attempts to reestablish the BGP session with LSR2. If the session is reestablished before the restart timer has expired, LSR1 stops the restart timer and continues to retain the stale information. However, if the session is not established within the restart time, the stale MPLS forwarding information is immediately deleted.

5. Assume that the LSR2 was able to preserve the MPLS forwarding state for the IPv4 address family across its BGP restart. After restarting, LSR2 examines the preserved MPLS forwarding state and marks it as stale. LSR2 starts a stale timer but continues to use the stale forwarding information. LSR2 tries to reestablish a BGP session with LSR1. During the session-reestablishment process, LSR2 sets the R bit to indicate the BGP restart. In addition, for each address family for which LSR2 was able to preserve the MPLS forwarding state across the restart, LSR2 sets the F bit. For this example, LSR2

would set the F bit to 1 for the IPv4 address family. In general, LSR2 would need to set the F bit for each address family for which it was able to preserve the forwarding state across the BGP restart.

6. On BGP session reestablishment, LSR1 stops the restart timer and processes the newly received graceful restart capability from LSR2. Because the F bit for the IPv4 address family is set to 1, LSR1 continues to retain the MPLS forwarding state for IPv4. However, if the F bit for an address family were not set to 1 in the newly received graceful restart capability, LSR1 immediately would have removed the stale MPLS forwarding state. To enable the restarting, LSR2 rebuilds its RIB and relearns FEC-to-out label mappings, LSR1 sends BGP updates to LSR2 for each address family. On completion of the initial update for an address family, LSR1 sends the End-Of-RIB marker to LSR2.

7. LSR2 receives BGP Update messages from peers, processes them, and rebuilds its Adj-RIBs-In. However, LSR2 defers (for a configurable time) its BGP route-selection process for an address family until the End-Of-RIB marker for that address family has been received from all peers. After LSR2 has selected a route, LSR2 updates the Loc-RIB, FIB, and Adj-RIBs-Out and advertises routes to peers.

    Assume that before the BGP restart, the edge LSR2 had originated a route with a label to LSR1 with itself as the next hop (which means the forwarding entry in LSR2 is of the form <in label, FEC, next hop>). After the restart, LSR2 must send an update for the route and the associated label to allow LSR1 to update its MPLS forwarding state. LSR2 uses FEC to determine the associated label in the preserved state. If such an entry is found, LSR2 clears the stale flag, selects the incoming label from the found entry, and advertises the route and the selected local label to peers (LSR1). If no such entry is found, LSR2 allocates an unused (new) label and advertises the new route to label binding to its peers. LSR2 has two options for the local label: advertise the old local label or select a new one.

8. After receiving routing updates from LSR2, LSR1 replaces/updates the stale MPLS forwarding state. On receipt of the End-Of-RIB marker for an address family, LSR1 deletes any MPLS forwarding state that is still marked as stale. LSR1 runs the decision process and updates the Adj-RIBs-In, FIB/LFIB, and Adj-RIBs-Out. To avoid waiting indefinitely for the arrival of all the End-Of-RIB markers and retaining stale routes and an MPLS forwarding state for an indefinite amount of time, LSR1 uses a (configurable) stale timer. When the stale timer expires, LSR1 deletes all remaining stale forwarding states.

9. Normal operation resumes.

Figure 7-11 *BGP with MPLS Graceful Restart Operation*

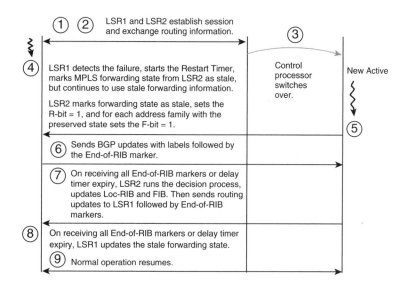

Network-Deployment Considerations

To avoid the harmful effects on MPLS forwarding caused by BGP restart, the restarting LSR and neighboring LSRs must support a certain set of control- and forwarding-plane capabilities. For example, the restarting LSR must support not only BGP with MPLS graceful restart extensions, but must also be able to preserve the MPLS forwarding state (and the IP forwarding state in some cases) across the restart. To be able to assist as a helper, at a minimum the helper LSR must support BGP with MPLS graceful extensions. However, the helper LSR might or might not be NSF-capable.

Clearly when an LSR cannot preserve its MPLS forwarding state across the BGP restart, although the concerned LSR would help to reduce the negative impact of a neighbor's BGP control-plane restart, the LSR under consideration won't be able to do so when its own BGP control plane restarts. This shows that to reduce the negative effects of BGP restart across the entire network, all LSRs must be capable of both graceful restart as well as NSF. Along these lines, another factor that can influence the overall benefit of BGP with MPLS graceful restart capability is the nature of coupling BGP and other IP/MPLS control-plane components. In a tightly coupled environment, the restart of one component is accompanied with the restart of other components. As discussed in Chapter 6, when BGP is inseparable from IP and MPLS control-plane components such as OSPF, IS-IS, and LDP, the LSR must be able to gracefully restart all affected components. The following scenarios describe the effect of BGP with MPLS restart on LSRs with a diverse set of control- and forwarding-plane capabilities.

Scenario 1: LSR1 and LSR2 Are Capable of Both BGP with MPLS Graceful Restart and of NSF

In this case, the BGP restart in either the LSR1 or LSR2 does not disrupt the MPLS forwarding state (see Figure 7-12). Therefore, for network-wide benefits from BGP with MPLS graceful restart mechanism, all LSRs in the network must support the full set of capabilities.

Figure 7-12 *BGP with MPLS Graceful Restart Interoperability*

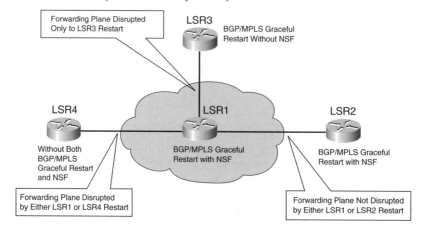

Scenario 2: LSR1 Is Capable of Both BGP with MPLS Graceful Restart and of NSF, but LSR3 Is Capable Only of BGP with MPLS Graceful Restart

In actual deployed networks, not all LSRs may be capable of supporting a full set of control- and forwarding-plane restart capabilities. In this case, when the BGP control plane in LSR1 restarts, its MPLS forwarding plane is not disrupted. This is because LSR1 supports BGP with MPLS graceful restart extensions and can preserve its MPLS forwarding state across the restart. However, to achieve this objective, neighbors recognizing that the restarting LSR is NSF capable must retain the forwarding state derived from the restarting LSR. This is made possible through the help of LSR3, which supports the BGP with MPLS graceful restart mechanism.

The situation is quite different in the case of LSR3 restart. Because LSR3 is not capable of preserving the MPLS forwarding state across the restart, it will not advertise <AFI, SAFI> for any address family before the restart. When BGP in LSR3 restarts, it loses the MPLS forwarding state. Therefore, from the moment LSR3 restarts until LSR1 detects the BGP session failure, MPLS data traffic from LSR1 is black holed in LSR3. On detection of BGP session failure, because LSR1 knows about the restart capabilities of LSR3 through the BGP graceful restart capability exchange before the restart, LSR1 immediately removes all MPLS forwarding states derived from (shared with) LSR3. (See Figure 7-12.) This in turn means that traffic from LSRs upstream of LSR1 (not shown in Figure 7-12) that are using LSPs passing through LSR3 and LSR1 would be discarded in LSR1 because LSR1 has deleted the forwarding state of the relevant LSPs. This process may continue and spread across multiple LSRs until alternative forwarding paths are discovered. All of this could have been avoided had LSR3 been NSF capable.

In summary, an LSR that is graceful restart-capable but NSF-incapable does not reduce the negative effects on the MPLS forwarding plane because of its own BGP control-plane restart. However, such an LSR still helps to reduce the negative effects by acting as a helper node when the BGP control plane of a graceful/NSF-capable peer restarts.

Scenario 3: LSR1 Is BGP with MPLS Graceful Restart- and NSF-Capable, but LSR4 Is Both BGP with MPLS Graceful Restart- and NSF-Incapable

In this case, a BGP restart in either LSR would disrupt the MPLS forwarding plane (see Figure 7-12). This means that to obtain any benefit from a BGP with an MPLS graceful restart- and NSF-capable LSR, at a minimum all its peers must be BGP with MPLS graceful restart-capable.

Summary

This chapter described the BGP with MPLS graceful restart mechanism, which allows the BGP control-plane restart without causing undesirable effects on the MPLS forwarding plane. The operation of the BGP with an MPLS graceful restart mechanism was explained through examples. And finally, several aspects of deploying BGP with an MPLS graceful restart mechanism were explained through multiple deployment scenarios.

References

[1] RFC 3031, "Multiprotocol Label Switching Architecture," R. Callon, E., Rosen, and A. Viswanathan, January 2001.

[2] RFC 2858, "Multiprotocol Extensions for BGP-4," T. Bates, R. Chandra, D. Katz, and Y. Rekhter, June 2000.

[3] RFC 3107, "Carrying Label Information in BGP-4," Y. Rekhter and E. Rosen, May 2001.

[4] RFC 3032, "MPLS Label Stack Encoding," A. Conta, D. Farinacci, G. Fedorkow, Y. Rekhter, E. Rosen, and D. Tappan, January 2001.

[5] Aggarwal, R., and Y. Rekhter, "Graceful Restart Mechanism for BGP with MPLS," IETF Draft, Work in progress.

[6] Chen, E., et al, "Graceful Restart Mechanism for BGP", IETF Draft, Work in progress.

[7] IANA-AFI, http://www.iana.org/assignments/address-family-numbers.

[8] IANA-SAFI, http://www.iana.org/assignments/safi-namespace.

CHAPTER 8

MPLS Control Plane: Restarting LDP Gracefully

This chapter describes the *Label Distribution Protocol*[1,2] (LDP) restart mechanisms that allow the LDP control-plane component of a *label-switched router* (LSR) to restart without disrupting its *Multiprotocol Label Switching* (MPLS) forwarding plane. The Internet *Engineering Task Force* (IETF) has defined two mechanisms for restarting LDP: LDP graceful restart[3] (GR) and LDP fault tolerance[4] (FT). The support of LDP GR in a majority of routers indicates that the LDP GR mechanism is expected to be the primary choice for restarting LDP. Therefore, this chapter focuses mainly on the LDP GR mechanism.

LDP has two modes of label distribution: downstream unsolicited and downstream on demand. Depending on the label-distribution mode in use, LDP GR uses slightly different state recovery procedures. This chapter covers the LDP GR mechanism for both label-distribution modes and elaborates on its operational aspects by considering various deployment scenarios. This chapter concludes with a brief summary.

Overview of LDP

Before packets can be forwarded using label information, a *label-switched path* (LSP) must first be established. To establish LSPs, LSRs need protocols for exchanging label information. MPLS architecture specifies multiple protocols for this purpose. LDP is one of the several methods by which LSRs signal label information.[1] Examples of other methods include *Border Gateway Protocol* (BGP; see Chapter 7, "MPLS Control Plane: Restarting BGP with MPLS Gracefully") and *Resource ReSerVation Protocol with traffic-engineering extensions* (RSVP-TE; see Chapter 9, "MPLS Control Plane: Restarting RSVP-TE Gracefully"). One of the reasons for using multiple label-distribution protocols is to handle the cases in which the routing protocol in use cannot be extended to piggyback the label binding information. In such cases new protocols have been defined for the explicit purpose of distributing labels. Another consideration for allowing multiple label-distribution procedures is the fact that MPLS technology encompasses a wide range of applications, such as *traffic engineering* (TE), *Layer 2 virtual private networks* (L2VPNs), and *Layer 3 virtual private networks* (L3VPNs). These applications and services have different sets of requirements for *quality of service* (QoS), routing, and placement of LSPs. For example, RSVP-TE is typically required when it is desired to establish LSP along explicit paths with bandwidth reservation (see Chapter 9). More details on the use of label-distribution protocols by various MPLS applications are provided in Chapter 10, "Improving Survivability of IP and MPLS Networks."

This section provides an overview of the LDP protocol with an emphasis on concepts that are relevant for LDP restart discussions.

LDP FEC-to-LSP Association

A group of packets that is forwarded along the same path is said to define a *forwarding equivalence class* (FEC). Each FEC is specified as a collection of one or more FEC elements. An example of a commonly used FEC element is the IP address prefix. Each LSP is associated with a FEC that specifies which particular set of packets is to be mapped onto the LSP. By associating a FEC that has multiple IP address prefixes with an LSP, an LSR can map any IP packet whose IP address matches at least one FEC element onto the LSP.

LDP specifies a set of procedures and messages to associate *Interior Gateway Protocol* (IGP) address prefixes with labels and to distribute these mappings between LDP peers. Because IGP routes traverse the shortest paths and because LDP provides IP address FECs to label mappings, LDP establishes LSPs along the shortest paths. It is for this reason that an LSP established using LDP is commonly referred to as a *hop-by-hop routed LSP*. In this case, the LSP tracks the shortest path of the associated FEC. That means that each time the next hop for the FEC changes, the LSP must also adapt its next hop accordingly (see Figure 8-1).

Figure 8-1 *LDP Adaptations to LSP Next-Hop Changes*

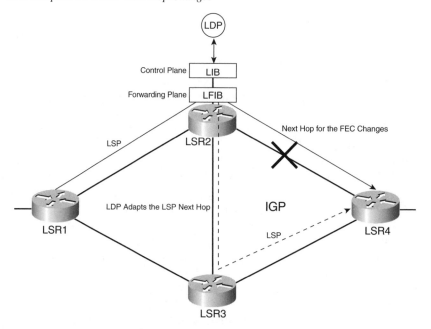

It is important to note, however, that LDP could also be used for associating other types of FECs, such as a Layer 2 circuit ID with an LSP. Such usage of LDP is discussed later in this chapter. (See the section "Establishing Pseudowires (PWs) Using LDP.") In general, an LSP may be associated with any types of FECs, including the following:

- IPv4/IPv6 session (for example, using RSVP)
- IPv4/IPv6 prefix (for example, using LDP)
- Layer 3 VPN IPv4/IPv6 prefix (for example, using BGP)
- Layer 2 circuit ID (for example, using LDP or BGP)

LDP Peers

LDP defines a set of messages (such as Label Request and Label Mapping; more details can be found later in this chapter) by which two LSRs inform each other about FEC-to-label mappings. However, before any two LSRs can exchange FEC-to-label mapping information, they must first establish an LDP session to become LDP peers. An LDP session is established using TCP to ensure the reliable delivery of protocol messages. The choice of TCP as a transport mechanism for LDP has important implications on the LDP restart behavior, as discussed in this chapter.

The first step toward the establishment of an LDP session involves discovering a potential LDP peer. Depending on whether a neighbor is directly connected at a link level or is indirectly connected at a network level, LDP uses two variants of the discovery mechanism, referred to as the *basic* and *extended discovery method*, respectively. After an LDP session has been successfully established between two LSRs, the LSRs are regarded as LDP peers and are ready for exchanging FEC-to-label mappings.

Hello Adjacency Establishment

An LSR periodically transmits LDP link Hellos on each LDP interface to discover potential peers directly connected at the link level. LDP link Hellos are transmitted as UDP packets addressed to the well-known LDP discovery port for this address: the "all routers in this subnet" group multicast address. An LDP link Hello contains the LDP identifier (LDP ID; a quantity of 6 bytes, of which the first 4 bytes uniquely identify the LSR using the router ID and the last 2 bytes indicate whether the LSR is using a platform-wide or interface-specific label space).

The reception of a link Hello on an interface establishes a Hello adjacency with a potential LDP peer that is directly reachable at the link level on the interface and the label space that the sender intends to use on that interface. To discover a potential LDP peer that is not directly connected at the link level, an LSR periodically sends LDP targeted Hellos as UDP packets addressed to well-known LDP discovery ports at the specific address. The reception of an LDP-targeted Hello on an interface establishes on the interface a Hello adjacency with a potential LDP peer reachable at the network level (as opposed to link level) and the label space the sender intends to use.

The formation of a Hello adjacency between two LSRs triggers LDP session establishment. The session establishment is a two-step process, namely establishment of the transport connection and initialization of the session. After having formed the Hello adjacency, the LSR determines whether it is going to play the active or passive role in the session-establishment procedure. The LSR makes this determination, for example, by comparing its own and neighbor transport addresses. If the determined role is active, the LSR tries to open a TCP connection. If the determined role is passive, however, the LSR waits for the neighbor to initiate the session-establishment procedure.

After the two LSRs have successfully established the transport connection, they negotiate session parameters by exchanging LDP initialization messages. Examples of the negotiated session parameters include LDP protocol version, label-distribution method (for example, downstream unsolicited or downstream on demand), keepalive timer values for the session, *Virtual Path Identifier* (VPI)/*Virtual Channel Identifier* (VCI) ranges for *label-controlled ATM* (LC-ATM) interfaces, and so forth.

Hello Adjacency Maintenance

LDP uses the receipt of LDP Hellos as a trigger to retain a Hello adjacency. For that purpose, an LSR maintains a hold timer for each Hello adjacency that is started on the reception of a Hello that matches the adjacency. A Hello adjacency is deleted if another Hello is not received on that adjacency before the associated hold timer expires.

Each interface requires one link Hello adjacency. For example, when two LSRs are connected through multiple parallel links, a separate adjacency is formed on each link. Even when there are multiple Hello adjacencies, as long as the parallel interfaces between LSRs are using a platform-wide label space, only one LDP session is established between the two LSRs. However, when the parallel links are using per-interface label space (which would be the case for ATM links, for example), a separate LDP session is established on each link.

When multiple Hello adjacencies are associated with a single LDP session, as long as there is at least one associated Hello adjacency, the LDP session is retained. As soon as the last Hello adjacency is removed, LDP terminates the LDP session (releasing all associated FEC-to-label mappings) and closes the TCP connection.

To monitor the integrity of a LDP session, LDP maintains a keepalive timer to ensure that an LDP *protocol data unit* (PDU) is received before the timer expires. To avoid premature expiration of the keepalive timer, an LSR either sends a protocol message, or if there is nothing else to send, a keepalive message. If the keepalive timer expires, the LSR terminates the LDP session by closing the TCP connection. For example, when an LDP control-plane component of an LSR restarts, for some time the restarting LSR is unable to communicate with a peer that causes the keepalive timer of the peer to expire. Therefore, the nonrestarting peer can use the keepalive mechanism to detect the failure of an LDP session. Figure 8-2 depicts the LDP session establishment and maintenance process.

Figure 8-2   *LDP Session Establishment and Maintenance Procedures*

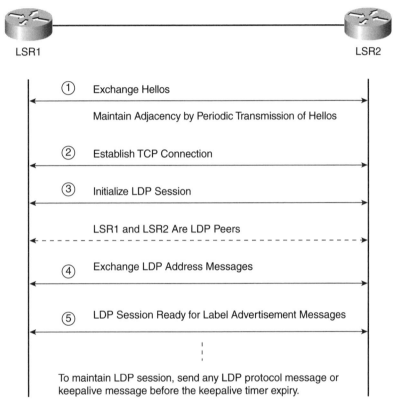

LDP Messages

After successful negotiation of session parameters, the two LSRs are LDP peers and ready to exchange LDP messages. LDP defines four types of messages:

- **Discovery**—Announce and maintain the presence of LSR in a network (such as link and targeted Hellos)

- **Session**—Establish, maintain, and terminate LDP sessions (such as initialization and keepalive messages)

- **Advertisement**—Advertise/withdraw interface addresses and FEC-to-label mappings (such as Address, Address Withdraw, Label Request, and Label Mapping messages)

- **Notification**—Indicate error and other advisory information

A brief description of the common LDP messages follows. The Address message is used to advertise the interface addresses when establishing a new LDP session or on activating a new interface. The Address Withdraw message is used to withdraw previously advertised interface addresses or on deactivation of a previously active interface.

The Label Request message is used to explicitly solicit a FEC-to-label mapping from the downstream peer. The Label Mapping message is used to advertise FEC-to-label bindings to a peer in response to a Label Request message (downstream on-demand mode) or unsolicited (downstream unsolicited mode). The Label Abort message is used to abort an outstanding Label Request message. An LSR sends the Label Withdraw message to an LDP peer when it wants to break a previously advertised FEC-to-label mapping. An LSR sends the Label Release message to an LDP peer to indicate to the peer that the LSR no longer needs the specific FEC-to-label mappings that were previously advertised by the peer.

Label Distribution Control Mode (Ordered Versus Independent)

Upon establishing a new LDP session, but before exchanging Label Mapping or Label Request messages, an LSR generally advertises interface addresses using Address messages. The Address messages are also advertised whenever a new LDP interface is activated, and withdrawn when a previously active interface is deactivated. The LSRs maintain Address messages in a database that provides a mapping between the peer LDP ID and the next-hop addresses.

For example, when an LSR receives a FEC-to-label mapping from a peer, the LSR consults a peer address list to verify whether that peer is the next hop for the FEC. The initial setup behavior of an LSP depends on whether LDP is operating with independent or ordered LSP control. When an LSR is operating in the independent label-distribution control (the label-distribution control mode of an LSR is determined through configuration), it does not wait for a remote FEC-to-label mapping before advertising the corresponding local FEC-to-label mapping to its LDP peers. In contrast, with ordered label-distribution control, an LSR waits for a remote FEC-to-label mapping (unless it is the egress LSR for that FEC) before advertising the corresponding local FEC-to-label mapping.

Label Advertisement Mode (Unsolicited Versus On Demand)

The term *downstream* means that the binding between a label carried by a packet and a particular FEC that the packet belongs to is created by an LSR that is downstream with respect to the flow of the packet from the LSR that places the label in the packet. For example, consider LSR1 and LSR2 with an LDP session between them (see Figure 8-1). Suppose data packets associated with a FEC 172.14.0.0/16 are sent from LSR1 to LSR2. When that happens in this direction of traffic flow for this particular FEC, LSR2 is known as the *downstream LSR*, and LSR1 as the *upstream LSR*. When using LDP (and generally when using other label-distribution methods), it is the downstream LSR for the FEC that assigns the FEC-to-label mapping. LDP supports two modes for FEC-to-label advertisement: downstream on demand and downstream unsolicited (see Figure 8-3).

Figure 8-3   *Downstream Unsolicited and Downstream On-Demand Label-Advertisement Modes*

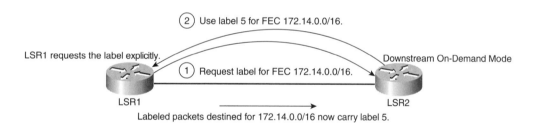

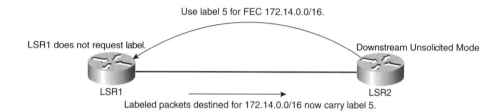

Downstream On Demand

In downstream on-demand label-advertisement mode, the upstream LSR makes an explicit FEC-to-label mapping request by issuing an LDP Label Request message to the downstream LSR. The Label Request message contains the FEC for which a label is being requested. The downstream LSR answers the Label Request message with an LDP Label Mapping message that provides the requested FEC-to-label mapping (see Figure 8-3). The downstream on-demand mode is typically used when you want to conserve label space (for example, in a cell-based LSR with a limited VPI/VCI range).

Downstream Unsolicited

In downstream unsolicited label-advertisement mode, the downstream LSR provides a FEC-to-label mapping by issuing an LDP Label Mapping message when the downstream LSR wants its upstream LSR to use this label.

In summary, an LSR receives FEC-to-outgoing label mappings (also called remote *FEC-to-label mappings*) from downstream peers, whereas the LSR locally assigns the FEC-to-incoming label mappings (also known as *local FEC-to-label mappings*).

Label Retention Mode (Liberal Versus Conservative)

Each LSR maintains locally assigned and remotely learned LDP FEC-to-label mappings in the *Label Information Base* (LIB). When an LSR is operating in conservative label-retention mode (typically used with downstream on-demand label distribution when it is desired to conserve label space), the LSR retains a remote FEC-to-label mapping from a peer only if it is the next hop for the FEC. In contrast, when an LSR is operating in liberal label-retention mode (typically used with downstream unsolicited label distribution), the LSR not only retains remote FEC-to-label mappings from the valid next hop, but also from a peer that is currently not the valid next hop for the FEC.

Interactions Between LIB, LFIB, and Routing

An LIB entry associates a FEC with an incoming label and one or more (peer, outgoing label) pairs. The LIB entry for a FEC is used to populate the MPLS forwarding state entry of the associated LSP in the *Label Forwarding Information Base* (LFIB). The MPLS forwarding state entry of an LSP is in turn used to forward data packets on that LSP. Even when a FEC entry in the LIB has more than one remote label mapping, the associated LSP entry in the LFIB always corresponds to the remote mappings received from the valid next-hop peer for that FEC.

Either routing updates or label advertisements from LDP peers might cause changes in the LFIB information. For example, when the IGP learns about a next hop for a FEC for which label switching is enabled, it informs the LFIB, which in turn requests the LIB for incoming and outgoing labels. The LIB searches the database using the FEC (destination IP address prefix) as an index to locate the corresponding entry. The LIB database entries are of the form

> <FEC-> {incoming label, (upstream peer LDP ID, for downstream on demand)}, {LDP ID, outgoing label}...{LDP ID, outgoing label}>

This means a particular LIB entry and the corresponding incoming label can be located using FEC. In contrast, the remote mappings for FECs are organized as (LDP ID, outgoing label) and can be located using LDP ID, which means the selection of the outgoing label from a next-hop peer requires mapping the next-hop address to the LDP ID. The peer address table provides the next-hop address-to-LDP ID mappings. When the next hop's LDP ID has been determined, the appropriate pair (LDP ID, outgoing label) can be located. Figure 8-4 shows the interactions between FIB, LFIB, and the LIB following the reception of a routing update.

Figure 8-4 *LIB, LFIB, and FIB Interactions Following Reception of a Routing Update*

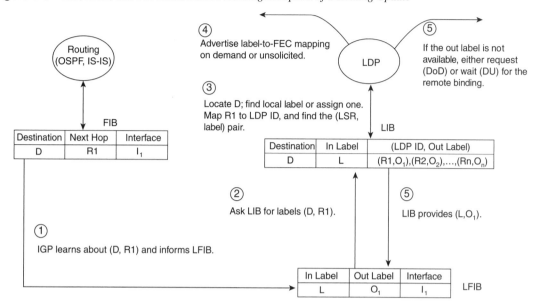

Similarly, whenever an LSR receives a remote FEC-to-label mapping via an LDP Label Mapping message, LDP determines whether the sender is currently the next hop for the advertised FEC. The next hop for a FEC (destination) is maintained by the FIB while the LIB entry maintains the FEC-to-local label and the remote-label mappings as (LSR ID, outgoing label) pairs. Therefore, the FEC is mapped to the next-hop address by looking up the FIB.

After the next-hop address has been found, and taking the next hop and the peer LDP ID as input, the LSR consults its peer address list to obtain the LDP ID-to-address mappings. Hence, if an entry in the peer address list matches the next-hop address, the receiver knows that the sender is the current next hop for the FEC. The receiver then allocates the incoming label, updates the LFIB with incoming and outgoing labels, and in turn advertises the local FEC-to-label mappings to peers. Figure 8-5 shows the interactions between FIB, LFIB, and the LIB reception of a remote FEC-to-label mapping that follows.

Figure 8-5   *LIB, LFIB, and FIB Interactions Following Reception of a Remote FEC-to-Label Mapping*

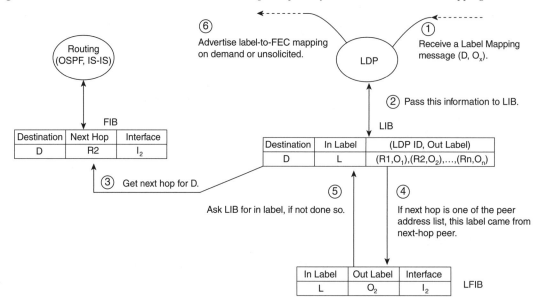

As mentioned previously, when operating with the liberal label-retention mode, the LIB might contain more that one pair (peer, outgoing label) for a particular FEC. To avoid traffic misrouting for an LSP, the outgoing label for the LSP must always use the outgoing label received from the valid next hop. To ensure that the outgoing label corresponds to the valid next hop, LDP monitors routing updates to keep track of next-hop changes for a FEC. Whenever the next hop for a FEC changes, LDP updates the LFIB information accordingly.

When LDP is operating in liberal label-retention mode, because the remote FEC-to-label mappings might already exist in the LIB and do not need to be requested, LDP can adapt to next-hop changes quickly. In contrast, when operating in conservative label-retention mode, because the LSR retains remote FEC-to-label mappings only from the valid next hops, LDP takes longer to adapt to the next-hop changes. The main benefit of conservative label-retention mode is that it conserves memory and label space. For example, cell-based LSRs such as ATM switches typically have limited VPI/VCI space. Therefore, cell-based LSRs most often use downstream on-demand label advertisement with the conservative label-retention mode to conserve the label space.

Establishing Pseudowires (PWs) Using LDP

So far in this chapter the discussion of LDP use has been confined only to the FECs of type IP address. However, it is important to note that LDP could also be used to associate an LSP with another type of FEC, such as Layer 2 circuit ID. For example, many types of L2VPN services involve encapsulating Layer 2 frames (such as ATM cells, Frame Relay frames, and Ethernet frames) and then transmitting them over Pseudowires. (See Chapter 10, "Improving Survivability of IP and MPLS Networks.")

A *pseudowire* (PW) is a mechanism that carries the essential elements of an emulated service from one provider edge (PE) router to another PE's over a packet-switched network (PSN) such as an IP or MPLS network.[5] The header of the PW contains a demultiplexor field that is prepended to the encapsulated frame before transmitting it on the PW. Typically, multiple PWs may be carried in a single tunnel (which in the case of MPLS is an LSP) across the PSN. When the packet arrives at the remote endpoint of the PW, the receiver uses the demultiplexor to identify the particular PW on which the packet has arrived. Depending on the tunneling protocol used to carry PWs across the PSN, the demultiplexor field might be based on an MPLS label, an L2TP session ID, or a UDP port number. In the case of an MPLS network, the demultiplexor field contains an MPLS label, which can be signaled using LDP between two PW endpoints. To accomplish this, new type length values (TLVs) have been defined for LDP that allow an LSR to identify PWs, bind a demultiplexor field value to a PW, and inform the remote peer about the binding.[6]

LDP Control-Plane and Forwarding-Plane Components

The state of an LSP that is established through LDP can be divided into two components: the LDP state (which is maintained in the control plane), and the MPLS forwarding state (which is maintained in the forwarding plane).

The exact format of the LDP state or the MPLS forwarding state of an LSP in an LSR depends on whether the LSR is ingress, egress, or transit for that LSP. For example, LSP ingress LSR uses a *FEC-to-NHLFE* (FTN) entry to map the associated FEC to one or more *next-hop label forwarding entry* (NHLFE). Similarly, an LSP transit LSR uses the incoming label to select a particular incoming label map (ILM) that in turn identifies a particular NHLFE. The NHLFE contains label-stack operation (such as swap, push, pop), next-hop address, and outgoing interface. (For further details, see Chapter 3, "MPLS Forwarding Plane: Achieving Nonstop Forwarding.") The separation of control- and forwarding-plane components makes it possible for the LDP control-plane component to restart without disturbing the forwarding plane. For disruption-free forwarding on LSPs that were established using LDP, the LSR must be able to preserve the MPLS forwarding state of the concerned LSPs across the LDP restart.

LDP Forwarding State

In this chapter, the term *control plane* means the "LDP component of the control plane," and the term *nonstop forwarding* (NSF) means the capability of an LSR to preserve the MPLS forwarding state for LSPs (that are established using LDP) across the LDP control-plane restart.

For the sake of conciseness, the phrase *MPLS forwarding state of an LSP* means information of the following forms:

- <FEC -> push (outgoing label), next hop> at an LSP ingress LSR
- <incoming label, swap (outgoing label), next hop> at an LSP transit LSR
- <incoming label, pop (label stack), next hop> at an LSP egress LSR

Keep in mind that parts of the MPLS forwarding state reside in the IP *Forwarding Information Base* (FIB). For example, forwarding of a packet at an LSP ingress LSR involves looking up the destination IP address in the FIB to identify the NHLFE. Similarly, forwarding of a packet at an LSP egress LSR might require one or more IP address lookups to determine the next hop.

For example, when the egress LSR assigns the same incoming label for multiple FECs with different next hops, the LSR might need to consult the FIB to determine the next hop for a FEC. In short, the LSR must preserve the required MPLS forwarding state regardless of where it resides.

LDP Control-Plane State

In this chapter, the phrase *LDP state of an LSP* refers to FEC-to-label mappings of the following form:

- <FEC->{outgoing label, next-hop address, LDP ID of the next-hop peer}> at an LSP ingress LSR
- <FEC->{incoming label, (and upstream peer LDP ID, in the case of downstream on-demand mode), (outgoing label, next-hop address, next-hop peer LDP ID)}> at an LSP transit LSR
- <FEC->{incoming label, (and upstream peer LDP ID, in the case of downstream on-demand mode)}> at an LSP egress LSR

The following sections examine the harmful effects of the LDP restart and describe procedures that you can use to alleviate these detrimental effects.

Understanding the Detrimental Effects of LDP Restart

At this point, the discussion turns to the issues that arise when the LDP control-plane component of an LSR restarts. As described earlier, an LDP session is established over TCP. When an LDP control-plane component on an LSR restarts, the restarting LSR (on which the control plane has restarted) loses LDP sessions with its LDP peers. RFC 3036 requires that whenever the TCP connection supporting an LDP session fails, LDP must immediately release all FEC-to-label mappings, including the MPLS forwarding state associated with the failed session. As a result, an LDP control-plane restart is said to impact MPLS forwarding. (See Step (a) in Figure 8-6, which shows the LDP restart behavior as specified in RFC 3036.)

However, this behavior is designed to keep the concerned routers from forwarding traffic into a black hole. When LSRs are capable of preserving the MPLS forwarding state across a control-plane failure, LDP restart describes methods that enable an LSR that has lost its LDP control plane to continue forwarding traffic. By using such restart methods, the LSR can relearn the LDP control state and refresh the associated MPLS forwarding state. (See Step (b) in Figure 8-6, which shows the LDP restart behavior using enhanced LDP protocol.) Achieving this, however, requires extensions to the LDP protocol.

Figure 8-6   *(a) LDP Restart Behavior Based on RFC 3036 (b) LDP Restart Behavior Based on Enhanced LDP Protocol*

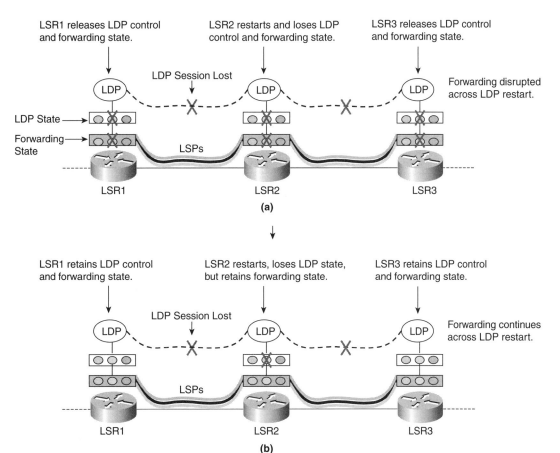

Mitigating Detrimental Effects of the LDP Restart

As discussed previously, when the LDP control-plane component of an LSR restarts, it causes the failure of LDP sessions between that LSR and its peers. As soon as a peer detects the failure of an LDP session with the restarting neighbor, that peer immediately terminates the concerned LDP session and releases FEC-to-label mappings and the MPLS forwarding state for all LSPs associated with the failed LDP session. Therefore this control-plane restart behavior results in disruption of forwarding on all LSPs associated with the failed session.

To make a bad situation even worse, because the LDP control-plane component restart is accompanied by the IP control-plane restart, and if the IP control-plane is not graceful restart-capable, the ripple effect caused by the LDP control-plane component restart can spread across multiple LSRs. (Recall that in this book control-plane software is considered to consist of inseparable components. For more information on IGP-related graceful restart mechanisms, see Chapter 4, "Intradomain IP Control Plane: Restarting OSPF Gracefully," and Chapter 5, "Intradomain IP Control Plane: Restarting IS-IS Gracefully.")

For example, on discovering IP control-plane failure, the IGP attempts to find alternative shortest paths that avoid the restarting LSR. As a result, next hops for certain FECs might change. This in turn causes LDP to adopt its FEC-to-label mappings accordingly. In short, the aforementioned control-plane restart event can cause a large number of LDP messages to be generated as LSRs withdraw previous FEC-to-label mappings and advertise new ones.

The separation of control and forwarding components should make it feasible for a restarting LSR to preserve its forwarding state and continue to forward traffic across the control-plane restart. However, preservation of the MPLS forwarding state across the control-plane restart alone is not sufficient to eliminate harmful effects caused by the control-plane restart, unless LDP protocol behavior is also modified.

For this purpose, IETF has specified two methods—LDP GR and LDP FT—that define LDP protocol extensions. These methods allow MPLS forwarding to continue across the LDP control-plane restart, and thus confine the effect of the control-plane restart to the restarting LSR and its peers. Both mechanisms require preservation of the MPLS forwarding state across the LDP restart, but greatly differ with regard to the amount of LDP state that must be preserved across the restart and the state recovery method.

An optimization of the LDP FT, known as the *Checkpoint Procedures for LDP* (LDP CKP), is also defined for a relatively static environment such as indirectly connected LDP sessions between PE LSRs in the L2VPN applications. Unlike LDP FT, the LDP CKP procedure relies on periodic but less-frequent incremental acknowledgments, which enables LSRs to reduce (at the risk of losing state for the most recent LDP exchanges) the amount of processing for acknowledging LDP messages. For example, an LSR can obtain acknowledgments for all label message exchanges containing FT Protection TLV (messages that carry this TLV must be secured and acknowledged) up to the time of the request by including the FT Protection TLV on an LDP keepalive message. The receiving LSR interprets such a keepalive message as a request to flush the acknowledgments for all previously received messages carrying FT Protection TLV.

Although the focus of this chapter is the LDP GR mechanism, it is beneficial to contrast LDP GR and LDP FT mechanisms.

Comparison of LDP Restart Methods

In one respect, the LDP GR and LDP FT approaches are similar; both attempt to avoid disruption of the MPLS forwarding plane across the control-plane restart As discussed earlier in this chapter, LDP-derived information comprises two components:

- LDP state that is maintained in the control plane (such as in the LIB)

- MPLS forwarding state that is maintained in the forwarding plane (such as in the LFIB and the FIB, when applicable)

The MPLS forwarding state that needs to be preserved across the control-plane restart is the same regardless of which particular restart mechanism is used. However, the two mechanisms have different requirements for preserving the LDP state, and they use different mechanics to recover and validate the LDP state.

- **FT Session TLV**—Both LDP GR and LDP FT (as well as the LDP CKP) use the same new TLV, referred to as the FT Session TLV (see Figure 8-7). The FT TLV is exchanged in the LDP initialization message. By the appropriate setting of the FT flags (S, C, L), an LSR can select the desired restart mechanism. For example, the LDP GR mechanism is selected by setting the L bit to 1 and the C and S bits to 0. The reserved bits should be set to 0 by the sender and ignored by the receiver.

Figure 8-7   *Encoding Format of the FT Session TLV*

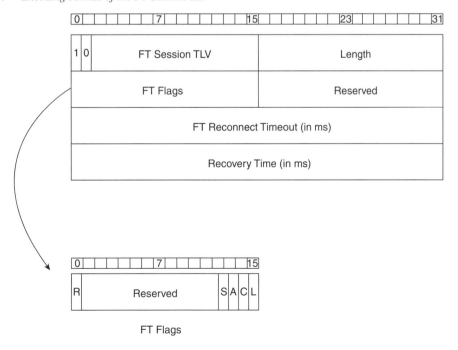

FT Flags

- **LDP Forwarding State**—Both mechanisms require that the restarting LSR must preserve the MPLS forwarding state for LSPs established through LDP across the control-plane restart. Moreover, the nonrestarting peers must also retain the MPLS forwarding state associated with the failed LDP sessions.

- **LDP Control-Plane State**—The LDP FT mechanism requires that in addition to the MPLS forwarding state for LSPs, the restarting LSR must preserve the concerned LDP state across control-plane restart. In contrast, the LDP GR mechanism requires preservation of none or reduced control-plane state. When using LDP GR, generally, local FEC-to-label mappings are preserved across the restart, whereas the remote FEC-to-label mappings are recovered from peers after the restart. Both mechanisms require support from neighbors. For example, the peers of an NSF-capable restarting LSR must not release their LDP states associated with the failed LDP sessions.

- **Recovery Speed**—In LDP FT, the presence of FT Protection TLV in an LDP message requires that the receiver preserve the LDP state derived from the message and additionally acknowledges it by including the FT ACK TLV in an LDP message. For example, the message could be a Label Mapping, Label Request, or keepalive message.

  Because the acknowledged FEC-to-label mapping information should have been preserved across the control-plane restart, LDP FT needs to recover the LDP state only for unacknowledged messages after the restart. Because the number of acknowledged messages typically should be small, the LDP FT mechanism can quickly recover the lost LDP state after the control-plane restart.

  In contrast, the LDP GR neither preserves nor acknowledges the LDP state derived from LDP messages. Therefore, LDP GR ends up recovering and validating the entire LDP state, which might take long time (in the order of seconds) depending on the number of FEC-to-label mappings that need to be relearned. A relatively longer recovery period means that the restarting LSR and its peers must use stale forwarding information for an extended period of time. Retaining stale forwarding state for an extended period of time is undesirable because if in the meantime the network topology changes and the forwarding state is not updated, forwarding traffic based on incorrect information might cause forwarding loops.

- **Congestion After Restart**—In LDP FT, only unacknowledged messages need to be resynchronized after restart, which means there is no real need to have a traffic-shaping mechanism to pace messages to avoid receipt of buffer overflows or receipt of control processor overload due to flooding of control messages. In contrast, LDP GR requires full LDP state resynchronization after restart in a relatively short time. Therefore, there is a potential for congestion in the receive buffer or for overload of the receive control processor. Although TCP provides a flow control, an additional shaping of LDP messages after restart might be needed in this case.

- **Congestion During Normal Operation**—As mentioned earlier, the LDP FT mechanism requires that all LDP message-carrying FT Protection TLVs be acknowledged. In contrast, LDP GR does not preserve any LDP-related state, and acknowledgment messages are not needed. Thus, during normal operation, the LDP GR reduces message flow between LDP peers.

- **Performance and Scalability**—The LDP FT mechanism typically is processing intensive (for example, messages needs to be acknowledged) and memory intensive (for example, both local and remote label mappings need to be preserved for a large number of FT labels). Therefore, as the number of FEC-to-label mappings increases, the LDP FT might not scale in a manageable fashion.

- **Label Space Usage**—When using LDP GR, remote FEC-to-label mappings are recovered from peers. To recover a local FEC-to-label mapping, LDP GR either retains the same label for the FEC or assigns a new one after the control-plane restart. The first option requires preservation of FEC-to-incoming label mappings across the LDP restart, which consumes additional memory. The second option does not require preservation of either local or remote mappings. However, as explained in detail later, the second alternative increases the risk of depleting the label space.

The comparison of the LDP GR and the LDP FT indicates that the two approaches offer design trade-offs for the following: different levels of scalability, implementation complexity, and speed of recovery. In general, LDP GR seems to be better suited for scalable implementations because it involves simpler protocol interactions and requires preservation of reduced LDP state information across the restart. The remainder of this chapter deals mainly with the LDP GR. As mentioned previously, the LDP GR has a slightly different recovery procedure for downstream unsolicited and downstream on-demand label distribution modes. The LDP GR mechanism for the downstream unsolicited label distribution mode is described in the following section.

LDP GR Mechanism for Downstream Unsolicited Mode

The LDP GR mechanism specifies protocol extensions that enable an LSR to express to an LDP peer its capability to preserve an MPLS forwarding state across the LDP control-plane component restart and the estimated time that it would take to restart the LSR to reestablish the LDP session with the peer. Afterward, when the LDP control-plane component of the LSR restarts, the restarting LSR loses its LDP session with the peers. On detecting that its LDP session with a neighbor has failed, the nonrestarting peer temporarily retains all its FEC-to-label mappings associated with the failed session, marks them stale, and waits for reestablishment of LDP communication with the restarting LSR. While waiting, the nonrestarting peer continues to forward traffic as normal using the previously learned MPLS forwarding state. The restarting LSR loses all or most of its LDP state for established LSPs. (An LSP is said to be fully established if its MPLS forwarding state has been installed in the LFIB.) The restarting LSR, however, continues to forward traffic on those LSPs across the control-plane restart using the preserved MPLS forwarding state.

After restarting its LDP control-plane component, the restarting LSR reestablishes LDP sessions with the previous peers. To prevent peers from releasing the FEC-to-label mappings that are associated with the failed LDP sessions, the restarting LSR establishes LDP sessions within the previously advertised time period.

If the restarting LSR successfully reestablishes LDP sessions within the allowed time, it will recover the LDP state and refresh the preserved (stale) MPLS forwarding state by exchanging FEC-to-label mappings with the peers. The FEC-to-outgoing label mappings are recovered from the remote peers. However, either the local FEC-to-label mappings are kept or new ones are assigned. If the first option is used, the restarting LSR must have some way to reclaim the pre-restart FEC-to-label mappings. Generally, this requires preservation of FEC-to-label mappings as an LSP's LDP state across the control-plane restart. If the restarting LSR chooses the second alternative, it can assign a new FEC-to-label mapping. When the LDP state for an LSP has been rebuilt, the associated MPLS forwarding state is also updated. The LDP GR mechanism for the downstream unsolicited label distribution mode can be described as a three-stage procedure.

Initial Capability Exchange

In the first phase, each LSR indicates its capability to support an LDP graceful restart by including the FT Session TLV (see Figure 8-7) in the LDP initialization message during the initial session establishment with the potential LDP peer. Setting the appropriate bit in the FT Flags field selects the desired mechanism. For example, to select LDP GR mechanism, the L flag (learned from the network) must be set to 1, and C and S flags bits are set to 0.

The FT Session TLV also contains FT Reconnect Timeout and FT Recovery Time fields. In the case of LDP GR, FT Reconnect Timeout indicates the time (in milliseconds) that the sender of the FT Session TLV wants the receiver to wait and keep its FEC-to-label mappings and corresponding MPLS forwarding state after the receiver detects failure of the LDP session with the sender. To prevent a peer from releasing FEC-to-label mappings and corresponding MPLS forwarding state prematurely, the sender should select a FT Reconnect Timeout long enough to allow it to reestablish an LDP session with the receiver after the control-plane restart. If the sender determines that it is incapable of preserving the forwarding state across the LDP restart, it must set the FT Reconnect Timeout to 0. By setting the FT Reconnect Timeout to zero, the sender signals a peer that it should immediately release all FEC-to-label mappings and the associated MPLS forwarding state after that peer detects failure of LDP session with the sender.

These protocol interactions indicate that the LDP GR mechanism requires support from nonrestarting LDP peers. The fact that an LSR is allowed to set the FT Reconnect Timeout to nonzero or zero shows that the LDP GR mechanism can be used by LSRs with or without the ability to preserve the MPLS forwarding state across the control-plane restart. As discussed later in this chapter, when an LSR supports an LDP GR procedure but is NSF-incapable, the LSR does not reduce the harmful effects caused by its LDP control-plane component restart. However, by retaining FEC-to-label mappings and continuing to forward as normal, such an LSR can still help reduce negative impacts on MPLS forwarding when the control plane of an NSF-capable neighbor restarts.

LDP Session Failure

The second phase begins with the restart of the LDP control plane and ensuing sessions failure. The restarting LSR continues to forward traffic across the control-plane restart using the preserved MPLS forwarding state. When LDP peers of the restarting LSR detect the failure of LDP sessions, assuming the restarting LSR has advertised a nonzero value for the FT Reconnect Timeout before the restart, the peers wait for the restarting LSR to reestablish an LDP session. While waiting, each peer retains all FEC-to-label mappings associated with the failed session but marks them stale and continues to use the corresponding MPLS forwarding state when forwarding data traffic on the concerned LSPs.

LDP Session Reestablishment and State Recovery

The third phase consists of reestablishing the LDP sessions, recovering the LDP state, and updating the stale MPLS forwarding state. After restart, during the session reestablishment procedure, the restarting LSR informs its peers about the recovery period by setting the Recovery Time in the FT Session TLV. The value of the Recovery Time is set based on an internal timer, as explained in the sections that follow.

The Recovery Time indicates the time (in milliseconds) after which the restarting LSR will not retain its MPLS forwarding state that it has preserved across the control-plane restart. The recovery time begins from the moment when the restarting LSR sends the LDP initialization message containing the FT Session TLV. For the restarting LSR, the LDP GR mechanism defines a configurable local timer known as the MPLS Forwarding State Holding Timer. After restart (before sending the LDP initialization message), the restarting LSR examines whether it has preserved the MPLS forwarding state across the LDP control-plane restart. If so, the restarting LSR starts the MPLS Forwarding State Holding Timer and marks its preserved MPLS forwarding state entries as stale. If the stale MPLS forwarding state is not refreshed before the MPLS Forwarding State Holding Timer expires, it is removed.

The restarting LSR advertises the current value of the MPLS Forwarding State Holding Timer in the FT Recovery Time field of the FT Session TLV. Therefore, to avoid harmful effects caused by (unintended) premature removal of the stale MPLS forwarding state, the LDP GR-capable peers must resynchronize all FEC-to-label mappings within the advertised FT Recovery Time.

On the other hand, upon restarting, if the restarting LSR determines that it has not been able to preserve MPLS forwarding state across the restart, the LSR sets the FT Recovery Time to zero. As soon as peers (who should be waiting for the peers to restart and reestablish sessions) see a value of zero in the FT Recovery Time, they immediately release FEC-to-label mappings and remove the corresponding forwarding state. An LSR is said to be in the process of restarting while its MPLS Forwarding State Holding Timer is running. Therefore expiration of the MPLS Forwarding State Holding Timer marks the completion of the LDP graceful restart procedure (see Figure 8-8).

Figure 8-8   *LDP GR Recovery States*

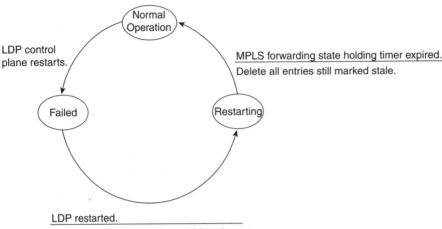

Nonrestarting LSR Behavior

For the nonstarting peer (the one that is participating in the graceful restart procedure with a restarting neighbor), the LDP GR mechanism defines a configurable local timer, referred to as the Neighbor Liveness Timer. Following detection of the LDP session restart with a peer, if the restarting peer had previously advertised a nonzero value for the FT Reconnect Timer before the restart, the nonrestarting LSR starts the Neighbor Liveness Timer, marks all FEC-to-label mappings exchanged with the restarting LSR as stale, and waits for session reestablishment. While waiting, the peer continues to retain the stale FEC-to-label mappings and uses the corresponding MPLS forwarding state when forwarding traffic on the associated LSPs. The nonrestarting LSR is expected to retain its stale MPLS forwarding information for a minimum duration. The duration is equal to the lesser of the Neighbor Liveness Timer and the FT Reconnect Timeout advertised by the restarting neighbor.

As mentioned earlier, the nonrestarting peer deletes all stale FEC-to-label mappings if the session is not reestablished within the allowed time or if the restarting neighbor advertises a value of zero in the Recovery Time after restart. However, if the restarting LSR advertises a nonzero value for the Recovery Time, the nonrestarting peer must continue to retain the stale FEC-to-label mappings. For a nonrestarting peer, the LDP GR mechanism also defines a configurable local timer, referred to as the Maximum Recovery Time. If the nonrestarting LSR successfully reestablishes an LDP session with the restarting neighbor within the allowed time (the lesser of the Neighbor Liveness Timer and the FT Reconnect Timeout advertised by the restarting neighbor), it examines the newly received Recovery Time value to decide whether to delete or continue to retain the stale FEC-to-label mappings. Specifically, if the nonrestarting LSR receives a nonzero value for the Recovery Time in the newly received FT Session TLV, it should retain stale label-to-FEC mappings for an additional duration (the smaller of the local Maximum Recovery Time and Recovery Time advertised by the neighbor).

Therefore, in entirety, a nonrestarting LSR can retain the stale MPLS forwarding information for a maximum duration equal to minimum of amount of time {the local Neighbor Liveness Timer, received FT Reconnect Timeout} plus the minimum time {local Maximum Recovery Time, received Recovery Time}. To allow time for updating the MPLS forwarding state entries, the LDP GR mechanism recommends that the nonrestarting peers should complete exchange of their FEC-to-label mappings with the restarting neighbor within one half of the Recovery Time.

When a nonrestarting peer receives a Label Mapping message, it searches its LDP state for a matching entry. If the newly received FEC-to-label mapping is the same as the stale entry in the LIB that already exists, it clears the stale flag. However, if a stale label mapping entry for the same FEC already exists but has a different label than the one received in the Label Mapping message, the LSR updates the existing LIB entry with the new label, clears the flag, and then follows the normal LDP procedure (for example, updates the LFIB if appropriate).

Restarting LSR Behavior

For an LSR in the process of restarting (an LSR whose MPLS Forwarding State Timer has not expired), LDP GR distinguishes between the behavior of egress and nonegress LSRs for an LSP. Following control-plane restart and session reestablishment, when the restarting LSR receives a Label Mapping message, it searches its MPLS forwarding state entry to determine whether it is noningress or an egress LSR for the associated LSP. Suppose following the control-plane restart and session reestablishment that a Label Mapping message for a FEC F with a label L is received from a peer N. The restarting LSR searches its MPLS forwarding state for an appropriate matching entry to determine whether it is a nonegress or egress LSR for the concerned LSP.

For example, a matching entry of the form

- <FEC=F -> push (outgoing label=L), next hop=peer N> or
- <incoming label, swap (outgoing label=L, or pop if outgoing label=Implicit Null), next hop=peer N>

indicates that the LSR is a nonegress LSR for the LSP. Similarly, a matching of the form <incoming label, pop (label stack), next hop=peer N> means that the LSR is an egress LSR for the LSP.

When the LSR has found a matching entry and the LSR has determined that it is the *nonegress* (meaning it is ingress or transit) LSR for the LSP, the LSR performs the following functions:

- Creates the LDP state for the LSP
- Updates the MPLS forwarding state for the LSP (clears the stale flag)
- In the transit case, associates either the same (same as the one allocated prior to control-plane restart) or a new one, and advertises the corresponding <FEC, incoming label> mapping to its peers

If the restarting LSR is an egress LSR for the LSP, depending on whether the LSR is configured to generate a non-NULL or NULL (either Implicit or Explicit), the LSR performs the following functions:

- Creates the LDP state

- Updates the MPLS forwarding state (clears the stale flag)

- Either advertises a <FEC, non-NULL> or <FEC, NULL> mapping to its peers, as appropriate

However, if a matching forwarding state entry is not found, regardless of a nonegress or egress case, the restarting LSR follows the normal LDP procedures. The detailed operation of the LDP GR mechanism is described in the following section.

LDP GR Operation in Downstream Unsolicited Mode

To summarize earlier discussions, the LSR itself assigns an incoming FEC-to-label mapping while it learns FEC-to-outgoing label mappings from peers. Each LSR maintains the locally assigned and remotely learned FEC-to-label mappings in a LIB. The collection of FEC-to-label mappings constitutes the LDP state for the established LSPs. The LIB in turn is used to populate the LFIB, which contains the MPLS forwarding state for the LSPs. In general, LFIB not only contains a forwarding state for LSPs established using LDP, but also for LSPs established via other protocols such as BGP and RSVP-TE. The following discussion, however, only concerns the LDP-derived MPLS forwarding state.

When the LDP control plane of an NSF-capable LSR restarts, the restarting LSR continues to forward traffic using the preserved MPLS forwarding state. After restarting, the LSR marks the preserved MPLS forwarding state as stale, but continues to use it for forwarding traffic on the associated LSPs. Then it reestablishes the session, recovers the LDP state, and refreshes the associated MPLS forwarding state in the LFIB. To rebuild LIB entries (LDP state) after the LDP control-plane component restart, FEC-to-outgoing label mappings are recovered from peers, while FEC-to-incoming label mappings are reclaimed locally as follows: For FEC to incoming label mappings, the restarting LSR has two options:

- Option A—Preserve the FEC-to-incoming label mappings across the control-plane restart.

- Option B—Assign a new FEC-to-incoming label mapping after the restart.

Option A has the advantage that the FEC-to-incoming label mappings are not changed after the restart, but option A consumes more memory space and requires a relatively complex implementation to preserve and manage label mappings across the restart. In contrast, option B obviates the need for preserving and managing the FEC-to-incoming-label mappings across the LDP restart, but consumes more labels. In particular, if the restarting LSR does not have at least as many unallocated as allocated labels during the LDP recovery period, using option B could lead to label depletion. The operation of LDP GR for both alternatives is described in the following sections.

Option A: LDP GR Operation for Downstream Unsolicited Mode

This section describes the operation of the LDP GR when the restarting LSR preserves the MPLS forwarding state and FEC-to-incoming label mappings across the control-plane restart. Therefore, the restarting LSR advertises the same FEC-to-incoming label mappings to its peers after the control-plane restart. The restarting LSR recovers the FEC-to-outgoing label mappings from peers. The following explanations are based on the assumption that the restarting LSR is a transit LSR. For the sake of brevity, egress and ingress restarting LSR cases are omitted. The operation is explained using the reference diagram shown in Figure 8-9.

Figure 8-9 *Operation of the LDP GR Mechanism (Option A).*

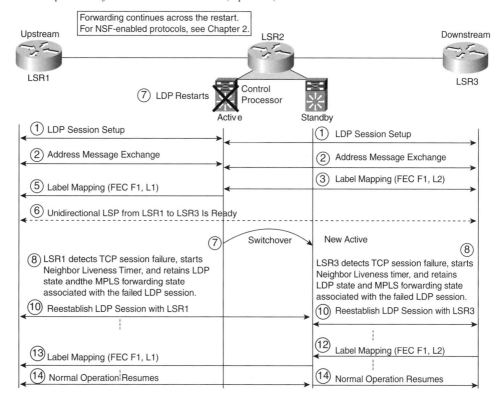

The sequence of LDP GR operational steps described in the following list does not necessarily imply that these steps are followed in a particular implementation. Note that some of the steps are not shown in Figure 8-9.

1. When establishing the LDP session, the neighboring LSRs exchange FT Session TLV in the LDP initialization messages. The FT Session TLV contains FT Flags, FT Reconnection Timeout (in milliseconds), and Recovery Time (in milliseconds). In the FT Flags field, the sender sets the L (learn from network) flag to 1 to select the LDP GR mechanism. All other FT flags are set to 0 by the sender and ignored by the receiver. Assuming the sender is NSF-capable, the sender sets the FT Reconnection Time to the period that it expects to take to be able to communicate following a LDP restart. During the initial session establishment process, the Recovery Time is set to 0 and is ignored by the receiver. The Recovery Time becomes meaningful after the LDP control-plane restart.

2. After the LDP session has been established, each LDP peer advertises its interface IP addresses using Address messages.

3. Assuming downstream unsolicited label distribution mode, for all FECs (here, for simplicity, consider a single FEC F1) reachable through LSR3, it sends LDP Label Mapping messages <FEC F1, label L2> to its peers (here, only peer LSR2). On receiving the Label Mapping message, LSR2 determines whether LSR3 is the valid next hop for the FEC F1. After validating that the label-to-FEC mapping came from the next hop for the FEC F1, LSR2 updates the MPLS forwarding state. Note that when LSR2 is operating with the liberal label-retention mode, it can retain a remote FEC-to-label mapping of a peer that is not the next hop for that FEC. However, the forwarding state in the LFIB should always correspond to the valid next hop for the FEC.

4. Independently, LSR2 learns via IGP that LSR3 is the next hop for the FEC F1. It assigns an incoming label L1 to F1 and updates the corresponding MPLS forwarding state entry in the LFIB.

5. LSR2 advertises its <FEC F1, label L1> mapping to all its peers (here, only LSR1) using an LDP Label Mapping message.

   After verifying that the <FEC F1, label L1> mapping came from a next hop for the FEC F1, LSR1 creates an LDP state entry in the LIB and an MPLS forwarding state entry in the LFIB.

6. Assume that the LSP from LSR1 to LSR3 has been established and is forwarding packets belonging to the FEC F1.

7. LSR2's LDP control plane restarts and it loses all LDP sessions with peers (LSR1 and LSR3).

8. On detecting LDP session failure, LSR1 and LSR3 retain the FEC-to-label mappings associated with the failed LDP sessions, but mark them stale. Moreover, LSR1 and LSR3 start the Neighbor Liveness Timer and wait for reestablishment of the LDP sessions. While waiting, they continue to forward using the stale MPLS forwarding state information.

9. Assume LSR2 has preserved its MPLS forwarding state and FEC-to-incoming label mappings across the LDP control-plane component restart. After restarting LDP, LSR2 marks the preserved MPLS forwarding state as stale and starts the MPLS forwarding State Holding Timer. During the LDP session reestablishment process, LSR2 sends the FT Session TLV with the Recovery Time field set to the current value of the MPLS Forwarding State Holding Timer. A nonzero value for the Recovery Time indicates that the restarting LSR has been able to preserve its MPLS forwarding state across the LDP restart. LSR2 needs to recover FEC-to-label mappings and update the stale MPLS forwarding state before the Forwarding State Holding Timer expires. LSR2 removes any remaining stale MPLS forwarding state when the MPLS Forwarding State Holding Timer expires.

10. Assume LSR1 and LSR3 reestablish LDP sessions with LSR2 within the allowed time (the lesser of the local Neighbor Liveness Timer and FT Reconnection Timeout advertised by the restarting neighbor before the restart). Moreover, assume LSR1 and LSR3 receive an FT Session TLV from LSR2 with a nonzero Recovery Time. Under these circumstances, LSR1 and LSR3 continue to retain stale FEC-to-label mappings and the corresponding MPLS forwarding information (the lesser of the local Maximum Recovery Time and Recovery Time advertised by the LSR2). Thus, LSR1 and LSR3 can retain stale FEC-to-label mappings and the corresponding MPLS forwarding state for a maximum total duration equal to the lesser of (local Neighbor Liveness Timer and the FT Reconnect Timeout advertised by LSR2) plus the lesser of (local Maximum Recovery Time, Recovery Time advertised by LSR2). However, if LSR1 and LSR3 receive the FT Session TLV from LSR2 with a zero Recovery Time that indicates that LSR2 was not able to preserve the LDP-related forwarding state across the LDP restart, they immediately release all stale FEC-to-label bindings and delete the corresponding MPLS forwarding state.

11. If LSR1 and LSR3 could not reestablish LDP sessions with LSR2 within the lesser of (the local Neighbor Liveness Timer and the FT Reconnection Timeout as advertised by LSR2), they should also delete all stale FEC-to-label mappings and the corresponding MPLS forwarding state associated with the failed session. Therefore, at a minimum, LSR1 and LSR3 should retain the stale FEC-to-label mappings for a duration equaling the lesser of (the local Neighbor Liveness Timer and the FT Reconnection Timeout as advertised by LSR2).

12. For each FEC reachable through LSR3, LSR3 sends an LDP Label Mapping message to its peers. Assuming there is only one FEC F1 reachable from LSR3, LSR3 sends a single Label Mapping message for FEC F1 to its peers (in this case, only to LSR2). A similar set of operations is performed by LSR1 for each FEC reachable through LSR1. LSR1 and LSR3 are expected to complete the exchange of FEC-to-label mappings with the LSR2 within one half of the Recovery Time advertised in the FT Session TLV by the LSR2.

13. Assume LSR2 is the transit LSR for the LSP associated with FEC F1. On receipt of Label Mapping message <FEC F1, label L1> from LSR3, LSR2 searches its MPLS forwarding state for an appropriate matching entry of the form <incoming label, swap (outgoing label=L1), next hop=LSR3>. If a matching entry is found, LSR2 creates the LDP state, updates the MPLS forwarding state (clears the stale flag), associates the incoming label from that entry with the FEC F1, and advertises the <FEC F1, incoming label> mapping to its peers (here, only LSR1). If a matching entry is not found, LSR2 follows normal procedures. For example, it creates the LDP state, allocates an incoming label, updates the MPLS forwarding state, and advertises that FEC-to-incoming label mapping to its peers (LSR1).

14. After having received a Label Mapping message, and having verified that the label binding came from a next hop for the FEC1, LSR1 updates the LIB entries. Using the new LIB information, LSR1 then updates the corresponding stale MPLS forwarding information in the LFIB. On receipt of a Label Mapping message from the restarting peer LSR2, LSR1 searches its LDP state for a matching entry. If the newly received FEC-to-label mapping is the same as the one already existing stale entry, LSR1 clears the stale flag. However, if a stale label mapping entry for the same FEC already exists but has a different label than the one received in the Label Mapping message, the LSR updates the existing LIB entry with the new label, clears the flag, and updates the LFIB, as appropriate.

15. The LDP restart is considered complete when the MPLS Forwarding State Holding Timer expires. On completion of the LDP restart, the restarting LSR and its peers remove the remaining stale information. Normal operation resumes.

Option B: LDP GR Operation for Downstream Unsolicited Mode

When using option B, the restarting LSR does not preserve FEC-to-incoming label mappings across the restart. (MPLS forwarding still must be preserved across the control-plane restart.) The restarting LSR recovers remote FEC-to-label mappings from the peers while it allocates and advertises new FEC-to-incoming label mappings after the restart. Because the restarting LSR must allocate new FEC to incoming labels after the restart, the restarting LSR might have two incoming label bindings for the same FEC in the LFIB:

- The first label binding that was allocated before the restart and has been preserved across the restart

- The second label binding that is allocated after the restart

Therefore, option B requires that the restarting LSR have at least as many unallocated as allocated local labels. Even though the LSR might have two incoming labels for the same FEC for a short time, they should always have the same outgoing label and the next hop. As a result, existence of two incoming labels for the same FEC does not pose any risk of traffic misrouting. The incoming label that was allocated before the LDP restart is not refreshed after the LDP restart and is removed when the MPLS Forwarding State Timer expires. With the exception of allocation of new FEC-to-incoming label mappings, LDP GR operation is identical in both cases.

LDP GR Mechanism for Downstream On-Demand Mode

The previous section described LDP GR mechanism for the downstream unsolicited label distribution mode.[7] This section describes the LDP GR mechanism for downstream on-demand label distribution by drawing on the concepts of the previous section.

To avoid repetition of information already described in the previous section, the following discussion first summarizes LDP GR procedures that are common to both modes. It then describes those procedures that are specific to the downstream on-demand label distribution mode.

LDP GR Common Procedures

During the initial LDP session establishment (before the LDP control-plane restart), an LSR that supports LDP GR downstream on-demand procedures advertises its NSF capability to its peers by setting the appropriate fields in the FT Session TLV. For example, the sender sets the L (learn from network) flag to 1 to select the LDP GR mechanism and sets the FT Reconnection Timeout to the estimated time that is required for the LSR to reestablish an LDP session with the peer.

When the LDP control-plane component on an LSR restarts, the restarting LSR loses LDP sessions with its peers and the associated LDP state, but the LSR preserves the MPLS forwarding state across the restart. The restarting LSR continues to forward data traffic using the preserved MPLS forwarding state across the restart. After restarting, the restarted LSR checks whether it has preserved the MPLS forwarding state across the restart. If so, the restarting LSR starts the MPLS Forwarding State Holding Timer and marks the preserved MPLS forwarding state information as stale. If the stale MPLS forwarding state is not refreshed before the MPLS Forwarding State Holding Timer expires, it is removed. While its MPLS forwarding state is running, the restarting LSR recovers the required LDP state and updates the stale MPLS forwarding state. Therefore, the recovery period begins when the MPLS Holding Timer starts and ends when it expires. This means that the restarting LSR must be able to recover the required LDP state and update the stale MPLS forwarding state within the recovery period. The exact behavior of a restarting LSR depends on whether the LSR is an ingress, transit, or egress LSR for the LSP (as described later).

Following LDP control-plane restart in a peer, a nonrestarting LSR detects failure of an LDP downstream on-demand session with the restarting peer. If the restarting peer has advertised a nonzero value for the FT Reconnect Timeout (indicating that it is NSF-capable), the nonrestarting LSR starts the Neighbor Liveness Timer, marks LDP state for established LSPs as stale, and waits for the session reestablishment. While waiting, the peer continues to retain and use stale forwarding state information. The nonrestarting LSR is expected to retain its stale MPLS forwarding information for a minimum duration equal to lesser of Neighbor Liveness Timer and the FT Reconnect Timeout advertised by the restarting neighbor.

If the session is not reestablished within the allowed time or if the restarting LSR advertises a value of zero in the FT Recovery Time (indicating that it has not preserved the MPLS forwarding state across the restart), after the restart the nonrestarting LSR immediately deletes the stale LDP state and removes the corresponding MPLS forwarding state. However, if the restarting LSR advertises a nonzero value in the FT Recovery Time field, the nonrestarting peer must continue to retain the stale forwarding state. If the nonrestarting LSR has successfully reestablished an LDP communication with the restarting neighbor within the lesser of the Neighbor Liveness Timer and the FT Reconnect Timeout advertised by the restarting LSR, the nonrestarting LSR examines the newly received Recovery Time value to decide whether to delete or retain the preserved LDP state and MPLS forwarding state.

The nonrestarting LSR determines the recovery period value as a lesser of {local Maximum Recovery Time, received Recovery Time}. The nonrestarting LSR must be able to revalidate LDP state and refresh the MPLS forwarding state within the recovery period. The exact behavior of a nonrestarting LSR depends on whether the LSR is an ingress, transit, or egress LSR for the LSP.

Downstream On-Demand Specific LDP GR Procedures

To this point, this chapter has described LDP GR procedures that are common for downstream unsolicited and downstream on-demand modes. The following section describes restarting and nonrestarting LSR behaviors during a recovery phase that are specific to the downstream on-demand label-distribution mode.

LDP GR downstream on-demand procedures distinguish between the behaviors of an ingress, transit, and egress nonrestarting neighbor. Therefore, in the following sections, each case is discussed separately.

Restarting LSR Behavior for Ingress LSRs

To understand the ingress restarting LSR's behavior, consider the example of an LSR1 and LSR2 with an LDP downstream on-demand session between them. (See the reference diagram in Figure 8-10.) These suppositions apply to the LSR1 and LSR2:

- The LSR1 is the ingress LSR for an LSP (associated with a FEC F1) that traverses LSR1 and LSR2.
- The LSR2 provides a <FEC F1, label L1> mapping to LSR1.
- The LDP control-plane component in LSR1 restarts.

Under these conditions, using LDP GR procedures described previously in this section, LSR1 and LSR2 reestablish the failed LDP session, recover LDP state, and refresh the MPLS forwarding state for the established LSPs. As a part of a nonrestarting peer restart behavior, LSR2 sends a Label Mapping message containing <FEC F1, label L1>. On receiving the Label Mapping message, LSR1 searches its MPLS forwarding state for an entry matching <FEC=F1,

{push (outgoing label=L1) or pop (outgoing label=Implicit NULL), next hop=LSR2}>. A matching entry indicates that the LSR1 is the ingress LSR for that LSP.

Therefore, LSR1 creates the LDP state (FEC=F1, {outgoing label=L1, next-hop neighbor=LDP ID of LSR2), and marks it stale. Then LSR1 sends a Label Request message to LSR2 and suggests the use of label L1 for FEC F1 by including it in the Label TLV. On receipt of a matching Label Mapping message from LSR2, LSR1 updates the LDP state and clears the stale flag. The Label Mapping message from LSR2 might carry the suggested label L1 or a different label for the FEC F1. If the received label matches the outgoing label (L1) in the forwarding state, LSR1 refreshes the forwarding state and clears the stale flag. Otherwise, LSR1 updates the forwarding state with the new label and clears the stale flag. If the MPLS Forwarding State Holding Timer expires while LSR1 is waiting for a reply to its Label Request message, it removes the forwarding state, sends a Label Abort message to LSR2, and then follows the LDP normal label-abort procedures.

For the sake of clarity, it is worth mentioning that an LSR might be an ingress LSR for some LSPs whereas it might be a transit LSR for others. If LSR1 does not find a forwarding state entry matching (FEC F1, outgoing label L1, next hop=LSR2), then LSR2 is not the ingress LSR for this LSP. In that case, for that particular LSP, LSR1 follows the appropriate behavior. The restarting LSR behaviors for egress and transit LSRs are described in the following sections.

Restarting LSR Behavior for Egress LSRs

To understand the egress restarting LSR's behavior, consider the example of an LSR2 and LSR3 with an LDP downstream on-demand session between them (see Figure 8-10). These suppositions apply to the LSR2 and LSR3:

- The LSR3 is the egress LSR for an LSP (associated with a FEC F1) that traverses LSR2 and LSR3.
- The LSR3 provides a <FEC F1, label L1> mapping to LSR2.
- The LDP control-plane component in LSR3 restarts.

Figure 8-10 *Reference Network Diagram of LDP GR Downstream On Demand*

Under these circumstances, using LDP GR procedures described previously, LSR2 and LSR3 reestablish the failed LDP session and attempt to recover the LDP state and refresh MPLS forwarding state for the established LSPs. As a part of a nonrestarting peer restart behavior, the upstream peer LSR2 sends a Label Request message to LSR3 and suggests the use of the label L1 for the FEC F1. On receipt of a Label Request message for the FEC F1 for which LSR3 is the egress LSR, LSR3 checks its configuration compatibility for generating the suggested label for the FEC F1. The suggested label might not be compatible with configuration. (For example, the suggested label might be asking for a non-NULL label, but LSR3 might be configured to generate Explicit or Implicit NULL). In this case, the LSR3 ignores the suggested label and processes the Label Request message following normal LDP behavior. If the suggested label is compatible with configuration, the LSR3 examines the incoming label to decide where to look for a matching forwarding state entry.

For example, if the received incoming label (L1) is non-NULL, LSR3 examines its MPLS forwarding state for a matching entry of the form <incoming label=L1, {pop (outgoing label), next hop}>. However, if the received incoming label is either Explicit or Implicit NULL, LSR2 looks up its IP forwarding state for a matching entry of the form <FEC=F1, next hop, outgoing interface>. If an MPLS or IP forwarding state entry is found, LSR3 clears the stale flag of the corresponding forwarding state entry and creates the LDP state <FEC=F1, (incoming label=L1, LSR2's LDP ID)>. Then the LSR3 responds with a Label Mapping message <FEC F1, Message ID=Message ID of the received Label Request message, Label TLV=incoming label L1>.

Restarting LSR Behavior for Transit LSRs

To understand the transit restarting LSR's behavior, consider the example of an LSR2 with an upstream LDP peer LSR1 and a downstream LDP peer LSR3. (See Figure 8-10.) These suppositions apply:

- The LSR2 is the transit LSR for an LSP (associated with a FEC F1) that traverses LSR1, LSR2, and LSR3.

- The LSR3 distributes a <FEC=F1, Label=L2> mapping to LSR2, which in turn advertises a <FEC=F1, Label=L1> mapping to LSR1. Hence, for FEC F1, LSR2 has an incoming label=L1 and outgoing label=L2.

- The LDP control-plane component in LSR2 restarts, and its LDP downstream on-demand session with LSR1 and LSR2 fails. In this case, the restarting LSR2 completes LDP GR procedures with both peers. The order in which LSR2 begins the restart procedure with a peer depends on which peer reestablishes LDP communication first.

The session with the upstream peer LSR1 reestablishes first. LSR1 sends a Label Request message to LSR2 suggesting the label L1 for the FEC F1. On receipt of the Label Request message from LSR1, LSR2 searches its MPLS forwarding state for an entry matching <incoming label=L1, swap outgoing label (or pop if outgoing label=Implicit NULL), next hop>. If a matching entry is not found, LSR2 ignores the suggested label and follows the normal LDP procedures. However, if a matching entry is found, LSR2 creates the LDP state for the LSP <FEC=F1, {incoming label=L1, upstream peer's LDP ID)> and marks it stale. Before proceeding further, LSR2 initiates interaction with LSR3. At this juncture, LSR2's interaction with the upstream peer LSR1 is said to be in the waiting for downstream state. The procedure with LSR3 starts on the receipt of a Label Mapping message.

After the session has been reestablished with the downstream peer, LSR3 sends a Label Mapping message <FEC=F1, label=L2>. On receiving the Label Mapping message from LSR3, LSR2 searches its MPLS forwarding state for an entry matching <FEC=F1, push (outgoing label=L2 or pop outgoing label=Implicit NULL), next hop=LSR3>. If a matching entry is found, LSR2 creates the LDP state <FEC=F1, {outgoing label=L2, next-hop neighbor=LSR3's LDP ID)> and marks it stale. Then LSR2 sends a Label Request message to LSR3 that suggests the use of label L2 for FEC F1. On receipt of a matching Label Mapping message from LSR3, LSR2 updates the LDP state and clears the stale flag.

The Label Mapping message from LSR3 may contain the suggested label L2 or a different label for the FEC F1. If the received label matches the outgoing label (L2) in the forwarding state, LSR2 refreshes the forwarding state. Otherwise, LSR2 updates the forwarding state. The stale flag is not cleared until interaction is complete with both upstream and downstream peers. At this point, the interaction with the downstream LSR peer is considered to be complete. Now LSR2 resumes its interaction with the LSR1 by replying with a Label Mapping message containing FEC=F1 to label=incoming label mapping. This completes interaction with the upstream LSR. Therefore, LSR2 clears the forwarding state stale flag. If the MPLS Forwarding State Holding Timer expires while LSR2 is waiting for a reply to its Label Request message, it removes the forwarding state, sends a Label Abort message to LSR3, and follows the LDP normal label-abort procedures.

So far, this chapter has discussed the restarting LSR's behavior. Next the chapter describes the GR restart behavior of the nonrestarting peers. LDP GR downstream on-demand procedures distinguish between the behavior of an ingress, transit, and egress nonrestarting peer.

Nonrestarting LSR Behavior for Ingress Neighbors

Consider LSR1 and LSR2 with an LDP downstream on-demand session between them. Suppose LSR1 is the ingress LSR for an LSP (associated with a FEC F1) that traverses LSR1 and LSR2. (See Figure 8-10.) Suppose LSR2 provides a <FEC F1, label L1> mapping to LSR1. Assume the LDP control-plane component in LSR2 restarts. Using LDP GR procedures described previously, LSR1 and LSR2 reestablish the LDP session and attempt to recover the LDP state and refresh the MPLS forwarding state for the established LSPs.

While LSR1 is waiting for reestablishment of the failed LDP session, if the next hop for a FEC changes from LSR2 to another peer, LSR1 clears the stale flag from the associated LDP state and follows the normal LDP procedures for next-hop changes, except that LSR1 does not send a Label Release message to LSR2.

When the session is reestablished, LSR1 scans its LDP state to determine all LSPs for which it is the ingress and for which LSR2 is the next hop. For each matching LSP entry, LSR1 sends a Label Mapping message with a suggested label. Assume LSR1 finds a single matching entry

<FEC=F1, push (outgoing label = L1), next hop=LSR2>. If this happens, LSR1 sends a Label Request message to LSR2 and suggests a label L1 for the FEC F1.

On receipt of a matching Label Mapping message from LSR2, LSR1 updates the LDP state and clears the stale flag. If the received label matches the outgoing label (L1) in the forwarding state, LSR1 takes no further action. Otherwise, LSR1 updates the forwarding state entry with the new outgoing label. If the MPLS Forwarding State Holding Timer expires while LSR1 is waiting for a reply to a Label Request message, it removes the forwarding state, sends a Label Abort message to LSR2, and follows LDP normal label-abort procedures.

Nonrestarting LSR Behavior for Egress Neighbors

Consider LSR2 and LSR3 with an LDP downstream on-demand session between them. (See Figure 8-10.) Suppose LSR3 is the egress for an LSP (associated with a FEC F1) that traverses LSR2 and LSR3. Suppose LSR3 provides a <FEC F1, label L1> mapping to LSR2. Assume the LDP control-plane component in LSR2 restarts. Using LDP GR procedures described previously, LSR2 and LSR3 reestablish the LDP session and attempt to recover LDP state and refresh MPLS forwarding state for the established LSPs.

While LSR3 is waiting for the reestablishment of the session, if the next hop for a FEC is lost, LSR3 follows the normal LDP procedures, except that where LSR3 is supposed to send a Label Withdraw message to the upstream peer LSR3 acts as if it had sent the message and in turn had received a Label Release message from LSR2.

After the session is reestablished with LSR2, LSR3 scans its LDP state to determine LSPs for which it is the egress and LSR1 is the previous hop. For each matching LSP entry, LSR3 sends a Label Mapping message. Assume LSR3 finds a single matching entry for FEC=F1 and incoming label = L1. In this case, LSR2 sends a Label Mapping message containing FEC F1 and label L1. When LSR3 receives a Label Request message for FEC F1 from LSR2 with a suggested label L1 from LSR2, it scans the LDP state for an entry matching FEC F1 and incoming label = L1. If the matching entry is not found, LSR3 ignores the suggested label and processes the Label Request message as per normal LDP procedures. However, if a matching entry is found, it updates the LDP state, clears the stale flag, and replies with a Label Mapping message to LSR2. If the MPLS Forwarding State Holding Timer expires while LSR3 is waiting for a Label Request message with a suggested label from LSR1, it removes the associated LDP and MPLS forwarding state entries.

Nonrestarting LSR Behavior for Transit Neighbors

Consider LSR2 with an upstream LDP peer LSR1 and a downstream LDP peer LSR3 (see Figure 8-10). Suppose LSR2 is the transit LSR for an LSP (associated with a FEC F1) that traverses LSR1, LSR2, and LSR3. Suppose LSR3 distributes a <FEC=F1, Label=L2> mapping to LSR2, which in turn advertises a <FEC=F1, Label=L1> mapping to LSR1. Hence, for FEC F1, LSR2 has an incoming label=L1 and outgoing label=L2. As LSR2 (the nonrestarting LSR) has an LDP downstream on-demand session with the upstream and the downstream neighbor, depending on whether the upstream peer, the downstream peer, or both upstream and downstream peers restart, and LSR2 completes the LDP GR procedure with either one or both neighbors. Thus a nonrestarting transit LSR behavior encompasses three distinct cases. In the following paragraphs, behavior for each case is described briefly.

As a first case, suppose the upstream neighbor LSR1 restarts. From the perspective of LSR2's behavior, this case is similar to the behavior described in the section "Nonrestarting LSR's Behavior for Egress Neighbors." It is similar, except that if the MPLS Forwarding State Holding Timer expires while LSR2 is waiting for a Label Request message, LSR2 clears the stale flag for the associated LDP state entry and behaves as if it had received a Label Release message and then follows the normal LDP label-release procedures.

As a second case, suppose the downstream neighbor LSR3 restarts. From the perspective of LSR2's behavior, this case is similar to the behavior described in the section "Nonrestarting LSR's Behavior for Ingress Neighbors." It is similar except that if the MPLS Forwarding State Holding Timer expires while LSR2 is waiting for a reply to its Label Request message, LSR2 deletes the LSP forwarding state, clears the stale flag from LDP state, and sends a Label Abort message to the downstream peer. It then follows the normal LDP label-abort procedures. As for the upstream peer, LSR2 behaves as if it had received a Label Withdraw message from the downstream LSR3 and following normal LDP procedures sends a Label Withdraw message to some or all upstream peers.

As a third case, suppose both the downstream and upstream neighbors restart. In this case, LSR2 needs to complete graceful restart procedures with both neighbors. The order in which the graceful restart interactions begin depends on the order in which the respective sessions are reestablished. The restart behavior in this case consists of concatenation of the previous two cases, with the exception that the restart interactions must take place with both peers. For example, if you assume the session with the upstream peer is established first, LSR2 starts interactions with LSR1. On receipt of a Label Request message with a suggested label from the upstream LSR, the interaction with the upstream is considered to be in the *waiting for downstream* state. At this point, LSR2 interactions with LSR1 for an LSP must wait until LSR2 has scanned the LSP LDP state with the downstream peer and put it in the waiting for the upstream state. Now for each such LSP, LSR2 sends a Label Request message to LSR3, and reception of a corresponding Label Mapping message completes the interactions with the downstream neighbor. At this point, LSR2 send a corresponding Label Mapping message to the upstream LSR and completes the interaction.

Comparison of LDP GR Mechanisms for Downstream Unsolicited and Downstream On-Demand Modes

Generally, there is a high level of commonality between the LDP GR procedures for downstream unsolicited and downstream on-demand modes. For example, in both modes, an

LSR includes the FT Session TLV to express its NSF capability to its peer before the restart. Specifically, in both modes, FT Flags, FT Reconnect Timeout, Recovery Time, MPLS Forwarding State Holding Timer, and Neighbor Liveness Timer are used in the exact same manner.

The major differences between the two modes can be confined to the LDP state recovery procedures. For example, in the case of LDP GR downstream unsolicited mode, an LSR receives remote FEC-to-label mappings from a downstream LSR without making an explicit request. In contrast, for LDP GR downstream on demand, even when an upstream LSR receives an unsolicited Label Mapping message from the downstream LSR, the upstream LSR makes an explicit request for a remote FEC-to-label mapping using a Label Request message.

Another major difference between the two mechanisms lies in the LDP state validation procedure. For example, on receipt of a Label Mapping message (assuming certain checks pass, as described later), the upstream LSR creates the LDP state information, marks it stale, and then revalidates it by sending a Label Request message to the downstream LSR. The upstream LSR includes an optional Label TLV (such as an ATM label, Frame Relay label, or generic label TLV, as appropriate) in the Label Request message to suggest which of its outgoing labels the downstream LSR should use (to use as the incoming label for the associated FEC).

The downstream LSR then replies with a corresponding Label Mapping message. On receipt of the matching Label Mapping message that contains the label suggested in the corresponding Label Request message, the upstream LSR clears the stale flag for the LDP state entry and updates the associated MPLS forwarding state entry. In contrast, the LDP GR downstream unsolicited procedures neither solicit remote FEC-to-label mappings from downstream peers nor suggest labels to them.

For an LSR in the process of restarting, LDP GR downstream unsolicited procedures distinguish between the behavior of LSP nonegress and egress LSRs. In contrast, LDP GR downstream on-demand procedures distinguish between the behaviors of LSP ingress, transit, and egress LSRs. LDP GR downstream unsolicited procedures do not distinguish between the behaviors of a nonegress or egress nonrestarting peer. In contrast, LDP GR downstream on-demand procedures distinguish between the behaviors of an ingress, transit, and egress nonrestarting peer.

Network Deployment Considerations

Among the LDP restart approaches, the GR mechanism is likely to be supported by a majority of networking equipment vendors. As a result, the main focus of this chapter is on deployment scenarios for the LDP GR mechanism. In general, however, the following discussion is applicable to both approaches.

To reduce harmful effects caused by control-plane restart, the LDP GR mechanism requires that

- The restarting LSR must be capable of preserving MPLS forwarding state across (as well as the pertinent IP forwarding state) the control-plane restart.

- The restarting LSR must support LDP GR extensions and the associated protocol behavior.

- All LDP peers of the restarting LSR must support, at a minimum, LDP GR extensions and protocol behavior.

Because the LDP control-plane component can fail on any LSR, to obtain maximum benefit from the LDP GR mechanism all LSRs must not only support the LDP GR mechanism but also be NSF-capable. If an LSR supports LDP GR procedures but is not capable of preserving the MPLS forwarding state, such an LSR does not help reduce detrimental effects caused by its own LDP control-plane restart. However, by retaining its FEC-to-label mappings across a neighbor's control-plane restart, an LSR with the aforementioned set of capabilities can still help reduce the harmful effects. Depending on the role of an LSR (such as ingress, transit, or egress) or if it is forwarding a mix of IP and MPLS traffic, in addition to the MPLS forwarding state, the LSR must also preserve its IP forwarding state across the restart. Particularly, if LDP is tightly coupled with the IP control-plane components such as *Open Shortest Path First* (OSPF), *Intermediate System-to-Intermediate System* (IS-IS), and *Border Gateway Protocol* (BGP), the LSR must be able to gracefully restart all affected components. The procedures for preserving the IP forwarding state across the restart are described in Chapters 4 through Chapter 6. The following sections describe the LDP peers with various combinations of LDP GR capabilities.

Scenario 1: LSR1 and LSR2 Are LDP GR- and NSF-Capable

In this case, the LDP restart in either LSR1 or LSR2 would not disrupt the MPLS forwarding plane, as shown in Figure 8-11. As a result, for an LDP GR deployment to benefit the entire network, all LSRs in the MPLS network should be LDP GR- and NSF-capable.

Figure 8-11 *LDP GR Deployment Scenarios*

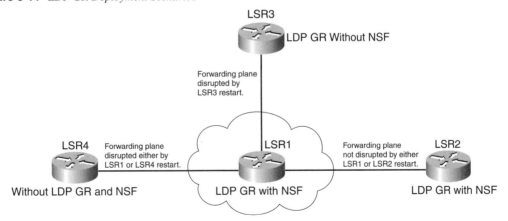

Scenario 2: LSR1 Is LDP GR- and NSF-Capable, but LSR3 Is Only LDP GR-Capable

In an MPLS network, not all LSRs may be able to support a full set of LDP control-plane restart and NSF capabilities. In this case, when the LDP control plane in LSR1 restarts, because it is LDP GR- and NSF-capable, the MPLS forwarding plane would not be disrupted. However, this behavior is possible with the help of LSR3, which is LDP GR-capable and retains FEC-to-label mappings (and the associated MPLS forwarding state) across LSR1's restart. In contrast, when the LDP control-plane component on LSR3 restarts, because LSR3 would have informed LSR1 about its inability to preserve the forwarding state before the restart, on detecting an LDP session failure with LSR3, LSR1 would immediately release FEC-to-label mappings associated with the failed LDP session. Therefore, after the control-plane restart on LSR3, forwarding on all LSPs associated with the failed LDP sessions is disrupted. Hence, to avoid the harmful effects caused by LDP and the control-plane component restart, NSF capability is a must for the restarting LSR.

Scenario 3: LSR1 Is LDP GR- and NSF-Capable, but LSR4 Is LDP GR- and NSF-Incapable

For this case, an LDP restart in either LSR1 or LSR4 would disrupt the MPLS forwarding plane. This scenario shows that for deriving any benefit from an LDP GR- and NSF-capable LSR, at a minimum all its peers should also be LDP GR-capable.

Summary

This chapter described the LDP GR restart mechanisms that allow the LDP control-plane component to restart without disrupting the MPLS forwarding plane. The operation of the LDP GR mechanism was explained through various examples and deployment scenarios.

References

[1] RFC 3031, "Multiprotocol Label Switching Architecture," R. Callon, E. Rosen, and A. Viswanathan, January 2001.

[2] RFC 3036, "LDP Specification," L. Andersson, P. Doolan, N. Feldman, A. Fredette, and B. Thomas, January 2001.

[3] RFC 3478, "Graceful Restart Mechanism for Label Distribution Protocol," R. Aggarwal, M. Leelanivas, and Y. Rekhter, February 2003.

[4] RFC 3479, "Fault Tolerance for the Label Distribution Protocol (LDP)," A. Farrel, February 2003.

[5] Bryant, S., and P. Pate, "PWE3 Architecture," IETF Draft, Work in progress.

[6] Martini, L., et al., "Pseudowire Setup and Maintenance Using LDP," IETF Draft, Work in progress.

[7] Raj, A., and R. Thomas, "LDP DoD Graceful Restart," IETF Draft, Work in progress.

MPLS Control Plane: Restarting RSVP-TE Gracefully

When the *Resource ReSerVation Protocol* (RSVP) control-plane component restarts, it disrupts the Multiprotocol Label Switching (MPLS) forwarding-plane operation. This disruption is similar to other MPLS control-plane protocols such as *Border Gateway Protocol* (BGP; see Chapter 7, "MPLS Control Plane: Restarting BGP with MPLS Gracefully") and Label Distribution Protocol (LDP; see Chapter 8, "MPLS Control Plane: Restarting LDP Gracefully").

This chapter describes an extension in the RSVP protocol called the RSVP *graceful restart* (GR) mechanism, which allows the RSVP control-plane component to restart without disrupting its MPLS forwarding plane. The operation of the RSVP-TE GR mechanism is explained through deployment scenarios.

Motivations for Traffic Engineering

To reduce the costs of operating and maintaining separate network infrastructures, an increasing number of service providers are migrating their legacy Layer 2 and emerging Layer 3 services onto a common packet-switched network. The converged network architecture is expected to deliver reliable and scalable differentiated services. To realize these objectives, service providers use special routing protocols and techniques to manage user traffic more effectively. For example, service providers commonly use *interior gateway protocols* (IGPs) such as *Open Shortest Path First* (OSPF) and Intermediate System-to-Intermediate System (IS-IS) within an autonomous system. Most IGPs compute their routes using the *Shortest Path First* (SPF) algorithm. A common drawback of an IGP is that when there are multiple feasible paths for a particular destination, IGP selects the path that minimizes an additive scalar link metric. Because the IGP path-selection procedure does not consider other attributes such as link available bandwidth and utilization, multiple SPF paths can converge on a link and cause that particular link to be overutilized, whereas links along alternative feasible, but longer, paths remain underutilized.

To distribute traffic more uniformly while avoiding known congestion and failure points in the network, service providers employ *traffic engineering* (TE). In brief, TE is the ability to direct traffic away from a conventionally routed SPF path and along a desired path, thereby enabling a more efficient use of the network resources. This in turn enables service providers to lower operational costs and deliver improved services to their end customers.

Traffic-Engineering Capabilities

Effective application of TE techniques encompasses the following capabilities:

- Classify packets into different traffic classes
- Aggregate packets with the same traffic class into a traffic trunk
- Specify explicit paths and reserve resources along these paths
- Steer traffic trunks along the explicit paths
- Smoothly reroute traffic trunks around link and node failures

MPLS Traffic Engineering

MPLS-TE is a unique solution and offers the following functions: integration of the MPLS label-switching functionality, enhanced RSVP, and constraint-based IGP routing. Specifically, MPLS-TE allows establishment of *label-switched paths* (LSPs) along explicit paths (which can be specified manually or computed automatically) with resource reservations. MPLS-TE also permits mapping of each traffic trunk onto a single LSP. An aggregate of unidirectional flows of the same class is called a *traffic trunk*.

Aggregation of data flows into traffic trunks and placement of each traffic trunk onto a single LSP is desirable because it enables scalable network architecture. For example, assume that an adequate number of LSPs has been placed in a network. As the traffic volume in the network increases, although the total bandwidth of the LSPs must continue to scale to meet the increased traffic volume needs, the number of LSPs does not increase. Another attractive feature of the MPLS-TE-based solution is the support for the *make-before-break mechanism*. For example, by establishing a new LSP before releasing the old LSP, MPLS-TE provides a graceful solution for rerouting traffic from old to new LSPs with no or minimal traffic loss. The move from an old to a new LSP could be caused by the fact that a more optimal path is now available for the LSP. On the other hand, the move could indicate that you need to allocate additional bandwidth for the LSP. In either case, you should establish a new LSP and move traffic from the old to the new LSP in a graceful fashion.

Overview of RSVP

This section provides an overview of RSVP and its enhancements to support MPLS-TE applications. In the remainder of this chapter, the directional terms such as *downstream*, *upstream*, *previous hop*, and *next hop* are defined with respect to the direction of data packet flow.

Originally, RSVP was designed as a protocol to install resource reservation states for individual data flows along a destination-based routed path (that is, along an IGP path).[1] An RSVP session is defined by its destination IP address, IP protocol ID, and optionally by its destination TCP/UDP port. A data flow is a single instance of the application-to-application flow of packets identified by source/destination IP address and port.

Path Message

When a sender application intends to reserve resources for a data flow, it invokes the RSVP module in the source node (a host or router) to originate a Path message toward the downstream node.

The Path message is sent with the same source and destination IP address as the data packets and traverses the same path as the data packets. RSVP messages are encapsulated in IP packets and are routed using destination IP address. An RSVP Path message contains several parameters, such as the following:

- SESSION object (which defines the RSVP session)
- RSVP_HOP object (which contains the IP address of the upstream node sending this message and the *logical interface handle* LIH of the outgoing interface)
- SENDER_TEMPLATE object (which contains the source IP address and the TCP/UDP port)
- SENDER_TSPEC object (which specifies the traffic parameters such as peak data rate, token-bucket rate, and token burst size)

Path State Block

When an RSVP-capable router receives an initial Path message, it creates a *path state block* (PSB) for that particular session (see Figure 9-1). Each PSB consists of parameters derived from the received Path message such as SESSION, SENDER_TEMPLATE, SENDER_TSPEC, RSVP_HOP objects, and the outgoing interface provided by the IGP routing. When an RSVP-capable router forwards a Path message, it inserts the IP address of the outgoing interface in the RSVP_HOP object. When the RSVP-capable downstream next-hop router receives the initial Path message, it also creates a PSB, inserts the IP address of the outgoing interface in the RSVP_HOP object, and in turn forwards the Path message to the next-hop downstream router. This process repeats until the Path message arrives at the target receiver. During processing of the Path message, if any errors are encountered on a node along the way, from that node a path error (PathErr) message is generated upstream toward the sender.

Figure 9-1 *RSVP Path and Resv Messages and PSB/RSB State Creation*

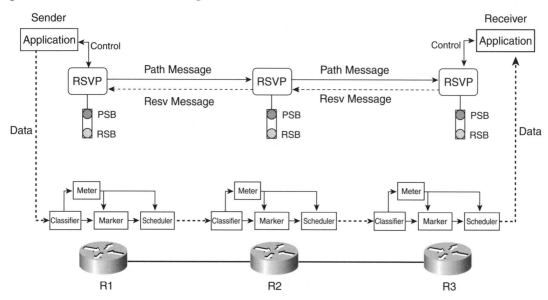

Upon receipt of an initial Path message, the receiver uses information carried in the Path message (such as traffic parameters carried in the SENDER_TSPEC object) to select the resource reservation parameters.

Resv Message

The receiver initiates a Resv message to request a reservation for a data flow. The Resv message is routed upstream toward the sender along the route taken by the Path message.

The IP source address of a Resv message is the address of the node (a host or router) that originates the message. On the other hand, the IP destination address corresponds to the address of the upstream node from which the associated Path message was received previously. Before forwarding the Resv message upstream, each RSVP-capable node modifies the IP destination address of the received Resv message. The IP destination address is modified to become the address stored in the RSVP_HOP object of the associated PSB. In this fashion, the Resv message is steered upstream along the route that was taken by the corresponding Path message in the downstream direction.

A Resv message carries a SESSION object, a RSVP_HOP object, flow descriptor objects, and a few other objects. Briefly, a RSVP flow descriptor consists of FLOWSPEC and FILTER_SPEC objects. The FLOWSPEC object carries TSPEC (traffic parameters) and RSPEC (requested resource such as bandwidth and delay) parameters. Traffic management procedures (such as connection admission control [CAC] and traffic scheduling) use the TSPEC and RSPEC parameters in nodes along the way to provide the requested *quality of service* (QoS). The FILTER_SPEC object specifies filters such as IP source address, source port, or other fields in the packet headers to select a subset of packets in a session that are to receive the requested QoS. The FILTER_SPEC is typically used to set parameters in the packet classifier in a node.

Reservation State Block

As a Resv message travels upstream toward the sender, it creates a *reservation state block* (RSB) in each RSVP-capable node along the way (see Figure 9-1). Each RSB stores information derived from objects in the received Resv message, such as the following:

- SESSION object
- RSVP_HOP object (the IP address of the interface through which the Resv was sent and the LIH on which the reservation is needed)
- FLOWSPEC object
- FILTERSPEC object
- STYLE object (which specifies reservation styles, such as whether the reservation is intended for an individual sender or shared by several senders)

During processing of the Resv message, if any errors are encountered along the way, a reservation error (ResvErr) message is generated and forwarded downstream toward the receiver. The successful propagation of the Resv message to the sender, results in the creation of a reservation state along the IGP routed path of the data flow from the receiver to the sender. RSVP reservation requests are for unidirectional data flows. Because bidirectional flows can travel separate paths in each direction, bidirectional data flows require two separate reservation requests.

Soft State

RSVP uses a soft state model. This means that to maintain the state created by the initial Path and Resv messages, each RSVP-capable node along the path must send Path and Resv refresh messages periodically. The refresh period value is derived from the TIME_VALUES object, which is carried in Path and Resv messages. If a particular node does not receive Path and Resv refresh messages within an associated cleanup time (the lifetime of the state), the node removes the corresponding PSB and RSB state. The RSVP periodic refresh mechanism allows maintaining the soft state and handling the occasional loss of messages caused by the inherently unreliable IP service, as discussed later in the section titled "Lifetime of RSVP-TE State."

Using RSVP in MPLS-TE

The actual use of RSVP in MPLS-TE is quite different from the use that was envisioned at design:

- RSVP in MPLS-TE is used to create a reservation state for a collection of flows (as opposed to individual data flows) that share a common forwarding path and have a common pool of reserved resources.

- RSVP in MPLS-TE not only creates a resource reservation state for an LSP, but also installs its forwarding state.

- The path along which this state is created is no longer restricted to a destination-based routing path; instead, it can be specified explicitly.

- An RSVP session in MPLS-TE is not confined to being used between a pair of hosts, but can also be used for a traffic trunk between a pair of *label-switching routers* (LSRs).

Using RSVP in MPLS-TE involves exercising mainly existing procedures for resource reservation and extending these procedures for establishing LSPs along explicit paths. The enhanced RSVP protocol, referred to as *RSVP-TE*, enables a new set of capabilities such as the following:

- Downstream on-demand label distribution

- Establishment of explicitly routed LSPs

- Reservation of resources along the explicit paths

- Rerouting of established LSPs using the make-before-break approach

- Preemption of a lower-priority LSP by a higher-priority LSP

The RSVP-TE specification[4] defines several new objects such as the LABEL_REQUEST object for requesting a label from the downstream LSR, the LABEL object for distributing an MPLS label to the upstream LSR, the EXPLICIT_ROUTE object (ERO) for specifying the explicit path, and the RECORD_ROUTE object (RRO) for recording detailed path information.

Generalization of the Flow Concept

A distinct aspect of RSVP-TE usage involves generalization of the notion of a flow as defined in the original RSVP specification. In RSVP-TE, a session can have an arbitrary aggregation of traffic flows (a traffic trunk) between the originating and terminating LSRs of the LSP. More precisely, the original RSVP specification defines a session as a data flow with a particular destination IP address and TCP/UDP port. In contrast, an RSVP-TE session is implicitly defined as a group of packets that are assigned the same label at the originating LSR of an LSP. The labels-to-packets mappings may be based on local policy (for example, using filters based on a packet header) and may include a subset of packets or even all packets between the LSP endpoints.

LSP Tunnel

The set of packets assigned the same label at the ingress LSR of an LSP is said to belong to the same *forwarding equivalency class* (FEC), and the label is said to define an RSVP-TE flow through the LSP. When a traffic trunk is mapped onto an LSP in this manner, it is called an *LSP tunnel* or just a *tunnel*. As depicted in Figure 9-2, MPLS-TE LSP tunnel is unidirectional, originates at the ingress LSR (known as the *head end*), passes through one or more transit LSRs (known as the *midpoint*), and terminates at the egress LSR (known as the *tail end*). A tunnel is characterized in terms of its ingress and egress LSRs, the FEC that is mapped onto it, and a set of attributes (such as traffic parameters, path selection, preemption, and re-optimization) that determine the tunnel's behavioral characteristics.

Figure 9-2   *Tunnel Head End, Midpoint, and Tail End*

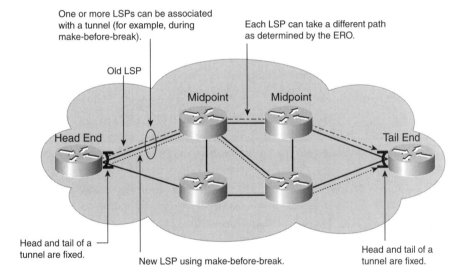

One or more LSPs can be associated with a tunnel (for example, during make-before-break).

Each LSP can take a different path as determined by the ERO.

Old LSP

Midpoint   Midpoint

Head End

Tail End

Head and tail of a tunnel are fixed.

New LSP using make-before-break.

Head and tail of a tunnel are fixed.

LSP_TUNNEL Objects

To support the aforementioned LSP tunnel features, the RSVP-TE specification has defined several new RSVP objects, including the SESSION object, the SENDER_TEMPLATE object, and the FILTER_SPEC object. The new objects are collectively referred to as *LSP_TUNNEL objects*. The SESSION object contains the following:

- A tunnel endpoint IP address (tunnel's egress LSR).

- A 16-bit tunnel ID that remains constant over the life of the tunnel.

- A 32-bit extended tunnel ID that is normally set to zero. However, the ingress LSR might set the ID to its IP address to narrow the scope of a session to the ingress-egress LSR pair.

In MPLS-TE applications, it is often desirable (as during LSP rerouting, for example) to associate multiple LSPs with the same tunnel endpoints (see Figure 9-2). In this case, the SESSION object together with the SENDER_TEMPLATE (or equivalently FILTER_SPEC) object uniquely identifies an LSP tunnel. The SENDER_TEMPLATE object contains the tunnel sender node's IP address and a 16-bit LSP ID that can be dynamically changed to allow a sender to share reservation resources for a new LSP with its older instance (for example, during LSP re-optimization using make-before-break). In short, five-tuples including tunnel endpoint address, tunnel ID, extended tunnel ID, sender node address, and LSP ID uniquely identify an LSP tunnel.

SESSION_ATTRIBUTE Object

To specify tunnel preemption priority and other attributes, the RSVP_TE specification has defined a new object class known as SESSION_ATTRIBUTE. Briefly, this object contains tunnel resource affinity filters (such as exclude-any, include-any, include-all) for including or excluding a link during path selection, tunnel setup, and holding priority. The object also contains the following types of flags:

- **Local protection desired**—To protect an LSP against a link or node that uses a backup tunnel. (Usage of backup tunnels is described in the Chapter 10, "Improving Survivability of IP and MPLS Networks.")

- **Label recording desired**—To have LSRs along the LSP path record their labels in the RRO.

- **SE style desired**—A *shared explicit* (SE) reservation style allows a receiver to explicitly specify the list of senders that can share the same reservation pool.

Because each sender is explicitly specified in the Resv message, even though different labels may be assigned to different senders to create separate LSPs, there is a single reservation for all senders on any common link. This is an extremely useful feature for LSP rerouting because it avoids double counting of the reservations on links that are common to the old and new LSPs. In addition to the new objects, RSVP_TE specification has also defined new error messages to signal notification of exception conditions, such as "Bad ERO object," "MPLS label allocation failure," "Tunnel locally repaired," and so forth.

To establish an explicitly routed LSP tunnel, the head-end LSR originates a Path message with the ERO to steer the Path message along the desired path. The head-end LSR also inserts the LABEL_REQUEST object in the message to solicit label mapping for the RSVP-TE session from the LSRs along the path. The head-end LSR builds an ERO based on a user-specified path or computes it automatically using an enhanced TE topology database. For further information on distinct aspects of MPLS-TE application such as TE topology database construction, path calculation, LSP re-optimization, and local protection, see Chapter 10.

Specifying ERO

An ERO can be specified strictly or loosely. A strict ERO specifies all nodes along the path, whereas a loose ERO specifies only a few nodes. The loose ERO object is typically used when the head-end LSR does not have the complete path information (as, for example, in the case of inter-autonomous system TE; see Chapter 10).

When a downstream LSR receives an initial Path message, it creates a PSB, stores the ERO in the PSB, and forwards the message to the next-hop LSR indicated by the ERO. If an LSR receives a loose ERO that needs to be expanded, the LSR stores both the loose as well as the expanded ERO in the PSB. As the Path message travels along the explicit path, it creates a PSB in each LSR along the way. When the Path message with a LABEL_REQUEST arrives at the tail-end LSR, it creates an RSB, assigns a label for the session and stores it in the RSB, installs it as the incoming label in the associated LSP forwarding state, inserts the assigned label in the LABEL object, and responds with a Resv message upstream.

When an upstream LSR receives an initial Resv message containing a LABEL object, it performs the following functions:

- Creates an RSB and stores the received label in the RSB
- Installs the received label as the outgoing label for the LSP
- Allocates a new label and inserts it in the LABEL object and stores it in the RSB
- Installs the allocated label as the incoming label for the LSP
- Sends the Resv message upstream

As the Resv message propagates upstream along the explicit path, it creates the RSVP and LSP forwarding state in each LSR along way. Moreover, as the Resv message propagates upstream, each LSR along the path performs a *connection admission control* (CAC) check (for example, to check whether the requested bandwidth is available) and reserves the requested amount of bandwidth. Each LSR manages its local outgoing link resources by maintaining available bandwidth pools at multiple priority levels. An LSP tunnel is said to be established when the associated Resv message arrives at the head-end LSR.

RECORD_ROUTE Object

RSVP-TE uses the *RECORD_ROUTE object* (RRO) to detect Layer 3 routing loops and forwarding loops inherent to the explicit path. By including RRO in the Path message and setting the appropriate flags in the SESSION_ATTRIBUTE object, a head-end LSR can discover detailed path information such as nodes that are being traversed, labels that are being used by nodes along the path, and whether local link/node protection is available along the path.

Initially, at the source node, RRO contains only one subobject that records the sender node's IP address. As the Path message propagates downstream, each node stores a copy of RRO in the PSB, records its IP address, attaches a new subobject to the RRO, and forwards the Path message to the next node. When the Path message finally arrives at the tunnel endpoint, the egress LSR adds the RRO to the Resv message and forwards it upstream. The RRO in the Resv message records the path in the reverse direction. If the Label Recording Desired flag is set in the SESSION_ATTRIBUTE object, each node also inserts its label in the RRO. As the Resv message travels upstream, each LSR stores a copy of the RRO in the RSB. In this manner, each LSR has the complete LSP path information from head to tail—head end to itself by means of the RRO received in the Path message and tail end to itself by means of the RRO received in the Resv message.

RSVP-TE Soft State

Similar to the original RSVP protocol, the RSVP-TE state must also be refreshed periodically. In the RSVP-TE, with the exception of LABEL_REQUEST and LABEL objects, all other new objects are optional. Therefore, in addition to the mandatory objects as defined in the original RSVP specification, the RSVP-TE Path refresh message must also contain the LABEL_REQUEST object. The RSVP-TE Path refresh message may also contain additional optional objects such as ERO and RRO, as appropriate. Similarly, an RSVP-TE Resv refresh message must contain the LABEL object and other optional objects, as appropriate.

Lifetime of RSVP-TE State

RSVP messages are transmitted using unreliable IP datagram transport. Each RSVP node periodically transmits Path and Resv messages to handle occasional loss of RSVP messages. The Path and Resv messages contain a TIME_VALUES object that specifies the value for the refresh period (R) used by the sender of the message. When a node receives initial Path and Resv messages and creates an RSVP state, the node uses the value of R to determine the value for the lifetime (L) of the state (the maximum time period for which the node will retain the RSVP state if no refresh messages are received from the neighbor). Therefore, depending on the duration of the lifetime, a node can tolerate the loss of periodic refresh messages. For example, if the effective lifetime is set to K times, and the refresh timeout period to R, RSVP can tolerate $(K - 1)$ successive RSVP packet losses without falsely deleting state. To avoid premature loss of RSVP state due to loss of $(K - 1)$ successive refresh messages, RFC 2205 recommends that L be set to at least $(K + 0.5) * 1.5 * R$. For example, if a node selects a value of 3 for K and receives a value of 30 seconds for R from a neighbor, that node should be able to retain the RSVP state for at least 52.2 seconds without receiving refresh messages from the neighbor.

On the one hand, a longer lifetime value allows a node to tolerate loss of a greater number of RSVP messages. On the other hand, it increases the time to detect a neighbor failure. For example, if the absence of refresh messages were not caused by the loss of messages but was actually caused by a neighbor failure, it would take a long time (in the order of minutes) for the node to detect the neighbor's failure and remove its RSVP state. This means that data traffic destined for the failing neighbor will be black holed for a long time. The prolonged packet loss is generally not acceptable for many applications (such as Voice over IP) that typically require packet loss to be limited to tens of milliseconds.

The necessity to refresh soft state means that depending on the number of established LSPs, a large number of refresh messages must be generated, transmitted, and processed. The RSVP refresh reduction extensions, however, address most of concerns about RSVP state refresh overhead and unreliable message delivery.[3] For example, these extensions define a new MESSAGE_ACK object for detecting a message loss and a new message (called SUMMARY_REFRESH message) for reducing the overhead of transmitting and processing state refresh messages. However, this does not address the issue of detecting node failure quickly.

The following section describes a mechanism by which a node can detect RSVP failures rapidly and yet still allow use of relatively large values for the refresh period to reduce the frequency of refresh messages.

Detecting RSVP-TE Failures

RSVP-TE specification also defines a new Hello message for rapid detection of node and RSVP control-channel failures. Node failures differ from control-channel failures as follows:

- **Node failure**—A failure in which a node loses its control plane (or a component of the control plane such as the RSVP-TE component), but its forwarding plane continues to function as normal

- **Control-channel failure**—A failure in which a node loses its control channel (when an RSVP communication link goes down, for example) to a neighbor, but the node otherwise continues to function correctly (for example, the node's control plane and forwarding plane remain unaffected)

The RSVP-TE Hello extension consists of a Hello message, a HELLO_REQUEST object, and a HELLO_ACK object. The HELLO_REQUEST and HELLO_ACK objects contain source instance (Src_Instance) and destination instance (Dst_Instance) fields. Src_Instance is a 32-bit field in which a sender advertises a unique instance value to an RSVP neighbor. A separate (unique) instance value is maintained for each RSVP neighbor. After a sender has advertised a nonzero source instance value to a neighbor, the node must not change this value unless it has restarted or its RSVP communication to the neighbor has been lost.

Dst_Instance is a 32-bit field in which a node reflects the last received Src_Instance value from a neighbor. If a node has not received any Src_Instance value from a neighbor, it sets the Dst_Instance field to 0. To detect a neighbor's control-plane or control-channel failure, a node collects and stores the Src_Instance value received from the neighbor and monitors its own Src_Instance values reflected back by the neighbor in the Dst_Instance field.

To monitor the status of a neighbor, a node periodically (at every Hello interval) sends Hello messages with request objects to the neighbor. Another mechanism, known as *bidirectional forwarding detection* (BFD), is described in Chapter 10. BFD can be used to detect failures on the forwarding-plane path. The neighbor is expected to respond with a HELLO_ACK object. On receipt of the HELLO_ACK object from the neighbor, the requesting node compares the new received Src_Instance value with the previous value. The requesting node presumes that the neighbor has failed if any of the following conditions apply:

- The newly received Src_Instance (a nonzero value) differs from the previous value.

- The neighbor is not reflecting back the correct requesting node's Src_Instance value.

- The requesting node does not receive any response from a neighbor within a configured period (by default, 3.5 Hello intervals). For example, if the Hello interval is set to 50 milliseconds, the node can detect a neighbor failure within roughly 175 milliseconds.

For further details on the Hello mechanism, refer to the RSVP-TE specification.[4]

RSVP-TE Control-Plane and Forwarding-Plane Components

Now that the usage of RSVP-TE in MPLS-TE has been reviewed, focus turns to the main topic of this chapter: the RSVP-TE control-plane restart. In this chapter, the term *FEC* refers to an aggregate of data flows defined in terms of filters such as source IP address and other fields in the packet header. Each LSP tunnel is associated with a FEC that specifies which particular set of packets is to be mapped onto the LSP tunnel. RSVP-TE is used to create both resource reservations and forwarding states along the LSP. Each LSR along the LSP tunnel's path obtains its outgoing label from the downstream next-hop LSR, but each LSR assigns the incoming label locally.

For each LSP tunnel that traverses an LSR, the LSR stores a locally assigned incoming label and a remotely learned outgoing label in the associated RSB. The incoming and outgoing labels are used to create an MPLS forwarding state entry for the LSP tunnel in the *Label Forwarding Information Base* (LFIB). The MPLS forwarding state entry of an LSP is used for forwarding data packets on the LSP tunnel. The form of an LSP MPLS forwarding state entry depends on whether the LSR is ingress, egress, or transit for the LSP tunnel.

The state of an LSP tunnel in its entirety can be divided into two categories:

- Control-plane state (that is, maintained in the RSVP-TE control-plane component)
- MPLS forwarding state (that is, held in the forwarding plane)

Detrimental Effects of RSVP-TE Restart

In theory, with the separation of control-plane and forwarding-plane components, the RSVP-TE control plane should be able to restart without disturbing the associated forwarding-plane state. This means that the LSR should be able to continue forwarding traffic on the established LSP tunnels as normal while the RSVP-TE control-plane component restarts and recovers. In practice, however, when the RSVP-TE control plane of an LSR restarts, the restarting LSR not only loses its RSVP-TE control state, but also deletes the associated MPLS forwarding state for all established LSP tunnels. This means that the forwarding of data traffic on the associated LSP tunnels is disrupted.

The undesirable effect of RSVP-TE control-plane restart is not confined to the restarting router, but also influences neighbors. This is because following RSVP-TE control-plane failure, the restarting LSR is unable to send or receive refresh messages or respond to neighbors' Hellos for some time. When a neighbor fails to receive refreshes or responses to its Hello messages, the neighbor removes the RSVP-TE control and MPLS forwarding state for all associated LSPs. In short, RSVP-TE control-plane restart results in disruption of MPLS traffic both in the restarting LSR and its neighbors (see Figure 9-3[a]).

Figure 9-3   *Effect of RSVP-TE Control-Plane Restart (a) Existing Protocol Behavior After Restart (b) New Protocol Behavior After Restart*

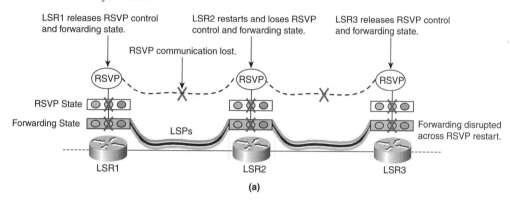

(a)

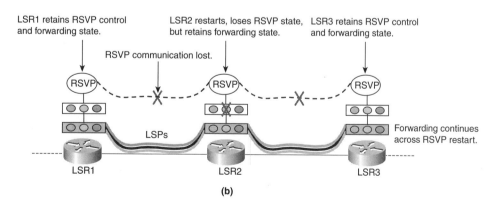

(b)

To reduce aforementioned harmful effects of RSVP-TE control-plane restart, the RSVP-TE *graceful restart* (GR) mechanism defines protocol extensions. These extensions allow an LSR to indicate its capability to preserve the MPLS forwarding state across the RSVP-TE control-plane restart to its RSVP neighbors before the actual restart. Afterward, when the RSVP-TE control-plane component of the LSR restarts, it loses its RSVP-TE control-plane state. The LSR, however, continues to forward data on established LSP tunnels using the preserved MPLS forwarding state. When neighbors detect this RSVP-TE control-plane restart, they continue to retain their control and forwarding state for all affected LSP tunnels and forward traffic as normal. After having restarted its control plane, the restarting LSR reestablishes Hello communication and resynchronizes its RSVP-TE control state with the previous neighbors. The end result is that disruption of MPLS traffic is avoided (see Figure 9-3[b]). The detailed mechanics of the RSVP-TE GR procedure are described later in this chapter.

Term Definitions

In the remainder of this chapter, terms are used as follows:

- **Control plane**—The RSVP-TE component of the MPLS control plane

- **Nonstop forwarding (NSF)**—The capability of an LSR to preserve the MPLS forwarding state for LSP tunnels across the RSVP-TE control-plane restart

- **RSVP-TE control-plane state of an LSP tunnel**—PSB and RSB (including incoming and outgoing label information, RRO, ERO, and other pertinent objects)

- **MPLS forwarding state of an LSP tunnel**—LFIB entry of the form:
  - <FEC -> push (outgoing label), next hop> at an LSP tunnel ingress LSR
  - <incoming label, swap (outgoing label), next hop> at an LSP tunnel transit LSR
  - <incoming label, pop (label stack), next hop> at an LSP tunnel egress LSR

Note that at the ingress LSR, forwarding of an unlabeled packet onto an LSP tunnel might involve looking up the destination address in the IP *Forwarding Information Base* (FIB) to identify the *next-hop label forwarding entry* (NHLFE) in the LFIB. Similarly, at the egress LSR, forwarding of a packet might require one or more FIB lookups to determine the next hop. In short, the LSR must preserve all states that are necessary for forwarding traffic (including IP state in the FIB, as appropriate) across the RSVP-TE control-plane restart.

Mitigating the Detrimental Effects of RSVP-TE Restart

As mentioned earlier, RSVP-TE control-plane restart causes detrimental effects on the MPLS forwarding plane. To reduce such harmful effects, the *Internet Engineering Task Force* (IETF) has defined the RSVP-TE GR restart mechanism.[5]

RSVP-TE GR Mechanism

RSVP-TE GR allows an LSR to express the following information to its neighbors:

* Its capability to preserve the MPLS forwarding state across its control-plane restart

* Estimated time within which the LSR expects to be able to reestablish Hello communication with the neighbors after restarting its control plane

* Recovery period during which the LSR is prepared to retain its preserved MPLS forwarding state after the restart and during which it expects its neighbors to resynchronize RSVP-TE state after reestablishing Hello communication

To be able to communicate this information, RSVP-TE GR defines the following three new objects: RESTART_CAP, SUGGESTED_LABEL, and RECOVERY_LABEL.

The RESTART_CAP object is carried in RSVP-TE Hello messages. During the recovery period, the SUGGESTED_LABEL object is carried in Path messages to provide the label preference of an upstream LSR to a downstream LSR. The RECOVERY_LABEL object is also carried in the Path messages from an upstream LSR to a downstream LSR during recovery period and conveys the most recently received label value in the corresponding Resv messages from the downstream LSR.

Initial Capability Exchange

From an overview level, the RSVP-TE GR mechanism can be regarded as a three-phase procedure. In the first phase, neighboring LSRs advertise GR capability to each other using the RESTART_CAP object in Hello messages. Each LSR that supports the RSVP-TE GR mechanism must include the RESTART_CAP object in all its Hello messages. The RESTART_CAP object contains two parameters: Restart Time and Recovery Time. Restart Time specifies the time duration in milliseconds within which the sender is expected to reestablish Hello communication with the receiver after restarting its RSVP-TE control plane. When a sender's control-plane restart is expected to take an indeterminate time and its forwarding plane remains unaffected across the restart, the sender advertises a value of 0xffffffff for the Restart Time (indicating an indefinite restart period).

RSVP-TE Control-Plane Restart

When the RSVP-TE control plane on an LSR restarts, the RSVP-TE GR restart procedure can be considered to enter the second phase. During this phase, the restarting LSR continues to forward traffic (across the control-plane restart) using the preserved MPLS forwarding state. When an LSR detects that a neighbor has restarted and the neighbor has previously indicated its capability to preserve the MPLS forwarding state using the RESTART_CAP object, the LSR retains its RSVP-TE control plane and MPLS forwarding state for all established LSPs that traverse links between the LSR and the restarting neighbor. Then the LSR waits for reestablishment of the RSVP-TE Hello communication with the neighbor.

Reestablishment of Hello Communication

The third phase begins when the restarting LSR, after having restarted its control plane, is ready to reestablish Hello communication with the neighbors. After restarting, the LSR checks whether it was able to preserve its MPLS forwarding state across the control-plane restart. If the answer is no, the restarting LSR informs its neighbors (by advertising a value of 0 in the Recovery Time field) that it was unable to preserve the MPLS forwarding state across restart. On receipt of this information, the neighbors (which should have been retaining their state) immediately remove the RSVP-TE control and forwarding states that they shared with the restarting LSR. However, if the answer is yes, the restarting LSR initiates the state recovery procedure and informs its neighbors about the recovery period. In this case, the neighbors continue to retain their RSVP-TE and MPLS forwarding state and attempt to resynchronize their RSVP states during the recovery period. The state information that has not been resynchronized during the recovery period is deleted at the end of the period (see Figure 9-4).

As mentioned before, RSVP is a soft state protocol that relies on refreshes to maintain connectivity with neighbors. Sometimes a node fails and is able to restart and recover (for example, the node has preserved the required control and forwarding-plane state and does not need neighbors' help) without neighbors noticing its failure. In such cases, the RSVP-TE GR mechanism is not required. The RSVP-TE GR mechanism is needed when failures of an RSVP node are noticeable by its neighbors, and the node requires support from its neighbors to maintain NSF and recover control-plane state. The following section presents further details on the GR behavior of a restarting LSR and its nonrestarting neighbors.

Figure 9-4 *RSVP-TE Control-Plane Recovery States*

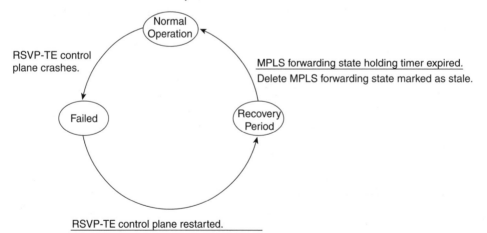

Restarting LSR Behavior

As discussed earlier in this chapter, if the restarting LSR was not able to preserve the MPLS forwarding state across the restart, it advertises a Recovery Time of 0 in its Hello messages.

If the LSR was able to preserve its MPLS forwarding state across its control-plane restart, however, it marks the preserved MPLS forwarding state as stale and initiates the RSVP-TE state recovery procedure by sending Hellos to neighbors. The *recovery period* is the time period during which an LSR is prepared to maintain its preserved forwarding state and resynchronize its state with neighbors. The restarting LSR advertises a nonzero recovery period value in the Recovery Time to inform neighbors that it has managed to preserve MPLS forwarding state across the restart. Moreover, to allow neighbors to determine whether the current fault was due to control-channel or control-plane failure, the restarting LSR advertises a different nonzero value (different from what it advertised before the restart) for the Src_Instance field and a value of 0 for the Dst_Instance field (which identifies the failure as a control-plane failure). During the recovery period, the restarting LSR must set the Recovery Time to the duration of the recovery period in its all Hello messages. When neighbors receive a Hello with a nonzero Recovery Time, they continue to retain their MPLS forwarding states and attempt to resynchronize RSVP-TE state using RSVP-TE GR procedures, as described in the following paragraphs. The neighbors are expected to resynchronize their RSVP-TE states within half of the Recovery Time. The RSVP-TE state information that has not been resynchronized is deleted at the end of the recovery period.

RSVP-TE state recovery involves exchanging Path and Resv messages. During the recovery period, when an LSR receives a Path message, it checks whether RSVP-TE state associated with the message already exists. If the RSVP-TE state is present, it follows the normal RSVP-TE protocol procedure for handling the Path message. If the RSVP-TE state does not exist and the received message does not contain a RECOVERY_LABEL object, however, the LSR treats this Path message as a setup for a new LSP and handles it according to the normal RSVP-TE procedure. If the RSVP-TE state does not exist but the message contains a RECOVERY_LABEL object, the LSR treats it as an established LSP. In the latter case, the LSR searches its preserved MPLS forwarding state for an entry whose incoming interface matches the received Path message's interface and incoming label matches the label received in the RECOVERY_LABEL object.

If a matching MPLS forwarding state entry is not found, the LSR treats this Path message as a setup request for a new LSP and handles it as normal. (For example, the LSR creates a PSB and forwards the message downstream as appropriate.)

However, if a matching MPLS forwarding state entry is found, the LSR creates the corresponding RSVP-TE state and refreshes the associated MPLS forward state entry (clears the stale flag, for example). The LSR includes the outgoing label from the restored forwarding entry in the SUGGESTED_LABEL object and in all other respects the LSR follows the normal RSVP-TE protocol procedure. In the event that the downstream neighbor is also restarting, the LSR uses the RECOVERY_LABEL object rather than a Suggested_Label to include the outgoing label in the outgoing Path message.

During the recovery period, Resv messages are processed as normal with the following exceptions:

- When an MPLS forwarding entry is refreshed, a new label or resource allocation is not required during Resv message processing.
- When a Resv message is received but there is no corresponding Path state, the Resv message is silently discarded without generating a ResvErr message.

Figure 9-5 depicts the summarized RSVP-TE GR recovery procedure.

Figure 9-5   *RSVP-TE GR Recovery Procedure (Restarting LSR)*

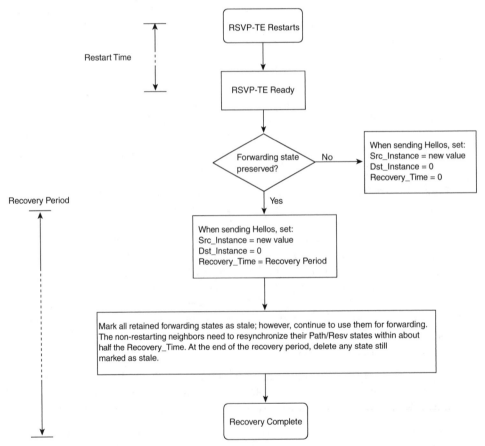

By now, it is clear that the restarting LSR must preserve its MPLS forwarding state across restart to avoid traffic disruption. However, preserving MPLS forwarding state alone is not adequate to support the RSVP-TE GR procedure. Specifically, the restarting LSR must also preserve Src_Instance and Dst_Instance values for each RSVP neighbor. Depending on whether it is a head end, midpoint, or tail end, a restarting LSR might need to preserve even more information. TE topology database construction, path calculation, and LSP tunnel establishment details are described in Chapter 10. At present, it suffices to know that the MPLS-TE feature utilizes various functional components at the head end, midpoint, and the tail end. For example, the head-end control module is used to manage any original LSP tunnels in the head-end LSR. The path calculation module is used in the head end and midpoint LSRs (only when a loose ERO is to be expanded). Each LSR has the TE topology database module to maintain the enhanced topology information. The link management module, which manages an outgoing link resource, such as available bandwidth pools, at up to eight priority levels, is needed at the head-end and the tail-end LSRs. In the case of a tail end, a tunnel traverses only an incoming link, whereas for head-end and midpoint LSRs the tunnel either traverses outgoing or incoming/outgoing links; therefore, the link management module might not be present in a tail-end LSR. In short, depending on its role, each LSR performs a different set of processing tasks, uses a different set of functional modules, and might need to preserve different additional state information, as discussed in the sections that follow.

Head-End Restarting

At the head end, the functional components that hold state information may include head-end control, link management, and the TE topology database. As described earlier, during the recovery period, the head end needs to send Path messages containing Suggested_Label (or Recovery_Label if the downstream LSR is restarting) for all the LSPs for which it is the head end. Clearly, the head end must have sufficient information to build a Path message containing the same values (as before the restart) for most of the objects. Based on the preserved tunnel configuration information, the head end can derive several objects such as SESSION, TIME_VALUE, SESSION_ATTRIBUTE, SENDER_TSPEC, and SENDER_TEMPLATE (with the exception of LSP ID, which is typically generated dynamically and should be preserved). Any information that cannot be derived from tunnel configuration or recovered from neighbors needs to be preserved. This includes LSP ID, ERO (to ensure that following the control-plane restart, the Path message traverses the same route that was taken before the restart), per-LSP bandwidth pools, and the precedence level. The per-LSP bandwidth pools information is needed only if during the recovery period a new LSP of higher priority is allowed to preempt an LSP with an established lower priority.

Midpoint Restarting

During the recovery phase, the restarting midpoint LSR receives Path messages with the RECOVERY_LABEL object from the upstream neighbor and Resv messages with the LABEL object from the downstream LSR. Using the information received in the Path and Resv messages, the midpoint LSR can re-create PSB and RSB state blocks. Any information that cannot be derived from tunnel configuration or recovered from neighbors should be preserved. Examples of this type of information include the loose ERO, the associated expanded ERO (if any), per-LSP bandwidth pools, and the precedence level.

Tail-End Restarting

In this case, the restarting LSR can rebuild PSB on receipt of the Path message containing the Suggested_Label from the upstream neighbor. Because CAC (which involves checking whether the requested bandwidth is available) is performed on an outgoing link, it is not required on a tail-end LSR. Therefore, at the tail-end LSR, per-LSP bandwidth pools and the precedence levels are not needed. In brief, the tail-end LSR has the required information to build the Resv message and re-create the RSB.

Nonrestarting Neighbor Behavior

After an LSR determines that an NSF-capable neighbor has restarted, it must wait for at least the restart time to allow the neighbor to restart and reestablish Hello communication. The LSR might wait different amounts of time based on local policy. While waiting, the LSR continues to retain its RSVP-TE and MPLS forwarding state for all established LSPs that traverse links between that LSR and its restarting neighbor. However, the LSR might time out the state for those LSPs that are in the process of being established when their associated state refresh timers expire. During this waiting period, when attempting to reestablish Hello communication with the restarting neighbor, the LSR sends all Hello messages with the Dst_Instance set to 0 and the Src_Instance unchanged (the same value that was being advertised to the neighbor before the restart).

If the Hello communication with the restarting neighbor could not be established before the waiting period expires, the LSR immediately removes its RSVP-TE and MPLS forwarding state that was being retained across the restart.

However, if the Hello communication with the neighbor is reestablished within the waiting period (a Hello is received from the neighbor), the LSR examines the newly received Src_Instance to determine whether the neighbor's fault was caused by control-channel failure or control-plane failure. For example, if the newly received Src_Instance value differs from the value that was received before the fault, the LSR treats the current fault as a node failure. Otherwise, the fault is treated as a control-channel failure.

If the LSR determines the fault to be a control-channel failure and the neighbor is able to preserve MPLS forwarding state across the failure, a nonzero Recovery Time is received from neighbor. Then the LSR updates its RSVP-TE state shared with the neighbor using normal Path and Resv refresh message procedures. To reduce the refresh message volume, the LSR may use summary refresh messages. To avoid the possibility of congesting a neighbor's control plane by bursting a large number of refresh messages in a short time, the LSR may utilize traffic shaping to spread these messages evenly in the recovery period.

However, if the LSR determines that the fault was caused by the neighbor's control-plane restart and the neighbor had preserved MPLS forwarding state across the restart, the node refreshes all Path states shared with that neighbor by including the RECOVERY_LABEL object in the Path message and using the normal path-refresh procedures. Specifically, the LSR includes the RECOVERY_LABEL object in all outgoing Path messages to the downstream neighbor to convey the outgoing label that was received in the latest Resv message from the downstream neighbor before the restart. The path state refresh should be completed within half of the Recovery Time advertised by the restarting neighbor.

The LSR uses the following procedure to update its Resv state. The LSR does not send a Resv refresh message to the restarting neighbor until it has received a corresponding Path message from the neighbor. This indicates a behavior change in the RSVP refresh procedure during the recovery period. Specifically, this requires that normal Resv and Summary Refresh processing be suppressed during the recovery period. However, as soon as a Path message is received, a corresponding Resv message is generated and RSVP reverts to the normal state processing behavior. The following section details the operation of the RSVP-TE GR mechanism.

RSVP-TE Graceful Restart Operation

This section describes the RSVP-TE GR operation for a restarting midpoint LSR. For the sake of brevity, restart behaviors of head-end and tail-end LSRs are omitted because their restart behaviors can be viewed as special cases of the midpoint restart behavior. For the following discussion, see the network topology shown in Figure 9-6. Assume a unidirectional MPLS-TE LSP tunnel originating at the LSR1 (head end) transiting LSR2 (midpoint), and terminating at the LSR3 (tail end).

Figure 9-6   *Operation of the RSVP-TE Graceful Restart Mechanism*

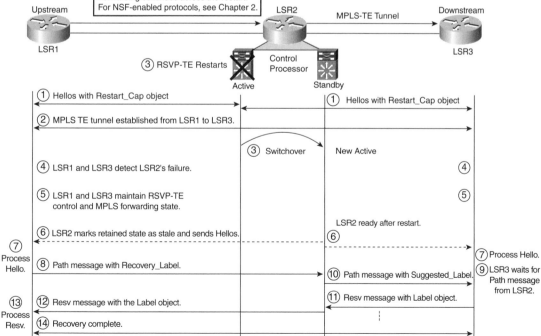

The sequence of operational steps does not necessarily correspond to a particular implementation, but rather is intended as a functional description.

1. LSR1, LSR2, and LSR3 exchange RSVP-TE Hellos containing the RESTART_CAP object to inform each other about GR capabilities.

2. Suppose an MPLS-TE tunnel is established from LSR1 to LSR3 and traffic is being forwarded on the tunnel.

3. Assume the RSVP-TE control-plane component on LSR2 restarts.

4. Using the RSVP-TE Hello mechanism, LSR1 and LSR3 detect loss of Hello communication to the LSR2.

5. On detection of failure, LSR1 and LSR3 wait at least the amount of time indicated by the Restart Time. During this waiting period, LSR2 and LSR3 send Hellos with the Dst_Instance value set to 0 and the Src_Instance unchanged. While waiting, LSR1 and LSR3 retain their RSVP-TE and MPLS forwarding states for the established LSPs that traverse links between LSR1/LSR3 and LSR2. In other words, LSR1 and LSR3 treat the RSVP-TE state of the established LSPs (that traverse LSR2, LSR1, and LSR3) as if they are still receiving periodic RSVP refresh messages from LSR2. In the waiting period, LSR1 and LSR3 suppress the normal refreshing of Resv and Path states.

6. On restarting, LSR2 checks to see whether it was able to preserve its MPLS forwarding state across its control-plane restart. If the answer is no, LSR2 sends a Hello with Recovery Time set to 0, Dst_Instance set to 0, and Src_Instance set to a nonzero value that differs from the value set before this restart. However, if the answer is yes, LSR2 initiates the state recovery process. It marks all MPLS forwarding states that were preserved across the restart as stale, but continues to use the stale state for forwarding. LSR2 advertises its total Recovery Period to LSR1/LSR3 in the Recovery Time parameter of the RESTART_CAP object. During the recovery period, LSR2 sends a Hello message that contains these elements:

   — Recovery Time set to the nonzero duration of the recovery period

   — Dst_Instance set to 0 (or instead reflecting a neighbor's Src_Instance value when a Hello has been received from the neighbor)

   — Src_Instance set to a new value (different than before this failure)

7. On receipt of a new Hello message from LSR2, LSR1 and LSR3 determine whether the fault was a control-channel or a nodal failure. Assume the fault is determined to be a control-plane failure. Furthermore, assume that the received Recovery Time is nonzero, which indicates that the LSR2 was able to preserve its MPLS forwarding state across the restart. Therefore, LSR1 and LSR3 mark all RSVP-TE states shared with LSR2 as stale, retain the stale state, and continue to use corresponding MPLS forwarding state for forwarding traffic on LSPs. LSR1 and LSR3 attempt to resynchronize their path states that

are shared with LSR2 in the recovery period. (See Step 8.) During the recovery period, LSR1 and LSR3 do not refresh their RSVP-TE Resv state shared with LSR2 until a corresponding Path message has been received.

8. Following the previous step, for each LSP that traverses LSR1 and for which LSR2 is the next hop (here a single LSP), LSR1 places its outgoing label (the label which was received in Resv message from LSR2 before LSR2's restart) in the RECOVERY_LABEL object of the Path message and sends it to LSR2.

9. For the reference network topology, a single LSP is assumed from LSR1 to LSR3. Because there is no LSP that traverses LSR3 and for which LSR2 is the next hop, LSR3 does not send a Path message to LSR2. To refresh Resv states, LSR3 waits until it has received a corresponding Path message from LSR2.

10. In the recovery period, LSR2 processes the received Path message according to the procedure described in the section "Restarting LSR Behavior" to refresh its RSVP-TE and MPLS forwarding states. Assume LSR2 does not find PSB corresponding to the received Path message. Therefore, LSR2 creates a PSB and sends the outgoing Path message with a SUGGESTED_LABEL object to LSR3. The SUGGESTED_LABEL object contains the outgoing label value in the restored forwarding entry.

11. LSR3 receives the Path message from LSR2 and finds a PSB associated with this Path message. LSR3 builds the Resv message, places its corresponding incoming label in the LABEL object, and sends it to LSR2.

12. LSR2 receives the Resv message, builds its RSB, and associates it with the PSB. Now both the incoming label and the outgoing label have been refreshed. LSR2 clears the stale flag and sends a Resv message with the LABEL object containing its incoming label.

13. LSR1 receives the Resv message, refreshes its RSB, and clears the stale flag. More precisely, when LSR1 receives a Resv message, it searches its RSVP-TE state for a matching entry. If the newly received label mapping is the same as the already existing stale entry, it clears the stale flag. However, if a stale label mapping entry for the same session exists but has a label different from that received in the Label Mapping message, LSR1 updates the RSB with the new label, clears the flag, and updates the associated LFIB entry.

14. The recovery period expires. LSR2 deletes any forwarding entry still marked as stale. Similarly, LSR1 and LSR2 delete all remaining state information. The recovery is complete.

Network Deployment Considerations for RSVP-TE Graceful Restart

By now it should be clear that the support of the RSVP-TE GR mechanism requires that the restarting LSR be capable of preserving its MPLS forwarding state across its restart, the restarting LSR must inform neighbors about its GR capability before the restart, and the neighbors must also help the restarting LSR recovery procedure by retaining their RSVP-TE control plane/MPLS forwarding state across the restart and resynchronizing RSVP-TE state during the recovery period. Because RSVP-TE control-plane component failure might occur in any LSR of the MPLS network, to derive maximum benefit from the LDP GR mechanism, each LSR not only must support RSVP-TE GR extensions but also be able to preserve its MPLS forwarding state across the restart. If an LSR supports RSVP-TE but is NSF incapable, the LSR does not help reduce the detrimental effects of its own restart. This is because in this case the restarting LSR loses its MPLS forwarding state and hence is unable to forward across the restart. By retaining its RSVP-TE control and MPLS forwarding state across a neighbor's control-plane restart, however, the LSR can still help reduce the negative effects of restart. In summary, to avoid the harmful effects of a particular LSR's RSVP-TE control-plane restart, at a minimum all RSVP neighbors must be able to support the RSVP-TE GR protocol extensions, as discussed in the paragraphs that follow and depicted in Figure 9-7.

Figure 9-7   *RSVP-TE GR Deployment Scenarios*

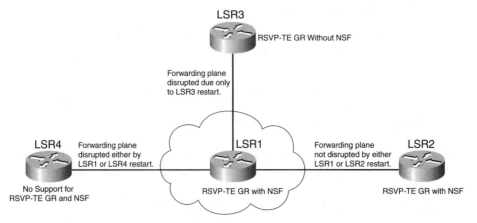

Scenario 1: LSR1 and LSR2 Are RSVP-TE GR- and NSF-Capable

In this case, RSVP-TE restart in either LSR1 or LSR2 would not disrupt the MPLS forwarding plane (see Figure 9-7). Therefore, for the most beneficial deployment of the RSVP-TE GR mechanism, all LSRs in an MPLS network must be RSVP-TE GR-capable and be able to preserve the MPLS forwarding state across an RSVP-TE control-plane restart.

Scenario 2: LSR1 Is RSVP-TE GR- and NSF-Capable, but LSR3 Is Only RSVP-TE GR-Capable

This deployment scenario is important because in practice not all LSRs can support a full set of control-plane restart and NSF capabilities. In this case, when the RSVP-TE control plane in LSR1 restarts, because it is RSVP-TE GR- and NSF-capable and its neighbor also supports RSVP-TE GR extensions, the MPLS forwarding plane would not be disrupted. In contrast, when LSR3 restarts, because LSR3 would have informed LSR1 about its inability to preserve the forwarding state before the restart, on detecting LDP session failure with LSR3, LSR1 would immediately remove RSVP-TE control and the associated MPLS forwarding state. Therefore, forwarding on all LSP tunnels traversing LSR3 is disrupted.

Scenario 3: LSR1 Is RSVP-TE GR- and NSF-Capable, but LSR4 Is RSVP-TE GR- and NSF-Incapable

For this case, RSVP-TE restart in either LSR1 or LSR4 would disrupt the MPLS forwarding plane. This shows that for deriving any benefit from the RSVP-TE GR capability of an LSR, at a minimum all its RSVP neighbors must be capable of supporting the RSVP-TE GR mechanism.

Summary

This chapter described the harmful effects caused by the RSVP-TE control-plane restart and covered the RSVP-TE GR mechanism, which enables the RSVP-TE control plane to restart without causing detrimental effects on MPLS forwarding. The operation of the RSVP-TE GR procedure was elaborated through various deployment scenarios.

References

[1] RFC 2205, "Resource ReSerVation Protocol (RSVP)—Version 1, Functional Specification," R. Braden et al., September 1997.

[2] RFC 2210, "The Use of RSVP with IETF Integrated Services," J. Wroclawski, September 1997.

[3] RFC 2961, "RSVP Refresh Overhead Reduction Extensions," L. Berger et al., April 2001.

[4] RFC 3209, "RSVP-TE: Extensions to RSVP for LSP Tunnels," D. Awduche et al., December 2001.

[5] RFC 3473, "Generalized Multi-Protocol Label Switching (GMPLS) Signaling Resource ReSerVation Protocol-Traffic Engineering (RSVP-TE) Extensions," Lou Berger et al., January 2003.

PART III

High Availability of MPLS-Based Services

Chapter 10   Improving Survivability of IP and MPLS Networks

Improving the Survivability of IP and MPLS Networks

Chapters 4 through 9 described various *Internet Protocol* (IP) and *Multiprotocol Label Switching* (MPLS) control-plane restart mechanisms for improving the fault tolerance of different individual control-plane components. Generally, each IP/MPLS application involves multiple control-plane components. This chapter focuses on applications rather than individual components. Overall network availability has two aspects: node-level availability (internal to the system) and network-level availability (external to the system). Node-level availability refers to fault-tolerance mechanisms that are internal to the system and which typically are invisible to an external viewer. For example, control-plane *stateful switchover* (SSO) in conjunction with *graceful restart* (GR) mechanisms can be used to improve the node-level fault tolerance against unplanned control-plane failures. Network-level fault tolerance involves the interaction of a node with other nodes through external interfaces. Thus network-level availability encompasses link/node protection schemes at multiple layers, including *wavelength-division multiplexing* (WDM), *Synchronous Optical Network Synchronous Digital Hierarchy* (SONET/SDH), and MPLS. Because both node internal and external faults contribute to the total network downtime, fault tolerance at both levels is essential to have any meaningful end-to-end network availability. This chapter discusses how different IP and MPLS control-plane restart mechanisms (described in previous chapters) and node external protection schemes can be used collectively to improve the end-to-end availability of an MPLS-enabled IP network against different types of failures.

A service provider can offer to a customer two fundamentally different types of *virtual private network* (VPN) services: *Layer 3 virtual private networks* (L3VPNs) and *Layer 2 virtual private networks* (L2VPNs). The VPN tunnel (a logical link between two devices such as *provider-edge* (PE) routers to carry customer traffic across the backbone) is a functional component that is common to both types of services. In MPLS, a tunnel corresponds to a *label-switched path* (LSP).

In general, MPLS LSPs can be set up either along *Interior Gateway Protocol* (IGP) paths or explicit paths. The mechanisms to establish an LSP along an IGP path are described in Chapter 8, "MPLS Control Plane: Restarting LDP Gracefully." Although the main concepts of MPLS *traffic engineering* (TE) are introduced in the preceding chapter, that chapter does not discuss the mechanics of establishing MPLS-TE tunnels. This chapter draws on and extends the concepts of the preceding chapter and explains how you can use MPLS-TE mechanisms to set up TE tunnels. After describing the common building blocks such as

VPN tunnels, the chapter provides an overview of L3VPN and L2VPN applications and discusses VPN-specific mechanisms such as signaling of the tunnel demultiplexer field. This chapter also discusses ways to protect PE-PE tunnels against unplanned control-plane failures using restart mechanisms.

In addition to improving network fault tolerance against unplanned control-plane failures, it is also essential to reduce service outages that result from unplanned transport-plane faults such as link and node failures and planned events such as software upgrades. Although detailed discussion of fault-tolerance mechanisms other than control-plane restarts is beyond the scope of this book, for the sake of completeness this chapter briefly covers a few other mechanisms such as SONET/SDH protection, MPLS Fast ReRoute (FRR), MPLS *operation, administration, and maintenance* (OAM), *Bidirectional Forwarding Detection* (BFD), and in-service software upgrades.

Layer 2 and Layer 3 Services over MPLS Networks

To meet growing telecommunication and data communication demands, most enterprises and organizations find that network connectivity between different sites has become a necessity. Traditionally, service providers have offered connectivity between enterprise networks over private leased lines using *Frame Relay* (FR) or *Asynchronous Transfer Mode* (ATM) networks. More recently, with the migration of legacy Layer 2 infrastructure over a converged packet-switched network, these services are predominantly offered over an IP/MPLS backbone.

Provider-Provisioned Virtual Private Networks

The term *virtual private network* (VPN) refers to a private network offered over a service provider backbone infrastructure that is shared by multiple customers. From the perspective of an individual customer, the backbone appears to be dedicated to that customer.

The term *provider-provisioned virtual private network* (PPVPN) refers to a VPN in which the service provider participates in the management and provisioning of the VPN. A PPVPN can be further classified into L2VPNs and L3VPNs:[1]

- In L2VPNs, *customer-edge* (CE) devices are interconnected using a mesh of point-to-point links (tunnels) over the shared backbone. As a result, customer addressing is not visible to devices in the service provider backbone.

- In L3VPNs, CE devices exchange routing information with the directly connected PE routers, and therefore some backbone devices know about customer addresses.

In any type of PE-based PPVPN, customer packets are carried in PE-PE tunnels.

VPN Tunnels

A VPN tunnel is a logical link between two devices such as PE routers that carries customer traffic across the backbone. One of the main reasons for using tunnels in VPN applications is to carry customer packets with nonunique addressing information between the VPN edge devices. Other important reasons for using tunnels include the need to isolate traffic from different VPN customers and to provide different *quality of service* (QoS) and security characteristics.

A tunnel that encapsulates one tunnel within another is known as a hierarchical tunnel. For example, L3VPNs and L2VPNs use hierarchical PE-PE tunnels to carry traffic from multiple VPN customers across the backbone between PE routers. In general, a tunnel is implemented by encapsulating packets within another header. More details on VPN tunneling can be found in the context of L2VPN and L3VPN discussion later in this chapter.

Tunnel Demultiplexing

Because each PE-PE tunnel can carry traffic from several customers, an individual customer's traffic within the tunnel is distinguished by using a tunnel demultiplexer field.

The format of the demultiplexer field depends on the underlying tunneling protocol and can be based on the following:

- IP header
- MPLS label
- Layer 2 Tunneling Protocol (L2TP) session ID[2,3]
- Generic Routing Encapsulation (GRE) key field[4]

In the case of MPLS, a tunnel corresponds to a *label-switched path* (LSP) and a hierarchical tunnel corresponds to nesting multiple LSPs within a single LSP using label stack. (See Chapter 3, "MPLS Forwarding Plane: Achieving Nonstop Forwarding.") In this case, the demultiplexer field consists of another MPLS label known as a *VC label* or *inner label*.

In general, a hierarchical PE-PE tunnel might have two or more MPLS labels (label stack). Without loss of generality, in this chapter only the top and bottom labels are considered. The top label is used to forward labeled packets across the backbone and is meaningful to label-*switched routers* (LSRs) along the tunnel's path, including PEs and intermediate LSRs. In contrast, the bottom label is meaningful to the tunnel endpoints, namely, the PEs. In L3VPN and L2VPN applications, the bottom label allows traffic from multiple LSPs to be carried in a single tunnel across the backbone and provides a mechanism for distinguishing one nested LSP from others.

In the remainder of this chapter, the term *tunnel label* refers to the top label, and the term *VPN label* refers to the bottom label. The term *L3VPN* label refers to the bottom label for L3VPN applications. Similarly, the term *L2VPN label* refers to the bottom label for L2VPN application.

Signaling of the Tunnel Labels and VPN Labels

In MPLS, a tunnel can be established either along a hop-by-hop or explicitly routed path. In general, tunnel labels corresponding to IGP routes are distributed either via *Label Distribution Protocol* (LDP) or RSVP-TE. For example, as discussed in Chapter 8, LDP can be used to establish LSPs along IGP paths. Similarly, as discussed in Chapter 9, "MPLS Control Plane: Restarting RSVP-TE Gracefully," RSVP-TE can be used to establish LSPs along explicit paths.

As far as signaling of the VPN labels is concerned, depending on L2VPN or L3VPN applications, different label distribution protocols can be used for this purpose. For example, in an RFC 2547-style L3VPN, L3VPN labels for customer addresses are distributed using *Border Gateway Protocol* (BGP). (See Chapter 7, "MPLS Control Plane: Restarting BGP with MPLS Gracefully.") In contrast, L2VPN labels can be signaled using LDP (or BGP).

NOTE   The L2VPN label-distribution option using BGP is not covered in this chapter.

NOTE   A *service* is the set of functions or tasks performed by the network on request from the user such as voice call, e-mail, and Internet access. A *service outage* refers to user inability to request new services or to continue to use an existing service because the service is no longer possible or is impaired.

Service Attributes Related to Network Availability

The following list outlines the important attributes of a service that need to be considered from the perspective of network reliability and availability:

- Importance (mission critical, critical, noncritical)
- Failure impact (number of users affected)
- Outage duration
- Failure rate (frequency of the failure)[5]

For example, a mission-critical service might not tolerate lack of service greater than a few milliseconds, whereas for noncritical services, loss of service in the order of a few minutes might be acceptable. A network outage is the loss of network resources such as routers, switches, and links caused by complete or partial failures of hardware/software components in routers, link failures resulting from fiber or cable cuts, operational errors, or acts of nature such as earthquakes and floods. Depending on the location and severity of faults and the network design, loss of network resources might cause partial or complete service outage, reduce available bandwidth, or just reduce network protection (for example, reduce redundant paths) without having any effect on service.

Network Fault-Tolerance Techniques

For your convenience and to provide the proper context for the flow of concepts being discussed in this chapter, this section summarizes the main points from Chapter 1, "Understanding High Availability of IP and MPLS Networks." A network is said to be a fault-tolerant or survivable network if it can maintain or quickly restore an acceptable level of performance during network failures. The design of fault-tolerant networks requires the use of a variety of techniques, including the following:

- Redundant hardware components (for example, redundant switch fabrics, line cards, links, control processors, and so forth)

- Redundant software components (such as redundant control-plane software), SONET layer and MPLS layer redundant paths for protection against link and node failures

- Effective OAM mechanisms to rapidly detect and recover from faults

- In-service software upgrades to reduce downtime due to planned software upgrades

MPLS Traffic Engineering

The objective of this section is to provide an overview of MPLS-TE functional components and discuss various deployment scenarios. The present discussion draws heavily on the concepts discussed in Chapter 9.

TE mainly deals with improving the operational efficiency of a network by effective placement of data traffic flows on the underlying network infrastructure. Currently, several techniques are used in IP/MPLS networks for this purpose, including manipulation of IGP metrics and establishing LSPs along explicit paths. This chapter covers MPLS-TE techniques that allow the establishment of tunnels along explicit paths (either specified manually or computed dynamically using constraint-based routing). Chapter 9 covers concepts related to the RSVP-TE protocol and graceful restart.

In conventional IGP protocols, the shortest paths correspond to routes with minimum additive scalar link cost (or link metric). Because the conventional IGP path-selection process does not consider link attributes such as available bandwidth, multiple shortest paths can converge on a link and cause it be overutilized, while at the same time links along alternative but longer routes remain underutilized. *Constraint-based routing* refers to routing algorithms that compute their paths subject to a set of constraints such as bandwidth, delay, resource class, and so forth.

Because conventional IGP protocols are incapable of propagating link attributes such as available bandwidth and resource class, extensions have been made to IGP protocols that allow propagation of additional link attributes as opaque *link-state advertisements* (LSAs).[6,7] Each router uses opaque LSAs that are propagated throughout the area to advertise the router's local link state. A collection of such opaque LSAs is known as an extended link-state database or TE topology database. Unlike a regular IGP topology database, the TE topology database contains additional information about link attributes that enables computation of *constrained shortest path first* (CSPF) routes.

MPLS-TE Functional Modules

MPLS-TE uses enhanced IGP protocols in the IP control plane, RSVP-TE in the MPLS control plane, and MPLS label switching in the forwarding plane (see Figure 10-1). An MPLS-TE tunnel is unidirectional (head to tail) and has three parts: the head end, the midpoint, and the tail end. An MPLS-TE application contains several functional modules such as head-end control, link management, TE topology database, and path calculation.

Figure 10-1   *MPLS-TE Control-Plane and Forwarding-Plane Components*

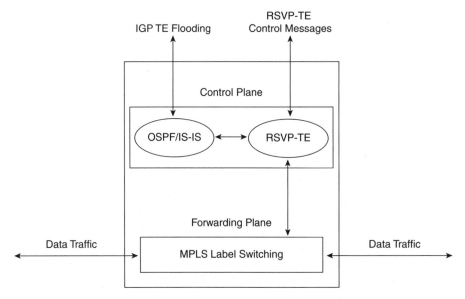

The head-end control module is used to manage MPLS-TE tunnels that originate on the node. The link management module is primarily responsible for managing local link resources, including available bandwidth at each of eight priority levels, optional link attributes (coloring), and optional link administrative weight. The link management module provides the latest link information to the IGP for propagating as opaque LSAs. The IGP and TE topology database interactions are depicted in Figure 10-2. The MPLS-TE topology database is a link-state database that contains network topology information built using opaque LSAs from the IGP. The path calculation module exists on nodes that might function as the head-end for MPLS-TE tunnels and on midpoints when the loose *explicit route object* (ERO) needs to be expanded. The basic function of the path calculation module is to compute the explicit path using the TE topology database.

Figure 10-2   *IGP and TE Topology Database Interactions*

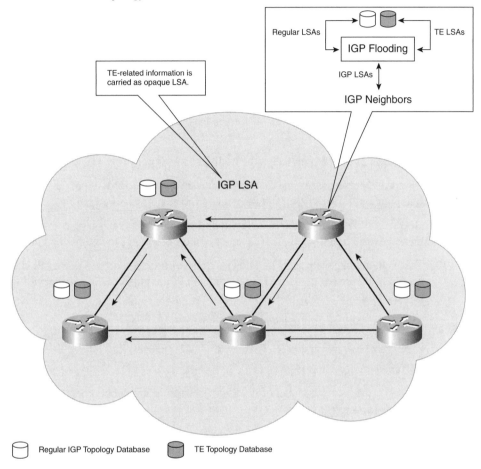

Establishment of an MPLS-TE Tunnel

The MPLS-TE tunnel establishment process begins with the configuration of tunnel parameters such as destination IP address, bandwidth, affinity, and so forth. The tunnel establishment process proceeds as follows:

1. The head-end control passes tunnel parameters to the path calculation module.

2. The path calculation module then computes the path subject to specified constraints and returns the selected path as an ERO.

3. The head-end control hands over the ERO to RSVP-TE to establish the tunnel.

4. RSVP-TE performs a *connection admission control* (CAC) to check whether the requested bandwidth is available on the outgoing link in the appropriate-priority bandwidth pool. The link management module maintains up to eight priority bandwidth pools on each link.

5. If the CAC bandwidth check passes, the link management module sets aside the requested bandwidth from the free bandwidth pool to the allocated pool and informs the RSVP-TE module.

6. RSVP-TE builds the Path message, includes the ERO, and forwards the message to the next hop.

7. On receipt of the Path message, the midpoint router performs a CAC check.

8. If the CAC check passes, the router allocates the requested amount of bandwidth from the free pool and forwards the Path message to the next hop using ERO.

9. However, if the CAC check fails, the midpoint router generates a path error (PathErr) message upstream toward the head end to report errors in processing the Path message.

10. This Path message is propagated downstream itself until it arrives at the tail end. On receipt of the Path message at the tail end, the following events occur. The RSVP-TE module of the tail end performs the following tasks:

    a. Allocates the incoming label for the tunnel

    b. Installs the incoming label in the *Label Forwarding Information Base* (LFIB)

    c. Builds the Resv message

    d. Inserts the incoming label of the Resv message in the Label object and forwards the Resv message upstream

11. When the Resv message arrives at the upstream (midpoint) LSR, the midpoint checks whether the previously allocated bandwidth is still available.

12. If the bandwidth check passes, the midpoint performs the following tasks:

    a. Reserves the bandwidth

    b. Allocates an incoming label

    c. Installs the remotely received outgoing and locally assigned label in the LFIB

    d. Inserts the locally assigned incoming label in the Label object

    e. Forwards the message to the upstream LSR

13. If the bandwidth check fails, the midpoint sends a reservation error (ResvErr) message downstream. The reception of a ResvErr message at a downstream node because of a CAC failure causes that node to create a local blockade state using a timer. When a blockade time expires, the associated blockade state is removed. (Refer to RFC 2205 for more information about the use of blockade states.)

Eventually, the Resv message arrives at the head-end LSR. On receipt of the Resv message, the head-end LSR checks whether the previously allocated bandwidth is still available. Assuming this is the case, the head end now reserves the bandwidth, installs the remote-received label in the LFIB, and informs the control module that the tunnel has successfully been established. The head-end control signals the IGP module to start forwarding data traffic onto the tunnel (see Figure 10-3).

Figure 10-3   *Interaction of MPLS-TE Functional Components During the Tunnel Establishment Process*

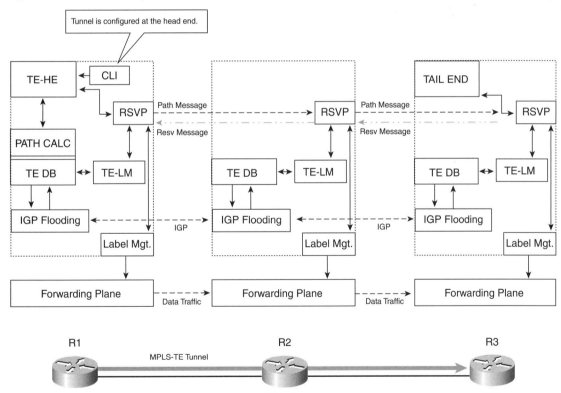

MPLS-TE Tunnel Reoptimization

After a tunnel is established, topology changes or other events trigger path recalculation that might render the existing LSP path no longer optimal with respect to specified constraints. The events that could trigger path recalculation include the periodic expiration of the reoptimization timer and the forcing by an administrator of changes to the reoptimization or bandwidth of the tunnel. The objective of tunnel reoptimization is to find a better path in terms of lower IGP cost, if such a path exists, and to reroute the tunnel along the new path. To avoid disrupting traffic on the existing tunnel, another tunnel is first established along the new path before tearing down the old tunnel. This approach is commonly referred to as *make-before-break* (see Figure 10-4).

Figure 10-4   *MPLS-TE Tunnel Reoptimization Using the Make-Before-Break Approach*

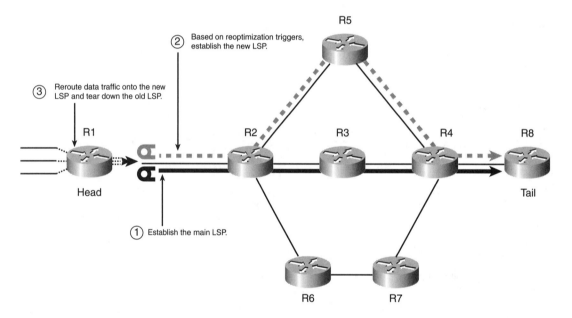

Protecting MPLS-TE Tunnels Against Control-Plane Failures

IGPs are used to distribute topology and routing information between routers within an *autonomous system* (AS). This fact has been previously discussed in Chapters 4 and 5, which are titled respectively, "Intradomain IP Control Plane: Restarting OSPF Gracefully," and "Intradomain IP Control Plane: Restarting IS-IS Gracefully." *Open Shortest Path First* (OSPF) and *Intermediate System-to-Intermediate System* (IS-IS) are two of the most widely deployed IGPs. For the purpose of routing scalability, each AS is partitioned into several smaller networks, known as OSPF areas or IS-IS levels. Within a given IGP area, routing is flat, which means each router within the area has the complete knowledge of the topology and routing information in the area. Across different IGP areas, however, routing is hierarchical, which means that routers inside a particular area have a partial knowledge of the routing information of other areas.

With regard to MPLS-TE control-plane failures, you need to consider three deployment scenarios: intra-area, inter-area (or intra-AS), and inter-AS. (See Figure 10-5 for an illustration of each of the three cases.)

Figure 10-5   *MPLS Intra-Area, Inter-Area, and Inter-AS Traffic Engineering*

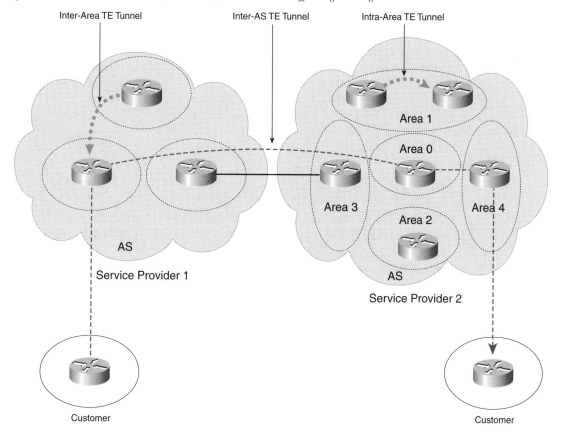

Intra-Area MPLS Traffic Engineering

This is the simplest case, in which both the head-end and tail-end LSRs of a TE LSP reside in the same IGP area, and thus TE LSP spans a single IGP area (see Figure 10-5). To avoid service outage on an intra-area TE tunnel that is caused by RSVP-TE control-plane failures, all nodes along the TE LSP path must support *nonstop forwarding* (NSF) and RSVP-TE GR capabilities. (For details on the RSVP-TE GR mechanism, see Chapter 9.)

Inter-Area or Intra-AS MPLS Traffic Engineering

Currently many network operators utilize MPLS-TE capabilities to deliver end-to-end Layer 2 and Layer 3 services with strict QoS guarantees. Using MPLS-TE optimizes network resources and provides fast recovery (in the order of milliseconds) against link and node failures. However, the existing set of MPLS-TE capabilities is confined to a single IGP area.

An undesirable side effect of the hierarchical routing (hierarchical routing that partitions the network into areas) is the loss of routing information for inter-area destinations. Only aggregated routing and topology information is propagated across an area boundary. Therefore, due to lack of knowledge about complete routing information, head-end LSRs in a particular area are unable to compute constrained-based optimal TE tunnels paths to the tail-end LSRs residing in other areas. (Constrained-based optimal TE tunnels paths have minimum end-to-end IGP or TE metrics.) However, service provider backbones often stretch multiple IGP areas and often traverse multiple autonomous systems. Therefore, it is essential to extend MPLS-TE capabilities beyond a single IGP area to enable service providers to offer QoS guarantees and allow efficient utilization of network resources across multiple IGP areas. The specification of inter-area MPLS-TE functionalities is currently underway in the *Internet Engineering Task Force* (IETF).[8]

From the perspective of protection against control-plane restarts, in the case of the inter-area deployment scenario, TE tunnels extend over multiple IGP areas (see Figure 10-5). This means all nodes along the TE LSP inter-area path should support NSF and RSVP-TE GR capabilities (see Chapter 9). It is worth reiterating that the goal of GR mechanisms is to reduce detrimental effects (such as loss of data traffic) due to control-plane failures that are internal to a node. These mechanisms do not address protection against failures external to the node, such as link and node failures along the tunnel path. To protect against link and node failures, other techniques such as SONET/SDH automatic protection switching and MPLS fast rerouting are used, as discussed later in this chapter.

Inter-AS MPLS Traffic Engineering

So far, this chapter has discussed using MPLS-TE functionalities within a single IGP area or across multiple IGP areas within a single AS. Many times, however, MPLS-TE tunnels need to traverse multiple autonomous systems that are part of one or more service providers' networks.[9] This type of deployment scenario calls for inter-AS TE capabilities in order to optimize network resources and deliver negotiated service-level agreements (SLAs).

With respect to control-plane failures, in the case of inter-AS deployment scenarios, TE tunnels extend over multiple autonomous systems (see Figure 10-5). Therefore, all nodes along the TE LSP path must support NSF and RSVP-TE GR capabilities. Additional recovery methods such as fast rerouting may still be required to protect data traffic against link/node failures.

Layer 3 Virtual Private Networks

An L3VPN interconnects customer devices (routers or hosts) at multiple sites and allows them to communicate using IP addresses. L3VPNs can be broadly categorized as VPNs that are either CE or PE based.

CE-Based L3VPNs

In CE-based L3VPNs, CE devices are connected through CE-to-CE tunnels such as L2TP, IPSec, and MPLS. The service provider manages and provisions the CE devices. Devices in the backbone, however, do not know about customer IP addresses.

PE-Based L3VPNs

In PE-based L3VPNs, PE devices exchange routing information with CE devices and thus know about customer IP addresses. Like CE-based L3VPNS, with PE-based L3VPNs customer packets are also transported over PE-to-PE tunnels. Unlike CE-based L3VPNS, however, with PE-based L3VPNs, customer addresses are visible to devices in the backbone.

There are two approaches for PE-based L3VPNs: RFC 2457 based and *virtual router* (VR) based.[11] In VR-style L3VPNs, the PE router emulates a separate logical router, runs a separate instance of routing protocols, and maintains a separate forwarding table for each customer VPN. In contrast, in RFC 2547-style L3VPNs, the PE router maintains a separate forwarding table for each customer VPN, but runs only a single instance of routing protocols.[7,10] The discussion in this chapter is restricted to the RFC 2547-style L3VPNs, in which the backbone consists of an MPLS-enabled IP network.

PE-Based L3VPN Reference Model

Figure 10-6 depicts the reference model for RFC 2547-style L3VPNs.

Different entities in the L3VPN reference model are briefly described herein. An access connection provides connectivity between a CE and a PE device. An access connection can be a physical (such as Ethernet interface) connection or logical (such as an IP tunnel, ATM virtual connection, or Frame Relay DLCI). The fact that a CE can connect to a PE device through a Layer 2 access connection (such as Ethernet or ATM) might seem to blur the differences between L2VPN and L3VPN services. However, you can easily make this distinction by recognizing that in the case of L3VPNs, when a CE device is connected to a PE device via a Layer 2 access connection, the PE still provides only an IP service (a Layer 3 service) to the customer. This means that in the case of L3VPNs, Layer 2 access connections must terminate at the PE devices. For example, in such cases, the PE extracts the customer's IP packets from any Layer 2 encapsulation and then sends them over PE-to-PE tunnels across the backbone. The access connection that carries IP packets from a CE router to a PE is known as the incoming (ingress) access connection. The access connection that carries IP packets from a PE router to a CE is known as the outgoing (egress) access connection.

Figure 10-6 *Reference Model for a Layer 3 PE-Based VPN with an MPLS Backbone*

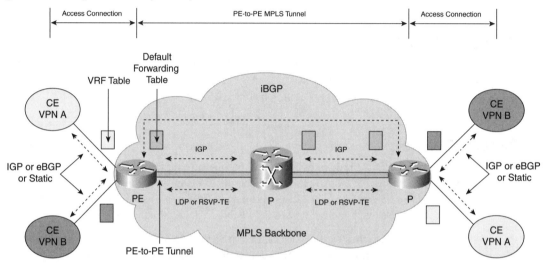

The service provider's backbone consists of interconnected PEs and *provider* (P) routers. The PE routers directly attach to CE devices, whereas P routers connect only to P and PE routers. A PE router may connect to CE routers belonging to different VPNs.

VPN Routing and Forwarding Tables

To provide per-VPN separation of routing information and to avoid erroneous forwarding of packets from one VPN to another, each PE router maintains a separate *VPN routing and forwarding* (VRF) table for each customer VPN. An access connection may be associated with one or more VRFs through configuration. If an IP packet arrives over an access connection that has been associated with a VRF, the packet is forwarded using the related VRF table.

Each PE router also maintains a default forwarding table that is used to forward packets from neighboring P or PE routers and packets arriving on access connections that have not been associated with any VRFs. PEs learn CE routes using IGP, external BGP (eBGP), or static routing. PE routers use *internal BGP* (iBGP) to distribute customer routes to each other. The customer routes are generally allocated from private address space. However, BGP requires IP addresses to be globally unique. Therefore, to disambiguate customer private addresses, a VPN-IPv4 address family is formed by concatenating a *route distinguisher* (RD) and the regular IPv4 address.

Within the service provider's network, the customer IP address is identified by a VPN-IPv4 address. Each VRF table is configured with a default RD, which is used for exporting a VPN-IPv4 route to BGP. In other words, PE translates customer addresses learned over PE-CE links into VPN-IPv4 addresses using a configured RD. The PE then exports VPN-IPv4 routes into BGP for distributing to other PEs. When there are multiple routes to a particular VPN-IP4 address prefix, BGP chooses the best route based on the BGP decision process. (See Chapter 6, "Interdomain IP Control Plane: Restarting BGP Gracefully.") Note, however, that PE does not leak customer routes to the IGP in the backbone.

In summary, each VRF table is populated from two main sources: routes learned over PE-CE links, and VPN-IPv4 routes learned from another PE router via BGP. The distribution of routing information is controlled using BGP route filtering. Every VRF is associated with one or more *route target* (RT) attributes. An RT uniquely identifies a VPN or set of VPNs to which the route should be distributed. When a PE creates a VPN-IPv4 route, it associates one or more RT attributes (referred to as export route targets) with the route. These attributes are then carried as BGP extended-community RTs. Similarly, there is a set of RTs (referred to as the import route targets) that a PE router uses to determine whether a route received from another PE router via BGP could be imported in the VRF associated with a particular VPN site.

A route learned from a CE router over a particular access connection is eligible for inclusion in the associated VRF. However, a route learned from another PE router is eligible for inclusion in a particular VRF if and only if the RT attribute of the learned route matches with one of the import route targets of that VRF that has been configured. Unlike VRFs, routes learned via IGP in the backbone are used to populate the default routing table.

PE-to-PE Tunnel

As mentioned previously in this chapter, a VPN tunnel is a logical link between two PE routers and can be used to deliver customer data packets across the backbone. The tunnel can follow an IGP or an explicit route. In the case of MPLS, PE-to-PE tunnels are established using LDP or RSVP-TE. MPLS allows multiplexing (nesting) of LSPs within other LSPs. Because a single PE-to-PE tunnel can be used to carry traffic from several VPN customers, a particular unit of VPN traffic within the tunnel is distinguished using a demultiplexer field, which consists of another MPLS label (referred to as inner label). When a customer data packet arrives at a PE, the PE encapsulates it with the appropriate MPLS label (the L3VPN label). The labeled packet is further encapsulated with another MPLS label (known as a tunnel label). In the case of a hop-by-hop routed VPN tunnel, the tunnel label is distributed using LDP. For an explicitly routed PE-PE tunnel, the tunnel label is distributed via RSVP-TE. The following section describes the method for signaling L3VPN labels.

Distribution of L3VPN Labels

How are the L3VPN labels distributed? Each VPN route is assigned an MPLS label by the concerned PE router. When BGP distributes a VPN route, it also carries an MPLS label for that route. As discussed in Chapter 7, the MPLS label for a VPN-IPv4 address is carried in *Multiprotocol Reachable Network Layer Reachability Information* (MP_REACH_NLRI). Therefore, the PE pushes not just one but two labels (or label stack) to customer data packets. The tunnel label is used for forwarding the labeled packet across the backbone LSRs. The L3VPN label is used to select the outgoing access connection in the egress PE.

PEs can distribute VPN-IPv4 routes and the associated MPLS label using an iBGP connection between them, or they can have an iBGP connection to a *route reflector* (RR). As discussed in Chapter 7, the RR is used to avoid iBGP session mesh and yet ensure propagation of BGP routing information to all BGP speakers inside an AS. The RR transparently reflects the label information along with the VPN-IPv4 route. For a more detailed description of L3VPN operation, refer to the L3VPN architecture specification.[11]

IPv6-Based L3VPN Services

To support IPv6-based L3VPN services, the RFC 2547b that is based on the method described in the previous section must be extended. For this purpose, the IETF has defined an IPv6 VPN address family and a corresponding route-distribution method.[12] A VPN-IPv6 address is a 24-byte quantity that begins with an 8-byte *route distinguisher* (RD) and ends with a 16-byte IPv6 address. Similar to the IPv4 case, a labeled IPv6 VPN route is encoded as MP_REACH_NLRI and distributed using BGP, but with different values for the *Address Family Identifier* (AFI) and *Subsequent Address Family Identifier* (SAFI) fields. For IPv6, the AFI field is set to 2, and the SAFI field is set to 128. Like the IPv4 case, with IPv6 VPNs, each PE maintains separate VRF tables for each IPv6 VPN.

Protecting L3VPN Service Against Control-Plane Failures

In the context of protection against control-plane failures, three deployment scenarios should be examined for L3VPNs, as follows:

- Single-AS backbone
- Multi-AS backbone
- Carrier supporting carriers (CSC)

Single-AS MPLS Backbone

With this, the simplest deployment scenario, two sites of a VPN attach to PE routers that are in the same AS (see Figure 10-6). In this case, an end-to-end data traffic path can be partitioned into the PE-CE access connection segment and into the PE-PE tunnel segment across the backbone. The IP and MPLS control-plane components that can fail along the data traffic path include the following:

- IGP (or eBGP) on the PE-CE link
- LDP (or RSVP-TE) on PE and P routers
- iBGP on PE routers
- IGP on PE and P routers

To avoid traffic disruption caused by IP control-plane failure on the PE-CE link, both PE and CE routers must be able to preserve the IGP (or BGP) forwarding state across the restart and support relevant GR extensions (see Chapters 4, 5, and 6). Similarly, along the PE-PE segment, all LSRs must be able to preserve the MPLS forwarding state and IP forwarding state (when applicable) across the individual MPLS control-plane component restart (such as LDP, RSVP-TE, BGP) that created the corresponding label bindings. When different control-plane components are tightly coupled (for example, whenever IGP restarts, BGP would also restart and vice versa), to reduce overall detrimental effects of control-plane restart in the AS, it is essential that all restarting control-plane components support the pertinent GR capabilities. Other recovery techniques such as fast rerouting are needed for protection against link or node failures.

Multi-AS MPLS Backbone

In this deployment scenario, two sites of a VPN are connected to different autonomous systems (see Figure 10-7). The multi-AS backbone enables a service provider to span multiple autonomous systems and offer L3VPN service in different geographic areas. In this case, PE routers use iBGP to redistribute VPN-IPv4 routes and the associated MPLS labels to an *autonomous system border router* (ASBR) directly or through an RR of which an ASBR is a client. Between autonomous systems, labeled VPN-IPv4 routes are redistributed using eBGP. For example, the ASBR from the first AS uses eBGP to redistribute those labeled VPN-IPv4 routes to an ASBR in the second AS, which in turn distributes them to the PE routers in that AS, or to another ASBR.

The use of eBGP to redistribute labeled VPN-IPv4 routes from AS to neighboring AS ensures loop-free exchange of routing information between autonomous systems. In this case, a data traffic path can be partitioned into the PE-CE attachment circuit segment, the PE-to-PE (or PE-ASBR) tunnel segment within the AS and ASBR-ASBR segment between two neighboring autonomous systems. The IP and MPLS control-plane components that can fail along the data traffic path include the following:

- IGP (or eBGP) on the PE-CE link
- LDP (or RSVP-TE) on PE and P routers

- iBGP on PE routers
- IGP on PE and P routers
- eBGP on ASBRs

Therefore, all nodes along the data traffic path must be able to support the relevant control-plane GR capabilities.

Figure 10-7   *Multi-AS Deployment Scenario for Layer 3 PE-Based VPN*

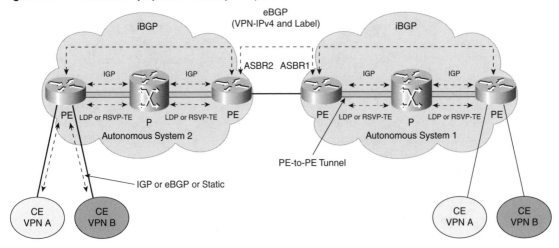

Carrier Supporting Carrier (CSC)

A carrier's carrier is an L3VPN deployment scenario in which a backbone service provider (referred to as a *carrier's carrier*) offers VPN service to another service provider (referred to as *customer carrier*) that in turn offers VPN services to its customers (see Figure 10-8). To offer carrier's carrier VPN service using RFC 2547 procedures, it is essential that the CE routers support MPLS. In this deployment scenario, LDP is used to distribute labels for routes between CE and PE routers. Thus, CE routers receive labels from the PE routers and send (receive) labeled packets to the PE routers.

Figure 10-8   *Carrier's Carrier Deployment Scenario for a Layer 3 PE-Based VPN*

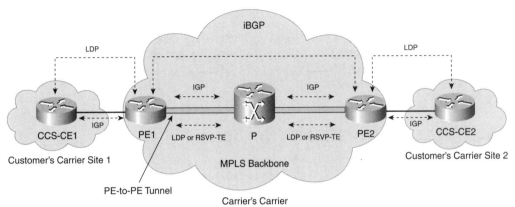

As discussed previously, in a single-AS deployment scenario, packets between CE-PE routers are not labeled. As before, the PE routers use iBGP to redistribute labeled VPN-IPv4 routes between them (for example, when PE2 learns a route from CE2 via IGP). This is the process:

1. PE2 translates the learned IPv4 address to a VPN-IPv4 address by attaching the appropriate RD.

2. PE2 assigns a label (incoming label L2) and installs it in the MPLS LFIB.

3. PE2 then advertises the labeled VPN-IPv4 route in the BGP update message to its iBGP peer PE1.

4. PE2 sets the BGP next-hop attribute in the BGP update message to the IP address of PE2.

5. On receipt of the BGP update, PE1 performs the following tasks:

   a. Installs the label received from PE2 as an outgoing inner label

   b. Allocates a local label L1 for incoming traffic from CE1

   c. Imports this route to the appropriate VRF table

   d. Translates the VPN-IPv4 address back to an IPv4 address

   e. Advertises this prefix to the CE1 via IGP

PE1 distributes the label-to-FEC mapping to CE1-PE1 using LDP. As usual, the outer label for the PE-PE tunnel is distributed either using LDP or RSVP-TE.

In the CSC deployment scenario, IP and MPLS control-plane components that can fail along the data traffic path include the following:

- IGP and LDP on the PE-CE link
- LDP (or RSVP-TE) on PE and P routers

- iBGP on PE routers

- IGP on PE and P routers

For example, PE2 maintains an incoming tunnel label (outer label distributed via LDP or RSVP-TE), an incoming inner label (which was allocated and distributed to PE1 via iBGP by PE2), and an outgoing LDP label (on the PE2-CE2 side.) Therefore, PE2 must be LDP restart- and BGP restart-capable.

Layer 2 Virtual Private Networks

An L2VPN interconnects customer devices (such as a host, a router, or a Layer 2 switch) at multiple sites and allows them to communicate using Layer 2 frames.[13] An L2VPN service provider can offer several types of L2VPN services to its customers, such as point-to-point and point-to-multipoint. In any type of L2VPN service, a PE performs the following tasks:

- Receives a Layer 2 frame from a CE over an attachment circuit (which could be an FR DLCI, an ATM VPI/VCI, an Ethernet port, a VLAN, and so forth).

- Encapsulates the frame in a *pseudowire* (PW) protocol data unit. (A PW is a mechanism that emulates the essential attributes of a service, such as FR, ATM, Ethernet, Time Division Multiplexing [TDM], and SONET/SDH over IP and/or MPLS network. A protocol data unit [PDU] that contains all of the data and control information necessary to emulate the desired service is known as a PW-PDU.)

- Transports one or more PWs over a tunnel across the PSN to another PE, which demultiplexes the PW.

- Removes the encapsulation.

- Sends the frame in its native format to the destination CE.

In L2VPNs, the set of procedures used for making Layer 2 forwarding decisions is called a *forwarder*. Conceptually, you might think of a forwarder as bound to an attachment circuit on one side and a PW on the other side. Different types of L2VPNs contain different types of forwarders. For example, a point-to-point L2VPN has a forwarder that binds exactly one PW to exactly one attachment circuit (see Figure 10-9 [a]). In contrast, a point-to-multipoint L2VPN contains a forwarder that binds one attachment circuit to one or more PWs (see Figure 10-9 [b]).

Figure 10-9   *L2VPNs Forwarder Architectures (a) Point-to-Point Case (b) Point-to-Multipoint Case*

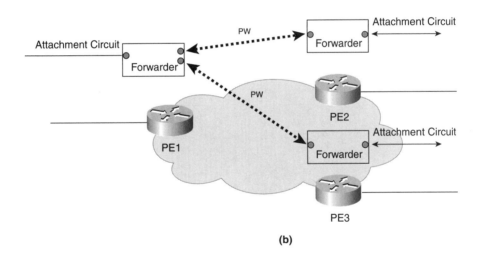

In the case of L2VPNs, PWs correspond to nested LSPs in the PE-to-PE tunnel in which an individual PW is identified based on the MPLS label. As in the case of L3VPNS, in L2VPNs PE-to-PE tunnels can be established using LDP or RSVP-TE. Thus PE-to-PE tunnels in L3VPNs and L2VPNs mainly differ in terms of the type of traffic carried within the nested LSPs and how VPN labels are signaled. For example, in L3VPNs, the PE-to-PE tunnels carry IP packets across the backbone. In contrast, with L2VPNs, PE-to-PE tunnels transport Layer 2 frames, such as FR, ATM, and Ethernet, across the backbone.

Protecting L2VPN Services Against Control-Plane Failures

With regard to protection against control-plane failures, two types of Layer 2 VPN services need to be considered: *virtual private wire service* (VPWS) and *virtual private LAN service* (VPLS). It is also possible to have a variant of the VPLS known as IP-only LAN-like Service (IPLS), but IPLS is not considered in this chapter. The discussion in this chapter is restricted to the control-plane-related functional aspects of MPLS-based L2VPN services. The control-plane restart of attachment circuits is not covered. The protocol details of VPWS and VPLS architecture, PW encapsulation methods, and interworking procedures are beyond the scope of this book.

Virtual Private Wire Service

Figure 10-10 shows the reference model for VPWS. A VPWS is a VPN service that provides Layer 2 point-to-point connectivity between two CE devices.

Figure 10-10 *Reference Model for the Virtual Private Wire Service with an MPLS Backbone*

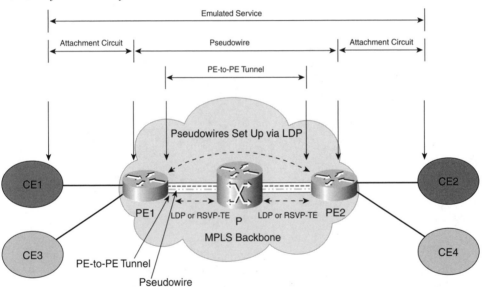

In VPWS, CE devices (routers, bridges, switches, or hosts) are connected to PEs in the service provider network via attachment circuits. In the MPLS backbone, PEs are connected via PWs, which correspond to PE-to-PE LSPs that are established using LDP. In turn, PWs are multiplexed (nested) and transported over PE-to-PE tunnels. The PE performs a one-to-one mapping between the attachment circuit and PW. The transport of PWs that contain Layer 2 frames across the MPLS network involves three layers of encapsulations:

- The tunnel header to carry PWs from an ingress PE router to an egress PE router

- The demultiplexer to distinguish individual PWs within a single tunnel

- PW encapsulation (a 32-bit control word used to carry information about the enclosed Layer 2 frames, such as Layer 2 header bits, sequence number for in-order delivery of the frame, and so forth)

In the case of an MPLS backbone, the tunnel header and demultiplexer fields are based on MPLS labels. The tunnel labels are distributed using LDP or RSVP-TE, whereas distribution of demultiplexers (L2VPN labels) for PWs is typically accomplished via LDP.

NOTE   Note that in Cisco products VPWS are sometimes called an earlier name—*Any Transport over MPLS* (AToM).

In a PE-to-PE data traffic path, the IP/MPLS control-plane components that can fail (and therefore must support a relevant graceful restart mechanisms) include the following:

- LDP on PEs that is used to set up PWs

- LDP or RSVP-TE on PE and P routers that establishes the PE-PE MPLS tunnel

- IGP on PE and P routers that distributes routing information inside the backbone

Note that VPSW service might also be disrupted by control-plane failures on PE-CE links. However, this book does not cover control-plane restart procedures for Layer 2 attachment circuits.

Virtual Private LAN Service

A VPLS is an L2VPN service that emulates the performance of a LAN across a packet-switched network and provides connectivity between several customer LAN segments. For users, sending data through an L2VPN seems the same as being connected via a single LAN. VPLS is similar to VPWS in that it makes its forwarding decisions without considering a Layer 3 header. However, VPLS is different from VPWS in the following two ways:

- First, VPLS PE forwards frames based on a frame's Layer 2 header.

- Second, VPLS allows frames from a single CE to be transmitted to multiple remote CEs.

In other words, VPLS is a point-to-multipoint service, whereas VPWS is a point-to-point service.

Figure 10-11 shows the reference model for VPLS. A CE device attaches to a PE device via an Ethernet port. PE devices are connected via point-to-point bidirectional PWs to carry frames between them. In the case of the MPLS backbone, a PW consists of a pair of point-to-point unidirectional LSPs (also referred to as *VC LSPs*). To a CE device, the set of PE devices interconnected via PWs appears as a single emulated LAN.

Figure 10-11 *Reference Model for the Virtual Private LAN Service with an MPLS Backbone*

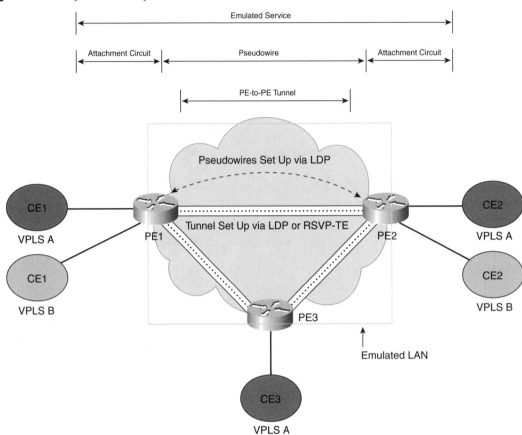

To aggregate traffic in the backbone, tunnels are established between PEs. In the case of an MPLS network, as in L3VPN, tunnels are set up using LDP or RSVP-TE. Multiple PWs can be carried inside a single tunnel. To distinguish a particular PW inside the tunnel, a unique demultiplexer value is assigned to each PW. In general, for a point-to-point PW, the egress PE of the tunnel selects the demultiplexer value and distributes the value using signaling protocols to the PE that is the ingress of the tunnel.

In the case of an MPLS backbone, the demultiplexer value for a PW is based on a label, which is signaled over an LDP session using LDP extensions defined for PW signaling. To set up a full mesh of point-to-point PWs, all PEs in a VPLS must have an LDP session between them. After an LDP session has been established between two PEs, they can exchange L2VPN labels (VC labels) for all PWs between them over this session. A PW is considered operational when both incoming and outgoing VC LSPs have been established. When the PWs are point to multipoint, they can be set up using either a point-to-point signaling protocol such as LDP or a point-to-multipoint signaling protocol such as BGP. Further discussion on point-to-multipoint PWs is beyond the scope of this book.

From the perspective of data-plane operation, when a PE receives a frame over an attachment circuit, it examines the MAC destination address and forwards the address to another local attachment circuit or over a PW to another PE. This second PE in turn forwards the frame out on another remote attachment circuit.

A conventional LAN provides broadcast and unicast services. This requires that each VPLS PE be able to perform the following tasks:

- Dynamically learn MAC addresses on physical ports and virtual ports (PWs)
- Associate learned addresses with the appropriate physical and virtual ports
- Replicate packets on physical and virtual ports
- Flood packets with unknown unicast destinations

When a PE learns a new MAC address on an inbound VC LSP, it associates the learned MAC address with the outbound VC LSP. Similarly, as a PE learns a MAC address over an inbound physical port, it associates that address with the corresponding outbound physical port. For further details, refer to the VPLS architecture specification.[13,14]

In the case of VPLS, IP/MPLS control-plane components along the PE-PE data path are identical to the VPWS except that PWs may be signaled using LDP or BGP. Hence, to avoid VPLS service disruption because of control-plane failures in the backbone, all nodes along the data path must support relevant IP and MPLS control-plane restart procedures (see Chapters 4 through 9 for details).

Network Fault Tolerance and MPLS-Based Recovery

To this point, discussion has focused on ways to protect service outages against control-plane failures. Although discussion of data-plane protection against network failures is not the main focus of this chapter, for the sake of completeness it would be useful to examine schemes that are commonly used to improve network survivability in the face of node and link failures.

Generally network outages are caused by failures of network elements such as links and nodes. *Network survivability* refers to the capability of a network to continue to provide an acceptable level of service in the presence of network failures. Design of survivable networks involves trade-offs between several conflicting objectives such as recovery speed, cost, and complexity. Network operators are generally interested in providing the fastest recovery mechanisms at the lowest feasible costs.

To satisfy these conflicting design objectives, survivable network architectures consider recovery at multiple layers, including WDM, SONET, MPLS, and the IP layer. At a particular layer, there are two main types of recovery approaches: protection and restoration (or rerouting).[15,16]

Protection and Restoration

In the case of protection, a backup path is pre-established for traffic on the primary path, and when a fault is detected the protected traffic is switched over to the backup path. In contrast to protection, when using restoration a backup path to reroute traffic on the primary path is established on demand after detection of a network failure.

A protection or restoration recovery scheme can be further categorized as local or global repair, based on the scope of recovery. A local recovery scheme protects a primary path segment in the vicinity of the fault against a single link or node failure, whereas a global recovery scheme protects an end-to-end primary path against any link or node failure (see Figure 10-12). Unlike global recovery, a local recovery scheme provides a backup path closest to the point of failure and thereby avoids extra delay by propagating failure notification to the upstream nodes to reroute traffic onto the backup path. Avoiding delay is highly desirable to reduce traffic disruption during failure. In general, recovery at a lower layer is faster than at a higher layer, but is costly. For example, recovery at the SONET layer is faster than at the MPLS layer, which in turn is faster than recovery at the IP layer. Moreover, local recovery is faster than global recovery, and at any given layer protection is faster than restoration, but costly.

Figure 10-12 *MPLS-Based Local and Global Recovery Schemes*

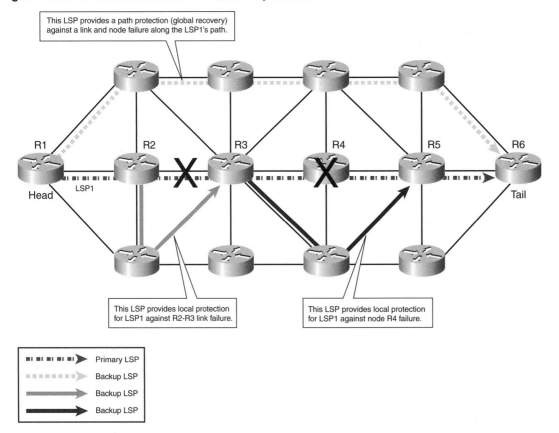

In L2VPNs, increasing the level of network availability with packet-loss duration not exceeding tens of milliseconds during network failures is required. This increase is necessary because emulated circuits can be carrying delay-sensitive data such as *voice over IP* (VoIP) and loss-sensitive data such as stock exchange data services. It is required to provide QoS comparable to the native emulated circuits. Therefore, to satisfy the negotiated SLAs, customer data traffic must be protected against link and node failures in the backbone and access network. The following sections describe recovery schemes at different layers.

Optical Layer Protection

Wave-division multiplexing (WDM) technology enables the aggregation of multiple channels (or wavelengths) onto a single fiber channel. Each WDM channel can carry traffic from multiple higher layers such as SONET, MPLS, and IP. The protection at the optical layer provides the ability to switch data traffic from one wavelength to a completely different wavelength.

In WDM networks, optical layer protection can be deployed in point-to-point and ring configurations. Figure 10-13 shows SONET equipment making use of optical layer point-to-point link protection. For example, if for some reason the working fiber is cut, the switch mechanism directs the traffic onto the protection fiber. Generally, handling of fiber cuts is faster at the optical layer than the SONET layer. This is because a single switch at the optical layer can restore all wavelengths on the failed link instead of restoring individual SONET links. Figure 10-14 shows an example of the optical layer protection in a ring configuration.

Figure 10-13 *Optical Layer Protection in Point-to-Point Architecture*

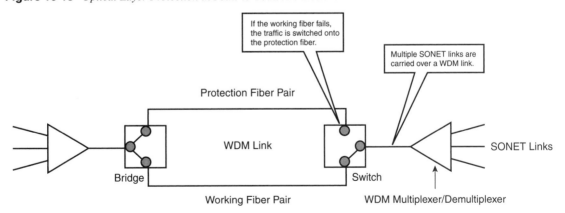

Figure 10-14 *Optical Layer Protection in Ring Architecture*

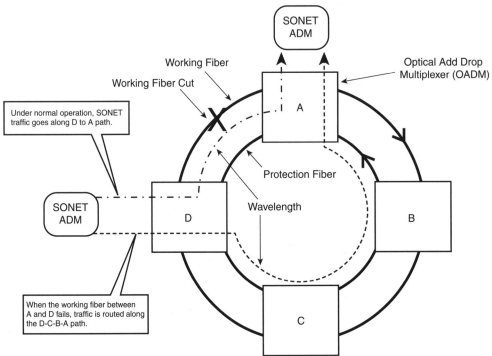

SONET/SDH Layer Protection

The SONET *Automatic Protection Switch* (APS) is a mechanism that protects SONET equipment against link failures (such as fiber cuts and transceiver failures). Like the optical layer, the SONET/SDH layer protection can also be used in point-to-point and ring architectures. After a failure has been detected, SONET APS makes it possible to switch from the working line to the protection line within 50 milliseconds.

IP Layer Restoration

You can also use the IP layer to reroute traffic around link and node failures. For example, an IGP maintains a synchronized link-state database that describes the network topology. Using this topology information, an IGP calculates a shortest-path tree. When a topology change is detected, a new route is quickly calculated, and the data traffic is rerouted along the new route. Depending on the routing protocol and the setting of various time parameters, it might take a long time (in the order of minutes) to reroute traffic around the failure. Although IP layer restoration might be acceptable as a recovery method for best-effort data traffic, IP layer rerouting typically is not suitable for time-sensitive and data-loss–sensitive applications (such as VoIP), which require recovery times in the order of tens of milliseconds.

MPLS Layer Protection—Fast ReRoute

Currently WDM and SONET/SDH-based recovery mechanisms are widely used in existing networks. However, deployments of higher-layer recovery schemes such as MPLS-based local and path protection are also increasing rapidly with the emergence of converged packet-switched networks. Generally a higher-layer recovery scheme is slower, but provides a more granular and cost-effective solution than a lower-layer scheme such as SONET/SDH protection. One such MPLS-based local protection scheme that limits packet loss in the order of tens of milliseconds during network failure is known as *Fast ReRoute* (FRR).

MPLS FRR provides a mechanism to set up backup label-switched paths and quickly reroute traffic from protected TE LSPs onto the backup tunnels on detection of local link and node failures.[17] Because the backup LSPs (referred to as *bypass tunnels*) are established before the failure and provide local protection, MPLS FRR can reroute traffic within tens of milliseconds (see Figure 10-15 for a summary of terminology). When the node immediately upstream of the failure point (known as the *point of local repair* [PLR]) detects a network element failure (based on a Layer 2 mechanism or using IGP/RSVP Hellos), it quickly reroutes the set of protected TE LSPs onto the appropriate bypass tunnel around the failed network elements. An LSP is said to be protected at a particular node if it has one or more associated backup tunnels originating at that node. MPLS FRR provides not only a backup path, but also a backup path with equivalent QoS (such as bandwidth) to the primary path.[18] In short, an MPLS FRR-based local protection scheme provides a natural, practical, and effective solution against link or node failures.

Figure 10-15 *MPLS Fast ReRoute Commonly Used Terms*

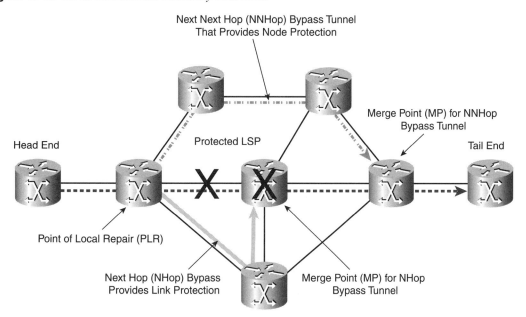

The two approaches of MPLS FRR are referred to as bypass and detour. Table 10-1 compares these approaches.

Table 10-1   *Comparison of the Bypass and Detour Approaches of MPLS FRR*

	Bypass Approach	**Detour Approach**
Link and node failures	Provides protection against link and node failures	Provides protection against link and node failures
LSP protection	Protects multiple LSPs by using a single bypass tunnel; offers a facility (or one-for-n) LSP protection	Requires a separate backup LSP for each primary LSP that needs to be protected; in other words, detour provides a one-for-one LSP protection
Label stacks	Employs label stack to nest multiple LSPs	Does not use label stack

As discussed in Chapter 9, RSVP has a soft state model, which means that the RSVP state is periodically refreshed. If the state is not refreshed within an associated refresh interval, it is removed. Following a link or node failure, if a node in the proximity of the failure were to remove the RSVP-TE state for the LSPs for which the node had not received refresh messages from the peer, this would cause traffic disruption on those LSPs and defeat the purpose of rerouting such LSPs over the bypass tunnel (see Figure 10-16). The bypass scheme provides an elegant solution for this problem (see Figure 10-17) .

Figure 10-16   *Undesirable Effects of Not Refreshing RSVP-TE Messages for Protected LSPs After the Link or Node Failure*

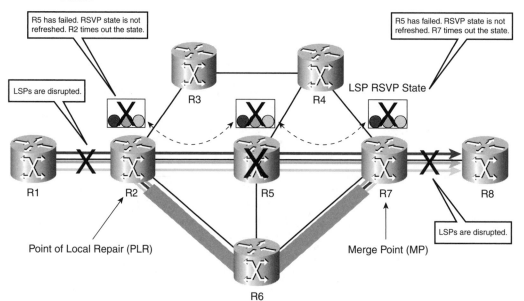

Figure 10-17   *Bypass Handling of RSVP-TE Messages After Link or Node Failure*

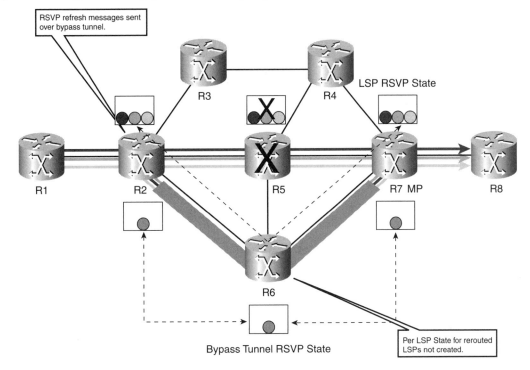

Bypass Tunnel RSVP State

To maintain LSP RSVP-TE state across link or node failure between PLR and *merge point* (MP) nodes, RSVP refresh messages are also sent over the bypass tunnel. Because of label stacking, RSVP-TE messages are not visible to any node along the bypass tunnel. As a result, even when several LSPs are being rerouted over the bypass tunnel, nodes along the bypass tunnel do not see RSVP messages and therefore do not create any RSVP state for the rerouted LSPs. From the point of view of scalability, this feature of the bypass approach makes it an effective solution for local protection. Detour, in contrast, does not use a label stack and as a result creates and refreshes per LSP state in all nodes along the backup path (see Figure 10-18).

Figure 10-18 *Detour One-for-One LSP Protection Solution*

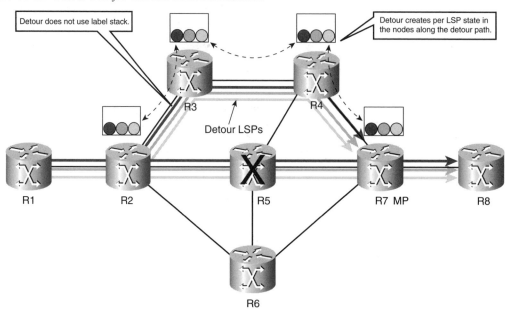

Protecting Bypass Tunnels Against Control-Plane Failures

A bypass tunnel is identical to any other regular TE tunnel in that it is established using RSPV-TE. However, the bypass tunnel is different from a regular TE tunnel in that it carries data traffic only when one or more protected LSPs are rerouted onto it following a link or node failure. Therefore, from the control-plane restart perspective, two cases deserve consideration. The effect of RSVP-TE control-plane restart on the bypass tunnel is harmless while no traffic is being rerouted over the tunnel. This is because even if the bypass tunnel state is lost because of a control-plane restart, it can be reestablished without effecting user traffic. A large number of LSPs could be protected over a single bypass tunnel. Therefore, in terms of service outage, the effect of a control-plane restart can be devastating when the bypass tunnel is carrying protected LSPs' traffic. If protected LSPs' traffic is being carried, to mitigate the negative impact of a control-plane restart, all nodes along the bypass tunnel's path must be capable of RSVP-TE GR and NSF.

With reference to intra-area, inter-area, and inter-AS MPLS-TE deployment scenarios, the existing MPLS FRR mechanisms can be used to provide local protection for a TE LSP against link or node failure, regardless of whether the LSP is an intra-area, inter-area, or inter-AS TE LSP. However, local repair notification procedures to trigger rerouting of the TE LSP might be somewhat different in the case of inter-area and inter-AS TE LSP.[19]

Interactions Between Different Protection Layers

A network might use different types of protection architectures because of cost and recovery speed requirements. Generally, different layers are better suited for handling different types of faults. For example, fiber cuts can be typically handled more efficiently at the optical layer, whereas equipment failures (such as laser failure) can be handled at the SONET layer. MPLS-based recovery methods allow faster recovery than the IP layer rerouting. Although recovery at the MPLS layer may be slower than the SONET layer, it allows more granular options and more bandwidth-efficient recovery options than SONET and optical layer protection. The physical topology of a network with multiple protection layers is shown in Figure 10-19 (a). The virtual topology as seen by the MPLS/IP layer devices such as routers is shown in Figure 10-19 (b).

In multilayer survivable network architectures, a client/server relationship exists between different protection layers (see Figure 10-20). For example, circuit-switched *time-division multiplexed* (TDM) services and IP/MPLS layer services are transported over SONET. Similarly, SONET is transported over the optical layer. This means the failure of a single WDM link can cause simultaneous failure of several optical channels (wavelengths), which can make recovery impossible at the higher layers (SONET, MPLS, IP).

Therefore, interworking between different layers becomes crucial to improve the end-to-end service availability during network failures. In other words, it is highly desirable to provide some coordination between protection mechanisms at different layers. You can achieve this coordination between different layers automatically by ensuring that a server layer recovers from a fault before its client layer detects that failure. For example, the SONET layer takes about 2.3 microseconds to detect a link failure. This means that as long as the optical layer can restore traffic within this time, the SONET layer will not even notice this failure. In general, it is difficult to achieve recovery times in the order of microseconds. You can also achieve this coordination between different layers by introducing an additional delay (hold-off time) at the client layer before it attempts to recover to allow adequate time for the server layer to complete its recovery.

Figure 10-19 *Multilayer Network Protection Architecture (a) Physical Topology (b) Virtual Topology*

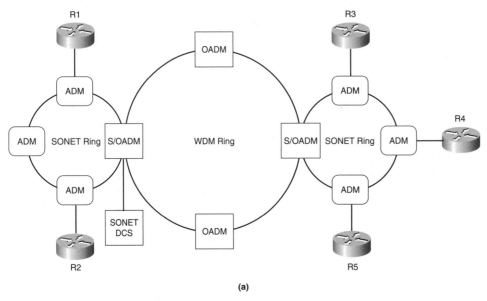

(a)

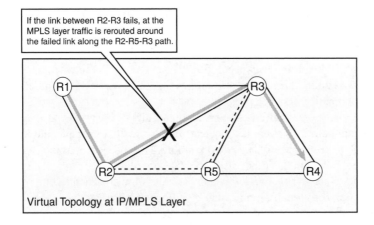

If the link between R2-R3 fails, at the MPLS layer traffic is rerouted around the failed link along the R2-R5-R3 path.

Virtual Topology at IP/MPLS Layer

(b)

Figure 10-20 *Layered Recovery Architecture*

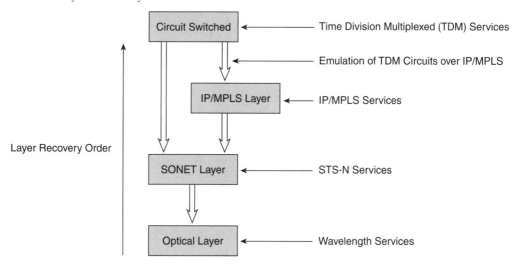

Network Fault Tolerance and MPLS OAM Mechanisms

Operation, administration, maintenance, and provisioning (OAM&P) encompass a broad set of management functional areas, including fault management, configuration management, accounting management, and security management.[20] A fault (or defect) is an interruption of the capability of a network connection caused by a network element such as link and node failures. Discussion of functions in this section is restricted to fault management and performance management:

- **Fault management**—A set of functions including fault detection, fault verification, fault isolation, and fault recovery

- **Performance management**—A set of functions for gathering and analyzing network QoS (such as packet delay, delay variation, and loss) and availability performance parameters for the purpose of measuring the quality of network performance against negotiated SLAs or to help with planning and provisioning of the network

From the perspective of end customers, network availability is measured by the frequency of service outages and the recovery time for each outage. In reference to L2VPN and L3VPN services, network availability depends on the fault tolerance of the PE-to-PE tunnel, pseudowire, and VPLS instance. Therefore, capability to quickly detect and recover from data-plane and control-plane faults is critical to reduce service-outage duration. In short, OAM mechanisms play a pivotal role in improving the network availability, and network providers rely heavily on these tools for swift identification and removal of network faults.

With the increased acceptance of MPLS as the technology of choice to deliver legacy Layer 2 and emerging Layer 3 services over the converged packet-switched networks, effective MPLS OAM capabilities become critical to manage, troubleshoot, and monitor SLAs. Standardization efforts are underway to specify a suite of MPLS OAM mechanisms to facilitate network operators in identifying defects, verifying network connectivity, and measuring network performance.

Examples of MPLS OAM mechanisms include LSP-Ping, Y.1711, pseudowire *virtual circuit connection verification* (VCCV), and VPLS OAM: [21–24]

- **LSP-Ping**—A tool to detect data-plane faults in LSPs and isolate faults. LSP-Ping offers two modes of operation called ping and traceroute. The ping mode is used to check basic connectivity of an LSP, whereas the traceroute mode is used to verify the forwarding path of data packets.

- **Y.1711**—A tool that provides fault management functions such as the following:
  - Connectivity verification (CV) to detect LSP connectivity
  - Forward defect indication (FDI) to inform downstream nodes about an upstream defect
  - Backward defect indication (BDI) to inform upstream nodes about a downstream defect.

- **VCCV**—Uses MPLS LSP-Ping to exchange sets of control messages between PEs to verify connectivity of the pseudo wire. VCCV defines two modes of operation: diagnostic mode and fault-detection mode. The diagnostic mode is used to verify the connectivity. The fault-detection mode is used to emulate attachment circuit-specific fault-detection mechanisms.

- **VPLS OAM**—Mainly consists of fault management and performance management functions. VPLS is an end-to-end service, which can span different types of access and core networks. For example, the access network might be a bridged network, whereas the core network might be an MPLS network. This means the VPLS OAM mechanisms must work end to end, independent of the underlying transport technologies such as Ethernet, IP, and MPLS.

Bidirectional Forwarding Detection

BFD provides a fast mechanism to detect faults in the bidirectional forwarding-plane path between pairs of directly connected or non-directly connected systems.[25] You can use BFD to provide fault detection on different types of forwarding paths such as direct physical links, MPLS LSPs, and tunnels. As you will learn shortly, you can use BFD to provide an efficient fault-detection component for many OAM-related functions.

Motivations

For many applications, the fault-detection times (in the order of seconds) of the existing mechanisms (such as routing protocol Hellos) are too slow and can cause a great deal of data loss during network failures. Moreover, there are certain media types, such as Ethernet, that currently do not have mechanisms for detecting interface or forwarding plane failures rapidly. To summarize, the main goals of the BFD are to provide the following:

- An efficient and fast fault-detection mechanism (with low processing overhead and with subsecond granularity)

- A common liveness-detection framework that is media and protocol independent and that allows a wide range of fault-detection times

How Does BFD Improve Network Availability?

As discussed in Chapter 1, "Understanding High Availability of IP and MPLS Networks," availability can be improved by reducing mean time to repair (MTTR). MTTR includes time required for failure detection, fault diagnosis, and actual repair. Thus, quick fault detection is a key for improving network availability.

How Does BFD Improve Network Convergence?

The time duration beginning with an event resulting in a topology or route change (such as link failure, router failure, and next hop change) until all routers have the consistent view of the network is known as the convergence period. Because the routers may have inconsistent topology and routing information during convergence period, there is increased likelihood of data loss or service outage. Therefore, it is extremely important to speed up the network convergence. It turns out that slow detection of neighbor failures is one of the main reasons for the delayed IGP convergence.[26] Thus, the BFD fast failure detection mechanism helps to improve network convergence.

BFD Protocol Mechanics

In some respects, the BFD protocol resembles the Hello mechanism of a routing protocol. For example, two systems that support the BFD protocol periodically transmit BFD control packets over each forwarding path between them. If a system does not receive BFD control packets from a neighbor on a particular path for a while, the system assumes that some component in that particular bidirectional path to the neighbor has failed.

Before two systems can exchange BFD control packets, they need to establish a separate BFD session for each communication path and data protocol in use between them. There are two modes of BFD operation: asynchronous mode and demand mode.

- **Asynchronous mode**—In this mode, two systems periodically transmit BFD control packets to each other; if a system does not receive a successive number of those packets, that system declares the BFD session to be down.

- **Demand mode**—In this mode, after the two systems have established a BFD session, they stop sending BFD control packets to each other. Afterward, when either system needs to verify connectivity explicitly, that system sends a short sequence of BFD control packets and then the BFD protocol quiesces.

In addition to these two modes, BFD also defines an Echo function that allows a local system to transmit a sequence of Echo packets to a remote system (see Figure 10-21). The remote system is expected to loop back these Echo packets through its forwarding path. If the transmitting system does not receive back a number of Echo packets in succession, it declares the BFD session to be down. The Echo function can be used in conjunction with either asynchronous or demand mode.

In general, different situations might require different BFD modes. For example, demand mode might prove advantageous in situations in which you want to reduce the processing overhead of periodic control packets. For example, demand mode might be advantageous for a system with a large number of BFD sessions. The advantage of the echo function is that it enables the transmitting system to verify the forwarding path through a neighbor with reduced jitter in the round-trip time. However, the echo function has the drawback of requiring twice as many packets to achieve a particular fault-detection time as the pure asynchronous mode requires.

BFD Applications

For different applications, BFD may be operating at multiple layers such as physical links, virtual circuits, and LSPs. You can implement BFD in the forwarding plane using a client/server model in which BFD provides services such as indication of session status (up/down) to its clients. BFD can also be implemented in the control plane; however, this may make it difficult to detect certain types of failures. In summary, many applications can take advantage of the BFD fast fault-detection mechanism to improve network availability. Some examples of such applications are described in the sections that follow.

Using BFD for Detecting IGP Neighbor Liveness

The Hello protocols of IGPs, such as OSPF and IS-IS, do not allow fast detection of an adjacency failure. For example, it can take OSPF and IS-IS on the order of a few seconds to detect an adjacency failure. Thus, the BFD fast detection mechanism can be used to overcome limitations of IGP Hello protocols. BFD usage for IGP neighbor liveness not only allows faster IGP convergence but also improves IGP adjacency scalability by allowing larger values for Hello timers to reduce processing associated with periodic IGP Hellos.

Figure 10-21 *BFD Modes of Operation*

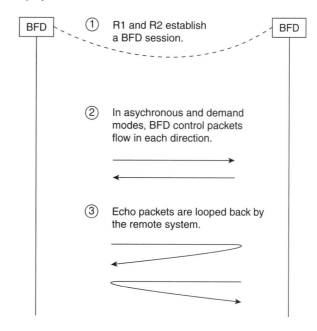

Using BFD for LSP Data-Plane Fault Detection and Control-Plane Verification

As you already know from the previous section, you can use LSP-Ping to detect an MPLS LSP data-plane failure and to verify the MPLS control plane against the data plane. In contrast, although you can use BFD for fast detection of a data-plane failure, it does not provide a mechanism to verify the MPLS control plane against the data plane. Because LSP-Ping includes extensive control-plane verification, it is computationally more onerous than BFD for detecting MPLS LSP data-plane faults. This is because BFD is designed as a lightweight means to detect forwarding-plane faults quickly, and BFD uses a fixed-packet format that makes BFD conducive to hardware- or firmware-based implementations. Therefore, it is advantageous to take the efficient and fast fault-detection capabilities of the BFD and combine them with the control-plane verification capabilities of the existing LSP-Ping mechanism to provide a scalable solution for LSP fault detection.[27]

To use BFD in conjunction with LSP-Ping for fault detection on an LSP, a BFD session is established between the ingress and egress LSR of that LSP. The ingress LSR encapsulates the BFD control packets in the MPLS label stack that correspond to LSP being verified. The labeled BFD control packets take the same path as the LSP being verified and are processed by the control plane of the egress LSR.

Using BFD for PW Fault Detection

Because PWs can be carrying data of delay-sensitive and loss-sensitive emulated services, fast failure detection might be highly desirable. One way to achieve this goal is to use the BFD mechanisms along with the VCCV fault-detection mode. For an illustration of BFD used for PW fault detection, consider the network diagram shown in Figure 10-22. Using the BFD mechanism, PE1 sends BFD control packets periodically to PE2. When PE2 stops receiving control packets for a defined period of time, PE2 declares that direction of the PW is down and notifies PE1 via control packets. Depending on the type of emulated service (such as ATM, FR, or TDM), the PEs might also need to send a native *alarm indication signal* (AIS) over the related attachment circuits to inform the endpoints about the fault condition.

Figure 10-22 *BFD-Based PW Fault Detection*

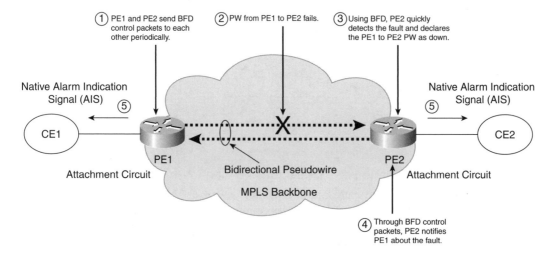

Using BFD for MPLS FRR Fault Detection

As discussed previously, in the event of a link or node failure data traffic from multiple protected LSPs is rerouted onto the bypass tunnel. The bypass tunnel might be carrying traffic from a large number of LSPs, and you can use BFD for fast detection of bypass LSP failures. Consider a scenario in which a number of LSPs are protected against the SONET link failure using a bypass LSP (see Figure 10-23). Assume there is a BFD session to detect failures on the bypass LSP and an additional BFD session to verify the forwarding path between R1 and R2. If the link between R1 and R2 fails, based on SONET alarms, R1 detects the link failure and attempts to reroute traffic from all protected LSPs onto the bypass LSP quickly. Although

MPLS FRR switchover can be accomplished rapidly, nevertheless it takes a finite amount of time (in the order of tens of milliseconds) to complete. During this time, data traffic on the protected LSPs is dropped. This means that following an MPLS FRR switchover due to a link or node failure, BFD control packets will be lost until the switchover is complete. Therefore, if the fault-detection interval of the BFD session between R1 and R2 is smaller than the MPLS FRR switchover time, a fault is declared for an LSP even though the LSP is in the process of being locally repaired. To avoid spurious BFD fault detections following MPLS FRR switchover, the BFD fault-detection interval should be greater than the MPLS FRR switchover time.

Figure 10-23 *Interactions of BFD and MPLS FRR Mechanisms*

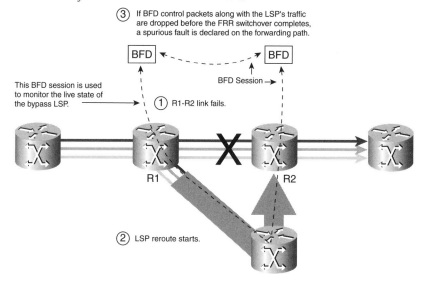

Using BFD for Fault Detection in the Access Network

To provide high-availability services such as VoIP, a CE device may be dual homed to guard against a PE-CE link failure. In this scenario, there are two forwarding paths: the primary and the backup. During normal operation, traffic flows on the primary path. In the event of a primary path failure, traffic is rerouted over the backup path. Thus, a BFD session can be used to monitor the liveness of each forwarding path (see Figure 10-24). If the primary forwarding path fails, the BFD can quickly be used to detect the link failure and reroute the traffic onto the backup path.

Figure 10-24 *BFD Use in the Access Network*

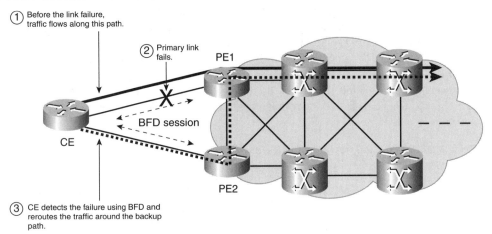

BFD Interactions with the IP and MPLS Control-Plane Graceful Restart
Mechanisms

As discussed in the previous chapters, to mitigate the detrimental effects to forwarding that
might result from IP/MPLS control-plane restarts, the restarting router and its neighbors must
support a certain set of control- and forwarding-plane capabilities. In particular, the restarting
router must support not only the appropriate graceful restart extensions, but also be able to
preserve its IP/MPLS forwarding state. In summary, the control-plane graceful restart
mechanisms depend on the existence of a separate forwarding plane that can continue to
function across the control-plane restarts.

Although most graceful restart mechanisms provide a way out of unsuccessful restart attempts
by reverting to normal restart procedures, it might take a while (in the order of seconds) before
a router determines whether a given graceful restart attempt with a neighbor is viable. For
example, suppose a router had indicated its capability to preserve the forwarding state, but
actually could not preserve it across the restart. The neighbors honoring the pre-restart
capability exchange that are unaware of the actual situation, would continue to forward data
traffic through the restarting router which would be black holed. In fact, in the event of an
unsuccessful graceful restart attempt, data traffic could be black holed a little longer (it could
be black holed for the time it takes to detect a session failure plus an additional waiting period
for session reestablishment) than it would be in the case of normal restart (only time to detect
session failure).

The BFD control packet contains a bit called the Control Plane Independent bit. By setting the
C bit to 1, a system announces independence of forwarding- and control-plane components. In
other words, if the C bit is set to 1, it indicates that the transmitting system's BFD is

implemented in the forwarding plane and can continue to function across the control-plane restart. This means the information in the C bit can be used to determine whether it is appropriate to continue with a graceful restart procedure or abort it. For example, consider two graceful restart-capable routers R1 and R2 with a BFD session and a graceful restart session between them (see Figure 10-25). Assume both routers have expressed their capability to preserve a forwarding state across the restart and both have been transmitting BFD control packets with the C bit set to 1. Suppose R2 restarts and loses its forwarding state across the restart. In this situation, if a BFD session fails while graceful restart is in progress, R1 should abort the graceful restart procedure.

Figure 10-25 *Interactions of BFD and Control-Plane Graceful Restart Mechanisms*

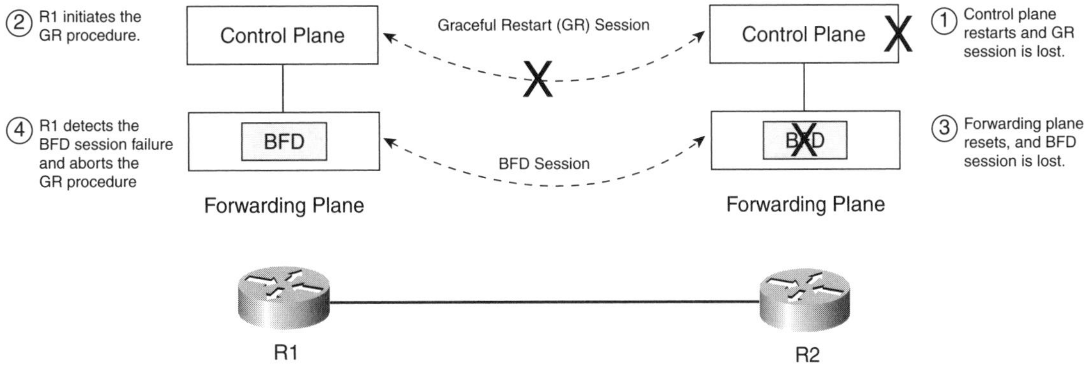

Network Fault Tolerance and In-Service Software Upgrades

In general, router outages can be caused by unplanned or planned events. An unplanned outage occurs because of unforeseen faults in hardware or software components. An MPLS control-plane restart is an example of an unplanned outage. In contrast, a planned outage occurs when a router is taken out of service for scheduled maintenance, such as during a software or hardware upgrade. Using redundant hardware and software components helps to mitigate the unplanned outages. As described previously, a combination of redundant control plane, IP/MPLS control-plane protocol enhancements, and NSF capability enable the nondisruptive *stateful switchover* (SSO) from an active to standby control processor. This switchover helps to reduce the downtime caused by unplanned control-plane failures.

To this point in the book, discussions have focused on mechanisms that assist in avoiding service disruption caused by unplanned control-plane failures. However, as mentioned in Chapter 1, operations related to planned software upgrades are the single largest source of router downtime. Therefore, carrier-grade services require reduction of not only unplanned outages, but also planned outages. The in-service software upgrade (also known as *hitless software upgrade*) mechanism enables you to reduce router downtime during planned software upgrade/downgrade operations.

The in-service software upgrade mechanism involves upgrading the standby control processor with a new version of software, synchronization of state information between the active control processor running with the old version of software and the standby control processor running with a new version of software, and making a nondisruptive SSO to the standby. The in-service software upgrade procedure entails a deliberate switchover (in contrast to automatic switchover, as in the case of unplanned control-plane failures) across which forwarding must not be disrupted. Therefore, the in-service software upgrade procedure relies on the SSO and NSF capabilities, which are used for unplanned control failures. Further details on in-service software upgrade are beyond the scope of this book.

Summary

This chapter described how you can use various IP and MPLS control-plane restart mechanisms to improve network fault tolerance against unplanned control-plane failures. The design of survivable networks has multiple aspects. To provide a broader view of network fault tolerance, this chapter also briefly touched on MPLS layer recovery schemes against network failures, the relationship of MPLS OAM to network availability, and reduction of unplanned outages through the use of the in-service software upgrade.

References

[1] Andersson, L., and T. Madsen, "PPVPN Terminology," IETF Work in progress, March 2004.

[2] RFC 2661, "Layer Two Tunneling Protocol (L2TP)," W. Townsley et al., August 1999.

[3] Goyret, I., J. Lau, and M. Townsley, "Layer Two Tunneling Protocol (Version 3)," IETF Draft, Work in progress, June 2004.

[3] RFC 2784, "Generic Routing Encapsulation (GRE)," D. Farinacci et al., March 2000.

[4] Committee T1-Telecommunications, "Technical Report on a Reliability/Availability Framework for IP-Based Networks and Services," Working Group T1A1.2 (Network Survivability Performance), Technical Report No.70, September 2001.

[5] RFC 3630, "Traffic Engineering (TE) Extensions to OSPF Version 2," D. Katz, K. Kompella, and D. Yeung, September 2003.

[6] RFC 3784, "Intermediate System to Intermediate System (IS-IS) Extensions for Traffic Engineering (TE)," H. Smit and T. Li, June 2004.

[7] RFC 2547, "BGP/MPLS VPNs," E. Rosen, et al., March 1999.

[8] Le Roux, J. L., et al. "Requirements for Inter-Area MPLS Traffic Engineering," IETF work in progress, March 2004.

[9] Vasseur, J. P. and R. Zhang, "MPLS Inter-AS Traffic Engineering Requirements," IETF work in progress, January 2004.

[10] RFC 2547, "BGP/MPLS IP VPNs," E. Rosen, et al., September 2003.

[11] Callon, R. and M. Suzuki, "A Framework for Layer 3 Provider Provisioned Virtual Private Networks," IETF Draft, Work in progress, October 2003.

[12] Clercq, J. D., et al., "BGP-MPLS VPN Extension for IPv6 VPN," IETF Draft, Work in progress, June 2004.

[13] Andersson, L., and E. Rosen, "L2VPN Framework," IETF Draft, Work in progress, September 2003.

[14] Lasserre, M., et al. "Virtual Private LAN Services over MPLS," IETF Draft, Work in progress, November 2003.

[15] Wu, T-H., "Emerging Technologies for Fiber Network Survivability," *IEEE Communications Magazine*, February 1995.

[16] RFC 3469, "Framework for Multi-Protocol Label Switching (MPLS)-based Recovery," F. Hellstrand and V. Sharma, February 2003.

[17] Pan, P., et al., "Fast Reroute Extensions to RSVP-TE for LSP Tunnels," IETF Draft, Work in progress, August 2004.

[18] Vasseur, J. P., et al., "MPLS Traffic Engineering Fast Reroute: Backup Tunnel Path Computation For Bandwidth Protection," IETF Draft, Work in progress, October 2002.

[19] Ayyangar, A., and J. P. Vasseur, "Inter-Area and Inter-AS MPLS Traffic Engineering," IETF Draft, Work in progress, February 2004.

[20] ITU-T Recommendation M.3400, "TMN Management Functions," February 2000.

[21] Pan, P. et al., "Detecting Data Plane Liveliness in MPLS," IETF Draft, Work in progress, February 2004.

[22] ITU-T Recommendation Y.1711, "OAM Mechanism for MPLS Networks," November 2002.

[23] Aggarwal, R., and T. D. Nadeau, "Pseudo Wire (PW) Virtual Circuit Connection Verification (VCCV)," IETF Draft, Work in progress, February 2004.

[24] Mohan, D., et al., " VPLS OAM Requirements and Framework," IETF Draft, Work in progress, July 2004.

[25] Katz, D., and D. Ward, "Bidirectional Forwarding Detection," IETF Draft, Work in progress, July 2004.

[26] Alaettinoglu, C., et al., "Towards Milli-Second IGP Convergence," IETF Draft, Work in progress, November 2000.

[27] Aggarwal, R., et al., "BFD For MPLS LSPs," IETF Draft, Work in progress, July 2004.

INDEX

Numerics

1+1 redundancy, 12
1:1 redundancy, 12
    Cisco IOS architecture, 39, 62
    control processor cards, 12
    control planes, 36
1:N redundancy, 12
5-9s availability, 6

A

ABRs (area border routers), 74
access networks, 293
address aggregation, 25
address classes, 24
Address Family Identifier (AFI) field, 153–154, 169, 174
address lookup, 24
    BGP, 147
    double lookups, 29
    edge LSRs, 56
    FECs, 44
    IP, 26–28
    label lookup (versus), 50, 53
    labels, 44
    LSRs, 164
    metrics, 26
    MPLS, 164
    route caching, 29
    routers, 26
    strides, 27
    temporal versus spatial locality, 29
    tries, 26–28
address mapping, 31
Address messages (LDP), 192
address prefixes, 25
Address Resolution Protocol (ARP), 31, 53
adjacencies, 31, 67
    ARP, 53
    broadcast networks, 76, 113
    cycling through down states, 115
    flaps, 71, 107
    graceful restart, 67
    Hello adjacencies
        establishing, 189-190
        maintaining, 190-191
        packets, 70, 109
        processing, 81
    holding timers, 110
    IS-IS, 107–110
    LDP, 189–191
    master/slave status, 76
    NBMA networks, 76
    OSPF, 75–76
    reacquisition, 118–119
    RouterDeadInterval timers, 75
    T1 timers, 123
    three-way handshakes, 109
Adj-RIBs-In, 148
Adj-RIBs-Out, 148
Advertisement messages (LDP), 191
advertisements (BGP), 144
AFI (Address Family Identifier) field, 153–154, 169, 174
aggregates (CIDR), 25
aggregation (addressing), 25
ALLSPFRouters addresses, 75
Any Transport over MPLS (AToM), 55, 275
APS (Automatic Protection Switch), 9, 12, 17, 280
area border routers (ABRs), 74
areas
    not-so-stubby, 78
    OSPF, 73
    stub, 77
ARP (Address Resolution Protocol), 31, 53
AS external LSAs (type 5), 77–78
AS_PATH lists (BGP), 146
AS_SEQUENCE lists (BGP), 146
AS_SET lists (BGP), 146
ASBR summary LSAs (type 4), 77–78
ASBRs (autonomous system boundary routers), 74
Asynchronous Transfer Mode (ATM), 48
AToM (Any Transport over MPLS), 55, 275
authentication, 19
Automatic Protection Switch (APS), 9, 12, 17, 280
autonomous systems, 67, 137, 146
availability, 6. *See also reliability*
    carrier-class, 6, 11
    control/forwarding planes, 35

DPM, 6
DPY, 6
edge routers, 9
fault tolerance, 7
five-nines, 6
MPLS networks, 256
MTBF/MTTR, 6
packet-switched networks, 11
redundancy, 7
reliability (versus), 6
service view, 11
software upgrades (in-service), 295–296
unavailability (versus), 6

B

backbone areas (OSPF), 73
backbone routers, 74
backup designated routers (BDRs), 76
backup paths, 7
backup tunnels, 55
BDRs (backup designated routers), 76
BFD (Bidirectional Forwarding Detection), 288–290
    access networks, 293
    detecting IGP neighbor liveness, 290
    FRR, 292–293
    IP/MPLS networks, 294–295
    LSPs, 291
    PWs, 292
BGP (Border Gateway Protocol), 8, 137
    advertising labeled routes, 171
    control processor cards, 138
    control-plane components, 138
    End-Of-RIB markers, 153–156
    external reachability information, 109
    FIBs, 138
    forwarding-plane components, 138
    FSM, 142
    label distribution, 169
    label-to-FEC bindings, 46
    labeled routes (withdrawing), 171
    LDP, 221
    line cards, 138
    messages, 141–142
    MPLS
        control planes, 168

graceful restart/NSF interoperability, 182–183
interrelationship, 168–169
NSF, 140, 166, 168
path attributes, 143, 146
    AS_PATH, 146
    LOCAL_PREF, 149
    MP_REACH_NLRI, 169
    MP_UNREACH_NLRI, 169
    NEXT_HOP, 147
protocol extensions, 168
recursive paths, 31
restarts, 140
    churns, 140
    detrimental effects, 139
    graceful restart, 151–161, 168
    helper BGP speaker behavior, 155–156
    mitigating detrimental effects, 150–151
    MPLS, 166–167, 173–182
    NSF interoperability, 159–161
    restarting BGP speaker behavior, 154–155
    route flaps, 138–140
RIBs, 138
routing, 140–144
    fluctuations, 138
    instability, 138
    reflection, 149–150, 171
    selection, 149
    tables, 25
speakers, 137, 141
    internal/external, 144
    RIBs, 148
    RRs, 150
states, 142–143
BGP with an MPLS graceful restart mechanism.
    See BGP/MPLS networks
BGP/MPLS networks
    advertising labeled BGP routes, 171
    control planes, 168
    protocol interrelationship, 168–169
    restarts, 166–167
    withdrawing labeled BGP routes, 171
BGP/MPLS restarts
    graceful restart, 173–175, 179–180
        helper LSR behavior, 178
        network deployment, 181–182

restarting LSR behavior, 175–178
mitigating detrimental effects, 173
binary tries, 26
Birectional Forwarding Detection (BFD), 288–290
access networks, 293
detecting IGP neighbor liveness, 290
FRR, 292–293
IP/MPLS networks, 294–295
LSPs, 291
PWs, 292
black holes, 70, 75, 83, 109, 114
Border Gateway Protocol. *See BGP*
bypass tunnels, 55, 284–285

C

carrier supporting carrier (CSC), 270–271
carrier-class networks, 6
router expectations, 11
CEF (Cisco Express Forwarding), 33–34
cell-mode LSRs, 48
Checkpoint Procedures for LDP (LDP CDP), 200
churns (BGP), 140
CIDR (classless interdomain routing), 25–26
Cisco Express Forwarding (CEF), 33–34
Cisco IOS architecture
1:1 redundancy, 39, 62
control-plane software, 15
label-distribution protocols, 53
MPLS SSO/NSF, 61
NSF, 39–40
SSO, 39–40
TFIB/MFI, 50
Cisco IS-IS restarts, 128–129
CSNPs, 129
IETF IS-IS restarts (versus), 128
interoperability, 132–134
operation, 130
PSNPs, 129
classful addressing, 24
CIDR (versus), 26
IP forwarding, 25
classless addressing, 25
classless interdomain routing (CIDR), 25–26
complete sequence number packets (CSNPs), 111

congestion indication (IS-IS), 112–113
constraint-based path calculation, 55
control capabilities (routers), 132
control planes, 8
1:1 redundancy, 36
adjacency flaps, 107
BGP, 138
BGP/MPLS networks, 168
Cisco IOS architecture, 15
control prcessor cards, 12
FIBs, 23
forwarding planes (separating), 19, 36
forwarding planes (versus), 35
IP, 23, 106
restart, 35–36
separating forwarding planes, 35
SSO, 37
tunneling protocols, 8
LDP, 197–198
mantaining state, 13–14
MPLS, 53–54, 61, 163–164
applications, 55
separating forwarding planes, 54
SSO, 57–59
MPLS-TE, 258
NSF, 37
OSPF, 69
recovery periods, 35
restarts, 13, 15, 132
routers, 12
RSVP-TE, 236
SSO, 15
stateful components, 35
stateless components, 35
unplanned restarts, 13
control processor cards, 12
1:1 redundancy, 12
active versus standby, 13
BGP, 138
reducing fault effects, 36
restartability, 16
RIBs, 69
router processors (Cisco), 39, 61
CSC (carrier supporting carrier), 270–271
CSNPs (complete sequence number packets),
111, 129

D

data encryption, 19
data planes, 277
  APS, 280
  FRR, 281–284
  protection/restoration, 278–280
    IP layer, 280
    MPLS layer, 281-284
    optical layer, 279-280
databases, 70, 110–112
  exchange process (OSPF), 75
  synchronization
    IETF IS-IS restarts, 119–120
    OSPF, 70–71
    timers, 118, 121
Database Description packets, 75
defects per million (DPM), 6
denial-of-service (DoS) attacks, 18
depths (label stacks), 45
designated IS (DIS) routers, 113
designated routers (DRs), 76
Dijkstra algorithm.
  See SPF (Shortest Path First) algorithm
DIS (designated IS) routers, 113
Discovery messages (LDP), 191
disposition (label), 52
distributed forwarding
  CEF, 34
  data rates, 30
  IP forwarding, 30–32
  MPLS, 56
  time criticality, 30
DOD (downstream on-demand) mode, 46, 193
  DU mode (versus), 219–220
  LDP
    graceful restart, 213–219
    nonrestarting LSRs (egress neighbors),
      218
    nonrestarting LSRs (ingress neighbors),
      217–218
    nonrestarting LSRs (transit neighbors),
      218–219
    restarting LSRs (egress), 215–216
    restarting LSRs (ingress), 214–215
    restarting LSRs (transit), 216–217

DoNotAge bits, 90
DoS (denial-of-service) attacks, 18
downstream modes (LDP), 192
downstream on-demand mode. *See DOD
  (downstream on-demand) mode*
downstream unsolicited mode.
  See DU (downstream unsolicited) mode
downtime, 5–6. *See also network outages*
  carrier-class routers, 11
  causes, 10
  link failures, 17
  software upgrades, 17
downtime per year (DPM), 6
DPM (defects per million), 6
DPY (downtime per year), 6
DRs (designated routers), 76
DU (downstream unsolicited) mode, 46, 194
  DOD mode (versus), 219–220
  LDP graceful restart, 203–204, 208–209, 212

E

eBGP (external BGP) sessions, 144
edge LSRs, 46, 164
  address lookup, 56
  label disposition, 52
  label imposition, 51
  Layer 2/3 services, 164–165
edge routers, 8
EGP (Exterior Gateway Protocol), 140
egress LSRs, 46
element nodes, 26
encoding (labels), 48
encryption (data), 19
End-Of-RIB markers, 153–156
enhanced IS-IS, 108
ERO (EXPICIT_ROUTE) objects, 233
established state (BGP), 142–143
Ethernet, 48
expansion (prefix), 27
EXPLICIT_ROUTE objects (RSVP-TE), 233
explicitly routed LSPs, 47
Exterior Gateway Protocol (EGP), 140
external BGP (eBGP) sessions, 144
external/internal speakers (BGP), 144

F

F (Forwarding State) bits, 154
failures (network/services), 5
Fast ReRoute. *See FRR (Fast ReRoute)*
fault tolerance, 7, 35
    availability, 7
    data-plane protection, 277
    MPLS networks, 257
        MPLS-based recovery, 277–285
        OAM mechanisms, 287–290
    network design, 11
    restarts, 201–203
    security, 18–19
    software upgrades (in-service), 295–296
FEC (forwarding equivalence class), 44, 164
    address lookups, 44
    label mappings, 45–46, 54, 176
    LSP associations, 188–189
    Layer 2 circuit IDs, 197
    NHLFE (FTN) entries, 197
    NHLFE (FTN) maps, 50
    next-hop mappings, 54
FIBs (Forwarding Information Bases), 23, 31, 106
    BGP, 138
    building, 32, 56
    line cards, 69
    m-tries, 31
    RIBs (versus), 30
    routers, 31
    RSVP-TE, 238
    SPF algorithm, 73, 111
    synchronizing with RIBs, 32, 56
filtering (packets), 19
FILTERSPEC objects (RSVP), 229
finite state machines (FSMs)
    OSPF, 85, 93
    BGP, 142
firewalls, 19
five-nines availability, 6
flags, 112
flaps (adjacency/route), 107, 138–140
flooding, 75, 105
    IS-IS, 112
    Link-State Acknowledgment packets, 75
    OSPF, 68–70
FLOWSPEC objects (RSVP), 229

forwarding
    ATM versus MPLS, 48
    FEC, 44
    FIBs, 23
    IP, 23–24, 35–36
    loops, 114
    routers, 132
    states
        IP, 12, 39
        LDP, 197–198
        MPLS, 12, 166
    tables
        FECs, 44
        IP forwarding plane, 23
        L3VPNs, 266–267
        route caching (versus), 29
        VPNs (166
forwarding planes, 12
    adjacency flaps, 107
    BGP, 138
    control planes, 19, 35–36
    FIBs, 23, 31, 106
    IP, 23
        control planes (separating), 35
        NSF, 36
        operations, 24
        tasks, 23
    LDP, 197
    MPLS, 53–54, 61, 163–164
        control planes (separating), 54
        label-stack operations, 51–54
        NSF, 43, 58
    MPLS-TE, 258
    NSF, 37
    OSPF, 69
    RSVP-TE, 236
    scalability, 35, 54
Forwarding State (F) bits, 154
FR (Frame Relay), 48
FRR (Fast ReRoute), 17, 50, 55, 281–284
    BFD, 292–293
    link failures, 17
FSMs (finite-state machines)
    BGP, 142
    OSPF, 85, 93
FT ACK TLV, 202
FT Protection TLV, 202

FT Session TLV, 201, 204–205
FTN (FEC-to-NHLFE) entries, 197
FTN (FEC-to-NHLFE) maps, 50

G–H

Generic Routing Encapsulation (GRE), 8
GR. *See graceful restarts (GRs)*
grace LSAs, 89
    planned/unplanned restarts, 92–93
    reason TLV, 90
graceful restarts (GRs), 67
    BFD, 294–295
    BGP, 151–161
    BGP/MPLS, 173–175, 179–180
        helper LSR behavior, 178
        network deployment, 181–182
        restarting LSR behavior, 175–178
    IETF OSPF Working Group, 100
    LDP, 201–203
        DOD mode, 213–219
        DU mode, 203–204, 208–209, 212
        exchanging initial capability, 204
        GR versus FT, 203
        interoperability, 221–222
        network deployment, 220–221
        nonrestarting peers, 206–207
        restarting peers, 207–208
        session failure, 205
        session reestablishment, 205
        state recovery, 205
    OSPF, 89–100
    reason TLV, 90
    RSVP-TE, 237–239, 245–247
        control-plane restart, 239
        exchanging initial capability, 239
        network deployment, 248
        nonrestarting LSRs, 244–245
        recovery procedure, 242
        reestablishing Hello communication, 240
        restarting LSRs, 241, 243–244
GRE (Generic Routing Encapsulation), 8

hardware redundancy, 11
head-end restarts (RSVP-TE), 243
Hello adjacencies
    establishing, 189-190
    maintaining, 190-191
    packets, 70, 109
    processing, 81
Hello packets
    OSPF, 70
    RS bits, 80
HELLO_ACK object messages (RSVP-TE), 235
HELLO_REQUEST object messages (RSVP-TE),
    235
helper nodes, 113
helper speakers (BGP), 154
hierarchical routing (IS-IS), 108–109
holding timers, 110
hop-by-hop routed LSPs, 47

I

I (Init) bits, 82
iBGP (internal BGP) sessions, 144
idle state (BGP), 142–143
IETF (Internet Engineering Task Force)
    LDP, 187, 200
    MPLS-TE, 264
    RSVP-TE, 238
IETF IS-IS restarts, 115–116
    adjacency reacquistion, 118–119
    Cisco IS-IS restarts (versus), 128
    database synchronization, 119–120
    interoperability, 132
    LSP generation/flooding, 120–121
    nonrestarting routers, 121–122
    operation, 124
        restarting routers, 126–128
        starting routers, 124–125
    restart TLV, 116–117
    restarting routers (with preserved FIB), 118–121
    SPF computation, 121
    starting routers (without preserved FIB),
        122–123
    timers (T1–T3), 118

IETF OSPF Working Group, 100
IGPs (interior gateway protocols), 72
IIHs (IS-IS Hellos), 109, 116
ILMs (incoming label maps), 50, 197
Implicit NULL labels, 52
imposition (label), 51
incoming label maps (ILMs), 50, 197
incoming labels, 45
ingress LSRs, 46
Init (I) bits, 82
in-service software upgrades, 295–296
Integrated IS-IS, 108
interarea paths (OSPF), 78
interior gateway protocols (IGPs), 13
Intermediate System-to-Intermediate System.
    See IS-IS
internal BGP (iBGP) sessions, 144
internal/external speakers (BGP), 144
Internet Protocol (IP), 23
Internet routing architecture, 67–69
interoperability
    BGP, 159–161
    Cisco IS-IS restarts, 134
    Cisco/IETF IS-IS restart, 132
    OSPF restarts, 100–102
    RSVP-TE, 248–249
interprocessor communication (IPC), 39
intra-area paths (OSPF), 78
intrusion detection/prevention, 19
IOS. *See Cisco IOS architecture*
IP (Internet Protocol), 23
IP forwarding, 23–24
    addressing (classful/classless), 25
    address lookup, 26–28
    architectures, 28
        distributed, 30–32
        route caching, 29
    CEF, 33–34
    NSF, 36
IP networks
    addressing, 24–25
    control-plane protocols, 37
    forwarding, 44
    forwarding planes, 12, 24
    forwarding tables, 28
    IS-IS, 107

load balancing, 31
NSF, 36–40, 106
routing protocols, 8, 12
SSO, 35–36, 40
IP over MPLS, 55
IP/MPLS networks, 5
    BFD, 294–295
    control-plane protocols, 12
    control-plane restart, 13
    control-plane software, 8
    forwarding planes, 12
    forwarding states, 12
    IP routing protocols, 8
    IP tunneling protocols, 8
    LSRs, 12
    migrating legacy services, 5
    MPLS signaling protocols, 8
    network design, 19
    OAM mechanisms, 17
    protocols, 8
    security, 18
    service/network views, 11
IPC (interprocessor communication), 39
IS-IS (Intermediate System-to-Intermediate
    System), 8
    dual routing, 107
    flags, 116
    Hello packets, 109
    IP networks, 107
    LDP, 221
    levels, 68
    LSPs, 68
    restart TLV, 116–117
    sequence number packets, 111
    three-way handshakes, 109
IS-IS Hellos (IIHs), 109
IS-IS restarts, 113–114
    adjacency flaps, 107
    Cisco, 128–131
    detrimental effects, 105, 113
    IETF restarts, 124–128
    IETF versus Cisco, 131
    mitigating detrimental effects, 113
        Cisco restarts, 128–129
        IETF IS-IS restarts, 115–128
    network deployment, 132
    original behavior, 105–107

restarting routers, 115
starting routers, 115
state information, 128
IS-IS routing, 107–108
adjacencies, 110
congestion indication, 112–113
designated routers, 113
discovering neighbors, 109–110
establishing adjacencies, 109–110
hierarchical, 108–109
LSPs, 110–112

K–L

Keepalive messages (BGP), 141–142
keepalive timers (LDP), 190

L bits, 80
L2TP (Layer 2 Tunneling Protocol), 8
L2VPNs (Layer 2 virtual private networks), 50, 55, 164, 197, 272–273
control-plane failures, 274
forwarding tables, 166
VPLS, 275–277
VPWS, 274–275
L3VPNs (Layer 3 virtual private networks), 55, 164, 265
control-plane failures, 268
CSC, 270–271
multi-AS backbone, 269–270
single-AS backbone, 268–269
forwarding tables, 166
IPv6-based services, 268
label distribution, 268
MPLS, 50
PE-based, 265–266
PE-to-PE tunnels, 267
routing/forwarding tables, 266–267
Label Abort messages (LDP), 192
Label Distribution Protocol. *See LDP*
Label Mapping messages (LDP), 192
Label Request messages (LDP), 192
Label Withdraw messages (LDP), 192

label-advertisement mode, 192
label-distribution control mode, 192
label-encoding techniques, 48
Label Information Bases. See LIBs
label-retention mode, 194
labels, 44
distribution (BGP), 169
DOD mode, 46
DU mode, 46
encoding techniques, 48
Implicit NULL, 52
imposition/disposition, 46
incoming versus outgoing, 45
label space, 50
label stacks, 45–46
label-to-FEC binding, 45
lookup, 50, 53, 163
MPLS forwarding, 51
label disposition, 46, 52
label imposition, 46, 51
label swapping, 51
recovering labels, 176
label-switched paths. *See LSPs*
Label-Switching Information Bases. *See LFIBs*
label-switching routers. *See LSRs*
label-to-FEC mappings, 176
Layer 2 Tunneling Protocol (L2TP), 8
Layer 2 virtual private networks. *See L2VPNs*
Layer 3 virtual private networks. *See L3VPNs*
LC-ATM (label-switching controlled ATM) interfaces, 48
LDP (Label Distribution Protocol), 8, 46, 187–188
active versus standby, 59
BGP, 221
Cisco IOS architecture, 53
control planes, 197–198
DOD mode, 193, 214
DU mode (versus), 219–220
graceful restarts, 213–219
restarting LSRs, 214
restarting LSRs (egress neighbors), 218
restarting LSRs (engress), 215–216
restarting LSRs (ingress neighbors), 217–218
restarting LSRs (ingress), 215

restarting LSRs (transit neighbors),
218–219
restarting LSRs (transit), 216–217
DU mode, 194
graceful restarts, 203–204, 208–209, 212
DOD mode (versus), 219–220
FEC-to-label mappings, 54
FEC-to-LSP associations, 188–189
FIBs, 198
forwarding planes, 197
forwarding states, 197–198
graceful restarts
DOD, 214–219
exchanging initial capability, 204
GR versus FT, 203
interoperability, 221–222
network deployment, 220–221
nonrestarting peers, 206–207
restarting peers, 207–208
session failures, 205
session reestablishment, 205
state recovery, 205
Hello adjacencies
establishing, 189–190
maintaining, 190–191
hop-by-hop routed LSPs, 48
IETF, 187, 200
ILMs, 197
Implicit NULL labels, 52
IS-IS, 221
keepalive timers, 190
label-to-FEC bindings, 46
label-advertisement mode, 192
label-distribution control mode, 192
label-retention mode, 194
LDP CKP, 200
LFIBs, 194
LIB/LFIB/routing interactions, 194–196
LSPs, 187, 197–198
Maximum Recovery Time, 206
messages, 191–192
MPLS, 43
MPLS forwarding state, 198
Neighbor Liveness Timer, 206
NHLFEs, 197
NSF, 197
OSPF, 221
peers, 189

PWs, establishing, 196–197
Recovery Time, 205
restarts, 198–199
methods, 201–203
mitigating detrimental effects, 200
routing, 194
TCP, 189
LDP CKP (Checkpoint Procedures for LDP), 200
leaf nodes, 26
level 1/2 LAN Hello (IS-IS), 109
LFIBs (Label-Switching Information Bases),
50, 163
building, 56
LDP, 194–196
RSVP-TE, 236
synchronizing with the LIB, 56
LIBs (Label Information Bases)
LDP, 194–196
RIBs (versus), 53
line cards
BGP, 138
CEF, 33
distributed forwarding, 30
FIBs, 69
forwarding-plane functions, 12
IPC, 39
MPLS networks, 8
synchronizing RIBs to FIBs, 32
link failures (mitigating), 17
link local signaling (LLS), 80
Link-State Acknowledgment (LSA) packets, 75
link-state advertisements. *See LSAs*
link-state databases. *See LSDBs*
link-state protocols, 68, 72, 105
Link-State Request packets, 75
Link-State Update packets, 75
LLS (link-local signaling), 80
load balancing, 31
locality (temporal versus spatial), 29
Loc-RIB, 148
LR (LSDB Resynchronization) bits, 82
LSAs (link-state advertisements), 13, 68
flooding, 70
grace LSAs, 89, 92–93
MaxAge, 77
OSPF, 76–79
self-originated LSAs, 85
types, 77

LSDB Resynchronization (LR) bits, 82
LSDBs (link-state databases), 68
   OSPF, 70–71
   purging LSAs, 77
   resynchronization, 81
LSP_TUNNEL objects (RSVP-TE), 231
LSPs (label-switched paths), 8, 106, 166
   adjacency flaps, 107
   BFD, 291
   congestion indication, 112–113
   CSNPs, 111
   database synchronization, 111, 114
   explicity routed/traffic engineered, 47
   flags, 112
   flooding, 112
   fragmenting, 112
   generation/flooding, 120–121
   hop-by-hop routed, 47, 188
   IS-IS, 109–112
   LDP, 187, 197–198
   MPLS, 61, 197–198
   MPLS-TE, 226
   nesting, 46
   tunnels, 231
   zeroth LSPs, 112
LSRefreshTime timer, 90
LSRs (label-switching routers), 45, 163
   address lookup, 164
   ATM, 48
   cell mode, 48
   DOD mode (LDP), 214–219
   edge LSRs, 46, 164–165
   frame mode, 48
   label-distribution protocols, 46
   LFIBs, 50
   penultimate LSP LSR, 46
   MPLS domains, 46
   NSF, 58
   recovery periods, 58
   RSVP-TE
      nonrestarting LSRs, 244–245
      restarting LSRs, 241–244
   transit LSRs, 46, 164

M

M (More) bits, 82
M/S (Master/Slave) bits, 82
make-before-break approach (MPLS-TE), 262
Master/Slave (MS) bits, 82
Maximum Recovery Time (LDP), 206
mean time between failures (MTBF), 6
mean time to repair (MTTR), 6
mesh connectivity, 8
MESSAGE_ACK objects (RSVP-TE), 235
messages
   BGP, 141–142
   LDP, 191–192
MFI (MPLS Forwarding Infrastructure), 50
midpoint restarts (RSVP-TE), 243
modularity, 15, 17
More (M) bits, 82
MP_REACH_NLRI attributes, 169
MP_UNREACH_NLRI attributes, 169
MPLS (Multiprotocol Label Switching), 7, 43–50
   applications, 55
   BGP, 168–169
   control-plane components, 163–164
   FECs, 164
   forwarding planes
      components, 163–164
      NSF, 43
   forwarding state, 166
      entries, 166
      LSPs, 197
   IP (versus), 163–164
   label lookup, 50, 53
   labels, 45
   LDP, 187, 198
   networks. *See MPLS networks*
   SONET/SDH (versus), 17
MPLS Forwarding Infrastructure (MFI), 50
MPLS Forwarding State Holding Timer, 205
MPLS networks, 46
   applications, 50
   ATM, 48
   backbone, 7
   components, 7, 9
   control planes, 59, 61
   distributed forwarding, 56
   domains, 46

edge LSRs, 164
Ethernet, 48
FEC-to-label mappings, 46
forwarding, 50, 53
    architecture, 56
    ATM (versus), 48
    forwarding planes, 12, 61
    IP (versus), 50
    label operations, 51
    state, 166
FR, 48
FRR, 50
IP forwarding (versus), 50–53
L2VPNs, 50
L3VPNs, 50
Layer 2/3 services, 254
    availability, 256
    fault-tolerance techniques, 257
    provider-provisioned VPNs, 254
    service attributes, 256
    VPN tunnels, 255–256
line cards, 8
LSPs, 47, 61
LSRs, 45
NSF, 43, 58–62
PPP, 48
protection layer interaction, 285
recovery, 277–285
routers, 7
separating control/forwarding planes, 53–54
signaling protocols, 12
SSO, 57–58, 62
MPLS/BGP networks
    graceful restart/NSF interoperability, 182–183
MPLS-TE (Multiprotocol Label Switching traffic
    engineering), 50, 55, 226, 257
    control-plane failures, 262–263
    establishing tunnels, 259–261
    functional modules, 258
    IETF, 264
    inter-area/intra-AS, 264
    inter-AS, 264
    intra-area, 263
    reoptimizing tunnels, 262
    using RSVP, 230
MS (Master/Slave) bits, 82
MSE (multiservice edge) routers, 7

MTBF (mean time between failures), 6
m-tries (multibit-tries), 27
MTTR (mean time to repair), 6
multibit-tries (m-tries), 27
Multiprotocol Label Switching. *See MPLS*
multiservice edge (MSE) routers, 7

N

Neighbor Liveness Timer, 206
nesting (LSPs), 46
network design
    core networks, 8
    edge networks, 8
    fault tolerance, 11
    IP/MPLS networks, 19
    redundancy, 7
network layer reachability information (NLRI), 141
network LSAs (type 2), 77–78
network outages, 10. *See also outages*
    causes, 10–11
    downtime, 5
    mitigating
        hardware outages, 11–12
        link/node failures, 17
        node-level outages, 17
        via OAM mechanisms, 17
        software outages, , 12–17
    planned, 10, 17
    unplanned, 10–17
network partitioning, 108
network summary LSAs (type 3), 77–78
NEXT_HOP attributes (BGP), 147
next-hop label forwarding entries (NHLFEs), 50,
    197, 238
NLRI (network layer reachability information), 141
NMBA (nonbroadcast multiaccess) networks, 75–76
node failures (mitigating), 17
nonrestarting routers (IETF IS-IS restarts), 121–122
nonstop forwarding. *See NSF*
Notification messages
    BGP, 141–142
    LDP, 191
not-so-stubby-areas (NSSAs), 78
NSF (nonstop forwarding), 15, 69, 106
    BGP, 140, 159–161, 166–168

capable versus incapable neighbors, 40
Cisco IOS architecture, 39–40
defensive techniques, 18
external view, 40
IP, 36–39
    control-plane SSO, 37
    forwarding, 36
    neighboring-node perspective, 40
    separating control/forwarding, 37
LDP, 197
MPLS
    control-plane SSO, 59
    neighboring-node perspective, 62
routers, 36
RSVP-TE, 238
NSSAs (not-so-stubby areas), 78

O

OAM (operation, administration, and maintenance)
    mechanisms, 17, 287–290
OL (overload) bit, 112–113
one-for-N (1:N) redundancy, 12
one-for-one (1:1) redundancy, 12
one-plus-one (1+1) redundancy, 12
OOB (out-of-band) resynchronization, 82
OOBResynch bits, 82
Open messages (BGP), 141–142, 151
Open Shortest Path First. *See OSPF*
operation, administration, and maintenance (OAM)
    mechanisms, 17, 287-290
optional nontransitive (BGP path attribute), 146
optional transitive (BGP path attribute), 146
OSPF (Open Shortest Path First), 8
    areas, 73
    control-plane components, 69
    databases
        Database Description packets, 75
        exchange process, 75
        synchronizing, 70–71
    discovering neighbors, 75
    flooding, 70
    forwarding-plane components, 69
    FSM, 85, 93
    Hello packets, 70, 81

inter-area paths, 78
intra-area paths, 78
LDP, 221
link-state protocols, 68, 72
Link-State Request packets, 75
Link-State Update packets, 75
LSAs, 75, 77
restarts. *See OSPF restarts*
routing, 72–73
    adjacencies, establishing, 75–76
    hierarchical, 73–74
    link-state databases, synchronizing, 75–76
    LSAs, 76–79
    paths, selecting, 78–79
    router classification, 74
    tables, 73–74
SPF algorithm, 72
type 1/2 external paths, 79
OSPF restarts, 69–70
    control-plane restarts, 69–71
    detrimental effects, 70–71
    graceful restarts
        neighboring router behavior, 95–96
        restarting router behavior, 93–94
    interoperability, 100–102
    mitigating detrimental effects, 79
        graceful restarts, 89–92, 96, 99
        graceful restarts versus restart signaling,
            99–100
        restart signaling, 80–81
    neighbor awareness, 70
    nonrestarting routers, 85–86
    planned/unplanned, 79, 92–93
    protocol extensions, 70
    restart signaling, 86–89
    restarting routers, 84
    SPF calculations, 85
outages
    causes, 10–11
    downtime, 5
    mitigating
        hardware outages, 11–12
        link/node failures, 17
        node-level outages, 17
        via OAM mechanisms, 17
        software outages, 12–17

planned, 10, 17
unplanned, 10–17
node/link, 277
services, 256
outgoing labels, 45
out-of-band (OOB) resynchronization, 82
Overload (OL) bits, 112–113

P

packet-scheduling algorithms, 31
packet-switched networks, 11
packets
filtering, 19
labeled versus unlabeled, 45
partial sequence number packets (PSNPs), 111
path attributes (BGP), 146
LOCAL_PREF, 149
MP_REACH_NLRI, 169
MP_UNREACH_NLRI, 169
Path messages (RSVP), 227
path state block (PSB) messages, 227
PathErr (path error) messages, 227
paths, 105
backup, 7
mesh connectivity, 8
next hop, 30
selecting (OSPF), 78–79
peer relationships. *See adjacencies*
penultimate LSRs, 164
penultimate-hop LSRs, 52
penultimate-hop popping, 46, 164
point-to-point Hello (IS-IS), 109
Point-to-Point Protocol (PPP), 48
point-to-point three-way handshakes, 109
portioning (networks), 108
PPP (Point-to-Point Protocol), 48
PPVPNs (provider-provisioned VPNs), 254
prefixes
addresses, 25–28
expansion, 27
CIDR, 25–26
supernets, 25
protection (data-plane failure), 278
provider-provisioned VPNs (PPVPNs), 254

PSB (path state block) messages, 227
pseudowires (PWs), 196–197, 292
PSNPs (partial sequence number packets), 111, 129
PWs (pseudowires), 196–197, 292

R

R (Restart State) bits, 82, 153
RA (Restart Acknowledgment) flags, 116
radix (tries), 26
reason TLV (graceful restarts), 90
RECORD_ROUTE objects (RSVP-TE), 233–234
recovery periods
MPLS, 58
routers, 35
RECOVERY_LABEL objects (RSVP-TE), 239
recursive paths, 30
redundancy, 7, 257
APS, 12
edge routers, 9
fault tolerance, 7
hardware, 11
IP control-plane protocols, 37
MPLS control-plane SSO, 59
schemes, 12
software approaches, 14
switchovers, 7, 15
refresh timers, 84
reliability. *See also availability*
availability (versus), 6–7
MTBF/MTTR, 6
routers, 9
service view, 11
reservation state block (RSB) messages, 229
resource exhaustion DoS attacks, 18
Resource Reservation Protocol. *See RSVP*
resources (networks), 18
Restart Acknowledgment (RA) flags, 116
Restart Request (RR) flags, 116
restart signaling
OSPF, 80–81, 86–89
graceful restart (versus), 99–100
Restart Signaling (RS) bits, 80
Restart State (R) bits, 153
restart TLV, 116–117
RESTART_CAP objects (RSVP-TE), 239

restartability, 15–17
restarting routers, 115
    adjacency reacquisition, 119
    CSNP, 120
    IETF IS-IS, 118–121
    timers, 118
restarting speakers (BGP), 154
restarts
    BGP, 140
        graceful restarts, 151–154
        mitigating detrimental effects, 150–151
        route flaps, 138–140
    fault-tolerant restarts, 201–203
    grace LSAs, 92–93
    head-end restarts (RSVP-TE), 243
    IS-IS, 113–114
        detrimental effects, 105
        IETF versus Cisco, 131
        mitigating detrimental effects, 113–116
        network deployment, 132
        original behavior, 105–107
    LDP
        detrimental effects, 198–199
        methods, 201–203
        mitigating detrimental effects, 200
    midpoint restarts (RSVP-TE), 243
    OSPF, 69–70
        detrimental effects, 70–71
        mitigating detrimental effects, 79
            graceful restart, 89–92, 96, 99
            graceful restart versus restart
                signaling, 99–100
            restart signaling, 80–81
    preserving state information, 131
    protocol extensions, 69–70
    RSVP-TE, 236–245
    tail-end restarts, 244
RestartState bits, 81
restoration (data-plane failure), 278
Resv messages (RSVP), 228–229
ResvErr (reservation error) messages, 229
Resynctimeout timer, 82
RIBs (Routing Information Bases), 30, 69
    BGP, 138
    BGP speakers, 148
    control processor cards, 69

End-of-RIB markers, 153, 155–156
    LIBs (versus), 53
    m-tries, 31
    SPF algorithm, 73
    updates, 31
route caching
    FIBs (versus), 31
    hit ratio, 29
    IP forwarding, 29
route flaps, 138, 140, 167
route reflectors (RRs), 149–150, 171
route selection, 149
router LSAs (type 1), 77–78
router processors (RPs), 39, 61
RouterDeadInterval timers, 75, 88
routers, 23
    ABRs, 74
    address lookup, 26, 44
    adjacencies, 76
    ASBRs, 74
    ATM LSRs, 48
    autonomous systems (AS), 137
    backbone routers, 74
    BDRs, 76
    BGP, 25
    BGP speakers, 137, 144
    bottlenecks, 23
    carrier-class routers, 10–11
    cell-mode LSRs, 48
    components, 8
    control/forwarding capabilities, 132
    control-plane availability, 16
    control-plane protocols, 12
    control-plane software, 12
    designated routers (IS-IS), 113
    distributed forwarding, 30
    downtime, 10
    DRs, 76
    edge routers, 8
    FIB, 31
    flags, 116
    flooding, 105, 112
    forwarding process, 24
    fragmenting LSPs, 112
    frame-mode LSRs, 48
    IGPs, 13

internal routers, 74
IP routers, 23
IS-IS restart TLV, 116–117
IS-IS restarts
    nonrestarting routers, 121–122
    restarting routers (with preserved FIB),
        118–121
    starting routers (without preserved FIB),
        122–123
link-state protocols (LSPs), 105
LSRs, 12, 45
MPLS networks, 7
MSE routers, 7
network partitioning, 108
NSF, 15, 36, 69
OSPF classifications, 74
OSPF restarts
    nonrestarting routers, 85–86
    restarting routers, 84–85
outages, 11
recovery periods, 35
reliability, 9
restarting routers, 115
    adjacency reacquisition, 119
    CSNP, 120
    IETF IS-IS, 126–128
    OSPF, 71
    T3 timers, 118
SPF algorithm, 111
SSO, 16
starting routers, 115, 124–125
traditional forwarding architectures, 28
routing
    BGP, 137, 140–144
    domains, 67, 72
    dual routing, 108
    IGP, 72
    interdomain routing, 137
    Internet architecture, 67–69
    IS-IS, 107–108
        congestion indication, 112–113
        designated routers, 113
        discovering neighbors, 109–110
        establishing adjacencies, 109–110
        hierarchical, 108–109
        LSPs, 110, 112
        maintaining adjacencies, 110

    LDP, 194–196
    OSPF, 72–73
        establishing adjacencies, 75–76
        hierarchical, 73–74
        LSAs, 76–79
        selecting paths, 78–79
        synchronizing LSDBs, 75–76
Routing Information Bases. *See RIBs*
routing protocols, 8, 12
    active versus standby, 37, 59
    control processor cards, 36
    control software, 106
    FEC-to-next hop mappings, 54
    RIBs, 30
routing tables
    BGP, 25, 143
    L3VPNs, 266–267
    OSPF, 73–74
    reducing the size of, 25
RPs (router processors), 39, 61
RR (Restart Request) flags, 116
RRO (RECORD_ROUTE) objects, 233
RRs (route reflectors), 149–150, 171
RS (Restart Signaling) bits, 80
RSB (reservation state block) messages, 229
RSVP (Resource Reservation Protocol), 8, 227
    label-to-FEC bindings, 46
    MPLS-TE, 230
    Path messages, 227
    PathErr messages, 227
    Resv messages, 228–229
    ResvErr messages, 229
    soft state, 229
RSVP traffic engineered (RSVP-TE), 48, 187, 225
    control/forwarding-plane components, 236
    detecting failures, 235–236
    EXPICIT_ROUTE objects, 233
    FIBs, 238
    graceful restart, 237–247
    Hello extensions, 235
    IETF, 238
    interoperability, 248–249
    LFIBs, 236
    LSP tunnels, 231
    LSP_TUNNEL objects, 231–232
    MESSAGE_ACK objects, 235
    new objects, 230–232, 239

NHLFE, 238
RECORD_ROUTE objects, 233–234
restarts, 236–245
SESSION_ATTRIBUTE objects, 232
soft state, 234
state lifetime, 234–235
SUMMARY_REFRESH messages, 235
traffic flows, 230
RSVP_HOP object (RSVP), 227, 229

S

SA (Suppress Adjacency Advertisement) flags, 117
SAFI (Subsequent Address Family Identifier) field,
153, 169, 173–174
scheduling, 24
security, 18
DoS attacks, 18
improving via fault-tolerant mechanisms,
18–19
send routing message flags. *See SRMflags*
send sequence number flags (SSNflags), 112
SENDER_TEMPLATE objects (RSVP), 227
SENDER_TSPEC objects (RSVP), 227
sequence number packets (IS-IS), 111
service-level agreements (SLAs), 11
services (networks), 10, 256
outages, 6-7
Session message (LDP), 191
SESSION objects (RSVP), 227, 229
SESSION_ATTRIBUTE objects (RSVP-TE), 232
Shortest Path First, 13
Shortest Path First algorithm.
See SPF (Shortest Path First) algorithm
signaling protocols, 8
SLAs (service-level agreements), 11
soft state
RSVP, 229
RSVP-TE, 234
software upgrades, 17, 295–296
SONET (Synchronous Optical Network), 280
SONET/SDH (Synchronous Optical Network/
Synchronous Digital Hierarchy), 7
APS, 9, 12
MPLS (versus), 17
speakers (BGP), 137, 141
internal/external, 144

RIBs, 148
RRs, 150
special locality, 29
SPF (Shortest Path First) algorithm, 13, 68, 105
LSPs, 111, 120
OSPF, 72
OSPF restarts, 85
RIBs, 73
zeroth LSP, 112
SRMflags (send routing message flags), 112
Cisco IS-IS restarts, 129
IS-IS restarts, 114
SSNflags (send sequence number flags), 112
SSO (stateful switchover), 15
capable components, 37
Cisco IOS architecture, 39–40
defensive techniques, 18
external view, 40
IP
control plane, 35–37
neighboring-node perspective, 40
MPLS
control plane, 59
neighboring-node perspective, 62
restartability, 16
starting routers, 115
IETF IS-IS restarts, 122–123
timers, 118
state transitions, 93
stateful components, 35–37, 57
stateful switchover. *See SSO*
stateless components, 35
states (BGP), 142–143
strides
address lookup, 27
patterns, 28
stub areas, 77
STYLE objects (RSVP), 229
Subsequent Address Family Identifier (SAFI) field,
153, 169, 173–174
SUGGESTED_LABEL objects (RSVP-TE), 239
SUMMARY_REFRESH messages (RSVP-TE), 235
supernets, 25
Suppress Adjacency Advertisement (SA) flags, 117
survivability. *See fault tolerance*
swapping (labels), 51
switching, 24
switching fabric (routers), 8

switchovers
    fault control processor cards, 36
    redundancy, 7
    restartability, 15
    SSO, 35–36
synchronizing databases, 114, 118
    IETF IS-IS restarts, 119–120
    OSPF, 70–71
    timers, 118, 121
Synchronous Optical Network/Synchronous Digital
    Hierarchy. *See SONET/SDH*

T

T1 timers, 118
    adjacency reacquisition, 119
    restarting versus starting routers, 123
T2 timers, 118
    adjacency reacquisitions, 119
    database synchronization, 120
    SPF computations, 121
    start-capable routers, 122
T3 timers, 118
    expiring before T2 timers, 121
    IETF IS-IS restart routers, 118
    inhibiting IIH transmissions, 119
Tag Forwarding Information Bases (TFIBs), 50
tail-end restarts (RSVP-TE), 244
TCP (Transmission Control Protocol), 189
TE (traffic engineering), 50, 225–226, 257
temporal locality, 29
TFIB (Tag Forwarding Information Bases), 50
three-way handshakes, 109
timers
    adjacencies, 110
    Hello adjacencies, 190
    IETF IS-IS restarts, 118
    LDP, 206
    LSP generation/flooding, 120–121
    LSRefreshTime, 90
    MaxAge, 77
    MPLS Forwarding State Holding Timer, 205
    refresh timers, 84
    ResyncTimeout, 82
    RouterDeadInterval timer, 88

TLVs (time length values)
    FT ACK, 202
    FT Protecton, 202
    FT Session, 201, 204
    reason TLV, 90
    restart TLV, 116–117
traffic engineering (TE), 50, 225–226, 257
traffic trunks, 226
traffic-engineered LSPs, 47
transit LSRs, 46, 51, 164
tries, 26, 28
tunnels
    bypass tunnels, 284–285
    MPLS-TE
        establishing, 259–261
        protecting, 262–263
        reoptimizing, 262
    RSVP, 231
    VPNs, 255
        demultiplexing, 255
        signaling labels, 256
tuples (CIDR), 25
type 1 LSAs, 77–78
type 1/2 external paths (OSPF), 79
type 2 LSAs, 77
type 3 LSAs, 77
type 4 LSAs, 77
type 5 LSAs, 77
type 7 LSAs, 77

U–W

unavailability, 6. *See also downtime; outages*
Update messages (BGP), 141–144
    distributing routing information, 171
    path attributes, 146–147
    Withdrawn Routes field, 171

VC labels, 165, 168
VCIs (virtual circuit identifiers), 45
Virtual Private LAN Service (VPLS), 275–277
virtual private networks. *See VPNs*
Virtual Private Wire Service (VPWS), 274–275
VPLS (Virtual Private LAN Service), 275–277

VPNs (virtual private networks)
    backbones, 164
    forwarding tables, 166
    L2VPNs, 272–273
        control-plane failures, 274
        VPLS, 275–277
        VPWS, 274–275
    L3VPNs, 265
        control-plane failures, 268–271
        IPv6 services, 268
        label distribution, 268
        PE-based, 265–266
        PE-to-PE tunnels, 267
        routing/forwarding tables, 266–267
    MPLS, 164–165
    provider provisioned, 254
    tunnels, 168, 255
        demultiplexing, 255
        signaling labels, 256
VPWS (Virtual Private Wire Service), 274–275

wavelength-division multiplexing (WDM),
   7, 279–280
well-known discretionary (BGP path attribute), 146
well-known mandatory (BGP path attribute), 146
    AS_PATH, 146
    NEXT_HOP, 147